About Island Press

Since 1984, the nonprofit organization Island Press has been stimulating, shaping, and communicating ideas that are essential for solving environmental problems worldwide. With more than 800 titles in print and some 40 new releases each year, we are the nation's leading publisher on environmental issues. We identify innovative thinkers and emerging trends in the environmental field. We work with world-renowned experts and authors to develop cross-disciplinary solutions to environmental challenges.

Island Press designs and executes educational campaigns in conjunction with our authors to communicate their critical messages in print, in person, and online using the latest technologies, innovative programs, and the media. Our goal is to reach targeted audiences—scientists, policymakers, environmental advocates, urban planners, the media, and concerned citizens—with information that can be used to create the framework for long-term ecological health and human well-being.

Island Press gratefully acknowledges major support of our work by The Agua Fund, The Andrew W. Mellon Foundation, Betsy & Jesse Fink Foundation, The Bobolink Foundation, The Curtis and Edith Munson Foundation, Forrest C. and Frances H. Lattner Foundation, G.O. Forward Fund of the Saint Paul Foundation, Gordon and Betty Moore Foundation, The JPB Foundation, The Kresge Foundation, The Margaret A. Cargill Foundation, New Mexico Water Initiative, a project of Hanuman Foundation, The Overbrook Foundation, The S.D. Bechtel, Jr. Foundation, The Summit Charitable Foundation, Inc., V. Kann Rasmussen Foundation, The Wallace Alexander Gerbode Foundation, and other generous supporters.

The opinions expressed in this book are those of the author(s) and do not necessarily reflect the views of our supporters.

Roads were NOT BUILT FOR CARS

HOW CYCLISTS WERE THE FIRST TO PUSH FOR GOOD ROADS & BECAME THE PIONEERS OF MOTORING

CARLTON REID

ISLANDPRESS

Washington | Covelo | London

Library of Congress Control Number: 2015934553

Printed on recycled, acid-free paper ⊕

Manufactured in the United States of America

10 9 8 7 6 5 4 3 2 1

ISBN (cloth) 978-1-61091-687-5
ISBN (paper) 978-1-61091-689-9

Copy-editor: Martin Rickerd **Indexer:** Nicola King
Front cover illustration: Pete English **Logo design:** Paul Robson

Back cover photo © National Motor Museum. The photo shows an 1898 Benz Velo in front of Glover Brothers Cycle Makers & Engineers of Windsor Street, Coventry. As well as signs for the CTC and Ariel bicycles there's a sign (on the spine) advertising Pratts Spirit, one of the earliest petrol brands in Britain. Bicycle shops were among the very few places that motorists could buy petrol. In 1912, Henry James Glover and Hubert Walter Glover manufactured a (short-lived) motor car of their own.

This book was supported with financial contributions from the Chartered Institution of Highways & Transportation, and the Rees Jeffreys Road Fund.

A catalogue record for this book is available from the British Library.

For Jude

CROWDFUNDING

Much of the research for this book was enabled by backers of a Kickstarter campaign run in 2013. The names of these backers – all 648 of them – can be found in the back of the book.

However, a number of individuals (and an organisation and a company) went above and beyond pre-ordering a book and I'd like to thank them here for their generosity.

Joe Breeze
Peter Berkeley
Emily Lang
Denis Caraire
Hackney Cycling Campaign
Trikke Tech
Patrick Russell Knox Sr.
Dave Walker
Terry Malouf
John Simpson

CONTENTS

FOREWORD

By Edmund King

I thought I knew a lot about roads, until I read this book. After all, I am president of the Automobile Association and, indeed, in the past, was campaigns manager for the British Road Federation. I have also had an interest in cars and cycles since the age of five, when my mother bought me my first bike (from Colin Chapman, founder of Lotus Cars). In my life, cycles and cars have always gone together.

I was astonished to read how closely cyclists and motorists were joined at the hip. Perhaps I shouldn't have been surprised? The history and origins of the AA owe much to cycling, as this book relates.

It wasn't just the AA that was influenced by cyclists. Carlton Reid skilfully traces back the extensive links between cycling and many automotive companies, such as GMC, Chevrolet, Land Rover and even Ford. (Henry Ford loved cycles; Hitler loathed them.) Ground-breaking technological developments, such as ball bearings and the pneumatic tyre, had their origins in cycling. The early drivers' bible *Autocar*, which still exists today, was founded by a cycle magazine editor. In the 1890s, Victorian cyclists and motorists were closely aligned, and worked together to improve roads (and create motoring).

This brilliantly researched book should help to demolish many of the Car v Cycle arguments, and put us all on a much safer road for the future. Motorists and cyclists are *not* two tribes. It would be healthy for some of the Mr. Toads out there to read this book; it amply illustrates that Roads Were Not Built for Cars.

Edmund King is President of the Automobile Association and Visiting Professor of Transport at Newcastle University.

PREFACE

Roads were invented for cars ... Roads are for cars, not bikes.
Daniel Meers, Gold Coast Bulletin, Australia, 2012

This is a highway history book, showing how we originally got our solid roads, roads that some motorists believe were built for their sole use. (Many now are, of course.) It's also about how Victorian and Edwardian cyclists helped motoring become globally pervasive. Motorists and cyclists – deemed by many to be poles apart – have an intimately shared history.

When, in 2011, Dutch urban anthropologist Line Algoed moved to London, she was shocked by the "two tribes" split between motorists and cyclists:

> You are either a cyclist, or a driver – as if people never switched between transport modes ... Both groups are moving farther away from each other, creating misunderstanding and conflict.

The president of the UK's Automobile Association, Edmund King, has urged "we must get past the dangerous *them and us* mentality." Optimistically, he concludes: "When we release our grip on the steering wheel or handlebars, the differences disappear."

He's right. Historically, at least. Cyclists and motorists have far more in common than many people realise. Early motoring was highly reliant on the cyclists of the 1890s. Not only did motorists later benefit from the improved roads first lobbied for by cyclists, but those motorists were often the same people who had originally done the lobbying. Cyclists and motorists of the late 1890s and early 1900s were not from separate tribes – they were often the exact same individuals.

It's usually assumed – and, thanks to some historians, often explicitly written – that motor cars evolved from horse-drawn carriages. This is not so. Carl Benz's *Patent-Motorwagen*, the first true automobile, was a motorised two-seater tricycle made from parts sourced from Germany's biggest bicycle shop. The key components for Henry Ford's *Quadricycle* – including the wire spoke wheels, bush roller chains and pneumatic tyres – were from bicycles. If a paternity test were possible, it could be shown that the first motor cars had much more cycle DNA in them than carriage DNA. The cycle was a vital part of the trunk of the automobile's family tree.

The first promoters of motoring were cyclists, and were used to lobbying thanks to their earlier promotion of cycling. Moneyed and socially elevated, these promoters had often been officials of cycling organisations. The long-time prime mover behind the Automobile Club of America (precursor to the Triple A) was Amos G. Batchelder, described as "America's foremost highway enthusiast." He had earlier been an official with the League of American Wheelmen cycling club. The ultra-exclusive Automobile Club of Great Britain and Ireland – later to add the Royal prefix – was founded in 1897, by cyclists. In 1904, many of its members, in their entries in a motoring annual, were still proudly displaying their love

Library of Congress

In the 1890s, cycling was a pursuit for the leisured elite.

for cycling. Ernest Shipton would have seen no irony in being a committee member of the influential Automobile Club as well as being, at the same time, the long-standing secretary of the Cyclists' Touring Club. Henry Sturmey was a cycling journalist to his dying day, wrote a classic 1877 book on cycling and gave his name to Sturmey Archer bicycle gears in the early 1900s, but he also founded *The Autocar*, the world's first weekly motoring magazine (which is still published, without the definite article). In the mid-1890s Sturmey was editor, at the same time, of both *The Cyclist* and *The Autocar*. He was one of many cycling-fixated committee members of the Automobile Club. The first automobile manufacturers tended to be cyclists, too: from the Dodge and Duryea brothers in America to the co-founders of Rolls-Royce and Aston Martin in Britain. At least 64 motor marques had bicycling beginnings, and in the appendix I discuss the cycle backgrounds of companies such as Cadillac, GMC and Chevrolet.

Without cycles and cyclists, motoring would have evolved very differently, and perhaps in a far inferior form. Cyclists became the first and staunchest evangelisers of motoring because they had been the first to awaken to the possibilities afforded by self-determined mobility – free from fodder, free from timetables, free from rails. And, as they were intimately aware of the benefits that came from the provision of smoother surfaces upon which to glide, pushy Victorian cyclists agitated for highway reforms. In America cyclists formed the hugely influential Good Roads movement. In Britain there was the trail-blazing Roads Improvement Association, a campaigning body founded by cyclists ten years before it was legally possible to drive a motor car on British roads.

That cyclists pioneered highway improvements before the advent of motoring is not heretical, it's hidden. To revive this hidden history I've spent umpteen hours immersed in Victorian and Edwardian journals, diaries, personal correspondence and newspapers. I've travelled from Coventry in the English Midlands to Detroit in America, to get up close and personal to the papers – and the geography – of the motoring pioneers. Before Coventry and Detroit became known as motor towns, they were cycling cities. One of the key reasons they became important centres for motor manufacturing was that, some years beforehand, they were important centres for cycle manufacturing.

This book is based on the opinions and knowledge of those who lived through the period I'm focussing on, which is roughly the early 1860s to 1914. The official organs of the League of American Wheelmen (L.A.W.) and the Cyclists' Touring Club (CTC) were produced by enthusiasts with a clear and obvious bias. Similarly, the pioneer motoring journals exhibit the same blinkered breathlessness, often because the journals were written by the same individuals – almost all of the first motoring journalists cut their teeth on cycling magazines.

THE TITLE of my book is polemical, but it's also a statement of historical fact. Roads were *not* built for motor cars. By and large, they were built for pedestrians. That roads were allowed to be colonised by cars is not something that happened by accident, nor was it inevitable. Powered road-going vehicles existed before Carl Benz attached a gas explosion engine to a Coventry-inspired tricycle but, for many interlocking reasons, the earlier road steamers did not catch on, and it wasn't for want of trying. Something different happened when Benz, Daimler and the other motor pioneers created the powered road-going vehicle that, eventually, caught on – or, rather, was allowed to catch on. Society, or at least the powerful parts of it, decided the fate of motor cars. The great majority of the Victorian public, with no prospect of owning them, hated motor cars, and this hatred continued, in some quarters, until the 1920s. Had more restrictions been placed in their way, motor cars would have evolved very differently – they may even have been stillborn. When motor cars arrived, it was the age of the train and, later, the tram. There was nothing inevitable about the acceptance of motoring. In the 1890s, very few people imagined motor cars would go on to dominate the world. That motor cars did so was partly due to cycling, and cyclists.

PEDESTRIANS (WHICH we all are!) may not always agree but, give or take the odd "scorcher" or two, bicycling is benign. Cyclists and pedestrians can mix far better in the same space than motorists and pedestrians. This is amply demonstrated at "car-free" events where roads are shut to motors. There are a growing number of these events around the world, usually organised on Sundays. They have been popularised by the *ciclovías* – or "open streets" events – of Bogotá, Colombia, first held in 1976. Major highways are closed to motorised traffic, and people take over, on skateboards, on roller skates, on foot, on bicycles. Space normally dedicated to movement for motors alone becomes public space where anything goes. Dance classes, pop-up cafes, leisurely chats, architectural tours and more transform streets back to what they originally were: public spaces, not spaces for motor cars alone.

Strictly speaking, as a British rights of way expert said in 1913, "a Highway is no place for a picnic, a public meeting, an al fresco dance, or an itinerant auctioneer's stand," but throughout history, roads have been about more than just transport. We have lost that aspect of roads, and this is a major amenity loss. Ciclovías – even when held on just one or two streets, and just once a week – remind people that roads need not be just for cars.

A great many residents of Leeds in Yorkshire discovered this when the Tour de France cycle race started in the city in July 2014. The congested A61 dual-carriageway north of Leeds was closed to "normal" traffic – it was busy, briefly, for the passing of the professional riders (and their support cars, team buses and trucks in the shape of tea-pots). After the riders and the motor convoy had passed, the roads remained closed to motor vehicles for some hours but were open to pedestrians and cyclists. Tens of thousands of people realised they could wander all over the road without fear of obliteration – tiny tots, wheelchair users and many others who wouldn't normally go anywhere near the A61 found they could share it quite happily with cyclists. It was party time! Children remained on the road long after the race had passed, laughing, playing, joking, having fun. This was liberating and uplifting for thousands of residents. Later the A61 returned to being an unwelcoming place for anybody not motor-propelled. The fun stopped.

I'm not an Arcadian, wishing for simpler times. Clearly, modern society relies on transport of people and goods by road but there are dangers in being in thrall to the motor car, and the reliance on propulsion in five-seater motor vehicles even when travelling alone and for the shortest of journeys is unsustainable in a number of well-understood but ignored ways. We all live in fear of those propelling motor cars – parents clutch their small children closer to them when walking near roads, and the "fear of traffic" compels people to retreat from the street. Sweden's "Vision Zero" – the principle that no level of "traffic efficiency" is worth a single pedestrian death – shows that it's perfectly possible to live in a modern democracy yet not have the "freedom" to treat speed limits as minimum targets. Vision Zero is infectious, many localities are inspired by it, including New York City which is gradually taming the motor car and transforming formerly motor-choked streets into thoroughfares where people matter.

ROADS BELONG to all, a shared resource. Too often, one user – the motorised user – has been allowed to dominate. This does not require any diktats from on high. Any and every road can become a "motor" way, because those piloting heavy, fast motor vehicles can use their speed and power to muscle all non-motorised users out of the way, often without knowing they're doing it. "Vulnerable road users" become either invisible, or irritants to be buzzed out of the way. Rule 170 in the Highway Code states: "Watch out for pedestrians crossing a road into which you are turning. If they have started to cross they have priority, so give way." Few motorists (or cyclists) know this rule exists, and pedestrians meekly scuttle out of the way, or risk being flattened. In America, the creation in the 1920s of the concept – and crime – of "jaywalking" shows how roads for all users quickly became defined as roads for motorists alone.

Try this experiment – ride a bicycle on a narrow road with cars parked on one side and play "chicken" with motorists heading towards you. You'll not get far because many British and American motorists won't pull to one side to let through a cyclist. (Actually, don't try this, it's potentially lethal.) Cyclists can be forced aside, unthinkingly, by nurses, nuns and White Van Man alike. Motor cars are deemed, by many, to have priority on roads. Might, it seems, is right. On a bicycle you often don't register on retinas. This results in SMIDSY – "sorry, mate I didn't see you" – a phrase commonly heard by upended cyclists (and motorcyclists).

When motorists *do* notice cyclists it's often because they are perceived to be "getting in the way." Motorists sometimes articulate that cyclists "slow down" what they consider to be the only legitimate road users. More normally, what slows down motorists is fellow motorists but it's human nature to scapegoat the "other".

A small minority of motorists believe they should inform the non-motorised what modern roads are for – the use of cars as weapons is well documented. Violence may be rare, but verbal abuse is not. In May 2014, Keith Maddox of Piedmont, Alabama, filmed himself ranting at cyclists he passed in his powerful SUV. He said he was "just trying to get to work," and didn't consider that the fellow road users he complained about were doing the same. After passing one cyclist, Maddox videoed himself on his smartphone saying: "I'm going to hurt one of them one of these days, I can't help it." He later gave two cyclists a "punishment pass", then pulled in front of them and proudly shouted: "That scare ya, boys? Get your pedalin' butts off the road." This type of unbidden hate is not limited to cyclists. Pedestrians and equestrians are also shouted at for daring to "share the road". In Pennsylvania there are a great many slow-moving horse-drawn buggies on the roads, and members of the Amish community are frequently abused by passing motorists. A courtesy guide produced for the Pennsylvania Department of Transportation uses a faux religious edict to put the guilt trip on those without internal combustion engines – it advises "plain people" in their buggies to " ... stop and let the faster traffic go by. Never think, 'I have just as much right on the road as he has.' That is true according to the law, but ... it is our Christian duty to ... not hog the road."

AMERICAN PHILOSOPHER Marshall Berman's powerful polemic of 1981, *All That is Solid Melts Into Air* – which influenced the 1990s "Reclaim the streets" and Critical Mass movements – stressed that the streets belonged to people on foot, not people in motor cars:

> [There is] revolutionary protest that transforms a multitude of urban solitudes into a people, and reclaims the city streets for human life ... the streets belong to the people.

In fact, streets belong to people on foot, people on bikes, people on horses, people on pogo-sticks, and, yes, people in motor vehicles. Yet it is now perfectly mainstream to argue that roads are the sole domain of only those people surrounded by steel overcoats. Unprotected propulsion, Shanks's pony or pedalling, is seen as perverse.

But change is in the air. That motor-car use ought to be restrained is becoming less of a minority position as the social, environmental, health and economic benefits of the "liveable city" are becoming better understood. Cities that put quality of life for all before amenities for motorists alone are finding that one of the first steps towards civic "attractiveness" is to rip out much of the ugly infrastructure that motorists are deemed to require. Some of this motor-centric infrastructure – roundabouts, crash barriers, sweeping corners with long sight-lines – encourages motorists to travel faster, making urban areas sterile and unpleasant.

HISTORY IS a social construct, written by the winners, and the winners in highway history have been motorists. Cycling's role in highway history was consciously downgraded – and, in some cases, deliberately deleted – when the bicycle morphed from the vehicle of rich transport progressives in the 1890s to "poor man's transport" in the 1930s. It's time that Victorian cyclists were given credit for what they helped bring about. Some became ardent motorists and were all too happy to forget their cycling roots, but many of the other motor pioneers continued cycling, and they celebrated the shared links between transport modes that are now deemed to be worlds apart. I'd like those links to be celebrated again.

CARLTON REID
Newcastle upon Tyne
August, 2014

INTRODUCTION

CAR v AUTOMOBILE

Throughout this book I use *motor car* and *automobile* interchangeably. (*Car*, too, but to a much lesser extent because, in the 19th century, car meant a train, tram or trolley *carriage*.) To British ears, the use of the word automobile sounds American. It's very much not a word in everyday use in Britain; ditto for the contraction *auto*. The Royal Automobile Club, founded in London in 1897 as the Automobile Club, shows that "automobile" was once a perfectly acceptable British English word. Automobile is a Latin and Greek mash-up, with the collision taking place in France in the 1890s. Even though the world's first automobile was developed in Germany, the first mass-market sales, promotions and brand building for automobiles took place in France. Why? Motoring pioneer and Cyclists' Touring Club trustee Sir David Salomons put it down to avarice, thanks to a bicycle magazine's challenge:

> The great success which cycling had in France, following upon the prize given by *Le Petit Journal*, which also gave so large an advertisement to that newspaper, led to the energetic proprietors offering a prize for quick self-propelled carriages, with the result which is so well known. Consequently the [new popularity of motoring] is not due to any new discovery or special invention, but simply that many minds were turned to the subject in the hope of gaining the large money prize.

French engineers – using German engines – dominated the (tiny) world market for automobiles until the late 1890s, just enough time for French words to predominate: words such as *chassis, garage, carburettor* and *chauffeur* – which, before 1905, meant "driver of a motor car" rather than a servant who drove a motor car. Other French motoring words – such as *coupé, limousine* and *cabriolet* (from which the word "cab" is derived) – had first been words for horse-drawn carriages. Limousine was originally a shepherd's cloak from the Limousin region of France. The first chauffeurs, who sat in the open air, adopted this heavy garment and the word transferred itself from a cloak, to a horse-carriage, to the covering for a driver, to the vehicle itself. Think of that the next time you see a stretch limo.

Other equestrian words – such as *driving* – transferred to motoring. *Motoring* wasn't the obvious word for the activity. An early favourite was *moting*.

There were many competing words for what one British Member of Parliament called "stinking engines of iniquity." Anticipating history, in 1879 American chancer George Seldon patented, but did not build, a *road engine*. Ford built a *quadricycle* (using bicycle parts). Other suggested names for the motor car included *Benzene buggy; diamote, self-motor, autovic* and, simply, *machine* – the Italian word for automobile is *machina*. *The Weekly Times and Echo* said its favoured name was *Greaser*.

In the late 1890s, people seemed to prefer *autocar*, especially the British magazine *The Autocar*, although Automobile Club founder Frederick Simms (a member of the Cyclists' Touring Club in his

Pioneering 1890s cycle infrastructure: the elevated California Cycleway in Pasadena (see chapter 11).

youth), rather cheekily wrote to the journal suggesting instead:

> Petrocycle, Motorfly, Automotive, Horseless Car, Motor Cycle, Oleo-Locomotive, Volvite, Autokenetic, Mechanical Car or Carriage, Automobile, Electrobat, Paramount, Locomotive Car or Carriage, Non-equine, Automatic Car or Carriage, and last but not least, the Autocar and Motor Car or Carriage.

An editorial in *The New York Times* had cause to hesitate when using the word automobile:

> There is something uncanny about these new-fangled vehicles. They are all unutterably ugly and never a one of them has been provided with a good, or even an endurable name. The French, who are usually orthodox in their etymology if in nothing else, have evolved "automobile," which being half Greek and half Latin is so near to indecent that we print it with hesitation …

WHEEL

There used to be many names for the cycle. In America, one of the most popular was *wheel*, even though a *bi*cycle, as the name suggests, had two wheels. The reason is writ large: the first mainstream bicycle was a high-wheeler, with a prominent front wheel and a tiny trailing wheel. The national cycling organisation in the US was the League of American Wheelmen, which is now known as the (non-sexist, tricyclist-offending) League of American Bicyclists. 19th-century American cycling magazines were littered with the wheel word, and it takes some time to get used to the fact the writer means the complete machine rather than one of its component parts. An 1895 advert for a New York bicycle insurance company said "if your wheel is stolen we recover it for you." This was a policy for whole bicycles.

Similar to *automobile*, the first name for bicycle was another Greek-Latin mash-up: *velocipede* (*velox*: fast plus *ped*: feet). At times, I am a velocipedestrianisticalistinarianologist (one who studies the study of studying cycling), a 40-letter concoction coined in 1869. The noun *bicycle* dates back to at least 1828 when a horse-drawn cabriolet was described as such.

The Polish word for bicycle is *rower*, with the *w* pronounced as *v*, named after J. K. Starley's Rover Safety bicycle of the mid-1880s. In other languages, the diminutive *bike* is *vélo* in French, *bici* in Italian, *fiets* in Dutch, *Rad* in German (from *fahrrad*), and, my personal favourite, *birota* in Vatican Latin – two-wheeler. This is very similar to *birotate chariot*, a term used in Charles Pratt's 1879 introduction to the joys of cycling. English and American magazines often referred to the cycle as a "steel steed" or even, in an American newspaper from 1879, a "mustang of steel."

Throughout this book I use the term *high-wheeler* for the type of early bicycle commonly known as the *penny-farthing*. This coinage-derived term was an 1890s disparagement, and collectors of antique bicycles used to steer well clear of the slur. Today, cycle historians and cycle collectors have softened, and often refer to high-wheelers as *pennies*. Period sources called the high-wheeler simply the bicycle, although after the introduction of the *Safety bicycle*, high-wheelers became known as *ordinaries*, or even, in some sources, *Grand Old Ordinaries*, or G.O.O.s.

I hope tricyclists will forgive me if I sometimes slip up but, throughout the book, I've tried to use the word *cycle* rather than *bicycle*.

TIME

This book mostly covers the period 1868 to 1896 and on to 1914 – from when bicycles were introduced, to when they boomed as part of a global "bicycle craze," and ending at the start of the Great War when, for the first time, automobile sales overtook bicycle sales. There is no single name for this period.

Instead, there are overlapping eras, the names of which I use interchangeably, depending on geography, period and whim.

In France, the late 1880s and 1890s formed part of what was known as the *Belle Époque*, the "beautiful era". In America, Mark Twain invented the term the *Gilded Age* for the off-golden era of US industrial expansion coupled with the excessive riches of the "robber barons." In Britain, it was the *Late Victorian* period, soon to merge into the *Edwardian* era. Motor historians often use the term *Brass Era*, the period when the early automobiles had brass lamps and brass radiator grilles.

The final chapter goes beyond 1914 in order to reveal how cycling and motoring went their separate ways, and how cycling became proletarian, and is still perceived to be "poor man's transport."

PAVEMENT v SIDEWALK

In Britain, the word *pavement* is not anywhere near as descriptive as *sidewalk*, the American term for the same sliver of pedestrian infrastructure. When Americans – and all nationalities of road engineers, including British – talk about *pavement*, they mean the road, not the sidewalk. In everyday speech, I use pavement, especially when bamboozling Americans: "That's right, in England, bicycles aren't allowed on the pavement." For clarity, in this book, I use "sidewalk".

FREEWAY v MOTORWAY

When talking about "motor-specific" roads in general I use the word *motorway*; when describing motorways in America I use *freeway*.

CYCLE PATH v CYCLEWAY

At the end of the 19th century America had the world's best cycle infrastructure – the California Cycleway and the Coney Island Cycle Path. I reckon *way* is a far more powerful word than *path*. In America and Britain, path became low status: a path is deemed to be narrow and for walkers. The words path and *pad* indicate earth beaten down by feet (either human or animal). In Victorian era magazines there was much discussion about "bicycle roads". The use of the right terminology can be important, especially in cultures which later downgraded the bicycle. In the Netherlands, a *fietspad* – or "bicycle path" – is not low status. Way denotes moving or travelling and comes from the same Sanscrit root (*vah*) as the words *wagon* and *vehicle*. Perhaps Eric Claxton, designer of the New Town of Stevenage in the 1960s, had the right idea when he insisted that the separated cycle infrastructure he created had to be called *cycleways*. Claxton's grand-daughter Joanna Brown told me he was very proud of his cycleways and insisted on calling them that:

> I remember as a child being pulled up for using the wrong term and being told "paths are for pedestrians, tracks are for horses, I built cycleways."

SETTS v COBBLES

Setts are quarried stones cut rectangular with flat surfaces. They are often colloquially known as "cobbles", yet true cobbles are naturally bulbous pebbles dredged from rivers or collected from beaches, a road surface popular in medieval times but way too bumpy for moderns. A cobbled street is, in fact, a setted street. The famous Paris–Roubaix cycle race has riders bumping over setts, not cobbles. Roubaix is close to Belgium – another name for setts is "Belgian blocks". The French word for setts is *pavé*. Cycling on setts is famously difficult – many professional riders won't ride the one-day classics which feature pavé. From the many disparaging comments in magazines of the time, it's clear that 19th century cyclists also disliked setts, preferring to ride on asphalte, wooden blocks or smooth macadam.

ASPHALT v ASPHALTE

There are differences between asphalt, asphalte, tarmac and Tarmac. When I feature pre-1900 asphalt I add an "e" to the end of that word because in most period sources it was called *asphalte* – this was different to today's blacktop. Chapter 7 provides more information on macadam, metalling and the experiments that eventually led to "asphaltic cement" – hard, smooth road surfaces were vital to the success of first cycling, and then motoring. A metalled, macadamised road is often thought to mean a road capped with asphalt: it's not. *Metal* is derived from the Greek word for road stone, and macadam is a road-building method using small stones that knit together to form an all-weather surface. Named for Scottish engineer John Loudon McAdam, macadamisation revolutionised road transport in the early part of the 19th century – but this revolution was short-lived as railways swiftly put roads to sleep.

WEIGHTS AND MEASURES

I'm no metric martyr, but I use Imperial measurements throughout this book, unless the context suggests otherwise. This is because I quote extensively from pre-metric British and non-metric American cycling and motoring pioneers. There are no conversions in brackets (apart from the one below). This looks messy and confusing in print and, should you want to know what 30 miles equals in kilometres, you can easily pop the figure into a well-known search engine.

Some roads book authors use the abbreviation Mm. This is the Megametre, not the millimetre. Mm is equal to one million metres or 1,000km (or 621.37 miles). Mm is a surveyor's measurement. Another, albeit older and shorter, system is the chain. Not the bicycle chain, Gunter's chain. This was designed in about 1610 by English clergyman and Oxford-trained mathematician Edmund Gunter, and was used to measure roads in Britain, America, Australia, India and other countries associated with the British Empire. Gunter used a 22-yard chain of 100 links. The length of a cricket pitch is 66 feet, or exactly one chain. This is not a coincidence.

SPELLING

When transcribing from original US sources I have attempted to keep American spellings even though my British English spellchecker tries to correct me when doing so. The word *aluminium* has proved to be especially taxing. When I feature aluminium, I include the extra "i"; when American quotes are included, I've used *aluminum*. Incidentally, the missing "i" is a spelling mistake, as demonstrated in chapter 14. For much of the 19th century and part of the 20th, Americans were perfectly happy spelling *aluminum* as *aluminium*. *Webster's Revised Unabridged Dictionary* of 1913 advises readers to turn to aluminium when seeking aluminum. Some Americans used to spell *tire* with a *y*. According to the *Oxford English Dictionary*, usage of both *tyre* and *tire* was acceptable in the 15th and 16th centuries. In the 17th century, *tire* became the settled spelling, in both Britain and America. Thomson's "aerial wheel" English patent of 1845 – which predated John Boyd Dunlop's pneumatic tyre patent – used the *i* variant. It was only in the 20th century that *tyre* became specifically British, and *tire* specifically American. I use "tyre" in this book, except when quoting from those American bicycle magazines which didn't ape English habits.

WHEEL*MEN*

Even when there were plenty of wheelwomen, the League of American Wheelmen kept its original name. The casual sexism – and racism – of earlier eras is shocking to our eyes but I haven't expunged every example of such *isms*. When I use the term "wheelmen", I don't mean men alone. The bicycle, of course, was a great emancipator of women – in dress and mores – and there were women who raced, toured the world and wrote about bicycling for a living. Cycling, and later motoring, attracted women

Frances Benjamin Johnston of Washington, D.C. was a professional photographer. This photo was a self-portrait – her extended foot is probably pressing a remote switch. Ms. Johnston was the official White House photographer for a time. If the high-wheeler was hers – and it appears to be the right size – this photograph was provocative for the time given that she's wearing mens' clothing and is even sporting a false mustache. Ms. Johnston was one of many high-society lesbians attracted to cycling.

participants but the main protagonists in the cycling and motoring organisations, in the push for Good Roads, in cycling and motoring journalism, and in the founding and running of cycling and motoring companies, were invariably men. Cycling and motoring were both transformational for the position of women in society but it was many years before women reached positions of power in either cycling companies and organisations, or motoring ones.

CYCLE DOMINANCE

When reading this book, you might get the impression I've pinned a cycle-credential on every character mentioned – finding a bicycling red under every bed. Do I really think *everything* has a cycling-related back-story, from roads to rockets? Of course not. I haven't done a *Forrest Gump*; there has been no insertion of cycling snapshots into historical episodes where they didn't exist. No need. There's plenty of evidence available, but it's evidence that rarely sees the light of day or has been suppressed.

NOTES

As much of this book is about resurrecting lost or deliberately obscured histories, there will be some who think I've made it all up. I've therefore been very careful to cite the source material for all the facts and quotes I've included. The copious notes would double the length of this book so I have placed them online: roadswerenotbuiltforcars.com/notes.

CHAPTER ONE

WHEN TWO TRIBES WERE ONE

*The roads you travel so briskly lead out of dim antiquity, and you
study the past chiefly because of its bearing on the living present
and its promise for the future.*
LIEUTENANT GENERAL JAMES HARBORD, 1946

**The improvements made to highways are normally assumed to have been started by motorists.
This assumption is mistaken. The "Good Roads" movement was created in the 1880s by cyclists.
Many of these cyclists were rich and influential, and would later morph into motorists and
continue campaigning for Good Roads. The first motorists drove automobiles that were heavily
dependent on technologies developed by the cycle industry, an industry at the cutting edge of
industrial design and which pioneered manufacturing processes absorbed by the automobile
industry, an industry dependent on former or existing cycle entrepreneurs and technicians.**

Many country roads in the 19th century were rutted in winter, dust-bowls in the summer and
churned with deep mud at most other times. Urban areas fared better, with macadam roads
capped with layers of dust-bound crushed stone. Major thoroughfares in cities were often topped not
with setts – don't call 'em cobbles – but with wood. In 1871, Pennsylvania Avenue in Washington, D.C.,
"America's Main Street," was laid with hardwoods. Five years later some of the wood blocks were lifted,
and a thin *asphalte* strip laid in their place. This was a test of a tar-and-gravel mix patented by a Civil
War cavalry general who had been inspired by a Belgian scientist's mountain-sourced French bitumen.
In effect, this was America's first bike path. Asphalte roads spread through the city – there were 45
miles of them by 1882. The District of Columbia's asphalte roads formed a "wheelman's paradise," said
Bicycling World. A writer in 1889 asked: "How is it possible for a man or woman to get along in that city
of magnificent surfaces without a cycle of some kind?"

Cyclists may have loved the pioneer blacktop, but it soon rippled and popped, and within a decade
the asphalte roads had been grubbed up; the perfect road surface was still some years away. However,
Gilded Age cyclists had seen the future – a future of hard, smooth roads. In the late 1880s the pushiest
of these well-heeled cyclists created an influential highways improvement campaign. The Good Roads
movement would go on to achieve much of what it wanted: Federal funding for roads, a national
plan, and the start of the world-reshaping American highway system. The Federal Aid Road Act of
1916 was signed by President Woodrow Wilson. When a law professor, Wilson had spent much time
in Europe, touring on his bicycle. The roads of France and England were far superior to the ones in
America and Wilson became an advocate of Good Roads, an interest he kept as he became a motorist.
By his side at the signing of the Federal Aid Road Act was Amos G. Batchelder, Executive Secretary
of the American Automobile Association. By 1916, the Good Roads movement was no longer led by
bicycle riders, but by motorists. However, Batchelder had first been a cycling official. A member of
the League of American Wheelmen since 1888 he had been the L.A.W.'s official handicapper, and
was also chairman of the National Cycling Association's racing board. A great many other motoring

1

officials, journalists, promoters, and manufacturers had also been heavily involved in cycling but in 1916 cycling's contribution to the improvement of America's highways was becoming obscured, partly by design.

The hiding was so successful that, by 1927, the Ford Motor Company could boldly claim that the "Ford car ... started the movement for good roads." The record was set straight in 2011 by Suzanne Fischer, curator of The Henry Ford museum in Dearborn, Michigan. "It might surprise you," she said, in a video, "but it wasn't car owners that first demanded better roads – it was bicycle riders."

AMERICA'S GOOD ROADS movement was modelled on Britain's Roads Improvement Association, created by cycling organisations in 1886. "Cyclists were the class first to take a national interest in the conditions of the roads," said William Rees Jeffreys in 1949. In the early 1900s, Rees Jeffreys led the influential Roads Improvement Association via his role as a council member of the Cyclists' Touring Club, one of the two cycling organisations which had established the pioneering roads lobbying organisation.

That it was bicyclists who first pushed for improved highways is today surprising, but it was clear and obvious in the 1890s. "The bicycle has done more for good roads, and will do more for good roads in the future, than any other form of vehicle," remarked Brooklyn's Mayor in 1896. An American newspaper said in 1899 that the reason bicyclists were "such advocates of good roads is that, having to furnish the motive power by the use of their own muscles, they learn at once what a mighty difference there is in the energy required to move the same load on a smooth, hard road or an uneven and muddy one." Another newspaper, in the same year, stated that cyclists had at first been despised because many thought they were demanding "that others should, without cost to him, smooth the roads that he alone might have more pleasure." When faced with rough or muddy highways, American farmers had acquiesced: "For years the farmer drives behind his horse with many a bumpety-bump, and the horse became stalled without ever swearing about it or writing a long protest to the county paper."

Cyclists, on the other hand, didn't keep quiet: "Here were people who could swear and write, pushing their vehicles by main strength on wretched paths when a [smooth] street ... permitted them to glide along almost without effort."

Spreading the "Gospel of Good Roads," cyclists cajoled, leafleted and sued, and flexed their political muscles. The campaigning continued when these moneyed cyclists morphed into motorists. Motoring pioneers were successful at – finally! – getting roads improved because they either benefited from the earlier lobbying work of cyclists or, just as likely, had started to lobby for Good Roads when, back in the day, they were cyclists.

Cycling's role in highway history started to be obscured when cycling became proletarian and when, even though cyclists were still the overwhelming majority on the roads, most of the money spent on highways was devoted to the needs of motorists alone. Motoring was modern; motoring was thrusting; motoring, thought almost everybody, was the future.

The critical part the bicycle played in the history of roads, automobiles, technology and, indeed, of society was played down because propulsion by anything other than motors was deemed old-fashioned. Pedalling became passé. "People may be divided into those who possess cars and those who want to possess them," chided aeronautical and automotive designer Sir Dennistoun Burney in 1931. Bicycles, went the slur, were "relics from the 19th century" (as though automobiles weren't).

HISTORIANS VERY often claim that cyclists and motorists of the late Victorian and Edwardian eras were from different classes. This book demonstrates the "two tribes" concept is incorrect: pre-1920s cyclists and motorists were often not just from the same (elevated) class, they were frequently the same individuals. Historians and social commentators started to get this wrong from the 1920s onwards, mainly because they were looking at history through a windscreen, and a narrow, grimy one at that. The early motorists celebrated their cycling backgrounds, but later, motor-myopic generations, ignored cycling's vital contribution to motoring and to highway history in general.

This isn't to say that cycling's history is a rosy one. In part, organised cycling had a rather inglorious past – elitist; metropolitan; militaristic; perfectly happy for roads to be improved via the sweat of

convicts; overwhelmingly white and male; at times openly racist (L.A.W. and some other American cycling clubs once had a bar on black members); fond of "scorching" (riding fast), to the detriment of pedestrians; and with a propensity to bicker over the smallest of differences (such as amateur versus professional racing status, and the good sense or otherwise of riding on "special roads" set aside for cyclists, an issue that still divides today). Rather more gloriously, cycling eventually provided transformative economic opportunities for workers, and had a major impact on equal rights for women. From suffragettes on two wheels through to the liberated "New Woman" who could openly wear looser, "rational" clothing, to the glamorous illustrations of Gilded Age "Gibson girls," cycling played a key role in women's emancipation at the end of the 19th century, as evidenced by the oft-wheeled out quote from women's rights activist Susan B. Anthony. In 1896, she told the *New York World*'s Nellie Bly that bicycling had "done more to emancipate women than anything else in the world."

Cycling also played a pivotal part in the emancipation of the horse: owners of Victorian livery stables complained that their takings were much reduced when the "steel steed" became all the rage in the 1890s. It is perhaps ironic therefore, that cyclists were hugely responsible for popularising what would push horses – and bicycles – off the roads. Prominent officials from the CTC and the L.A.W. were pioneer motorists and helped form some of the early motoring organisations, sitting on their boards and shaping their futures. The Automobile Club de France, the world's oldest motoring organisation, was founded by, among others, a number of former racing cyclists. It was much the same in other countries. Today, in the Netherlands, the main motoring and road rescue organisation is the ANWB, popularly known as the Royal Dutch Touring Club. A more accurate translation of *Algemene Nederlandse Wielrijders-bond* is the General Dutch Cyclist Union. The ANWB was established in 1883 as a cycling club, before the advent of motoring.

Cycling's contribution to motoring was common knowledge before the 1920s but once cycling became "poor man's transport" the contribution was deliberately downgraded in Britain and America, and officially obliterated in Germany. The Nazi propaganda department wrote to German encyclopaedias ordering them to delete the debt motoring owed to an Austrian Jewish engineer – and, surmises one historian, the debt owed to cycling, too.

The world's first motor car was a tandem tricycle and was created by a cyclist (Carl Benz raved about his cycling days). The first heavier-than-air powered flight was made by a cyclist (Wilbur piloting, Orville Wright running alongside; the brothers funded their aviation experiments from the profits generated by their upmarket own-brand bicycles sold from their Dayton, Ohio, cycle shop).

Most early motorists learned their road craft on bicycles. The parliamentarian Lord Montagu of Beaulieu was known as one of the most ardent motorists of his generation. In 1956, his son's extensive collection of cars, housed at the family's stately pile in the New Forest, was opened to the public as the Montagu Motor Museum, later becoming the National Motor Museum. In the 1880s and 1890s Montagu *père* was an especially keen cyclist. An 1896 *Vanity Fair* profile of him said the MP "cycles with ease" and cycling was still listed as one of his interests in the 1927 edition of *Who's Who*. Montagu is noted for being the first person to drive a motor car into the grounds of parliament. Far less well known today is that six years earlier he had been a cycling MP. In a parliamentary debate on what became the Motor Car Act of 1903, Montagu said: "I remember coming to this House in 1893 riding a bicycle …"

In the 1890s, cycling was seen as scientifically advanced, and the favoured travel mode of transport progressives. According to an 1896 editorial in the *Detroit Tribune*, "the invention of the bicycle was the greatest event of the 19th Century." The US Census of 1900 praised the bicycle thus: "Few articles created by man have created so great a revolution in social conditions." A full 16-pages of this publication were devoted to cycles and cycling, while just five pages were devoted to the nascent automobile industry.

"As a social revolutionizer it has never had an equal," said an 1896 editorial on the impact of bicycle in the *New York Evening Post*. "It has … changed completely many of the most ordinary processes and methods of social life. It is the great leveller, for not till all Americans got on bicycles was the great American principle, that every man is just as good as any other man, and generally a little better, fully realized. All are on equal terms, all are happier than ever before …"

Those who rode the revolutionary bicycle pushed for changes that benefited society as a whole. In 1900, motoring enthusiast Sir Arthur Pearson, a British newspaper owner, said: "It is the cyclists who are largely at the bottom of what has already been accomplished [in the cause of good roads]. In working for their own good, they have extended a benefit to the whole community, the magnitude of which could hardly be exaggerated."

BRITISH ESTABLISHMENT figures like Pearson had their equivalents in America. Cycling was for society's elite. The L.A.W. was founded in 1880 in Newport, Rhode Island – the epicentre of Gilded Age upper-crust culture and location for the grand "cottages" of the fabulously wealthy. By 1898, the cycling organisation had more than 103,000 members, including socialites John Jacob Astor, "Diamond" Jim Brady, and John D. Rockefeller, three of the richest men in the world. Rockefeller – the oil baron who became the world's first billionaire – made a cycle path to the summit of his summer estate at Forest Hill in Cleveland, Ohio.

In 1888, the L.A.W. formed a National Committee for Highway Improvement, putting the issue of Good Roads at the centre of what the organisation wanted to achieve. This campaign was vigorous, spirited and well-funded (mostly by bicycle barons). Millions of Good Roads pamphlets were distributed, to farmers, national and local politicians, and surveyors, indeed to whoever would listen. The circulation of the wheelmen's ground-breaking *Good Roads* magazine soared, and reached out far beyond the ranks of bicyclists.

Like Rockefeller, the wheelmen had a hill to climb. There were many interests ranged against them, from the rail lobby to farmers. The railway interests were all-powerful in the 1880s. Agents and lawyers employed by the rail barons dominated the US Congress and state capitols. Conservative farmers were suspicious about the claims from bicyclists that improved roads would boost agricultural prosperity.

Farmers believed the real beneficiaries of better roads – which they feared they would have to pay for – would be urban cyclists. At the time, roads were maintained by the "working out" method, under which farmers provided their own time and tools, a few times a year. This was an inefficient system, open to abuse, but, for farmers, at least it didn't involve an outlay of hard cash.

"The great majority of the farmers of the United States never saw a good road and do not know what it is," snapped an editorial in the *New York Times*. "A road that is a morass in Spring, a Sahara in Summer, a series of ruts and ridges frozen stuff in later Autumn, and a slough whenever there is a thaw in Winter is to them the normal means of rural communication ..."

Farmers weren't blind to the inadequacies of rural roads, but they mistrusted paying money to a centralised source, something that would be required for a road system to be improved as a whole. And farmers most certainly mistrusted the "peacocks" on their bicycles, riding out from cities and lecturing country people on what was good for them.

The rural community had long talked about the poor quality of the roads but had done little about it. "Let anyone drive over most American roads in the spring, with open eyes and wits, and see what unchecked destruction is at work," commented a writer in *Country Gentleman* in the Spring of 1884.

Eventually, after much hard work by campaigners, farmers came round to the idea of Good Roads, and the rail interests decided that better roads would be good for them, too. Bicyclists were given the credit. In 1892, *The New York Times* said: "The [Good Roads] movement ... was very largely promoted ... by the efforts of the wheelmen, who have done a great deal of public good ..." Eight years later, with thousands of automobiles on the streets, the *New-York Tribune* reminded its readers that "the part which the bicycle has taken in the promotion of highway improvement is acknowledged to be important. Perhaps it might not be exaggeration to say that the influence exerted by wheelmen in support of that work has been stronger than that proceeding from any other source ..."

IN THE 1890s there was a cross-over period when there was no dominant mode of transport in the cities of Britain, America and most other countries, too. Pedestrians, cyclists, equestrians and motorists, all shared the usually ill-defined roads. Add to the mix trams and omnibuses – both originally pulled by horses, later by motors – and the answer, as period films show, looks chaotic to modern eyes. A 35-minute 1906 film of San Francisco, shot from a moving trolley-car, shows pedestrians and cyclists darting hither and thither between motor cars, horse-pulled omnibuses and hand-pulled carts. Motor cars drifted between slower-moving vehicles. The large number of motor cars in the film is often said to point to early automobile domination of San Francisco's streets when, in fact, the same cars keep doubling back to appear multiple times in the film, a deliberate ploy by the film-makers. One of the motor cars appears ten times in the space of one and a half miles.

The film shows peaceful co-existence between the different road users. Motorists had not yet succeeded in using speed and power to claim road space as theirs alone. Roads were transport conduits, but they were also still linear parks, brimming with life, not the roads we know today – sterile, mono-use and largely personality-free.

BEFORE MOTORING became mainstream, motor car drivers were far from popular. Pioneer motorists were disparaged for the dust they threw up from macadamised roads, despised for their speeding, and derided for their desire to make the public highway into a conduit for transport alone. When the majority of MPs and peers owned motor cars the official dislike for "stink wagons" waned but it is instructive that, in 1903, many MPs spoke against the greater road rights being demanded by motoring interests (including the 123 MPs who were already motor car owners).

"The roads of England were made for the people," blasted Sir Frederick Banbury, the Conservative MP for Peckham, "and they should not be monopolised by a certain section, no matter whether they belonged to the poor or the rich."

Cathcart Wason, Independent Liberal MP for Orkney and Shetland (and famous for knitting during debates), continued on the same theme, claiming motorists were aiming to "monopolise the public roads," and that people would have to "fly for their lives at the bidding of one of these slaughtering, stinking engines of iniquity."

Former preacher George Harwood, the Liberal MP for Bolton, said he had witnessed cars using roads as race-tracks, "palpitating, throbbing, and turning the whole of the thoroughfare into chaos and confusion. This is unjust ... The many ought not to be thrust on one side for the few ..."

Parliament's most pro-automobile MP, Scott Montagu, claimed that "roads were intended for vehicles."

This claim was countered in a follow-up debate in August 1903 when Sir Ernest Soares, the Liberal MP for Barnstable, pointed out "the public has the use of the road by common law, whereas the motorists have only the right by statute."

He added the public have a "birthright to use the road." Furthermore, "the public have a right to come and say 'These roads are ours, and we have a right to use them, and you must not pass any legislation which conflicts with our interests.'"

Soares pressed his point: "Motorists are in the position ... of statutory trespassers on the road." Then, in a flourish that summarises the subject of this book, he concluded "roads were never made for motor-cars. Those who designed them and laid them out never thought of motor-cars."

MANY OF the pioneer motorists made no secret of their desire to make roads into racetracks, and weren't terribly tactful. "A powdery layer of lime dust lay 5cm deep on the road in the Piave valley," wrote the engine designer Rudolf Diesel, in 1905. He continued:

> George and I raced along it at full throttle. A vast plume swelled out behind us. We terrorised the pedestrians; it was like making a gas attack; their faces contorted and we left them behind us in a world without shape ...

The satirical magazine *Punch* poked fun at this sense of entitlement from the newest users of the road:

> I blow my horn and the people scatter ... I move and kill dogs. I skid and chickens die ... The roads were made for me; years ago they were made ... Roads I break and Rules of the Road. Statutory limits were made for me. I break them. I break the dull silence of the country ... I am I and She is She – the rest get out of the way ...

That motor cars would take over the world – pushing all other road users aside – was no fait accompli. And that the conditions for this colonisation were right in the 1880s and 1890s was no accident. There had been earlier attempts to create horseless carriages, in the late 1700s and in the early and mid-1800s. By the 1830s, it was perfectly logical for engineers to attach steam engines to road-going vehicles but, in the main, these "road steamers" did not catch on. Motoring historian Timothy Nicholson said there were two main periods of activity in Britain when such vehicles could have sparked a revolution, but didn't. The first was 1831-2, when steam engines were already becoming successful on rails, and a number of engineers thought putting steam engines on the road was the obvious next step. It wasn't to be. The second phase was in 1861. Again, the road engine, you could say, ran out of steam.

Why did the first two generations of self-propelled road vehicles fail to take root? Nicholson said it wasn't due to legal restrictions, for "at both these stages the self-propelled road vehicle had just been given legal recognition … sufficient to allow it to develop." Nor was it due to being priced off the turnpike toll roads. "What, then, was special about the state of affairs in Britain after 1896?" asked Nicholson.

What was special, and different, were attitudes towards roads and horse-free mobility. There was also now a large pool of people who had travelled long distances without recourse to rails (and who, by dint of circumstance, also now knew how to repair their own vehicles out in the sticks, leading to an appreciation for practical self-sufficiency that would be essential for early motoring). The missing link Nicholson was searching for was the cycle. But he dismissed cycling, even though those who were in the thick of things at the time *did* credit it as the missing link. Motoring pioneer Hiram Percy Maxim, writing in 1936 about his 1890s experiences, said the bicycle created motoring, for it "directed men's minds to the possibilities of independent long-distance travel over the ordinary highway." In 1892, Maxim was itching to attach a petrol engine to his fixed-wheel bicycle and later headed up the electric automobile division at America's biggest and oldest bicycle company, and it was clear to him "the bicycle created a new demand" for independent travel.

Other contemporary opinion also credited cyclists with being the prime movers where road travel was concerned. Economists Beatrice and Sidney Webb said in 1913: "What the bicyclist did for roads, between 1888 and 1900, was to rehabilitate through traffic, and accustom us all to the idea of our highways being used by other than local residents."

The copious credit given to the bicycle by those who were present at the birth of motoring is ignored by most historians due to modern prejudice against cycling – too many think of cycling as "poor man's transport," a concept that did not kick in until the 1920s and 1930s.

Nicholson is one of many eminent motoring historians who mistakenly dismiss cycling in Britain in the Victorian age as proletarian or, at best, lower middle class. Writing about the 1890s, Nicholson claimed, somewhat scandalously:

> Car ownership was for carriage folk, and bicycles for the masses. Carriage folk were not given the idea by riding bicycles, for by and large they did not do so. Carriage folk could imagine owning a motor car, because they could afford it, but the average bicycle owner, a shop assistant or City clerk on his £2 a week or less, could never seriously contemplate it.

Nicholson's woefully inaccurate view of 1890s cycling is a common one and still very much voiced today, part of the collective myopia of "motorism" that believes motoring is progressive and bicycling is backward; and that motor cars are superior to bicycles.

This belief in the motor car's superiority started early. In 1900, American author Gardner Dexter Hiscox damned the bicycle, John-the-Baptist fashion: "The bicycle has throughout its marvellous development been preparing the way for a vastly greater vehicle than itself."

The "marvellous" bicycle was portrayed merely as a stepping-stone towards the perfect vehicle, the motor car. The Darwinistic view of the motor car as "superior" reshaped our world, with roads becoming motor-only roads. What was once space for all quickly became space for those in motor cars alone. Other road users – including cyclists – were marginalised, stigmatised. It's assumed this trajectory will continue. It may not.

CHAPTER TWO

PIONEERS

All social progress resolves itself into the building of roads.
WILLIAM REES JEFFREYS, 1949

Many of the key motoring pioneers had first been pioneers of cycling. This chapter – a cast of characters, really – contains profiles of ten of the most influential.

Famous motoring pioneers – such as Henry Ford, Louis Chevrolet and Sir Charles Rolls – had bicycling backgrounds. Other motoring pioneers, less well known but key figures nevertheless, were also important in the world of cycling, although you wouldn't know this from their profiles in automotive history books. Sir David Salomons, Frank Duryea, Sir Alfred Bird, Lord Harmsworth, Viscount Nuffield and John Jacob Astor were prominent motorists in the 1890s and early 1900s, and they made no secret of their bicycling backgrounds. These characters will be encountered throughout this book. However, there are ten individuals who deserve longer profiles. All of them – bar one – were pivotal cyclists who went on to shape early motoring. The exception is Carl Benz – he was an enthusiastic cyclist for a time but he made no contribution to cycling. The others were inventors, entrepreneurs, officials and promoters who honed their skills in the world of cycling before transferring to motoring.

CARL BENZ
On Easter Sunday 1933, in front of a huge crowd and beneath fluttering red flags emblazoned with swastikas, a stone monument was unveiled in Mannheim, Germany. The monument was to Carl Benz. It's still there and features a bas-relief of a middle-aged Benz standing beside a pin-sharp representation of the "world's first motor car." As a piece of art it's unremarkable; as a piece of history it stinks. The Benz motor car is shown with carriage wheels. In front of the commemorative slab, there's a later memorial, an historically more accurate one. It's an exact facsimile of Benz's first vehicle: it has tricycle wheels. Carl Benz's 1886 *Patent-Motorwagen* wasn't a "horseless carriage," but was constructed from steel cycle-tubing and was shod with the same wheels used on the Coventry-designed tricycles of the day. Parts for the "world's first motor car" were bought from the House of Bicycles, Germany's biggest bike shop. Carriage wheels were chiselled on to the stone slab because to have depicted tricycle wheels would have suggested the first motor car had origins in England's cycle factories, a double no-no for the Nazis.

The elevated status afforded to Benz is partly due to the plaudits heaped upon him while he was still alive. Benz had the good fortune to survive into the late 1920s and was therefore worshipped by enthusiasts as a living link to the founding of motoring. In the 1930s, Adolf Hitler was said to have had a "special fondness and respect" for the Benz Patent-Motorwagen and would often ride in an early replica, making "little effort to conceal his delight."

Such delight didn't extend to Hitler's countryman Siegfried Marcus. Marcus was an Austrian engineer who some believe had a working gasoline automobile at least ten years before Benz. But Marcus was Jewish and the Nazis erased his name from history in 1940. They also erased the cycle origins of the Benz Patent-Motorwagen. It was clear to all who chose to see – then and now – that the original Benz vehicle was a tricycle with a motor attached. One of the patents filed by Benz described the vehicle as a "tricycle." The world's first automobile was a direct and blindingly obvious transfer of technology from cycling. For the Nazis, however, such linkage was anathema: cycling, by the 1930s, was for poor people and its origins were not gloriously Germanic – cycling was well known to have been perfected in "perfidious Albion." Historian and Benz expert Hans-Erhard Lessing believes it's highly likely that the Reich Ministry for Public Enlightenment and Propaganda ordered German encyclopaedias to wipe out all reference to the cycle origins of the Motorwagen just as it ordered the removal of Siegfried Marcus. Benz had no problems discussing motoring's cycling origins. He was a pioneer cyclist in the late 1860s and in a 1909 newspaper interview he was very open about his bicycling beginnings:

> A good friend of mine paid me a visit … He had just returned from a journey to Stuttgart. My friend had acquired a curious vehicle [a velocipede] and had returned to Mannheim with the same enthusiasm for the vehicle as mine. However, all his attempts learning to ride it came to a shameful end. So it wasn't sheer goodness of his heart when he gave me the velocipede. Rather he wanted another guinea pig to see if somebody else would suffer as many bruises and injuries as himself. Well, that turned out to be the case. But fourteen days later I had mastered it. Nobody was prouder than me at that time! What a sensation it was when I pedalled through the streets of Mannheim, and what a sensation when I stopped off at some inn somewhere down the road! I soon became accustomed to the mockery, all the more since I soon found out that actually everybody would have liked to ride it …

In an "autobiography" ghost-written by Karl Volk, his son-in-law, Benz is supposed to have rejected and discarded his "boneshaker" bicycle, even though it's known Benz was a rider for longer than just a few months:

> One fine day the heavy wooden monster had to make its way to the junk room, despite all the enthusiasm. Its iron hoops were eaten away by rust and the wooden wheels were succumbing to the ravages of time.

Volk seemed to relish describing the rotting away of the "monster" in a "junk room" but, in reality, Benz – who never owned a horse-drawn carriage – remained interested in cycling and especially the high-wheelers which, in the 1870s, were starting to be imported from England. Professor Lessing has described Benz as an "enthusiastic cyclist." It's also highly likely that Benz owned at least one pedal-powered tricycle before he made his motorised one.

IN THE 1880s Benz was an almost bankrupt machine shop owner and engine designer. His life – and wealth – changed when he met enthusiastic cyclist Friedrich Wilhelm Esslinger. *Automobile Quarterly* in

1986 said that this meeting came about because of Benz's "acute interest in the then-booming bicycling movement." Esslinger was involved with a Mannheim business owned by Jewish engineer Max Kaspar Rose. This business was the local agency for the cycle brands manufactured by Heinrich Kleyer, owner of House of Bicycles in Frankfurt, Germany's largest cycle shop. Esslinger and Rose joined with Benz to form, in 1883, Benz & Cie. [Company], which manufactured stationary internal combustion engines of Benz's design. The firm flourished, enabling Benz to experiment with cycle technology to create his first road-going motor vehicle. Unlike the horse-drawn carriages of the day, which used heavy, wooden-spoked wheels, Benz used lightweight, wire-spoked tricycle wheels for his first Patent-Motorwagen. He also used lightweight cycle-tubing, cycle chains and innovations such as the differential gear developed by James Starley of Coventry. A newspaper, reporting on the Benz vehicle in 1886, called it a "Motoren-Velociped," or motorised velocipede.

By the 1930s, when bicycles were seen as lowly and anti-progressive some historians and motoring writers went out of their way to obscure the fact motor cars sprang, in large part, from the cycle industry. In 1936, Max Rauck, an engineer and first curator of the Daimler-Benz archive, claimed that Benz fashioned his 1886 chassis with no external influences.

In a 1938 motoring history book, Wilfrid Bade, an official within the Nazi's propaganda ministry, trumpeted Germany's significant contributions to motoring history without once mentioning cycling. (Bade wasn't a terribly reliable historian – he also wrote a glowing biography of his boss, Joseph Goebbels.) But erasing cycling from the history of motoring wasn't just a Nazi flaw. English writers in this period, and beyond, were just as bad. Eminent motor writer St. John C. Nixon (who was a motorist in the early 1900s and knew many of the motoring pioneers) claimed in 1933 that the "Benz car had a chassis-frame made up of boiler tubes and had no resemblance to any other form of vehicle." Boiler tubes? No resemblance to *any* other vehicle? Either Nixon spent his 1890s schooldays blindfolded, preventing him seeing the two-person tricycles common at the time or, by 1933, he was suffering from a severely defective memory.

The see-no-tricycle malady was infectious. In a 1955 history of the Mercedes-Benz marque, motoring writer David Scott-Moncrieff wrote of Benz that "every part of [the first Benz vehicle] had to be designed out of his own head and made with his own hands." *Every* part?

Pre- and post-war motoring writers either genuinely believed what they wrote about Benz's machine – despite copious evidence to the contrary, including just looking at photographs of the first Motorwagen – or they deliberately downplayed cycling's part in motoring's birth narrative.

Benz used a great many off-the-shelf cycle parts, and, as the fellow directors of Benz & Cie. were formerly the Mannheim agents of Heinrich Kleyer's cycle shop, it's probable that Esslinger and Rose helped Benz source these parts from the House of Bicycles. French writer Louis Bonneville believed the parts for what he called Benz's "two-seater Sociable tricycle velocipede" were highly likely to have been sourced from Kleyer's shop. Bonneville is a more reliable source than Rauck, Bade, Scott-Moncrieff or Nixon. For a start, he had seen the original Benz tricycle in the flesh. At the age of 24, Bonneville studied the Benz tricycle when, in 1889, it was exhibited at the Paris Exposition. Bonneville wrote a report on this interesting new tricycle-with-motor-attached for French cycle magazine *Sport Vélocipédique*.

The first true motor car was a powered version of the two-person Sociable tricycle then in vogue with the leisured middle-classes and the well-heeled elites. Using mostly cycle technology, the tricycle design was modified to be propelled by a gas explosion engine. Benz's lightweight steel Patent-Motorwagen had almost no DNA from heavy, cumbersome wooden horse-drawn carriages.

Tricycles were first developed in England in the 1870s. James Starley's Coventry Rotary Tricycle used Renold's breakthrough bush-roller chain, and was soon joined by the Salvo, a tricycle made world-famous after Queen Victoria ordered a pair, and asked for them to be delivered by Starley himself, in

Carl Benz bought the parts for the world's first automobile from Heinrich Kleyer's House of Bicycles of Frankfurt. This nine-storey bicycle shop was modelled on Colonel Pope's bicycle shop in Boston, America.

1881. The Sociable tricycle, a two-person version of the Salvo, was well known in Germany in the 1880s. Kleyer's cycle shop opened in 1880 and, while it was a high-wheeler specialist, it probably also sold tricycles from the beginning – English imports at first but German-made soon thereafter. By 1886, the tricycle market was mature and growing, and there would have been little difficulty for Benz and his associates in laying their hands on parts suitable for making a motorised tricycle.

Griffith Borgeson, described by the Society of Automotive Engineers as one of the world's pre-eminent automotive historians, wondered in 1986 how the "direct and obvious link between the Benz vehicle of 1885–86 and the volume-manufactured … sociable trike could have been lost sight of so quickly and so thoroughly." He believed, as do I, that the obfuscation amounted to a "wilful smothering of the truth."

Benz made a number of changes to his early vehicle but, for two years, the incrementally-improved machines were still tricycles. Heinrich Kleyer had a good customer in Carl Benz (Kleyer would later go on to make automobiles of his own).

A later iteration of Benz's Motorwagen, made available for sale in 1888, was heavier than the prototype, looked a lot more like a horse carriage and had wooden-spoked wheels rather than cycle wheels. Sales were poor but the cycling connection continued – the 1888 vehicle was bought by a bicycle manufacturer, Emile Roger of Paris. In 1893, Benz introduced the Viktoria, another carriage-based motor car. Again, sales were poor. Carriage owners, for now, saw little need to swap their horses for engines. The demand for these new motor cars, believed Josef Brecht, in charge of sales for Benz, would not come from the traditionalist, horsey crowd but from those of a more progressive bent. Brecht impressed on Benz that the company should produce a vehicle more like the original cycle-based Motorwagen. This would have greater appeal to avant-garde customers who were alive to the potential of oats- and timetable-free travel – customers who owned and rode bicycles and tricycles. These potential customers were urban and urbane, moneyed but not necessarily fabulously wealthy. Many may not have had the wherewithal to afford a coach, a stable, servants and horses, but they had enough money to afford expensive tricycles. In 1893, Europe was still recovering from an economic depression, yet bicycling was starting to boom and Brecht figured that the cycling crowd, on their relatively expensive cycles (a few covered in gold leaf and encrusted with jewels), would be far more likely to buy into the concept of motoring if the vehicle offered to them looked more like the vehicles they had used and loved for the past ten or twenty years. Brecht got his way and the Benz *Velo* was the result. This, like the prototype, was equipped with cycle wheels, and was far lighter than the carriage-based Viktoria. It was an almost instant hit, partly because of its cycle-like looks but also because it was half the price of a Viktoria. The Benz Velo was one of the top-selling cars of its day: 500 were sold between 1894 and 1896.

The Benz Velo is widely considered to be the world's first series production automobile. When it was introduced it was called the Benz *Velocipede*, a clear reference to the world of cycles, and it was so named to appeal to transport progressives – cyclists. (Benz liked the French word for bicycles: he had also used it on a patent – "driving gear for velocipedes" – granted in 1888.)

In 1910, cycles were not yet seen as proletarian and a Benz & Cie. publication of that year, writing about the history of the company, featured the 1888 carriage-like Benz Motorwagen next to two high-wheeler cyclists. *The Benz Car* also listed the fact that Mannheim was the city where Karl von Drais had invented his "running machine", an 1816 forerunner to the bicycle:

> The city of Mannheim, which famously gave the world the first bicycle, can therefore be proud two of the most modern means of transport came from within its walls.

When Adolf Hitler revealed that it would be Ferdinand Porsche who was to design his much-trailed "people's car" – the Volkswagen – he did so in 1936 at the opening of the Berlin Auto Show. In order to promote this proposed new car, and stress the Germanic origin of motoring, the show had an exhibit of the first motor cars, including a reconstructed Benz Patent-Motorwagen and other early automobiles.

1936 was the 50th anniversary of the creation of both the Benz and Daimler cars. The show organisers, perhaps under instructions from the Nazi propaganda department, changed some vehicle names. A Benz Velocipede from 1896 was displayed in front of a placard saying it was the Benz Velo. The Daimler *Velocipede*, a quadricycle, was renamed the *Stahlradwagen*, "wire-wheel car." In the show's promotional literature, the Benz Patent-Motorwagen was described as having been a complete novelty in 1886 – an innovation that had been influenced by no other vehicle. Pointedly, there was no mention of its cycle-based beginnings. Cycling had lost all of its Belle Époque cachet by the 1930s. Bicycles were deemed a relic of the past – the future was motoring and bicycles could no longer have any place in motoring's nativity story.

There was a very personal reason for the vilification of cycling in 1930s Germany: Hitler hated bicycles. It's probable he developed this loathing while serving as a soldier in the First World War. His military records reveal he had been a lowly bicycle messenger. One record showed he had been a *Radfahrer*, a cyclist. The 25-year-old Hitler was the "runner" for a Bavarian regiment, taking messages from the command staff to the fighting units. This was a dangerous job (historians have never doubted Hitler's bravery) but not a terribly glamorous one. Hitler may have preferred to have been motorised: it would have been more glamorous to have been a *Kradfahrer*, a motorcycle messenger.

When in power, Hitler's Nazi party – fixated on the notion that the weak must be wiped out by the strong – enacted a number of anti-cycling laws, aiming to get "weak" cyclists off the roads, leaving more space for "strong" motor cars. Hans-Erhard Lessing believes that "to restore the cycle as a parent of the automobile, we will have to de-Nazify automobile history."

JOHN KEMP STARLEY

John Kemp Starley is generally considered the creator of the modern bicycle. He also made a pioneering electric car and today the company he founded makes the Range Rover Evoque and others in the "Rover" stable. The first Rover vehicle was Starley's Rover Safety, the bicycle that according to company adverts "set the fashion to the world." This bicycle inspired a global boom, revolutionising social mores in the process and reshaping streets as well as bodies.

J. K. Starley was the nephew of James Starley, the "father of the cycle industry" in England, one of the key popularisers of the high-wheel bicycle. Many manufacturers had attempted to create a Safety bicycle – safe in comparison to riding a high-wheeler, that is. J. K. Starley's first design for a Safety was introduced in 1884, while his company – Starley and Sutton of Meteor Works, Coventry – was still making tricycles.

The first Rover Safety was an indirect-steering, rear-wheel drive, chain-driven low-mount bicycle, unlike the direct-drive high-wheeler. It had a 36-inch front wheel and bridle rods rather than a raked front fork, and was far from perfect – Starley modified the design, creating in 1885 the second Rover, a bicycle with nearly equal-sized wheels and, critically, direct steer forks. It was introduced at the Stanley Cycle Show, Britain's main annual bicycle exhibition, held in a marquee on the Thames Embankment next to Blackfriars Bridge in London from January 28th to February 3rd, 1885.

High-wheeler riders looked down on Safeties – literally and figuratively. They called them "dwarf machines", "beetles" and "crawlers." However, the 1885 Rover – still with solid tyres – was shown to be anything but a crawler when a number of them beat the time record in a 100-mile promotional race, on the macadamised Great North Road between Norman Cross, near Peterborough, and one mile beyond Twyford in Berkshire. This race was staged by Starley and Sutton on September 25th 1885 and helped convince people that the Safety was here to stay. By 1888, the design-registered Rover had two equally-sized wheels and a "diamond-shaped" frame. When shod with John Boyd Dunlop's pneumatic tyres – a race winner in 1889 and commercially available in 1890 – the Rover Safety proved itself to be the perfect bicycle and, in essence, the main features on Starley's 1888 machine are still used on the majority of bicycles sold and ridden today.

In 1888, J. K. Starley built Britain's first electric car. In 1897, J. K. Starley & Co. became the Rover Cycle Company. After J. K. Starley's death his son started to manufacture Rover motor cars. Later the company would make Land Rover vehicles, a brand still setting "the fashion to the world."

Albert A. Pope

COLONEL ALBERT AUGUSTUS POPE

In June 1905, a motor car carrying US President Theodore Roosevelt was stopped for speeding by two policemen on bicycles. The car was a Columbia, the house-brand of America's then most powerful and successful bicycle firm, the Pope Manufacturing Company, a company founded, owned and run by a ruthless monopolist and ardent bicyclist, Colonel Albert Pope. In 1878, the Columbia was the first high-wheel bicycle in America to go into "mass" production (50 bicycles was mass for the time). By the 1890s, the Pope Manufacturing Company sprawled over five huge factories in Hartford, Connecticut. There were two bicycle factories, a tyre plant, a mill for drawing lightweight steel tubing and, from 1897, an automobile factory.

At the same time as producing Columbia bicycles, Pope Manufacturing created some of America's first electric cars, also branded Columbia. However, the Columbia car in which President Roosevelt was caught speeding was a gasoline car. (He was a passenger, not the driver.) Roosevelt had another connection with Albert Pope's bicycle and automobile firm. On August 22nd 1902 Roosevelt had been the first US president to be seen in public in a motor car. In effect, this was the first-ever presidential motorcade. It took place in Hartford. A report in *The New York Times* said that President Roosevelt was greeted by "10,000 workingmen." As this greeting took place in Pope Park (a recreational lung created by Pope for his workers, designed by the same firm that laid out New York's Central Park), it's likely that many of the men in this rent-a-crowd were provided by Pope Manufacturing.

The motor car was also provided by Pope's firm. It was a Columbia Electric Victoria Phaeton, and was flanked by policemen on bicycles. Columbia bicycles, of course. (See photograph on page 284.)

In 2005, Pope was placed third in the League of American Bicyclists' "list of 25 people who indelibly changed the face of cycling in America." Lance Armstrong was voted in as number one (this was before his doping infamy); Tour de France winner Greg LeMond was fifth; mountain bike innovators Gary Fisher and Joe Breeze were 11th and 14th respectively. That somebody born in 1843 could still be high on a list of industry influencers in 2005 says a lot for Pope's staying power as an industry icon.

Known as the "father of the American bicycle industry," Pope was a Civil War colonel who became

Pope is second from the left in this "wheel around the hub" photograph taken near Boston, Massachusetts in September, 1879. His patent attorney – Charles Pratt – is on the far left. Pratt was one of the founders of the League of American Wheelmen.

a pioneer cyclist and helped to popularise cycling in America. "To succeed, Pope had to sell not just Columbias, but cycling itself," wrote bicycle historian Bruce Epperson in 2010. "The allure and popularity of the bicycle did not just happen … It was a deliberately crafted and stage-managed creation, and the Colonel was its impresario."

Pope was a portly fellow – his patent attorney called him Colonel Bounce – and an astute businessman. His empire was built on advertising. Pope's enthusiasm for advertising was such that he's an icon in that sphere, too. Ad campaign measurement was pioneered by Pope – he did this by using different addresses on adverts – for the same building. "It was a maxim of Colonel Pope's that 'some advertising was better than others, but all advertising was good," said Sam McClure, a Pope employee who later became editor and publisher of the influential *McClure's Magazine*. Asked by a magazine what were the three essentials of selling bicycles, Pope responded: "Advertising! Big advertising! Bigger advertising!" Pope's bicycle adverts were ubiquitous in the 1890s: "Every boy in the West knew the Pope Manufacturing Company," said McClure, "the Pope advertisements [were] everywhere."

Pope was also an expert at cultivating the press. As well as launching and subsidising magazines that were largely fronts for his business, Pope was an astute user of what is today known as media relations. "Pope kept the daily press supplied with matter," said a reporter in 1902. "He flooded every paper in the country with bicycle stuff. The bicycle was a new thing, and little was known about it. The editors were hungry for news; they wanted either serious stuff or humorous stuff. Pope gave them all kinds, and billions of words were printed about the bicycle."

Pope's enthusiasm for bicycling wasn't just sales-driven, however, and he was a passionate user of his own products; he started Pope Manufacturing Company because he believed others would like what he liked. His first view of the product that would take over his life came in 1876 when visiting the Philadelphia Centennial Exhibition, America's first World's Fair. A display of five English high-wheeler bicycles caught Pope's eye: "They attracted my attention to such an extent that I paid many visits to this exhibit, studying carefully both the general plan and the details of construction, and wondering if any but trained gymnasts could master so strange and apparently unsteady a mount."

Pope learned to ride a high-wheeler in 1877, and started to import these exotics from England in 1878. They were expensive to import so Pope commissioned Weed Sewing Machine Company of Hartford to produce them in the US. A Hartford trade directory of 1889 takes up the tale:

> When, in May [1878] Col. A. A. Pope rode circuitously from the station to the office of [Weed Sewing Machine Company] on a bicycle of English make, excited throngs swarmed into the streets through which he passed to catch a view of the strange vehicle … As the Colonel disappeared through the door, the surprise and curiosity were transferred from the outside to the inside of the factory. The object of the visit was not only to place a preliminary order, but to arrange for the manufacture of similar machines on a large scale … From their utility as a means of quick and pleasant travel, these machines … little known ten years ago, and popularly regarded as a curious but idle toy, have become the staple of a very large trade.

Pope needed a brand name for his bicycle. Columbia was chosen because there was talk in America, even as early as 1878, of holding a Columbian World Fair in 1892, the 400th anniversary of Christopher Columbus's arrival in the New World.

The first American-made Columbia bicycles were cheaper than the English imports, but still luxury items, and were sold to young, affluent, thrill-seeking males. Sales weren't meteoric at first but momentum built up through the 1880s.

High-wheel bicycles became the fastest things on the road, with riders setting out from towns and cities to explore the countryside. Hundred-mile rides – "centuries" – were common, but only in those cities where the surrounding roads were relatively good. Pope understood that to sell more bicycles he would have to lobby for somewhere for riders to ride. He became one of the leading lights in what became the Good Roads movement. As well as lobbying for improved roads the American Good Roads movement led to a social reappraisal of the bicycle. Originally thought of as an urban peacock's toy, the bicycle became a vanguard for change, and Colonel Pope was the *de facto* leader of the movement that changed the way people thought about bicycles. And this shift in perception benefited the next transport revolutionaries on the scene – motorists.

Urban historian Clay McShane describes the shift as an "increased taste for high-speed, street-using transportation." Bicycles changed how people thought about the use of streets. McShane observed that by 1900 most American city dwellers perceived motor wagons, trolley buses, bicycles – and the odd motor car – as legitimate users of the public highway. "This represented a dramatic shift," said McShane, "from the prohibitions on mechanical vehicles that had prevailed in the 1880s."

Pope pushed for these changes to happen, and he did so with his immense wealth. Where his pet projects were concerned, money was no object. He bankrolled cycling magazines, and was one of the largest contributors to the L.A.W.'s Good Roads campaign. He paid for the printing and distribution of pamphlets, seed-funded road engineering departments in American universities, and masterminded an oversize petition, which was delivered to the US Senate. It called for the creation of a government roads department.

In 1892, Pope wrote a five-page article in the influential magazine *The Forum*. "I have for years urged improvement in the building and maintenance of public roads for practical business reasons," he asserted, adding:

> So far as I could use and extend my influence and the influences that I could quicken, I have sought to kindle and to fan a flame of enthusiasm for improved carriage roads, on the grounds of prudence in the expenditure of money, of foresight in the development of plans, and of practical results – that is to say, of profits measurable as money-returns on investment.

The work on the behalf of Good Roads continued when Pope's factories started to manufacture automobiles. As his business was transport-related he took an early interest in what would become motoring. His automobile division came into being in 1895 but his interest had been piqued as early as 1891, when he dispatched a team to check out an electric car that a Boston inventor had reportedly developed. This came to nothing, but four years later it was probably Pope who – anonymously – told *Scribner's Magazine*, from the New York Cycle Show, that "between electric cars in the cities and the bicycle in the country, the value of horseflesh will drop to almost nothing within twenty years."

It's unclear whether Pope – if he was the bicycle baron interviewed by the *Scribner's* reporter – meant electric automobiles or electric trams. If the former, that was a prescient comment, and it's likely that Pope was talking about individualised "trackless locomotion" because that had been his life's calling, first with bicycles. Pope isn't as well known as Henry Ford but, had electricity taken off as the main motive force for motor cars instead of petroleum it could have been Pope who was fêted as the father of mass motoring. Pope's electric cars were the best-selling automobiles of the 1890s but this early success meant he was less able to foretell the eventual market dominance of the internal combustion engine.

In his autobiography, motoring pioneer Hiram Maxim – an internal combustion expert – related how soon after he joined Pope Manufacturing Company's motor carriage division, in 1895, Colonel Pope told him: "Maxim, I believe this horseless-carriage business will be one of the big businesses of the future!"

However, motoring historians have jumped on the fact that Pope is also reported to have said, "You cannot get people to sit over an explosion," a quote often rolled out to demonstrate how the electric car pioneers were wrong about the internal combustion engine.

When having their fun with this explosion quote, many motoring historians neglect to mention that Pope was hugely responsible for the movement that hastened the success of the petrol-powered automobile. Towards the end of his life, Maxim reminisced about Pope's role in pioneer motoring and claimed that one of his "great regrets is that Colonel Albert A. Pope, the father of good roads in the United States, could not have lived to see his predictions come true a thousandfold."

In 1897, *The Horseless Age* said:

> The Pope Manufacturing Company began its work in the motor carriage field in January, 1895 and during the two years and a quarter that have elapsed since that date investigation and experiments have been going on, without regard to expense, to determine what is the best type of carriage and to devise and construct a vehicle which could be most successfully put before the public at the present time.

The motoring magazine added, "Everything about the carriage is made on a bicycle basis …"

HENRY STURMEY

Henry Sturmey straddled the worlds of cycling and motoring and was a leading voice in both. Today he is best known for the gears named after him, a staple on English roadster bicycles since the early 1900s. That his name was part of Sturmey–Archer gears is a product of company politics, not historical fact. But what's not in doubt is Sturmey's great contribution to cycle and automotive journalism. In the late 1890s, he was editor of *The Cyclist* and *The Autocar* at the same time. One of the earliest motoring pioneers, he was also a cycling pioneer. In 1879 he was a high-wheel rider and one of the leading officials in the nascent Bicycle Touring Club, which became the Cyclists' Touring Club in 1883. In the 1890s and early 1900s Sturmey was an official in the Automobile Club, which became the Royal Automobile Club.

Originally a science teacher, Sturmey became a cycle journalist after writing one of the first bicycle blockbusters. *The Indispensable Bicyclist's Handbook* of 1878 was an instant sales success and went through numerous printings. It was the first "bible" of bicycling, popular in America as well as Britain. Printer William Iliffe of Iliffe and Son secured the printing of the second and subsequent editions of Sturmey's handbook and agreed to his suggestion of producing a cycling magazine separate from the one his Coventry firm already published. This was the start of a long and profitable relationship for Sturmey and Iliffe. *The Cyclist* became the leading cycling magazine.

Iliffe published other magazines that interested Sturmey. The first, in 1888, was *Photography* (which still exists, as *Amateur Photographer*), and the second was *The Autocar*, first published in 1895 and still produced today, the world's longest-running weekly motoring magazine.

The Autocar, edited by Sturmey until 1901, was not the most independent of magazines. It – that is, Sturmey – was in cahoots with Harry Lawson, the magazine's biggest advertiser. Sturmey sold Lawson one of his motor car patents and was a large investor in Lawson's Great Horseless Carriage Company, which had interests in many of the first motor car brands available in Britain, including Daimler. Sturmey became an executive of the Daimler Motor Company and in October 1897 he drove from John o'Groats to Land's End in a British-built Daimler – quite some journey for a motor car, and a driver, at this time. Sturmey's clear and obvious bias estranged him from Iliffe and Son, and, after injuring himself while road-testing a car, he parted from the company in 1901. While still writing for cycling magazines – and a rival motor car magazine – Sturmey became the short-lived British importer of the Duryea motor car. Duryea was the first mass-produced American automobile and no doubt Sturmey had an affinity with company principal Frank Duryea who had earlier been a bicycle mechanic.

SELWYN FRANCIS EDGE

S. F. Edge was a pioneering British racing driver. *The Petrol Age*, a four-part celebration of motorsport on British satellite broadcaster Sky TV in 2012, said Edge had "near-mythological status" and was "our first true hero of speed." He was one of the first members of the Automobile Club, founded in 1897, and sat on its committee. In 1905, he also helped to crank into life the Automobile Association. Furthermore, Edge was a motoring promoter and a car company creator.

Edge's speed skills had been nurtured during an earlier – and very successful – career as a racing

cyclist. Edge won his first race when he was 19. He went on to work for bicycle companies, and used his many connections in cycle sport to good effect when he, like many other cyclists, morphed into motorists.

Born in Australia, Edge moved to England when he was three. He may not have been a member of the English aristocracy like many pioneer motorists (and cyclists), but Edge was born into a life of comfort. His parents bought a large house in Penge, south-east London, and the family had four servants. In 1891, Edge started working as a "commercial traveller" for the Rudge Cycle Company of Coventry, rising to become general manager. At this time he was also racing (his speciality in cycling, and later in motoring, was breaking long-distance records). Edge became general manager of the New Howe Machine Company, a bicycle manufacturer in Chatham, Kent, before moving to the (Dunlop) Pneumatic Tyre Company in 1893: "I saw that the pneumatic tyre would soon oust the solid tyre for bicycles," he said. At the time, Dunlop was producing tyres for bicycles only. The company should start creating tyres for automobiles, too, pressed Edge.

When Edge wanted to become a driver he contacted French racing driver Fernand Charron for his first ride in a motor car:

> It was at the beginning of 1895 that I first heard that Charron – a very noted French racing cyclist – was running a car and had resigned his position with the Humber [bicycle] Company. I was told further he was actively engaged in the motor business in partnership with two other ex-racing cyclists, Girardot and Voigt, who were running an agency for Panhard-Levassor, Peugeot, De Dion-Bouton and a few other cars … [in Paris]. In February, 1895, I wrote to Charron and enquired whether he would give me a run in his car if I came to Paris … I had a reply from him … He reminded me of various incidents in cycle races in which we had both taken part … I crossed over to France [and] wrote to my old friend, H.O. Duncan, another noted old racing cyclist, who lived in Paris, and asked him to dine with me … Duncan was then in partnership with Louis Suberbie as agents for Gladiator cycles and I knew he had some experience of motors …

Up to this point Edge had never seen an automobile, and he was looking forward to doing so:

> My appointment with Charron was not until the evening of the following day, so I spent the whole of that day visiting the various bicycle shops in Paris in the hope that I might catch a glimpse of a motor-car …

There must have been none, for Edge said his first view of an automobile came when the French cycle racer "led the way to the rear of his premises and then, for the first time in my life, I saw a motor car …" Charron took Edge for an hour-long drive. "For the first time in my life I was 'being pushed by a pint of paraffin,'" said Edge.

Edge was present at many of early motoring's key events in Britain, including the Horseless Carriage Exhibition at the Tunbridge Wells Agricultural Show Grounds on October 15th, 1895. This was organised by Sir David Lionel Salomons, Mayor of Tunbridge Wells, and a trustee of the Cyclists' Touring Club.

Salomons' event wasn't an all-day affair; it was run from 3 pm to 5 pm. But there were only five vehicles to see, all of them French. One of the promised vehicles, a powered tricycle "exhibited by Monsieur Guedon for the Gladiator Cycle Co. of Paris" never turned up.

Nevertheless, Salomons' exhibition was a first, and Edge had to be there: "When I heard of this Exhibition I determined to go to Tunbridge Wells and see it," he later wrote. Naturally, he "rode down there on my bicycle."

Edge later became friends with racing driver Charles Jarrott – another former racing cyclist – when the two started working for motoring promoter Harry Lawson. Edge and Jarrott were dapper dressers, famed for their long, fur-lined leather driving coats. (The well-dressed motorist of the late 1890s and early 20th century kept warm with fur from animals as diverse as leopards, squirrels and polar bears.)

Edge and Jarrott formed a company with former racing cyclist Herbert Duncan, securing the British rights for the De Dion-Bouton car, operating out of the Dunlop building on Regent Street in London. Later, Edge formed a partnership with cycle racer Harvey Du Cros of Dunlop fame, and Montague Napier, who in 1895 had started producing machine tools for the bicycle industry.

Napier, too, was a former bicycle racer, as Edge recounted in his autobiography:

> I had been a member of most of the important cycling clubs, one of the most prominent of which was the Bath Road Club. In the late eighties I had ridden as a member of this club, on what was then termed an "Ordinary," but which is now known as a Penny-farthing machine … Montague Napier and I were both members of the "Bath Road" at the same time and often met in club competitions … there were three [clubs] in which I kept in fairly close touch – the Bath Road, the Catford and the Anerley. To this day I count among my best friends certain members of these three clubs.

By 1898 Edge had lost touch with Napier but another former Bath Road Club member found his address: "I wrote to [Napier], reminding him of the several cycling competitions we had ridden in together and asked him when I could call. Within a few days I had a reply inviting me down to his small factory in Lambeth."

Napier had been working on his own design for a car but Edge told him that it was old-fashioned and that he should, instead, work on upgrading Edge's Panhard-Levassor, albeit with modifications, including a steering wheel instead of a tiller. Napier went on to make further modifications to Edge's "Old Number 8," including to the engine. Edge realised Napier's engineering works could make complete cars, and that an English car marque would have cachet. He asked his boss at Dunlop for start-up capital and by autumn 1899 Edge had contracted with Napier to buy six cars, creating the Motor Vehicle Company. The Napier brand was born, and would soon become England's most sought-after motor car. The Motor Vehicle Company was owned and run by three former cycle racers: Edge, Napier and Du Cros.

Napier was the top-selling luxury car marque in Britain until 1906. Edge drove a Napier car to victory in the 1902 Gordon Bennett Cup held in France – the first British victory in an international motor race.

Yet Edge nearly didn't make the race. Luckily, his cycling past rescued the day. Edge was rushing to a car "weigh-in" in Paris when a policeman stopped him. Edge didn't want to hand over his driving licence as he feared it might be confiscated and he wouldn't be able to enter the race:

> [The policeman] wished to see some document … so I produced everything I had in my

pockets … My season ticket, my Cyclists' Touring Club badge … everything I poured into the policeman's hand, but he was still not satisfied. Finally, I showed him my watch … and as soon as he caught sight of this his face lighted up with a smile of recognition. He explained that we had both been competitors in the Bordeaux–Paris cycle race of 1891, and that he would not think of detaining further an old comrade like myself!

Some early motor-car reliability events were timed by cyclists, such as a 1,000-mile track event held on November 21st, 1900 at the Crystal Palace cycle track in London. Edge knew the timers at these motor-car events because they were the same people who had timed Edge's record-breaking cycling events. H. J. Swindley, official timekeeper of the National Cyclists' Union, and F. T. Bidlake, who held the same office at the Road Records Association, were the two key timers of the day.

Bidlake was "my old friend," according to Edge. And Swindley – who went on to become a motoring journalist with *The Autocar* – was "my old friend of the cycling days."

In the 1904 edition of the *Motoring Annual and Motorists Year Book*, Edge described himself as "England's foremost racing motorist, and one of the most progressive of British business motorists." He added he was "formerly a racing cyclist, and holder of many records on track and road."

During the First World War, Edge was controller of the agricultural machinery department of the Ministry of Munitions, having started in the agricultural trade thanks to his business dealings with cycle manufacturer Dan Albone, another former racing cyclist, who had produced one of the very first farm tractors. Albone's tractor (a term that was not coined until later) was patented in the UK in February 1902. The directors of Ivel Agricultural Motors Limited were Edge, Jarrott, and two others.

Edge was a technical adviser to the creators of Brooklands, the world's first purpose-built racing circuit, and opened it in style in 1907 by driving his Napier for 24 hours at an average speed of 65.905 miles per hour, covering 1,581 miles – a record not broken for 18 years.

Edge's 24-hour challenge was a novelty in motoring but it wasn't a novelty in cycling: "These contests were well known in the cycling world," wrote Edge. "I had taken part in more than one of them myself … and I saw no reason why a similar feat should not prove highly interesting with a motor car."

JOHN BOYD DUNLOP and HARVEY DU CROS

On Friday November 19th, 1909 in Hotel Cecil, London's largest, swankiest hotel, 475 invited guests sat down to a lavish banquet celebrating the 21st anniversary of the introduction of the pneumatic tyre, the key innovation that boosted cycling and allowed motoring to go mainstream. The industry big-wigs and gathered dignitaries heard fulsome tributes paid to the founder of a "world-wide industry." Presided over by the Royal Automobile Club's chairman Prince Francis of Teck, brother of the soon-to-be Queen Mary, the banquet had been arranged to bestow the French Government's highest honour, *Chevalier de la Légion d'honneur*, on the evening's principal guest. Representatives of motoring and cycling organisations were present to witness the ceremony. Barrister Arthur J. Walter made the first speech, applauding the founder of "an industry which has conferred immense benefits upon the industrial world." Turning to face a patriarchal gentleman with a long grey beard, he continued: "Mr. John Boyd Dunlop, on the 23rd July, 1888, totally ignorant of anything that had been done before, reinvented the pneumatic tyre." The assembled guests cheered loudly.

"Let me pause here for a moment to emphasise … that you want two things," said Walter. "You want an inventor, and you want somebody who sees the merit of an invention, and who has the nous and the energy and the go to make the public see that the invention is a good one." (Cries of "Hear, hear.") "Every invention needs a sponsor, and that sponsor we have here to-night, and we are delighted to honour him – I mean Mr. Harvey Du Cros."

A huge cheer went up. The banquet, the royal guests, the Légion d'honneur, and a commemorative casket signed by 1,000 motoring and cycling pioneers were not for the Scottish veterinarian who had patented the pneumatic tyre in 1888, but for the Irish cycle champion who became the energetic promoter of the Scottish veterinarian's innovation.

"The names of inventors live in their inventions," continued Walter, adding presciently, "but too often the name of the man who has fostered the industry is forgotten after those who lived at the time with him have passed away."

This is certainly true of William Harvey Du Cros. In his day fêted and fabulously wealthy, he is now forgotten. John Boyd Dunlop, on the other hand, is still famous, his name living on as a sports brand, which is ironic, given Dunlop's hypochondria. Dunlop wasn't terribly enamoured of his own

"invention" once he discovered, in 1890, that his patent had been anticipated. Air-filled tyres for road-going vehicles had been introduced in 1845 by a fellow Scot, Robert Thomson, invalidating Dunlop's patent of 1888. Dunlop was so disillusioned that he tried to invent technologies to improve on pneumatic tyres, such as bicycle spring suspension systems, developments that had been tried – and rejected – by others before him. Dunlop gave his name to the tyre brand and his face to the company's first logo but it was Du Cros (pronounced *doo crow*), a paper merchant, who was the real populariser of pneumatics.

Without Du Cros, pneumatics may not have gone around the world, but might have stayed an oddity from Belfast, where Dunlop was living at the time. There was nothing inevitable about the success of pneumatics, and they weren't an overnight success story. It took a great deal of time, effort and money to popularise the concept. The confident words written by Du Cros in the company prospectus of 1889 sound reasonable now, but that's only because of hindsight. Du Cros wrote: "Racing machines fitted with Pneumatic tyres appear to be invincible … it will be apparent that nothing so calculated to revolutionize cycling has ever before been invented …"

As well as noting that "the pneumatic tyre will be almost indispensable for ladies, and persons with delicate nerves," Du Cros added: "There is every reason to expect that a large business can be done in fixing the Pneumatic Tyre to the wheels of carriages …"

To make the words come true Du Cros had to graft, scheme and fight. Later, once the confidence of Du Cros had been proved to be justified, pneumatics were recognised as a defining breakthrough.

Pneumatic tyres were critical to the rapid uptake of motoring, but they were not developed for motor cars – they had been introduced to make bicycles more comfortable and, critically, faster. Dunlop's 1888 patent said pneumatics were for use on bicycles and tricycles when "immunity from vibration is desired to be secured, and at the same time ensuring increased speed in travelling." The first air tyres required special wheels that had to be factory-fitted, couldn't be easily repaired and looked decidedly plump compared to the skinny "bootlace" solid tyres of the day. The saving grace for "pudding tyres" was their speed – they turned donkeys into racehorses. Track racers weren't fussed about comfort but when so-so racers on pneumatics beat top riders on solid tyres, the days of the hard tyre were numbered.

The transformational potential of pneumatic tyres dawned on Du Cros in May 1889, when he was managing the cycling team he had created around his six strapping young sons. Du Cros came to realise the worth of riding on air because two of his sons, riding solid tyres, were beaten in a track race in Belfast by a lesser racer riding pneumatics.

Du Cros Senior had been a boxing and fencing champion of Ireland. He later gravitated to the boom sport of cycling, riding high-wheelers. After his racing career was over he became the cycle sport trainer and manager of his six sons. He also became president of the Irish Cyclists' Association, and in so doing, rubbed shoulders with William Bowden, a Dublin cycle agent. Bowden had earlier acquired the rights to Dunlop's pneumatic tyre patent and at the May 1889 Belfast race meeting Arthur Du Cros saw at close quarters how the air-filled tyre could be superior in speed to solid tyres, and he told his father about the innovation.

Dunlop's first pneumatic tyre had been made and tested in Belfast, where the Scottish veterinarian had based his large and successful practice since 1867. Dunlop's 11-year-old son, Johnnie, had asked his father to somehow soften – and speed – the ride of his solid-tyred bicycle on the granite setts of Belfast. By 1887, Boyd Dunlop had done so. He patented the idea the following year, and with W. Edlin & Co. of Belfast – and Finlay Sinclair, later to work for the Dunlop company – made a batch of fifty pneumatic-equipped bicycles, their frames adapted to take the fatter tyres. As fitting pneumatics required new frame and fork shapes, and the wheels had to be factory-fitted, the English bicycle industry remained sniffy about pneumatics for some time. Consumers were less averse. The first advert for the world's first commercially-available pneumatic tyre was published in *The Irish Cyclist* on December 19th, 1888:

ANTI-VIBRATION. Look out for the new "PNEUMATIC" SAFETY. Vibration impossible, Sole Makers, W. Edlin & Co. 33 Garfield Street, Belfast.

These fifty bicycles, promoted for their comfort rather than speed, sold with "spontaneous success" to the Belfast cycle-racing community. While Edlin & Co. thought they had a done deal to produce more pneumatic-equipped bicycles, Dunlop had other ideas and switched his allegiance to business partners in Dublin. He roped in William Bowden who, in turn, involved J. M. Gillies, the manager of *Freeman's Journal*, a Dublin newspaper. Bowden and Gillies asked the well-connected Du Cros to form a company with them to exploit the innovation, and the Pneumatic Tyre and Booth's Cycle Agency Ltd. was born. Du Cros took the majority shareholding and assumed control. Dunlop sat on the board but had little say in how the company was run. He later sold the majority of his shares (for a fraction of the profit he would have made had he kept them), sniped from the sidelines, joined a rival pneumatic tyre company and, in a great many letters to the press, spread misinformation about his role in the promotion of pneumatics.

The first pneumatics made by Du Cros Snr. were manufactured in Lincoln Place, Dublin, but, because of complaints about fumes, the factory was forced to relocate. It made sense to be where most of the customers were based (especially because the tyres were factory-fitted), so the Dunlop factory was reopened in Coventry, home of the British cycle industry.

Du Cros Snr. brought his sons into the fledgling business. They were soon integral and important players in the new company, spreading the pneumatic gospel globally. Arthur was sent to England; Fred and William went to Belgium and France; Harvey Jnr., Alfred and George were dispatched to America.

On Christmas Day 1890, Du Cros Snr. stepped off a liner in New York with the first pneumatic tyres ever seen in America. These fat, white, tubular bicycle tyres – called "German sausages" by doubters – were about to face their first major challenge. Du Cros was wired with the news that Dunlop's patent for pneumatic tyres had been overturned, thanks to the belated discovery of Robert Thomson's patent of 1845. This was "one of the most disagreeable days of my existence," admitted Du Cros. With his investment at risk, he acted quickly, wiring instructions back to base for new patents to be found. Sooner than planned, he returned to Coventry. By graft and guile, he acquired the patents for detachable tyres of the "cheerful chubby-faced" English inventor Charles Kingston Welch, cannily employing him in the process.

London-based Irish cycling journalist E. J. O'Reilly said in 1909 that Welch's patent was more important to the success of the pneumatic tyre industry than Dunlop's of 1888:

> Thinking he had a valid patent [Du Cros] set out to found the pneumatic tyre industry. When the Dunlop patent was found to be invalid he had not only established an industry, but had made his business independent of that patent, and … when the Dunlop patent, through invalidity, became the property of the world … no one succeeded in shaking the hold that Mr. Harvey Du Cros had established on the industry.

At the banquet given in his honour, Du Cros said that had Thomson's patent been discovered earlier, he wouldn't have risked all to popularise the concept of pneumatics.

"No invention of the age was subjected to more ridicule than Dunlop's epoch-making tyre," said Selwyn Edge in his memoirs. "When it was exhibited on a few stands at the Stanley Show in 1890, it caused no end of criticism, comment and disfavour. A huge joke was created by one of the bicycles, fitted with [rival] cushion tyres, bearing a ticket saying it had 'rheumatic' tyres."

However, at the following show, held in London in January 1891, pneumatics were "prominent everywhere," said cycling champion and later motoring pioneer Herbert Duncan.

> There was hardly one set of exhibits in which it did not figure. It had become a familiar sight and the ejaculations of astonishment – even fright – which the few specimens evoked [at the 1890 show] were not heard at the 1891 show. Its round proportions … seemed to excite the public in much the same way as do the fat pigs and bullocks at a cattle show.

Pneumatics were "smackable," said Duncan. "No man passed a machine so 'attyred' without prodding and poking it in its soft parts."

While squeezable pneumatics became more popular and eventually killed off solid tyres, there was another category of tyre that, for a year or so, was more successful than pneumatics. This was the cushion tyre, a solid tyre that had some "give" in it and couldn't puncture. Even Boyd Dunlop made one, claiming it was superior to his 1888 creation. Cushion tyres promised much, but delivered little – they were more harsh to ride than the lively pneumatic. By 1895, thanks to Du Cros, pneumatics had cornered the market.

Pneumatics were promoted aggressively to the retail market. In 1893, Du Cros Snr. created the John Griffiths Cycle Corporation, which opened large bicycle shops in a number of British cities, always with Dunlop products to the fore. Du Cros later diversified, taking on cycle and car agencies, including the distribution of Panhard & Levassor cars from France. In 1896 Du Cros floated his renamed company alongside the speculator Terah Hooley. They made £2 million between them in the process. Du Cros Snr. and Arthur Du Cros became joint managing directors of the Dunlop Pneumatic Tyre Company. The company produced its first motor-car tyre in 1900.

However, it was not the first to do so. Michelin of France was the first to apply Dunlop's innovation to automobiles. Michelin was founded by brothers André and Édouard Michelin who took control of a struggling rubber products business in Clermont-Ferrand in 1889. They patented a detachable pneumatic bicycle tyre that was easier to repair than Dunlop's. Sniffing the wind, in 1895 the brothers produced a set of pneumatic tyres for motor-car use.

While Dunlop had a logo featuring a patriarchal Victorian gentleman – old man Dunlop – Michelin plumped for Bibendum. The "Michelin man" came to life in 1897 as an upper-crust soak made out of white bicycle tyres. Bibendum was drawn by Marius Rossillon, who went by the pen name of O'Galop. An 1898 Michelin poster by O'Galop showed the firmly inflated character flanked by flaccid rivals. The rivals – presumably deflated by the broken glass and nails held aloft in a champagne goblet by Bibendum – were the then chief of Continental Tyres of Germany and, with a beard fashioned out of punctured tyres, John Boyd Dunlop. (See colour plates.)

HENRY JOHN LAWSON

Con man or tireless promoter? England's Harry Lawson was both. This fascinating little man – five-foot nothing in his stockinged feet – died penniless yet, for a while at least, he was a mini-colossus who bestrode the interconnected worlds of cycling and motoring, in England and in America. In the 1870s he created a Safety bicycle, and in the 1890s he was the organiser of the Emancipation Run, the kickstarter event for motoring in Britain. He spent lavishly and hobnobbed with royalty. His business administration skills left a lot to be desired but he attempted to make up for that in enthusiasm. However, his cooking of the books landed him in prison, an experience that left him a broken man. Prior to his fall from grace he had influential acolytes willing to sing his praises – calling him the founder of both cycling and motoring in Britain, overzealous claims that Lawson encouraged – but history was less kind to him and he's now largely unknown.

Motoring historian Timothy Nicholson wrote in 1982 that "Lawson … did more than anyone else to create public opinion on the motor car …"

In his 1926 book on motoring history, upper-class motor pioneer and cycle racing champion Herbert Duncan called Lawson "the most extraordinary English pioneer of all." Lawson was "a keen cyclist" and, said Duncan, "was the founder of the motor-car industry in England and of the world's cycle and motor trade."

Lawson's interests in America included, in 1899, fronting the Anglo-American Rapid Vehicle Company, a syndicate that attempted to set up an electric taxi and haulage firm in New York in competition with the likes of Colonel Albert Pope's Columbia Manufacturing Company. Pope and Lawson probably never met but, as veterans of the bicycle business, they would have been aware of each other.

Wheeling in 1885 called Lawson the "wheeling inventor … favourably known in the trade." Lawson later made many claims for his early bicycles but not all stand up to scrutiny. In 1879, while working for Rudge & Co., he patented the Bicyclette Safety bicycle. This was never a commercial success and lacked key features compared to modern bicycles but it was six years in advance of J. K. Starley's historic Rover Safety bicycle. The name has lasted: *bicyclette* is one of the French words for "bicycle." An 1880 patent for a powered tricycle foresaw an engine powered by compressed gas. The patent was sketchy and light on detail – it's highly unlikely Lawson ever made one, although he later boasted that he "invented" motoring because of this patent. By the early 1880s

Lawson's company promotion interests had taken over from his engineering interests. There was more money to be made in such ventures. Energetic, extroverted and brimming with self-confidence, Lawson may have been a shyster in the making but this wasn't, at first, apparent and he had some early financial successes, certainly enough to sweeten deals with landed gentry who, strapped for cash, would lend their names to Lawson company promotions – a tactic that had been developed by Terah Hooley, a shady business associate of Lawson's.

By the beginning of the 1890s Lawson had spotted the potential of the embryonic motor car industry, and surmised that it could one day be as big – or possibly even bigger – than the cycle industry.

Many intelligent figures in early motoring attached themselves to Lawson's orbit – figures such as Frederick Simms, consulting engineer to all of Lawson's promotions, a member of the Cyclists' Touring Club and later founder of the prestigious Automobile Club. Despite his well-placed friends and employees, the City was wary of Lawson. None of his company promotions succeeded in raising all of the capital requested. Nevertheless, the general public were easier to hoodwink and he was able to gloss over his dubious track record with fanciful claims. Some of these claims – such as that the motor industry would become all-powerful – came true, yet were dismissed at the time by all but a very few. Lawson's Motor Car Club wasn't a club but a business, and one in which Lawson believed he could control the whole of Britain's motor industry, if he was able to control all of the main motor car patents.

Selwyn Edge said Lawson "… made a vast fortune out of the cycle and its allied trades …" and then

> turned his attention to the future of the motor car … His plan was to make a corner in motor cars in this country, by purchasing every patent on which he could lay his hands in the hope that some would turn out to be genuine master patents … huge sums of money flowed from his pockets on patents … He paid away ten thousand pounds as the ordinary man would a five-pound note.

Edge, writing in 1934 – more than ten years after Lawson had died – painted a rare, post-1900 positive picture of the man:

> Although one cannot agree with the highly speculative nature of Lawson's various enterprises, one cannot help admiring the boldness of the man in risking huge sums of money on an industry which did not then exist, and the products of which it was illegal to use on the roads.

In a full-page advertorial in *The Times* of May 1896 – probably the first ever full-page newspaper automobile advertisement – Lawson was praised to the hilt, as were his endeavours on behalf of the motor car. Lawson's typically overblown puffery on the prospects for the motor car were contained alongside a great many references to Lawson's bicycling background. In 1896, it was clearly necessary for the fledgling and nowhere-near-successful motor car business to ride on the coat-tails of the obviously successful bicycle business. Lawson's bicycling background was first mentioned in the advertorial's third paragraph and then repeated many times on the rest of the page.

"[The motor car's] effect … will unquestionably be enormous," predicted the advertorial in its opening paragraph, "… and will mark the new departure as one of the most marvellous features of reform which the future historian will have to record in connexion with an age unprecedented in its wealth of discovery and scientific research."

One can't escape the feeling that the advertorial was penned by Lawson himself. As well as linking Lawson to the still-booming bicycle business, the article talked of him as surpassing the fame of the early railway promoters: "Not even the triumphs of Stephenson's ingenuity and genius … are likely to be regarded as of more importance … than the new method of locomotion of which Mr. Harry J. Lawson is the brilliant pioneer." This was a startling claim to make in 1896. The advertorial continued:

> As the inventor of the first British Motor Car, of which the force was supplied by petroleum, patented by Mr. Lawson, September 27, 1880 … he undoubtedly inaugurated the first practical step leading up to the present triumph of the auto-car movement … As the inventor of the first safety cycle, Mr. Lawson had already written his name largely on the pages of history … The "Safety" was at first treated almost with ridicule, as was the pneumatic tyre: yet to-day we find them established in the public confidence to an extent almost incredible of belief.

Referring to the impending legislation which would legalise the use of motor cars in Britain, the advertorial reminded readers that:

> The effect of this much needed reform will be evidenced in the remarkable impetus given to the new industry of which Mr. Harry J. Lawson is the pioneer, and which owes in great measure its already assured success to his all-powerful personality. Mr. Lawson has been conspicuously identified with wheeling matters since his earliest years, and if only as the inventor of the safety bicycle fully merits the title of the "Columbus" of this now all-pervading pastime of the hour.

This "all-pervading pastime" was nothing of the sort. Driving a motor car was still all but illegal in Great Britain, and only a handful of motor cars were owned by Britons at the time.

The advertorial featured the speeches given at a banquet to celebrate the opening of the Motor Car Club's 1896 exhibition at the Imperial Institute. Sir John Puleston proposed the first toast, and he too referred to the motor car industry through the prism of the cycle industry, saying how "in the past the cycle industry, from a very small beginning, had grown into not only huge commercial importance, but one which influenced our daily lives."

Henry Sturmey responded to Sir John's toast by "referring to the bicycle industry, he remarked that twenty-two years ago he formed one of a small band of enthusiasts who made themselves ridiculous in the eyes of the general public by mounting on two wheels and proceeding along the road without the aid of horse … In his wildest flights of imagination he never conceived that cycle manufacture would reach the enormous proportions that it had to-day."

The advertorial said Lawson responded to Sturmey's address with a reference to the steam railway. Again, Lawson pushed his cycling credentials, this time claimed he actually founded the whole shebang:

> The next great industry in self-propulsion I myself had the honour to found. I refer to the safety bicycle industry. Introduced with the same singular opposition and ridicule, twenty years ago it seemed that I took hold of no paper but what some term of opprobrium was applied to my invention. It was called an abortion, a freak of nature, and a crocodile. (Laughter). To-day, however, it blesses the world, and every large nation is making millions of money every year out of that industry which I so founded …

The advertorial also dedicated space to mentions the motor car industry had received in editorials in other newspapers, again including references to bicycling. Here's the *Daily Telegraph*:

> There will [soon] be an immense demand for Horseless Carriages both for public and private use. What this may mean to trade the enormous development of the cycle industry exemplifies.

Cycling has created towns like Beeston, re-created places like Coventry, and recalled to life from their sleepy hollows hundreds of wayside inns dear to the traveller. In Coventry alone the manufacture affords employment to fifteen thousand people …

And here's the *Financial News*:

The great use of the bicycle has opened people's eyes to the advantage of a means of transit which is practically always available, and is not subject to such innumerable ills as horseflesh is heir to. In country districts one sees ladies bicycling into towns to give their orders, instead of driving [a horse carriage] as of old …

The last two words in the advert, appropriately enough, were the words "cycle industry." The advert said that, thanks to Lawson's "indomitable energy," the launch of the Beeston Tyre Company, a bicycle-accessories supplier, had the "most brilliant promise of success."

In 1896, Lawson founded the Daimler Motor Company with Gottleib Daimler, having purchased the rights to the Daimler engine from Frederick Simms. A factory in Coventry was opened, and production started. Lawson and his lieutenants shuttled between Coventry and London, aiming to produce English-built motor cars for the domestic market – not that there *was* much of a domestic market. The use of motor cars was still highly restricted, much to the annoyance of the motor pioneers, including Lawson. While Sir David Lionel Salomons, another great motoring pioneer, bent the ear of government ministers, urging them to pass legislation that would legalise motoring, Lawson preferred promotional events. He organised a motor show in London, which was attended by the Prince of Wales and many other dignitaries. Meanwhile, Salomons' sweet-talking had worked its wonders, and the so-called Emancipation Act was passed in the autumn of 1896. The Locomotives on Highways Act freed motor cars to drive on the roads of Britain. Stealing Salomons' thunder, Lawson organised the Emancipation Run, the London–Brighton "race" that celebrated the passing of the Act.

This event proved to be the zenith of Lawson's success. His factories didn't produce cars, his expensive patent collection proved to be worthless and, by 1904, his past had caught up with him and he was imprisoned for fraud.

WILLIAM REES JEFFREYS

In 1910, William Rees Jeffreys became secretary of the Road Board, the first central authority for roads in Great Britain since the Roman era. The Board was created by the Liberal government of the day to administer the money raised from the Road Fund, a new direct taxation on motorists – this would become known as "road tax". This tax (in fact, it's a duty, a slightly different thing) was no longer operational by 1927, and was formally killed off in 1936. The Road Fund was created to pay for the damage done to the roads by the growing number of motorists.

Chaired by a dictatorial railway man, the Road Board was never a terribly effective body – there were many complaints about it in Parliament, from the Treasury, and from motoring organisations. The Road Board released funds to resurface some roads, and provided some finance for a handful of short new roads to be built. "Why did the Board neglect to build any of the new roads for motor traffic it was called into being to provide?" complained Rees Jeffreys. In 1919, the Road Board was disbanded and its role taken over by the newly created Ministry of Transport. Payment of the Ministry of Transport's Motor Licence Duty came to be viewed by British motorists as a road usage fee. Non-motorised road users were deemed to be "freeloaders." This misapprehension is still with us, and it's a toxic one. Cyclists – and, to a lesser extent, equestrians – are believed by many to be "tax dodgers," and to have no rights to be on roads, which are said to be "paid for by motorists" when, in fact, roads are paid for by general and local taxation.

In 2009, I created a website to counter the "you don't pay road tax" claims from some motorists. When researching the history of the Road Fund for ipayroadtax.com I started to research the story of Jeffreys who, by many accounts (especially his own), was the person most responsible for the 20th-century expansion and improvement of Britain's road network. "The conception of the construction of wide, new roads in this country is due to Mr. W. Rees Jeffreys ..." said the City Engineer of Liverpool in 1925. I was intrigued to discover that Jeffreys started his 50-year career as a champion for improved roads as an official with a cycling organisation. He took over the running of the cycling-based Roads Improvement Association in 1900, while a council member of the Cyclists' Touring Club. His first experience of the new science of road crust manufacturing came while he was employed by the CTC. He would run the Roads Improvement Association until the 1950s, and it became known as a motoring organisation – especially noted for its campaigning for motorways – but it had been founded in 1886 by the CTC and the National Cyclists' Union, forerunner to today's British Cycling Federation.

In a 1937 speech, British Prime Minister David Lloyd George said: "I know something about roads. I started the Road Fund in England when I was Chancellor of the Exchequer." This fund-raising body lived for just eight years before being absorbed into the newly formed Ministry of Transport. Its secretary for those eight years was Rees Jeffreys. Lloyd George described Jeffreys in the same speech as "the greatest authority on roads in the United Kingdom and one of the greatest in the whole world." According to Jeffreys, the "road problem [would] be solved only by the construction of roads suitable for rapid traffic along which motor-cars may travel without being subject to any artificial limits of speed." Jeffreys was at one time the Secretary of the Royal Automobile Club, and until 1933 was honorary treasurer of the Institution of Automobile Engineers. When Parliament researched roads – such as during a public inquiry into highways in 1903 – invariably the first witness called would be Jeffreys. In 1905, *Commercial Motor* said of Jeffreys, "... there is no doubt that many of the privileges enjoyed by automobilists are directly or indirectly due to his efforts." The trade magazine added that "Mr. Rees Jeffreys is associated with cycling as well as with automobilism. He has been for many years, and still is, a member of the Council of the Cyclists' Touring Club."

Jeffreys, the roads-promoting arch-motorist, started his 50-year highway administration career as a touring cyclist. In 1890, at the age of 18, he cycle-toured in Scotland. "With other members of the Council of the Cyclists' Touring Club, I took a cycling holiday in Scotland each summer inspecting the roads, sampling the hotels and hydros, and accumulating information required for the guidance of touring cyclists." He also cycled in Ireland, experiencing at first hand the "boggiest, ruttiest roads impossible nowadays to conceive." While in Ireland he met former cycle racer R. J. Mecredy, editor of *Irish Cyclist* since 1886. In the late 1890s Mecredy helped form the Irish Roads Improvement Association, and he would later become one of Ireland's foremost motoring journalists and editor of *Motor News*. "I have stayed with [Mecredy] in his picturesquely-situated house under the shadow of the Sugar Loaf Mountain in Co. Wicklow," reminisced Jeffreys, "talking far into the night about Irish roads and how to improve them."

In a motoring yearbook for 1903 Jeffreys said he had toured "awheel in eleven countries; and … cycled over twenty-eight of the Alpine passes." At this time it was not unusual to list cycling credentials in such a yearbook. In fact, it was perfectly normal, and many of the rich, high-society individuals in the yearbook – to be a motorist in 1903 was an explicit admission of wealth – also highlighted the fact they were cyclists.

Jeffreys was given the Road Board role thanks to his leadership of the Roads Improvement Association. He had been made Secretary of the RIA in March 1901, while a council member of the CTC. He was to remain a CTC council member until 1909, and was chairman of the CTC's rights and privileges committee from 1901 to 1906. In the early 1900s, being an official in a cycling organisation was no bar to being an official in a motoring organisation. Cyclists and motorists wanted the same thing: better roads. Via the RIA Jeffreys became an advocate for spreading tar on Britain's roads, travelling the world on behalf of cyclists and motorists.

The RIA was obsessed with road dust. "It is … impossible, for the present generation to appreciate what their parents and grandparents suffered from dust and mud," wrote Jeffreys in 1949. "Not only were houses made distressingly uncomfortable by dust, but household work was increased greatly by the mud and dust which children brought into the house on boots and clothes. The dust caused many ailments and diseases of the eyes, nose and throat." Dust at the time was part dirt, part horse manure, increasing fears that it might spread disease. "Few reforms brought so much direct benefit to the people as a whole as that which in so few years made the British roads dustless," claimed Jeffreys.

He started cycling in the 1890s while a student at the London School of Economics. The LSE was founded in 1895 by four Fabian socialists Beatrice and Sidney Webb, Graham Wallas and George Bernard Shaw. All four were cyclists. The institution's motto, *rerum cognoscere causas* – "to know the causes of things," from Virgil's *Georgics* – was suggested by Professor Edwin Cannan, another cyclist. Jeffreys attended Cannan's economics lectures. "Outside the school we were associated as members of the Council of the CTC," said Jeffreys. "Cannan was a great cyclist. He made full use of the bicycle as a means of transport."

From 1901 to 1910 Cannan worked with Jeffreys at the RIA. Jeffreys transformed the organisation from a cycling-only one that pamphleted, aiming to influence road surveyors and local authorities, to one that was highly politicised, aiming to change national government policies.

"The methods of propaganda then adopted would not secure any important results," said Jeffreys. "Local road surveyors were inclined to resent instruction in the technique of their business by a voluntary body possessing no official authority." A professional lobbying organisation was needed and Jeffreys said that he had "full authority from the cycling and motoring bodies to organize political propaganda in favour of a Central Highway Authority and a State grant for highway purposes."

What Jeffreys wanted – and eventually got – was the first central administration for British roads since the Roman era. In effect, this was the nationalisation of Britain's main roads. Jeffreys said in 1906 that, "[The] roads so selected … should be specially subsidised by the State and termed 'national roads'. It should be left to an 'authoritative and impartial body' … to decide which roads should be subsidised." Prior to the creation of the Road Fund, roads were the responsibility of hundreds of local authorities, with an appalling disparity in quality of road upkeep from parish to parish, region to region. Even strategically important roads – roads now taken care of by Britain's Highways Agency – could be poorly maintained in places. The creation of a central highway authority was key to Jeffreys' reform platform.

The call for the nationalisation of Britain's roads was first mooted by Jeffreys in an article in the CTC *Gazette* in 1900. The CTC man got the first chance to put his view before Parliament during a Highways Committee research meeting in 1903. Rees Jeffreys told the committee: "… a certain sum should be allocated and placed in the hands of the central department for the purpose of building new roads and improving existing ones, and that, as these improvements will be required mainly for national purposes in the national interests, we think it but fair that the State should contribute fairly liberally towards them."

This wish was granted, something an editorial in an automobile journal in 1903 could hardly believe: "A national system of road control! How many of us have dreamed of it – dreamed of it as something nigh impossible of realisation? And yet the report of the Departmental Committee of the Local Government Board … opens up an alluring possibility of something being done to nationalise our roads …" The journal said this was a "Triumph for the Roads Improvement Association."

The RIA was later taken over by motoring interests but in the early 1900s it was very much a bicycle organisation. Its work was funded by the National Cyclists' Union and the CTC, with the Automobile Club as the minor partner. In 1901, the Annual General Meeting of the RIA was held at the offices of the CTC, which also owned the RIA's furniture. Before 1905, there were more cyclists on the RIA board than motorists, although some RIA officials sat on motoring and cycling organisation boards at the same time. CTC council members Joseph Pennell and E. R. Shipton were on the RIA committee. Shipton was also an Automobile Club board member. At council meetings of the RIA before 1905 there were generally five representatives from the CTC (including Jeffreys), five from the NCU and two or three from the Automobile Club. Those representing the Automobile Club included William Worby Beaumont, assistant editor of *The Engineer*, and a member of the Cycle Engineers' Institute; and John Scott-Montagu MP, an arch-motorist but who used to pedal to Parliament in the 1890s.

When Jeffreys represented the RIA in parliament he did so as both a cyclist and a motorist. In 1903, the CTC *Gazette* praised Jeffreys's securing of a highways improvement inquiry:

> After two years unremitting labour the Roads Improvement Association have induced His Majesty's Government to institute an inquiry into Highway Administration and Highway Authorities in England and Wales … [The terms of reference] are everything that could be desired from the cyclist's point of view …

Jeffreys clearly had motorists in mind when he told the CTC *Gazette* that "… old roads should be widened, straightened and severe gradients reduced …" and that "… loop roads for the fast traffic should be built round towns and villages …", but he also admitted that "… to no class in the community are good roads so important as to cyclists."

In his evidence to the parliamentary inquiry he stressed his cycling credentials:

Chairman: You are, I understand, the Honorary Secretary of the Roads Improvement Association?

Jeffreys: That is so.

Chairman: I suppose you have travelled a good many miles on the roads yourself?

Jeffreys: Yes, in all parts of the United Kingdom, and also a good deal abroad.

Chairman: On both motor cars and bicycles?

Jeffreys: More upon bicycles than upon motor cars. The bicycle is perhaps the best road inspector there is.

Jeffreys used his cycle touring experience to flesh out his evidence:

> I have cycled through the mountainous districts of the Alps, in Austria, in Italy, in Switzerland; I have been across the Juras, the Vosges, and the Black Forest, and we have nothing in this country to compare with the magnificently engineered roads in those countries. They have been built by road engineers, but they have been built with the assistance and support of the State, and it is because we have not had this assistance and support from the State that we do not get properly engineered roads in this country.

The following year Jeffreys gave evidence to the Royal Commission on London Traffic and, again, he did so as a cyclist and a motorist. He was asked: "Are you chairman of the Roads Improvement Committee of the Cyclists' Touring Club?" He replied: "That is so … I am authorised to appear here on behalf of the Roads Improvement Association … I am in touch with the feelings of automobilists and cyclists."

When asked whether he thought London needed the construction of many wide new roads he referenced cycling's boom years:

> Yes, I think that is our chief need in connection with the traffic problem … Like many of our existing roads out of London, the old Bath Road is not adequate now for the local traffic, much less for the tremendous through traffic which the development of cycling has brought upon it.

Jeffreys told the panel he was in favour of a "circular boulevard around London," but that, unlike the modern M25, it wouldn't just be for motors: "the motor car and cycle traffic coming into London by any of these main roads, as soon as it reached the boulevard would switch on to it … instead of making its way to the centre."

Jeffreys was also in favour of separating cars from bicycles. He didn't wish cyclists to be banished from the new roads he proposed but rather to be provided with their own parallel roads, the sort of separation later perfected in the Netherlands. In a paper he read at the Automobile Club in London in 1903 he proposed the "building [of] eleven new main roads out of London and encircling it with a boulevard." The eleven new roads would be "four track roads" which were to "consist of a number of separate tracks" including one for slow-moving traffic and others for "automobiles and cycles." One road was to be from Shoreditch to Snaresbrook and "would give a new exit from London where it is most sorely needed … Many are the fervent prayers uttered daily by cyclists and all other classes of road users for a way out of London that would enable them to avoid the terrors of the Lea Bridge Road."

He insisted upon "… the slow going traffic keeping close to the kerb … The banishment of all crawling cabs from main roads … The removal of all unnecessary obstructions from the centre of all streets, including lamp posts, electric standards, public conveniences and cab ranks …" While he was sympathetic to cyclists, he was less mindful of the needs of pedestrians, for he proposed "the enforcement of a rule of the road upon pedestrians using the carriageway."

In his lifetime, Jeffreys saw many of his road proposals come to life, or at least get planning permission. He died in 1954, four years before the opening of England's first motorway, the 8¼ mile M6 Preston By-pass. The next stretch of motor-only road to be opened, in September 1959, was the Chiswick flyover, which later became part of the M4 motorway to Slough and Windsor. Jeffreys had first suggested such a road in 1901. He had called it the Royal Road to Windsor. The third and longest stretch of motorway to be opened – and Britain's first recognisably modern motorway, complete with service stations and cloverleaf junctions – was a 67-mile section of the M1, between Crick and Berrygrove. It was opened in November 1959 by Ernest Marples MP, a founding partner of a Westminster-based civil engineering contractor that built motorways. In a delicious irony that would have tickled Jeffreys, Marples was a touring cyclist and the first CTC member to rise to the role of Minister of Transport.

HORATIO S. EARLE

The Michigan Department of Transportation recognises Horatio Earle as the "father of Good Roads." Born in Vermont but domiciled in Detroit, Earle made it his mission in the early 1900s to dethrone "the mighty monarch mud, who rules the road to the exclusion of everyone." He was a key figure in

motoring history, in charge of the roads in the capital of America's nascent automobile industry. From 1905 to 1909, he was Michigan's first Highway Commissioner having earlier been a State senator, responsible for legislating to create what is now known as the Michigan Department of Transportation. In 1902, he founded what became the American Road and Transportation Builders Association, still an important part of the influential American "roads lobby."

Earle started his roads administration career as a member of the League of American Wheelmen. He became L.A.W's Chief Consul of Michigan in 1899, and in 1900 was elected to the Michigan Senate on a L.A.W. ticket. In the same year, Colonel Aaron T. Bliss was voted in as Governor of Michigan; he too was a member of the L.A.W. Bliss joined the L.A.W. for its stance on Good Roads rather than for any abiding love of cycling – Earle was a utilitarian rider, not a racer or tourer. His first task as Chief Consul was to "eliminate bicycle racing and push the good roads movement." He said: "There is no more sense in the L.A.W. running bicycle races, than the poultry association, cock fights; or the dairy association, bull fights."

Earle joined the L.A.W. in 1896, and from 1898 headed the Michigan chapter's Highway Improvement Committee. He had good reason to be interested in both cycling and roads: his businesses included the Earle Cycle Company, the Genesee Gravel Company and the Good Roads Supply Company. Earle also had an agricultural implements business, and was able to pursue outside interests – such as roads – when he netted $110,000 after winning a patent infringement court case for a sickle he had invented.

His bicycling background was always important to him. "Of all honors bestowed on me by my fellow beings," he said, "none are remembered with so many pleasant incidents and prized so highly as that of having had the honor and pleasure of serving as president of the L.A.W."

Earle promoted the cyclists' Good Roads message in the Michigan Senate by pushing for a State Highway Committee (and making himself chairman), but his key road-improvement tools had been show-me-how-it's-done ones. Between 1900 and 1902, he organised travelling exhibitions to promote the science of creating better roads and, ironically to modern eyes, he did this not with motor cars or motor wagons but with the willing cooperation of railway companies. Earle claimed to be the first to organise a Good Roads Train rolling exhibition. The Good Roads Train – with 40 carriages – would disgorge road builders, a traction engine, a road roller, a sprinkler and broken stone, from which an "object lesson" road would be constructed at prearranged stopping points. The first such road was built at the First International Good Roads Congress, organised by Earle in Port Huron, Michigan in July 1900. These short stretches of well-engineered, macadam "dirt" roads wowed the rural crowds, who were used to rutted, dusty or muddy "corduroy" roads made with logs (which usually sank). The Good Roads Trains had originally been the idea of the US Office of Road Inquiry (ORI), a Federal body founded thanks to the L.A.W.'s 1890s lobbying for Good Roads. In 1900, Earle was appointed as a salaried "special agent" of the ORI for the Midwest, and organised a number of Good Roads Trains. A year later he was made the (unpaid) national president of the L.A.W. In 1909, thanks to his role as a Wayne County road commissioner (another was Henry Ford), Earle created his most famous "object lesson" road: this was more permanent than his macadam roads, and built on Woodward Avenue in Detroit, between the Sixth and Seventh Mile Roads. Today, a commemorative cast-iron sign by the side of the road marks the point where the world's first concrete highway ended. "From far and near road builders came to see how concrete stood up under the heavy traffic of that period," says the sign. "The success of this experiment speeded the development of modern automobile highways."

In 1914, Earle was responsible for acquiring the land upon which was built Detroit's imposing Grand Lodge, headquarters for the Freemasonry movement in Michigan. Earle had been a Freemason since the 1890s. Henry Ford was a member of the same lodge, the largest in the world. (In the 1880s and 1890s cycling was described as "freemasonery of the wheel".) Earle identified with cyclists for many years, reminding readers of his 1929 autobiography who were the first to call for Good Roads. Cyclists, said Earle, were "the pioneers of road building in this country."

CHAPTER THREE

MASTODONS TO MOTORWAYS

Roads have in all times been among the most influential agencies of society; and the makers of them, by enabling men readily to communicate with each other, have properly been regarded as among the most effective pioneers of civilization.
SAMUEL SMILES, 1867

The Road ... is the greatest and most original of the spells which we inherit from the earliest of our race. It was the most imperative and the first of our necessities. It is older than building and than wells ... The Alps with a mule-track across them are less of a barrier than fifteen miles of forest or rough land separating one from that track.
HILAIRE BELLOC, 1923

Roads have been important conduits for passage, carriage, commerce and play since time immemorial. But in the 19th century, and even into the 20th, it was assumed roads had an insignificant future – politicians and planners were fixated on railways. Few people imagined roads would regain their importance or become dominated by motor cars.

Roads did not appear recently, out of nowhere, lowered on to virgin land by modern-day navvies in hard hats and hi-vis. Most roads – in fact, the overwhelming majority of roads – have long, rich histories, carved by boots and hooves, with little thought for wheels, petrol-propelled or otherwise.

In due course, I'll touch on the rich history of British roads but antiquity can also be ascribed to North America's supposedly modern roads, many of which were, in fact, created by Native Americans as trading or hunting trails. There are many examples, but here are just four. Broadway in New York was originally the Wickquasgeck Trail, stamped into the brush of *Mannahatta* by Native American tribespeople. Detroit's Woodward Avenue, later famous for having the world's first concrete road surface, and the automobile factory constructed by Henry Ford, follows the route of the long-distance Saginaw trail. Route 209 in New Jersey is based on the Minisink trail of the Munsee people. US Highway 12 began as the Great Sauk Trail, named after the Sauk people's hunting trail, originally trodden down by buffalo. The trail's transhumant origins probably pre-date the buffalo: palaeontologists from the University of Michigan discovered the trail was blazed by migrating mastodons. Motorists driving today between Washington, D.C. and Detroit are following a route padded out 10,000 years ago by now-extinct megafauna.

VITAL THOUGH we now view them, roads have gone through a number of phases, not all of them busy ones. Right now, we're 80 or so years into a fast, long-distance phase, and a motor-dominated one. Roads are viewed as vital to economic prosperity, even though they are sometimes the exact opposite: in 1993, in an article for *Geographical*, author Oliver Tickell wrote: "If access by road is the key to economic prosperity then Birmingham should be the wealthiest city in Britain. It is not."

Roads are today perceived as motor thoroughfares, with "vulnerable road users" perhaps allowed to share a sliver of the infrastructure – grudgingly, and it's usually the gutter. The current phase will not last for ever. Double-decker motor roads that appear permanent can be removed on a whim, and many cities around the world are demolishing – or remodelling – urban motorways and replacing them with linear parks and people-friendly boulevards.

Seoul's Cheonggyecheon elevated highway is the poster child of "freeway removal." Built in 1976, the eight-mile South Korean multilane flyover was demolished in 2005, replaced with a country park and a bus route. What happened to the motorists and their cars? They dispersed, with no noticeable impact on congestion. Benefits have included the reduction of carcinogenic airborne particulate matter by 21 percent and lowering the city's summer temperature by 3.6 degrees Celsius.

Many cities are now realising they built too many motor-centric roads, especially in the 1960s and 1970s, when the only future was supposed to be a motor future. With many elevated arterials now past their use-by date, urban authorities are weighing up the costs for renovation, replacement or removal. Remodelling is often the cheapest option, and certainly the greenest. In Liverpool, England, the "Friends of the Flyover" received crowd-funding in 2014 to proceed with a design to remodel the city's "brutal" Churchill Way flyover into a "pedestrian and cycle-friendly promenade in the sky."

In 2000, the Harbor Drive Freeway in Portland, Oregon, was replaced by the Tom McCall Waterfront Park. Toronto, Ontario, knocked down part of the double-decker Gardiner Expressway, and replaced it with a ground-level, multi-use boulevard with an adjacent cycle path. When, in 1989, a one-mile elevated section of San Francisco's Embarcadero Freeway was felled by the Loma Prieta earthquake the original plan was to rebuild like-for-like. This was eventually scrapped, and the end result was a traffic-calmed, multi-use waterfront road. Boston's famous "Big Dig," which started in 2008, buried major freeways underground and, on a smaller scale, Dallas did the same with the Woodall Rodgers Freeway: both cities built "freeway cap" parks above the buried roads. Los Angeles – one of the world's most motor centric cities – is proposing to rip out stretches of US Route 101, and not replace them.

Each time it's proposed that a city is to decommission a highway, there are apocalyptic predictions of gridlock: in reality, when roads are ripped out, traffic planners find, to their surprise and delight, that congestion tends to drop. Seventy-five percent of the motor traffic re-routes, while the other 25 percent disappears. The "Highways to Boulevards" movement – "reclaiming urbanism, revitalising cities" – is gaining momentum, and world cities planning to dismantle more freeways include Auckland, Washington, D.C., Montreal and Tokyo. The routes roads follow may endure but the motor-centric accoutrements upon them might not.

WHEN, IN 1831, Sir William Molesworth of Pencarrow in Cornwall planned out the route of a railway line, from Wadebridge to Wenfordbridge, he had haulage in mind. The Bodmin and Wadebridge Railway was intended to carry sand from the Camel estuary to inland farms for use as fertiliser. This use changed in 1846 when the London and South Western Railway purchased the line to transport slate from trackside quarries. The quarries are still there – mainly grubbed out – but the steel rails and the wooden sleepers are long gone. The last passenger train was in 1967 and freight carriage on the line ceased in 1983. The 17-mile former railway line is now the Camel Trail, one of Cornwall's top tourist attractions, a walking and cycling route enjoyed by more than half a million people each year.

Sir William Molesworth could not have predicted that his industrial "sand line" would turn first into a line that carried excursionists to executions and then morph into a "bucket-and-spade" trail for pedal-powered tourists. His Permanent Way proved to be not at all permanent. Another former railway line became the hugely popular Bristol and Bath Railway Path, the 13-mile cyclist and pedestrian trail that, via Sustrans, kick-started Britain's National Cycle Network. The route might be popular but that hasn't prevented the local authority from toying with the idea of converting part of the trail into a guided busway.

That things change is a given. The motorways of today – so incredibly vital that billions must be spent on new ones at every opportunity – may suffer a similar fate to the railway lines that are now rail-trails. We've built ourselves a motor-centric society and we can only imagine a slightly different future: more roads, dotted with faster, sleeker motor cars, perhaps powered with electricity but still car-shaped. 18th-century folk thought canals would last for ever. 19th-century folk thought the same about turnpikes, and then trains. "People of to-day … were born in a railway world, and they expect to die in one," said H. G. Wells in 1901.

When the use of stagecoaches tailed off thanks to competition from railways, Britain's expensive turnpikes went through a period of "desuetude and disrepair." Roads were considered outdated, no longer needed. The only future imagined was of steel rails and steam trains. Victorian towns and cities were eviscerated to incorporate the transport mode of the future. Nothing was allowed to stand in the way of progress. In the 1890s, no policymakers, no bureaucrats, no planners, no government ministers had any inkling that the "railway age" was but a blip, and that towns and cities so ripped apart by the unstoppable train would be ripped apart again by the seemingly insignificant motor car. MPs and ministers were influenced mainly by railway interests until well into the 1920s. Motor cars came to dominate our lives not by design but by stealth. Few predicted the motor car's eventual dominance and it's reasonable to assume that the same inability to accurately predict the future afflicts us, too.

There could come a time when motor cars are perceived as historically quaint, like steam trains. Holidaymakers of the future may go on "motorway heritage" day trips, wallowing in the nostalgia of journeying on preserved sections of Britain's dismantled motorway network. This is unthinkable now, but history teaches us that transport modes don't just evolve, but can flip, and usually in the most unexpected ways. Google is banking on "driverless cars" becoming the next disruptive transport technology but extrapolation is a poor predictor of the future, and removing the driver may not be as disruptive as Google thinks. Removing the car would be the real disrupter, and some cities are thinking of doing just that – Helsinki has plans to phase out use of the private motor car by 2025, and the writing is on the wall when the head of roads and transport policy at Britain's Automobile Association believes that cars will "become redundant in cities," something that's already "happening organically" because cars "cannot be fully enjoyed or used to potential."

While some governments are banking on roads becoming busier and busier – and thanks to no drivers, safer and safer – this might not happen. The next transport technology could be something we've never even thought of, or not thought of for a very long time.

Should 1950s science fiction become science fact in the 2020s, with capsules on rails shooting us from A-to-B in the blink of an eye, roads – even ones made from solar panels – may once again fall into "desuetude and disrepair," where a traveller on a British main road could, like Charles Edward

Montague in the early 1900s, hear only the "multifarious buzz of grasshoppers, flies, bees and the rest … swelling insistently towards the dry roar of Dog-day noons."

Montague, the long-time chief leader writer of *The Guardian*, was writing in 1924 about an early 1900s solo cycle ride from Manchester to London, on the formerly busy Holyhead road, "all untarred in that age." His 19-hour journey was done for the hell of it. (He was a mountaineer, not a cyclist.)

> You certainly see most when you walk, but you cannot walk to London in a day, and one unbroken day's view of the whole stretch of road was the object. By car the thing would be easy, but then travel by car is only semi-travel, verging on the demi-semi-travel that you get in trains. You must feel a road with your muscles, as well as see it, before even your eyes can get a full sense of it.

When Montague recounted his tale in the 1920s, the idea of being able to undertake a quiet and peaceful bicycle journey on what had become one of Britain's major trunk roads must have seemed a lifetime away. In just 25 years a previously quiet road had been transformed into a maelstrom of motors. Montague's early-1900s ride had been over the "brutal white … macadam dust" of Telford's great turnpike road built atop the Roman Watling Street. By 1924, the Holyhead road had become the anodyne A5. Motorists, the men from "the ministry" decided, had no need of history – they were in a hurry and needed codenames for *their* roads, not those cumbersome, romantic names. Roads were modernised overnight not with asphalt but with a number and the letter A. On April Fool's Day, 1923, the Ministry of Transport finally listened to Rees Jeffreys, and classified the Great North Road as the A1, the Dover Road as the A2, the Portsmouth Road as the A3 and so on, naming English roads via "spokes" radiating out from London.

"The face of any old road," wrote Montague, "is as visibly filled with expression and lined with experience as any old man's." That was still the case in 1924, despite the road re-naming exercise, and it remained so for about another 30 years. Motorways – when the letter A was joined by the letter "M" – changed all that, transforming roads with personalities into you-could-be-anywhere motor-centric roads. Yet for all the modernist concrete bridges, standardised blue signs and four or more lanes demarcated with disfiguring thermoplastic paint, much of Britain's motorway network, started in the late 1950s, is, to those who care to recognise it, ancient. A great many stretches of motorways were built over the top of turnpikes – which, in their turn, had levelled out the *agger* road lips thrown up on the orders of centurions.

Not that the Romans should be given automatic top billing as the progenitors of the British road network. Celtic chariots suggest that Britons had hard roads before Roman times, and neolithic pathways lie beneath many of today's trunk roads. These pathways may have kinked and dog-legged but this was often due to ancient obstructions – even something as temporary as a fallen tree – rather than the drunken meanderings of the ancient Britons, as imagined by G. K. Chesterton's famous 1914 poem:

> Before the Roman came to Rye or out to Severn strode,
> The rolling English drunkard made the rolling English road,
> A reeling road, a rolling road, that rambles round the shire,
> And after him the parson ran, the sexton and the squire;
> A merry road, a mazy road, and such as we did tread
> The night we went to Birmingham by way of Beachy Head.

It was the Romans who put British roads on the map. Roman roads were also statements of intent, built as fast lines of communication. Just as motorways proclaim "these roads are for motors," or – and it's really much the same thing – "here be dragons," Romans proclaimed that their roads were for soldiers, and only gradually did they become roads for more peaceful purposes.

Roman roads can be considered the third major phase in British road history, with transhumance being the first. As in America, animals created the first British roads, at first by themselves in natural seasonal migrations, and later as livestock when the ancient Britons moved their beasts between winter and summer pastures. At roughly the same time, high-level trading routes were also created, above the marshes, on ridges, over hill and dale.

On these early British roads it's likely that survival was more important than speed. The Romans accelerated road transport. Speed, however, is relative. A Roman legion was expected to march the ten miles between military camps in three and a half hours, at a speed of just under three miles per hour, with the one-mile-per-hour oxen-pulled baggage trains trailing in much later. If required, soldiers could march at twice this speed and complete 20 to 30 miles in a day. Once protected and developed, the Roman road network allowed for even greater speed. There would be a rest-house – or *mansio* – every 15 to 18 miles, which is a good indication of how far a pedestrian or a rider could be expected to travel in a day. (In exceptional circumstances impressive distances could be accomplished on Rome's European roads. In 9 B.C., the future emperor Tiberius was able to ride almost 200 miles across Germany in 24 hours to join his dying brother, Nero Claudius Drusus.)

The Roman road system in Britain eventually extended for 6,500 miles, and many of these roads – or, at least, their routes – are still in use today. It's usually believed that, following the end of Roman rule in Britain by 410 A. D., Roman roads quickly fell out of use once they were no longer maintained, but this is not the case. In a book published in 2014, archaeologist Mike Bishop echoes other scholars when he states that Britain's Roman roads were crucial to later English history, "try to find a medieval battle that is not near one," he suggests. "When Richard III allegedly offered his kingdom for a horse, it was beside a Roman road." Dr. Bishop believes the Roman legacy is "still clear in the building of 18th century military roads and in the development of the modern road network."

While many of Britain's "modern" roads – especially the main ones – follow the alignments of known Roman highways, many stretches of Roman road have yet to be discovered. As well as using aerial surveys, ground-penetrating radar or extrapolations from known Roman alignments, there's a sweet-smelling way of spotting a hidden Roman road: follow the flowers. Roman soldiers would accidentally deposit seeds as they trudged. Linear accumulations of invasive species such as greater celandine, corn cockle, cotton thistle, scarlet pimpernel, white mustard and the field woundwort, all flowers used by Roman soldiers, can suggest the proximity of a long-forgotten Roman road. Blackthorn hedges, too, can hide Roman roads beneath them.

ROAD PHASES can be linked by a common factor: mileage, and whether that mileage was considered psychologically local or national. The first roads in Britain were largely thought of as local roads. Roman roads, on the other hand, were very much considered long-distance roads. They may have been split into daily chunks but, mentally and geographically, they reached out – mostly straight (because that was cheaper and easier) – from one part of the country to another, national and international rather than local.

Medieval roads, even those that followed Roman routes, were mostly thought of as local, although, of course, some traders (and their packhorses), and lots of pilgrims and pedlars, trod long distances on them, village to village. Some of our modern roads were laid out in the 17th and 18th centuries as a result of private Inclosure Acts. Large landowners consolidated and parcelled up their landholdings to the detriment of the smaller ones, and enclosure commissioners created new "public roads" between towns and villages. These "carriageways" were generally far wider than the "cartways" they replaced, but a carriageway did not, at this stage, mean a way for wheeled vehicles but for all forms of transport that involved carrying, and that included sleds and other primitive means of carriage.

The next long-distance roads, roads that bypassed many villages, were those of the turnpike era, reaching out to towns and their coaching inns, where horses were switched. On turnpike roads stagecoaches would reach heady speeds of 12 miles per hour, but prior to this road era wheeled vehicles weren't always made very welcome. In a classic highway history book of 1913, economists Beatrice and Sidney Webb wrote that parliament – and many people – remained opposed to wheels almost until the modern era:

> ... successive knots of amateur legislators [laid] down stringent rules as to the breadth of the wheel; the form of its rim; the use of iron tires and headed nails; the height of the wheel; the position of the felly, the spokes, and the axle ... [The] implicit assumption [was] that the wheeled carriage was an intruder on the highway, a disturber of the existing order, a cause of damage – in short, an active nuisance to the roadway – to be suppressed in its most noxious forms, and, where inevitable, to be regulated and restricted as much as possible.

Skinny wheels cut into soft roads so, in a series of Acts in the 1600s and 1700s, the British parliament decreed that wheels should be made fatter, the number of horses pulling carts and carriages should be capped and the weight per load should be fixed at a level that would not cause carriages to sink in to the roads. These laws, widely and ingeniously flouted, were an attempt to adapt wheels for roads. The famous road engineers of the late 18th century and very early 19th, turned this concept on its head: they adapted the roads for wheels.

The first turnpike was built on a stretch of the Great North Road in 1663, in the town of Wadesmill, near Ware, 25 miles north of London. (I know the village well. My brother and his family live there. The turnpike gate is long gone, but there's a concoction of wooden posts to commemorate the original – not that many drivers who speed past it give it a second glance. This is the old A10, which, even further back in time, was the Roman Ermine Street.)

Daniel Defoe, author of *Robinson Crusoe*, was a great traveller and, in 1726, he described the improvements made to the Wadesmill turnpike:

> ... the road there, which was before scarce passable, is now built up in a high, firm causeway; the most like those ... of the Romans ... Turn-pikes ... are very great things, and very great things are done by them; and 'tis well worth recording, for the honour of the present age, that this work has been begun, and is in an extraordinary manner carry'd on ...

Defoe hoped to see "the roads all over England restor'd in their time to such perfection, that travelling and carriage of goods will be much more easy both to man and horse, than ever it was since the Romans lost this island."

Defoe would have been disappointed, for few other great thoroughfares were turned into turnpike roads until the second half of the 18th century when, finally, a large number of trusts were set up to create the gates that blocked free passage on the soon-to-be improved highways.

And improved they were, although the results were patchy, with some parts of the country getting better improvements than others. Very few new roads were constructed by turnpike trusts, the tolls paid for upgrades of the former Roman roads – all-weather surfaces and, sometimes, well-engineered cuttings and embankments to ease gradients. (The Romans, and early and later medieval travellers, mostly used packhorses rather than wheeled transport so steep gradients were not insurmountable, as it were.) Lord Byron was certainly impressed with the improved roads he travelled on. In his epic poem *Don Juan*, he wrote:

> What a delightful thing's a turnpike road!
> So smooth, so level, such a mode of shaving
> The earth, as scarce the eagle in the broad
> Air can accomplish, with his wide wings waving.

Turnpikes would have been an abject failure but for the great civil engineers of the day, keen to use scientific methods to create resilient road surfaces fit for the industrial age. British engineers tend to get much of the credit for introducing modernised road-building techniques, but they were anticipated in Italy and France. In 1585, Italian engineer Guido Toglietta wrote a treatise on a road surfacing system using broken stone and good drainage. France was the first country to apply the new methods. Europe's first civil engineering university, the pre-revolutionary *École Nationale des Ponts et Chaussées*, the National School of Bridges and Highways, was founded in Paris in 1747. It exists to this day. The first of the great 18th century road engineers was Frenchman Pierre-Marie-Jérôme Trésaguet. In 1775 Trésaguet developed a new type of relatively light road surface, based on the theory that the foundation should support the load, and there should be multiple layers, topped with gravel. The newly improved French roads – essential for the later military campaigns of Napoleon – were the best in Europe until the first part of the 20th century and, with their excellent surfaces, attracted pioneer motorists like moths to a flame. However, French road-building techniques were expensive, and it was a British method that was taken up by much of the rest of the world, and is still used today.

The first of the three great British road engineers was "Blind" John Metcalfe of Knaresborough, who between 1765 and 1797, supervised the re-making of more than 180 miles of turnpikes in Lancashire and Yorkshire. The second was Thomas Telford, a self-made man, the son of a Scottish shepherd. Romantic poet Robert Southey called his friend "Pontifex Maximus," the great bridge builder. Telford's bridges and aqueducts were the wonders of the age. (In his day, Telford was just as famous for the canals he built, which became obsolete in his lifetime.) Fêted by parliament and favoured by turnpike trusts, he made a not unsubstantial amount of money from his surveying and surfacing of hundreds of miles of British roads, including the strategically important turnpike road between Marble Arch in London and the Admiralty Arch in Holyhead, the highway to Ireland. Telford designed not only the road (much of which follows the Roman Watling Street) but also the milestones and the toll houses, 80 percent of which are still standing. His road-building technique involved a strong but expensive foundation of large, flat stones topped with a gravel surface. When the A5 was "improved" in the 1920s, little needed to be done to Telford's supremely well-engineered road: many stretches were merely topped with tarmac.

Tarmac the brand name and tarmac the noun were both unknown in Telford's day but the "t"-word would have likely sent a shiver down his spine. The "mac" comes from the "Mc" of McAdam. John Loudon McAdam was known in his day as "McAdam the Magician". He was the third of the great British road builders, and no friend of Telford's. The men clashed on a number of occasions. While the Telford name lives on in an English New Town – Telford in Shropshire was so named in the 1960s – it's the blacktop named after McAdam that has become better known. Tarmac is the reason McAdam's name has remained in public view, yet this is ironic since McAdam, even though he owned a tar factory, never spread tar on his roads. It's not the only terminological mistake connected with McAdam. A common misnomer is to call a road covered in tarmac a "metalled" road, no doubt thinking that metal in this case means a hard surface. In fact, "metal" means road-stone, and is from the Latin word *metallum*, or "stone quarry." A metalled road is a specific type of well-constructed dirt road with a "macadamised" surface. This was named after McAdam: macadam is a compacted layer of small broken road stones. ("Dirt roads" are not natural features, and are more sophisticated than many people imagine.)

Telford and McAdam may have clashed at times but it was McAdam's road building technique that won out in the end. But all three road systems – Metcalfe's, Telford's and McAdam's – worked for one critical reason: drainage. These road engineers recognised what the poorly paid and unskilled surveyors of previous centuries had failed to grasp – on a rainy island, roads have to be made impervious to water. Some earlier road-building theories supposed that roads could be built below the level of the surrounding land because it was noticed that river beds were made up of solid stony surfaces. Roads were therefore made by digging trenches; the entry of water was believed to be unavoidable. Before the 19th century, road surveyors were not professionally trained or well-paid (and often not paid at all). Road surveying was a part-time, onerous task. The famous Sadler's Wells dance theatre in London owes its existence to a 17th-century road surveyor. In the summer of 1683, while searching for road-stone in his garden, Richard Sadler – a Surveyor of the Highways – found not gravel but a spring. The waters from this spring – Sadler's well; he dug more later – could cure "dropsy, jaundice, scurvy, green sickness and other distempers to which females are liable," claimed the canny road surveyor. To entertain the society types who flocked to what would be today called a spa, Sadler built the Musick House. This was a far more profitable use of his time than repairing roads.

McADAM DISCOVERED that with a well-drained road there's no need for an expensive foundation of large flat stones. The stiffness of the road's base layer mattered little if the top layer shed water, and a McAdam road did this by raising the level of the road above the ground upon which it was built, and cambering it so rain drained away. His road layers rested on the sub-soil, and did not require complex foundations: McAdam's method – which was only followed to the letter under strict supervision – was simple, stronger than the Telford method, and highly economical compared to all other systems.

McAdam's definition of what a road was for almost wholly ignored the pedestrian. A road, said McAdam, was "an artificial flooring, forming a strong, smooth, solid surface, at once capable of carrying great weight, and over which carriages may pass without meeting any impediment."

The surface of a McAdam road – "impervious and indestructible," he claimed – was created from the compaction of a ten-inch layer of small angular stones, precisely broken. These stones were at first compacted by passing traffic, but later in the 19th century they were compacted by heavy rollers. Knapped angular stones were used instead of rounded gravel – even if gravel was easily available locally – because, under load, broken angular stones knitted together. Large stones deflected wheels, small ones did not. "Every piece of stone put into a road," said McAdam in 1811, "which exceeds an inch in any of its dimensions is mischievous." No binders were required in a true McAdam road, no sand, or clay or other "flashings."

Road builders using the McAdam system were instructed to use small stones, and were provided with measuring rings. McAdam was also said to have made stonebreakers put road metal between their teeth: only those stones that could be placed in the mouth would be suitable for knitting together into a road crust. His road-building method – minus the mouth test – is still used today, with layers of cambered broken stone floated over the subsoil. The final modern layer – a skin of asphalt – may be new but the deep layers beneath, compacted by heavy rollers, are straight out of McAdam's road-building books. (A road roller built in 1882 was used in the construction of the first stretch of the M1 motorway in 1959.) McAdam's administrative reforms were also revolutionary, although less long-lived than his road-building technique. These reforms aimed to professionalise the management of turnpike trusts and create a competent body of trained surveyors. He lobbied hard for national administration of the British road system, but was thwarted by a reluctant parliament.

McAdam's surveying, surfacing and road administration ideas were later popularised through the Roads Improvement Association, a body created in 1886 by the CTC and NCU. Cyclists wanted smooth road surfaces and knew that, to get these, county surveyors would need to be both prodded and professionalised. Cyclists also lobbied for central administration of roads, basing their calls on the same arguments used a generation earlier by McAdam. (The Roads Improvement Association also supplied surveyors with McAdam-style stone-measuring rings.)

Thanks to Metcalfe and Telford, but mostly to McAdam, Britain's roads in the 1830s were well-surfaced, and the stagecoaches and mails that ran on these mostly macadamised roads were able to achieve speeds undreamt of by travellers just a generation earlier. Coaches may have been relatively infrequent – about one an hour – but, with speeds in excess of 12 mph, they were fast for the time and rural folk knew not to linger on turnpike roads.

"OUR SHOPS, our horse's legs, our boots, our hearts have all benefited by the introduction of macadam," wrote Dickens. However, despite the best efforts of McAdam, and his three sons and four grandsons who continued his work, many of the turnpike trusts eventually slipped into insolvency when, thanks to trains, long-distance road travel withered. At the beginning of the railway age, there were more than a thousand turnpike trusts in England and Wales managing 22,000 miles of road between them. In 1838 there were 7,796 toll gates, 3,535 administrators and 20,000 gate keepers. In 1864 a parliamentary select committee recommended that turnpike trusts should be abolished. The last tollgate, on the Anglesey stretch of the London-to-Holyhead road was raised for the last time in 1895.

Rail historian Michael Robbins wrote that travel by stagecoach was "snuffed out" with "dramatic suddenness" by rail travel. This was true of some of the major long-distance routes, such as London to Bristol. In 1843 it was reported that "within the last week the only coach that was left on the road from Bristol to London ceased running. The railroad monopoly is now complete." But the decline in the country as a whole was less precipitous than that. Those towns and cities not quickly connected by rail saw an *increase* in stagecoach travel. It took 20 to 30 years for the stagecoach business to die.

Novelist Flora Thompson described how England's macadamised turnpikes, once heaving, became hidden highways. What is now the busy A421, near Buckingham, was described as "a main road [with] scarcely any traffic ... deserted for hours together. Three miles away trains roared over a viaduct, carrying those who would, had they lived a few years before or later, have used the turnpike. People were saying that far too much money was being spent on keeping such roads in repair, for their day was over; they were only needed now for people going from village to village ..."

In his 1887 novel *The Woodlanders* Thomas Hardy described – with his usual poetic beauty – the "tomb-like stillness" of these formerly busy main roads:

> The physiognomy of a deserted highway expresses solitude to a degree that is not reached by mere dales or downs, and bespeaks a tomb-like stillness more emphatic than that of glades and pools. The contrast of what is with what might be probably accounts for this. To step, for instance, at the place under notice, from the hedge of the plantation into the adjoining pale thoroughfare, and pause amid its emptiness for a moment, was to exchange by the act of a single stride the simple absence of human companionship for an incubus of the forlorn.

Hardy would later come to appreciate the solitude on these deserted highways. At his wife's insistence, in his fifties he became a cyclist. Thomas and Emma Hardy would ride for many miles on the quiet turnpikes of Dorset. Their relationship was quiet so he also frequently rode alone, believing that the literary cyclist could pedal for long distances "without coming in contact with another mind – not even a horse, and in this way there was no danger of dissipating one's mental energy."

When he did ride with others, it was with fellow novelists such as Rudyard Kipling. Both rode sedately. There would have been little else on the roads other than fellow cyclists.

IN 1913, when Beatrice and Sidney Webb wrote their highway book, they were enthusiastic motorists. Earlier they had been keen cyclists, riding on Safety bicycles. Instead of writing "what the bicyclist did for roads," they should have written "what the cyclist did for roads," for tricycles were very popular in the Victorian era, especially with the middle and upper classes. In 1885, Carl Benz placed a petrol engine on a tricycle, creating the world's first automobile. What took him so long? Others had been talking about "manumotive engines" for quite some time. (The 13th-century English philosopher and Franciscan friar Roger Bacon was jailed for predicting that "chariots will move with an unspeakable force, without any living creature to stir them …") Before Benz there were tricycles powered experimentally with steam and with batteries. *The Spectator* magazine foretold of a time when tricycles would be supplied with "intermittent power to be used only when required." This prediction was made in 1869:

> Nothing is more wanted in modern life than a means of getting swiftly about on common roads without incessant expense, of going, say, thirty, or even twenty, miles without very great fatigue … In most English counties, with their swelling undulations, and roads built apparently with a view rather to the enjoyment of scenery than to the saving of labour … this objection, unless it can be overcome, is fatal to anything approaching the universal use of the velocipede … Certainly it cannot be while the only power employed is that residing in the traveller himself. No conceivable ingenuity of adjustment can seriously relieve him up-hill, or enable him to get to the top without carrying his own weight and that of his machine … Is there the possibility of obtaining fresh and intermittent power to be used only when required? With it, the tricycle might become a valuable addition to our locomotive resources …

It was the start of the cycling era – with many paeans to pedal power due to be published over the next 25 years – and yet here was a magazine suggesting that Brits would rather be carried up hills by a motive force rather than use their own muscles. *The Spectator* was spot on.

During the first few years of the motoring age the effort-free aspect of motoring was welcomed and celebrated. The act of motoring was even said to promote health, especially by doctors, who were among the earliest to benefit from the convenience and speed of motoring (a motor car extended reach, allowed a doctor to arrive at destinations in some comfort, and enabled many more calls per day – and each call attracted a fee).

Sir Henry Thompson, a professor of surgery and pathology at the Royal College of Surgeons, wrote that: "The easy jolting which occurs when a motor-car is driven at a fair speed over the highway conduces to a healthy agitation … it aids the peristaltic movements of the bowels and promotes the performance of their functions."

Sir Henry added:

> I have been told by men who are occupied long and closely with brain-work, that the automobile

has filled a great want in their lives. They have found themselves too much exhausted to be able to take a long bicycle ride into the country; while railway travelling excites their overwrought nerves, and increases their sense of fatigue.

But he warned that those who drove everywhere would soon become "flabby," a warning not terribly well heeded:

> The vigorous man who has been used to take exercise on horseback, on his bicycle, or on his legs, must beware lest the fascination of motoring lead him to give up his physical exercise. Unless he systematically maintains habits of muscular exertion he may find that he is putting on flesh, becoming flabby, and generally losing condition.

IN POPULAR imagination the usual chronology in the history of the motor car is this: bicycles and horse-drawn buggies were set aside; motor cars took over; everybody wanted a motor car; as soon as they could afford one they got one; increased wages allowed all to afford cars; everybody lived happily ever after. Reality was different to that. The hegemony of the automobile is now such a given, and the car-is-king mentality so ingrained, that it's surprising to discover motor cars were not universally welcomed when they came spluttering onto the scene at the end of the 19th century. Many motoring history books include only the praise, neglecting the antipathy. Much of the praise for motor cars came from cyclists, who were among the first automobile purchasers, the first motoring journalists, the founders and first officials of motoring organisations, and the first motor-company promoters. But motoring was not an overnight success story and many years of incessant promotion were needed before motor cars sold in numbers.

It was easier to sell the concept of motoring to urbanites. Even in car-mad America, conservative, rural interests remained suspicious for more years than many motoring histories care to disclose. One of the reasons for the myth that the motor car was an instant hit is the propaganda from what would become one of the dominant motor car manufacturers, the Ford Motor Company. In 1903 a company photograph showed Henry Ford using a Model A as a stationary source of power – to chop wood – and from this it's assumed that farmers used motor cars similarly. In fact, such use – which eventually became common on American farms – took some years to catch on. Farmers were among the first and loudest critics of what some called "devil wagons." And many farmers didn't want "their" roads used by motorists.

A farmer's wife told a New York newspaper in 1904 that

> we … think that the people who are able to own and run an automobile are able to build their own roads to run them on, and leave the public highways for the use of people who do not care to be sent from this mundane sphere by a horse maddened by one of those pesky automobiles.

In the same year, an American farm magazine called automobile drivers "a reckless, bloodthirsty, villainous lot of … crazy trespassers." A number of localities banned the "devil wagon." In the late 1890s, when the civic leaders of Mitchell, South Dakota, heard that someone over 100 miles away, in Pierre, the state capital, had built an automobile, they prohibited motor car use on their streets. Mackinac Island, Michigan – ironically, a summer playground of the early 20th-century elites from the "motortown" of Detroit – is one of the few American localities to retain, to this day, its prohibition of motor vehicles.

Some of the most restrictive polices against automobiles in North America were enacted in Canada. In Kings County, Nova Scotia, no automobiles were allowed on public highways at the weekend, a rule enforced until at least 1910. Nova Scotia was a hotbed of anti-automobilism. The editor of New Glasgow's newspaper said that motor cars were "gasoline devils," and – predating the rule in Nazi Germany that all Jews had to wear yellow badges – local bylaws in New Glasgow forced "auto people" to wear distinctive badges on their clothing, marking motorists as misfits even when not driving their "running stinkers."

A 1907 editorial in the *Eastern Chronicle* pointed out that roads had not been built for cars:

> New Glasgow during the past week has got another of the "devil wagons." Possibly more will follow. This is a free country – within certain limits. However, we feel fairly certain that besides the danger and injury inflicted, these "devil wagons" will lose the merchants of the town thousands of dollars worth of trade, because the country people will not … risk their lives, coming or going from town, by meeting one of these machines … If we have to put up with them, drivers of horses will be driven off the roads. Drivers of horses are mostly on business, but the "devil wagons" are used for fun. Has the whole county, whose people built the roads for their own use in order to do their work, to put up with these pleasure jaunters?

The newspaper called for automobiles to be banned: "The law should give municipalities the power to forbid [devil wagons] the use of our roads."

An American anti-automobile society lobbied for laws designed to make motoring downright impossible. In 1903, residents of Evanston, Illinois formed the Farmers' Anti-Automobile League to "mete out justice to reckless [drivers]" after a woman was injured by a speeding motorist. This society, while never mainstream, became national and held small-scale rallies in many US states. At a convention held in Montana in 1909 the Farmers' Anti-Automobile League urged its members to "give up Sunday to chasing automobiles, shooting and shouting at them." The society demanded restrictive laws to repel motorists. These laws were never enacted but the demands often surface today in newspaper articles and on websites listing "wacky motoring laws" as though the Farmers' Anti-Automobile League had been politically successful. A mainstream 1961 American documentary on the history of the motor car – fronted by Groucho Marx – claimed the laws were real and, to raise a laugh, spent a number of minutes of precious airtime re-enacting the supposed rules, such as having to dismantle a car should a horse take fright, or covering a car with a tarpaulin painted to represent the surrounding scenery:

> Any self-propelled vehicle must come to a complete halt upon approaching a cross road. The engineer must thoroughly examine the roadway ahead and sound his horn vigorously, then hello loudly or ring a gun after which he must fire a gun of sufficient calibre to be heard at great distance, thereupon he will dismount and discharge a Roman candle, a vesuvius bomb or other warning device as final warning of his approach … [When nearing a horse, he must] discharge his passengers, convince the horse the car wasn't there by covering it with a cloth painted to resemble the surrounding countryside. The [motorist must] further take the machine apart as rapidly as possible and conceal the pieces in grass at side of the road.

There was a great deal of genuine anti-automobile feeling in England. In her weekly column in the popular magazine *The Graphic*, in 1899 Lady Violet Greville painted a picture of a countryside blighted by automobiles:

> Alas! all the grace and beauty [of the countryside] must be spoiled as the craze for auto-cars

increases. Roads are churned up, dust flies in clouds, the air is filled with hideous sounds and odious smells as these terrible inventions fly along, scattering foot-passengers and carriages and destroying all the sweet solitude of the country. Last Sunday three auto-cars abreast might be seen rushing at twenty-five miles an hour along the Guildford Road and raising terror and abhorrence in the minds of all who beheld them. While every country road becomes a mere railway track, rural haunts will have for ever lost their charm.

Later the same month, in *The Autocar*, editor Henry Sturmey suggested that Lady Greville would be converted to the pleasures of motoring if only she tried it herself:

Will someone who owns a really nice auto car persuade Lady Violet Greville to take a good, long drive in it? She does not know what is ailing her, but it is evident that she requires a little practical experience of autocaring … Why the automobile should destroy the charm of the countryside we cannot even guess, so, though it pains us to do so, we fear we must conclude that Lady Violet Greville [is] suffering from a slight attack of envy or prejudice, and that after she has tasted the delights of a brisk drive on a good car she will think and write differently.

Many from the upper classes remained unconvinced. The "friends of the horse" movement – that is, the whip makers, quipped Harry Lawson, the motoring promoter – feared that motorised transport would supplant equine transport. Working class people felt embittered that they were being shunted to the margins of the road by "rich mens' toys." Pioneer motorists were pelted with stones. There are many recorded examples of this from Germany and Switzerland, but missile-throwing was endemic in the Netherlands, claimed a German woman motorist, who recorded in her diary in 1905 that "a journey by automobile through Holland is dangerous, since most of the rural population hates motorists fanatically. We even encountered older men, their faces contorted with anger, who, without any provocation, threw fist-sized stones at us."

Motorists were physically attacked in America, too. Between 1903 and 1907, farmers shot at motor cars in Minnesota; motorists were pulled from their vehicles in Wisconsin; and in rural New York motorists were whipped. Roads were sometimes booby-trapped with rakes, glass or tacks and ropes or barbed wire were strung across rural roads known to attract motor "scorchers."

Part of the antipathy was due to class. Woodrow Wilson, the president of Princeton University – and a cycle tourist of some note – declared in 1906 that "nothing spread socialistic feeling in this country more than the use of automobiles." Asked for his opinion about Wilson's claim, one motor car manufacturer said:

We have become accustomed to the outburst from time to time of occasionally discontented minds not familiar with the subject of automobiling … but if [Wilson] will investigate he will find that there are not as many crazy drivers of automobiles as there are crazy drivers of horses [and] bicycles.

(Wilson later became an enthusiastic motorist, and President of the United States.)

In Europe, many politicians initially abhorred motorists. At a session of the Prussian parliament in 1908, Baron von Eynatten scolded a brochure published by the Imperial Automobile Club. To laughter and applause from his colleagues, Eynatten read out lines from the brochure in a scornful tone. He mocked that the brochure claimed that "panic on the part of the public" caused most accidents, that coachmen must be made to realise "quiet times on country roads are a thing of the past," and that "the road is for vehicles, not for pedestrians."

August publications from around the world voiced concerns about the increasing popularity of motoring. In 1911, *The Economist* asked whether the advent of the motor car had been a good thing: "Has the invention of motors brought with it a balance of profit or pleasure? Would the nation as a whole be richer and happier if motor vehicles of all kinds had been absolutely prohibited?"

In 1905, an English newspaper complained that motor cars were "being driven 60 or 70 miles an hour" on the unimproved roads of England and consequently "children were not safe going to school without attendants." Such excessive speeds – as well as honking horns and kicked-up dust – led to campaigns against the fast new users of the road. Many of these new users were moneyed toffs, but not all English aristocrats swooned over motor cars. Some even founded anti-motoring organisations. Similar to the anti-motoring societies in rural America, the Highway Protection League never went mainstream but that it existed at all will be a surprise to many. The League, with an office in London, had for its aims "the protection of the public from excessive motoring speed and the introduction of legislation to remove the terrorism of the flying motor." Founded in 1902 the organisation was led by Tory peer Lord Leigh. The vice-president, and soon to be president thanks to the death of Lord Leigh in 1903, was Baron Willoughby de Broke. He was "a genial and sporting young peer, whose face bore a pleasing resemblance to the horse ... and was not more than two hundred years behind his time."

The Highway Protection League was highly conservative, most definitely "horsey" and supported by at least parts of the rural community. Major J. W. Dent of the Yorkshire Agricultural Union chaired a meeting in 1905 which "strongly supported the Highway Protection League in their endeavours to prevent the infringement by persons using motor power of the common law rights of the public to the free and full use of the highways." Likewise, the Warwickshire Chamber of Agriculture also supported the League's aims, as did many other rural interests.

At a league meeting held in Warwick in 1905, motorist T. Hamilton Barnsley of Birmingham said the league should not be supported as he felt it desired to see "motorists wiped off the road altogether." England was a manufacturing country, he told the meeting, urging delegates "not to do anything to cripple what [was] going to be an enormous industry."

Sir James Fergusson MP presided over a Highway Protection League meeting at the Westminster Palace Hotel in London in 1905, where delegates were told "the reckless conduct" of some motorists amounted to "tyranny on the highways" which was "shameful." Motorists were getting away with murder, the meeting heard: "The old legal maxim that if a man fired a gun into a street and killed a person without meaning to do so he was guilty of murder, should be applied to motor drivers who recklessly [rode] down inoffensive people."

MPs Cathcart Wason and Brooke Robinson were at the London meeting. "Lord North, Sir Walter Gilbey, and the Master of Emanuel College, Cambridge, sent their regrets at their absence."

The league demanded that leaders of automobile interests should "keep the rank and file of their own army in decent and respectable order" if the "common law rights of the public [were to be] preserved as their undisturbed and peaceable possession." The league paid for an advert in the pro-motoring *Daily Mail* showing a speeding motorist kicking up dust (the car pictured was a high-powered Napier, the leading English marque – and a company founded by two racing cyclists). The advert said: "All persons who are alive to the danger and discomfort now caused by those who travel at an excessive speed on the Public roads are STRONGLY URGED to support this league."

The league was not for pedestrians and equestrians only. "We particularly hope to gain the sympathies of the cyclists," said the organisation's secretary in 1904. Cyclists were "more liable to danger from motorists than pedestrians are, because cyclists have less control over their movements."

In 1907, supporters of the League were still lambasting "selfish motor savages" who did not feel the full force of the law for their sins. However, by this time, even the most vocal anti-motoring high-society types were being won over to the new form of locomotion, and the League for Highway Protection, like its American counterpart, gradually slipped into obscurity.

However, there were hold-outs. Charles Frederick Gurney Masterman, a charismatic Liberal politician and journalist, wrote a withering attack on speeding motorists in his 1909 book, *The Condition of England*. At this time he was the Parliamentary Secretary to the Local Government Board and hence in a position of power but clearly powerless to do much about what he said was destroying the peace and tranquillity of England. "Wandering machines, travelling with an incredible rate of speed, scramble and smash and shriek along all the rural ways," he complained. He remarked that car ownership was a marker of status and that excessive speed was a natural outcome of this ownership:

> [A] large proportion of those who have employed motor cars in habitual violation of the speed limit, and in destruction of the amenities of the rural life of England, have done so either because their neighbours have employed motor cars, or because their neighbours have not employed motor cars; in an effort towards equality with the one, or superiority over the other.

Speeding motor cars on England's rural roads made people frightened to venture out of doors, said Masterman: "From those villages ... not only the evidence of activity has departed, but the very memories of it."

Many of those who remembered the slower, safer horse-drawn days regretted their passing. Speaking in a House of Lords debate in 1946, Viscount Cecil of Chelwood blamed speed for a "great slaughter":

> It has not always been the case that there has been this gigantic slaughter on the roads. It began with the introduction of motors. There is no doubt about that; that is a mere historical fact. The primary and main difference between the motor and the previous vehicle was that the motor went much faster and was much heavier, so that a blow struck by the motor was a much more serious matter than the blow struck by a horse-carriage ... This great slaughter ... of 7,000 people a year ... and the injuring of hundreds of thousands every year – is entirely new. It did not exist in the old days at all. Few accidents happened then. Every now and then a horse ran away, and somebody in the carriage was injured, or somebody who got in the way of the horse was injured and, occasionally, killed, but it was a very rare event. Now the thing is common and has become a very, very serious danger to our whole civilization ... I do not deny that [motor cars] have their importance; but the question of congestion on the roads and things of that kind, important though they may be, are quite insignificant compared with the slaughter and maiming and injury of vast numbers of our fellow-subjects.

In 1925, *The Spectator* argued that "very high speed cars ... should be altogether forbidden on public thoroughfares ..." and that "... heavy cars ... should be forbidden to use country lanes." The magazine stated that:

> The King's Highway is the common track for all classes of traffic – foot passengers, perambulators, bicycles, milk-carts, farm wagons and cattle – and no person has the right to behave on the common highway in such a manner as to imperil the safety of fellow-users of that track. Yet a large number of high speed motorists behave as if they had that right ... Habitually, too, a large number of motorists behave as if they believe that the whole roadway belongs to them ... It is the power to do ill deeds that makes ill deeds done ...

Motorists very often brought on anti-motoring antipathy by their own actions, scaring slower road users by "skimming" them when passing, or by making inflammatory statements in print sure to raise the hackles of those likely to be on the receiving end of aggressive motoring.

Talking in the 1930s about the 1890s, Lieutenant-Colonel J. T. C. Moore-Brabazon, vice-chair of the Automobile Club and an MP, told the House of Commons:

> It is true that 7000 people are killed in motor accidents, but it is not always going on like that. People are getting used to the new conditions ... No doubt many of the old Members of the House will recollect the number of chickens we killed in the old days. We used to come back with the radiator stuffed with feathers. It was the same with dogs. Dogs get out of the way of motor cars nowadays and you never kill one. There is education even in the lower animals. These things will right themselves.

A similar point of view had been put forward in 1904 by Sir Horace Plunkett, president of the Irish Automobile Club. He believed "dogs, ducks and policemen" would soon learn the new order of things:

> The speed of motors on the road will ... cease to be a serious difficulty in the near future ... I notice that judgment of speed is quickly developing in the animal kingdom. Dogs, ducks, and policemen are the slowest to bring their standards of comparison up to date ... Ducks puzzle me most, as they were far the best judges of the speed of old-fashioned vehicles ... their little locomotor machinery always managed to drag their cumbrous, amphibious after-carriages out of the way of ... wheels. Now the chauffeur has to do the calculation for the duck. Policemen are improving rapidly. I have not been fined for a year.

The preoccupation with animals – and humans – failing to get out of the way of motorists was global. French playwright Octave Mirbeau wrote in 1908: "How frustrating, how thoroughly disheartening it is that these pigheaded, obstructive villagers whose hens, dogs and sometimes children I mow down, fail to appreciate I represent Progress and universal happiness." He added: "I intend to bring them these benefits in spite of themselves, even if they don't live to enjoy them!"

The idea that animals had to get out of the way of revolutionary road vehicles was nothing new. Cyclists had said the same back in the boom years: "Apparently the dogs of London do not for a moment realise how fast a bicycle travels," wrote a high-society cyclist in 1895. "They will have to be educated up to the new order of things." This education could be shrill and potentially aggressive if the very loud Cyclists' Road Clearer whistle of the 1890s was anything to go by.

Nevertheless, cyclists tended to be more aware of the risks of collision (as is still the case) because in any impact – even in cases of impacting soft things such as small children – they were just as likely to injure themselves as to cause harm to the soft thing they hit. Writing in an 1897 cycling guidebook, Arthur T. Poyser warned: "There is a long descent through Auchterarder, becoming rather steep latterly, and requiring care owing to the children who make the road their playground ..."

A steep descent would have been tricky for a cyclist in 1897 as the bicycles of the day didn't have freewheels. Without the ability to "coast," cyclists were warned when approaching descents by signs erected by cycling organisations. While "scorching" by some cyclists was most definitely a problem in the last quarter of the 19th century, a speeding cyclist was of comparatively little danger compared to a speeding motorist of the early 20th century, especially since many of the early motorists were so clearly intoxicated by the velocities they could achieve.

Mirbeau might have been an uncaring cad, but he recognised why. He realised that getting behind the steering wheel did awful things to his moral compass:

> When I am in the car, possessed by speed, humanitarian feelings drain away. I begin to feel
> obscure stirrings of hatred and an idiotic sense of pride. No longer am I a miserable specimen
> of humanity, but a prodigious being in whom are embodied – no, please don't laugh – Elemental
> Splendor and Power. And given I am the Wind, the Storm, the Thunderbolt, imagine with what
> contempt I view the rest of humanity from the vantage-point of my car.

Road "bullying" did not start with motorists. It has a long history, as recounted in chapter 4. However, the ease with which the early motorists could force aside other road users meant that ancient roads very quickly became thought of as "motoring roads." Non-motorised users became the "other." Writing in an Austrian motor magazine (founded by an Olympic gold medal-winning racing cyclist), one contributor observed in 1909 that a

> large proportion of accidents happen because the other users of the street refuse to acknowledge
> and adapt to the changed circumstances brought about by the appearance of the motor car. The
> heedlessness with which the public still crosses the busiest streets is beyond belief; and many
> parents let their children use the street as a playground, as if streetcars and automobiles simply
> don't exist.

(Children have always played out close to their homes but, with the coming of cars, they were expected to play elsewhere – and if they did not, it was their fault if they were knocked over and killed.)

In 1942, German sociologist and philosopher Theodor W. Adorno wrote ironically of the feeling of power over supposedly lesser road users: "And which driver is not tempted, merely by the power of the engine, to wipe out the vermin of the street, pedestrians, children and cyclists?"

Those without motors who dared to carry on using streets were doing so "improperly," thought an American writer, in 1916: "With an automobile properly driven there is no menace to life, except that precipitated by those on foot who make improper uses of the streets and thoroughfares."

The view that non-motorised use of streets was "improper" went mainstream, especially among planners and civic leaders. Roads became motor roads, and their earlier – and far longer-standing – use as highways for all became increasingly redundant. In the 1930s, the Cyclists' Touring Club lobbied alongside Britain's motoring organisations to secure "motorways" for motor cars. The CTC hoped that motorists, given their own roads, would use those in preference to the country's "ordinary roads." The same hope was expressed by Alfred Barnes, the Minister of Transport. In a post-war statement in the House of Commons, he said:

> If Parliament sees fit to grant the necessary powers, it would be my intention to start on a
> further number of motor roads where that course is found to be preferable to the widening
> or by-passing of the existing roads. The latter, freed from fast-moving through traffic, would
> then remain available for pedestrian, cyclist, and local motor traffic, which would use them in
> greater comfort and security.

Clearly, the belief that special "motor roads" would leave the remaining roads free of motorised vehicles was a misjudged fantasy – Britain's roads rapidly clogged with cars.

URBAN USE of the private motor car – which can accommodate five or more people but generally only carries one – is only truly fast and efficient when car ownership is low, such as in the very early days of motoring, or when the population density is low but the provided motor-centric infrastructure is copious (some American, cities spring to mind). In 1971, when car ownership in Britain was already deemed to be at "saturation point" with 12 million cars in use (it has nearly trebled since then), William Plowden, author of a book about the political influence of motorists, wondered

> … how had we got into a situation in which it was apparently possible for the users of private cars, without serious question, to dictate the pattern of traffic to every other road-user, and to maximise their own comfort and convenience at the expense of the vast majority travelling by other means.

Today, the vast majority of Britons choose to travel by private motor car, and the government dismisses the idea of "peak car" and believes the 30 million motor cars currently in use will increase by 46 percent within 30 years. The official estimates of traffic growth in most developed countries predict similar levels of growth in car ownership. Consequently, congestion is also predicted to increase. In 2010, car satnav maker TomTom produced an outdoor poster which told motorists: "You are not stuck in traffic. You are traffic." The ironic campaign didn't seem to result in any greater understanding that the problem isn't just the cars in front, but the car you're sitting in, too.

British urban planner Thomas Sharp made a similar point in 1932:

> A motorist is apt to complain of the "overcrowded" condition of the road if he finds he has not continually got a whole mile-long stretch of it to himself … He will declare there is no pleasure in motoring under such conditions. He will search his map for some alternative route by quiet lanes where he can speed along with the road to himself. And when others find that alternative route and all further alternatives are exhausted, he proceeds to demand a new road system so that his motoring may again become a pleasure.

THERE'S PLENTY of road space to go round, but it's how we use it at peak times that's the problem. At 3am, most British motorways are empty. These roads are plenty wide enough most of the time – the bottlenecks occur sporadically, and usually at wholly expected times yet there are regular calls for more roads to be built. Not learning from past mistakes, and hoping that failed solutions will somehow work "this time," is a sure sign of madness. Yet it's a shared madness – a group hallucination that's costly, wasteful and quickly ineffective.

Just as in the 1960s and 1970s politicians still nod through hugely expensive road building schemes, ignoring warnings, dreaming instead – it seems – of ribbon-cutting photo-opportunities. In 2011, a Public Local Inquiry in Scotland recommended that a five-mile urban motorway in the centre of Glasgow "should not be authorised". The inquiry's report concluded that "[the] benefits of the new road would be progressively eroded by the continuing traffic growth which would be facilitated and induced by the new road." The £692 million M74 motorway would only "temporarily ease traffic congestion," and would "seriously hinder the achievement of important Scottish Executive commitments and objectives for traffic reduction, public transport improvements, and CO2 emissions." Politicians went ahead and commissioned it anyway.

Measures to get people out of cars are rarely mooted, and funded even more rarely. Social thinker and historian Lewis Mumford said in 1955,

> … motor transportation is the sacred cow of the … religion of technology, and in the service of this curious religion no sacrifice in daily living, no extravagance of public expenditure, appears too great… A large part of the present difficulty … is caused by the over employment of one method of transportation, the private motorcar – a method that happens to be, on the basic of the number of people it transports, by far the most wasteful of urban space. Because we have apparently decided that the private motorcar has a sacred right to go anywhere, halt anywhere, and remain anywhere as long as its owner chooses, we have neglected other means of transportation.

By "other means of transportation", Mumford meant trams, buses and walking. In his writings he made little mention of cycling – in the 1950s, the bicycle was not considered a vehicle for the future. In the Netherlands, the bicycle remained a national icon and from the 1970s onwards the extensive network of Dutch bicycle paths was extended. Germany, too, built segregated roads for both motorists and cyclists; Britain (and America) did not.

In Britain, the belief that roads are for motor vehicles alone was very much due to the ancient claim of the public's "uninterrupted possession" of the "right of way." From the early days of motoring there were demands for new roads, but motorists wanted no restrictions placed on their use of existing roads.

CHAPTER FOUR

WHO OWNS THE ROADS?

*Highways have been forced to change from enabling short distance
movement at walking pace, to carrying high-speed, short, medium and long distance
motor traffic. Most were never originally intended for high-speed motor vehicles.*
UK Highways Liability Joint Task Group, July 2009

*If I [ask] what's a street for somebody is going to say car right away. It's like
free-association in psychology. It's just automatic. [But] if you'd asked that same
question to a random person a hundred years ago ... none of them would have
said that a street is for cars, even though there were a lot of cars then.*
Peter Norton, 2014

**Roads belong to all and need to be shared by all. However, there's a
long history of some road users believing they have priority over others.**

Social scientists theorise that humans believe in three kinds of territorial space. One is personal territory, like home. The second involves space that is only temporarily available, such as a gym locker. The third kind is public territory, such as roads.

"Territoriality is hard-wired into our ancestors," believes Paul Bell, co-author of a study on road rage. "Animals are territorial because it had survival value. If you could keep others away from your hunting groups, you had more game to spear, it becomes part of the biology."

When they are on the road, some motorists forget they are in public territory because the cues surrounding them – personal music, fluffy dice, protective shells – suggest they are in private space.

"If you are in a vehicle that you identify as primary territory, you would defend that against other people whom you perceive as being disrespectful of your space," added Bell. "What you ignore is that you are on a public roadway – and you don't own the road."

A standard quip from bicycle advocates, aimed at a certain type of mine-all-mine motorist, is "You own a car, not the road."

Some motorists insist it's cyclists who have the entitlement issues. "Cyclists think they own the roads," is a typical retort, common on forums and in local newspaper letters pages the world over, but most especially in America, Canada, Britain, Australia and New Zealand. In July 2014, Courtland

Milloy, a columnist for the *Washington Post* wrote, in all seriousness, that "biker terrorists" are "out to rule the road". (He later apologised.)

Belief in road "ownership" – even if it's just the few metres in front and behind the road user – leads to disagreements, but probably what many motorists and cyclists would agree on is that roads are thoroughfares for travel. Pioneer motorists would amplify and expand the idea of roads being for transport only but the transformation of the road's role was already well advanced by the time the first automobiles came along. The bicycle, the fastest vehicle on the road in the 1870s through to the mid-1890s, certainly played a part in redefining what a road was for, but apart from a smooth surface, the slim, single-track bicycle needed little in the way of built infrastructure. Trams, on the other hand, needed a great deal of dedicated space. With their rails and, once electrified, their overhead cables, trams very much transformed the concept of what roads were for, and that large parts of them could be appropriated for travel, and travel alone.

Later, motorists benefited from the land grab made by private tram companies. This was done by ripping out the rails put down at such great expense, and replacing them with motor-centric asphalt. The hegemony of the motor car was accelerated by countries co-operating to ease its passage. In Europe, in the early 1900s, it was extremely difficult to drive between nation states. Motor cars had to be "imported" at every border and pay punitive duties in each country visited. Many countries required motorists to pass national driving tests. Automobile clubs – many of them founded as cycling clubs – lobbied hard to get such restrictions lifted.

The lobbying took place at an international level, and would quickly transform "public highways" into "motoring roads." By 1908, just twelve years after Britain's "Emancipation Act" had legalised the use of motor cars, the officials at an international roads conference – many of them motorists, some of them former campaigning cyclists – took it upon themselves to define what roads were for. The Permanent International Association of Road Congresses excluded horse-drawn traffic from its remit at its first conference, held in Paris in 1908. PIARC delegates started to exclude cycling traffic from its work at the congress held in Brussels in 1910. At the London conference held in 1913, cycling was removed completely. Roads, decided the PIARC delegates, were only for A-to-B travel propelled by motors. There were only 105,734 motor cars in use in Britain in 1913 yet they had already driven many traditional users off the roads. "The right of the pedestrian to use the King's highway is one of the most valuable and cherished public possessions," wrote rambler and rights of way expert G. H. B. Ward in a 1913 pamphlet. "Notwithstanding the legal right of the pedestrian to the full and free use of any part of the King's highway … the modern multitude of motor-cars have, to all intents and purposes, driven him off the main trunk, county, and interurban roads …"

The legacy of the PIARC decision in 1913 is still with us: roads are deemed to be motor thoroughfares. Those without motors may be granted access, perhaps, but only under sufferance, and only under strict, motor-centric conditions. Cyclists must ride in the gutter; pedestrians must stay on the sidewalk (if one is provided, and if one isn't, that's a motor-only road); and both shall interact with motorists only at designated crossing points, which are usually far apart, militating against those without motors but "smoothing the traffic flow," the transport wonk term for squeezing as many motor vehicles through a junction as possible. And don't expect to cross any time soon – British and American traffic planners clearly believe roads are for cars, and pesky pedestrians and cranky cyclists can damn well wait.

ACCORDING TO town planning academic Carmen Hass-Klau, there are historical differences between German and British "city cultures," differences that help to explain how British cities (and perhaps, by extension, cities in America, Australia, Canada and New Zealand) came to be overwhelmed by motor cars. Counter-intuitively, it's to do with national concepts of freedom. Professor Hass-Klau said German cities often restricted passage of wheeled vehicles because of a desire for order. British cities, on the other hand, were more egalitarian: "There appears to have been (and still is) a greater acceptance of wheeled, and later motor, traffic as a way of life from very early on and a possible fear of conflicts if "equal" rights of all participants were not provided."

The so-called "liberty of the subject" was of great importance in Britain long before the 19th century. The public – even the lowest of the low – had the right to use any highway for passage because of the public's "uninterrupted possession" of such "ways". Lawful movement was not a privilege, but a fundamental right, held by the king, "for all the king's subjects."

The right to use the public highway applied to all highways, which today translates into the freedom for British motorists to drive their motor vehicles on almost all roads, not just the ones designed for their exclusive use, the *motor*ways. In Germany (and the Netherlands) it's far easier for planners to separate different road users because there is a greater appreciation that these users will have different needs, concerns and desires. Dutch planners can and do designate some roads as more important for motor-vehicle use and others as more important for cyclists, or for the exclusive use of pedestrians. Dutch motorists are prevented, or mightily discouraged with design, from using those roads that have been designated as important routes for other users. In Britain, the ancient and much-cherished freedom of *people* to use roads – any and all roads – has led to a system where motorists "rat run" on minor roads despite adjacent arterial roads. While some British motorists argue that cyclists ought to stick to cycle paths (of which there are but few), they would find it perverse to be restricted only to motorways and arterials. Likewise, British pedestrians bristle at the idea of being channelled on sidewalks – a Fast Lane/Slow Lane campaign for Oxford Street in London was laughed into oblivion in 2000. The British affection for queuing has resulted in a strongly held belief in first-come first-served but different rules apply on the roads – the British system of affording road users the "freedom" to travel howsoever they choose results in the heaviest, fastest and widest users creating their own priority.

THE LAWFUL movement on the British high*way* was, in the main, not movement on wheels. People walked, or rode on horseback, or took to water*ways*. When coaches became more prevalent, this was unsettling for some. In 1622, Thames waterman poet John Taylor wrote "this is a rattling, rowling, rumbling age," with people in coaches "tossed, tumbled, rumbled, and jumbled about in them." But, for all their discomforts, coaches became increasingly popular with the upper classes and Taylor grumbled that the "world runs on wheels."

Another writer, anticipating the very similar barbs aimed at pioneer motorists, complained that coach travel made the men of England effeminate and weak; destroyed trade; and was a great evil:

> Most gentlemen, before they travelled in coaches, used to ride with swords, belts, pistols, holsters, portmanteaus, and hat-cases, which, in these coaches, they have little or no occasion for: for, when they rode on horseback, they rode in one suit and carried another to wear when they camp to their journey's end, or lay by the way; but in coaches a silk suit and an Indian gown, with a sash, silk stockings, and beaver-hats, men ride in, and carry no other with them, because they escape the wet and dirt, which on horseback they cannot avoid; whereas, in two or three journeys on horseback, these clothes and hats were wont to be spoiled …

While coaches carried high society folk, carts and wains carried goods, locally. For long-distance transport, when waterway access wasn't possible, packhorses were used. A horse and cart would have been unsuited to the roads of the day. A train of, say, twelve packhorses could carry the same as two carts but could move faster over bad surfaces, and if one packhorse went lame its load could be redistributed. Lose the use of a carthorse, and the load goes nowhere.

While all classes of traveller had equal rights on the highway, that didn't stop complaints about those felt to be – literally – "in the way." Describing the "wayes, which are so grossly foul and bad," Thomas Mace, one of the clerks of Trinity College, Cambridge, wrote that passage along the Great North Road in the time of Charles II was often slowed by "innumerable controversies, quarrellings, and disturbances" caused by packhorse trains. The truck drivers of their day, blocking the road, were felt to be a nuisance, with Mace claiming, rather unfairly, that "disturbances, daily committed by uncivil, refractory, and rude Russian-like rake-shames, in contesting for the way, too often proved mortal, and certainly were of very bad consequences to many." Naturally, Mace, as an important traveller – the BMW driver of his day – felt these lowly "whifflers" ought to step aside:

> No man should be pestered by giving the way ... to hundreds of pack-horses, panniers, whifflers, coaches, waggons, wains, carts, or whatsoever others, which continually are very grievous to weary and loaden travellers; but more especially near the city and upon a market day, when, a man having travelled a long and tedious journey ... shall sometimes be compelled to cross out of his way twenty times in one mile's riding, by the irregularity and peevish crossness of such-like whifflers and market women; yea, although their panniers be clearly empty, they will stoutly contend for the way with weary travellers, be they never so many, or almost of what quality soever.

From "You Have Been Warned",
Fougasse & McCullough, 1935.

Mace clearly believed his "important business" gave him superior rights on the road but, as the packhorse train had might on its side – just like today's trucks – he had to wait until the horses went on their merry way:

> I have often known many travellers, and myself very often, to have been necessitated to stand stock still behind a standing cart or waggon, on most beastly and unsufferable deep wet

57

wayes, to the great endangering of our horses, and neglect of important business: nor durst we adventure to stirr (for most imminent danger of those deep rutts, and unreasonable ridges) till it has pleased Mister Garter to jog on, which we have taken very kindly.

According to Sidney and Beatrice Webb, writing in 1913, wheeled traffic in Britain remained mainly an urban phenomenon:

> Right down to the middle of the eighteenth century – in remote parts of these islands we may even say down to the middle of the nineteenth century – the passage of a wheeled vehicle of any kind remained … an exceptional event of the day. To an extent that we find it now difficult to realise, the seventeenth and eighteenth century roads were trodden by animal feet … The "New Users" of the roads in the seventeenth and eighteenth centuries, whose aggressions on the pedestrians and on the road surface were made the subject of persistent complaint in their day, are now themselves resenting the quite analogous aggressions of the "New Users" of the roads in the twentieth century.

With the road surface improvements of Metcalfe, Telford and McAdam – discussed in chapter 7 – roads began to be adapted for wheels, not wheels adapted for the roads. This was a radical change. Pedestrians, despite being the majority users of British roads, were pushed to the margins; they were slower and softer, and deemed inferior. Naturally, pedestrians didn't take kindly to this marginalisation, this bullying out of their "birthright." *The Beggar's Opera* author John Gay kicked out against these "proud chariots" in his 1716 poem *Trivia: or the art of walking in London*. He started by describing what pedestrians already had to look out for – muck. The "miry Lane" had to be "pick'd" through …

> And the rough Pavement wounds the yielding Tread;
> Where not a Post protects the narrow Space

But now the pedestrian – often poor or vulnerable – had to look out for the speeding carriages which splashed through the mire:

> Proud Coaches pass, regardless of the Moan,
> Of Infant Orphans, and the Widow's Groan …

And …

> What Walker shall his mean Ambition fix,
> On the false Lustre of a Coach and Six?
> Let the vain Virgin, lur'd by glaring Show,
> Sigh for the Liv'rys of th' embroider'd Beau.

Lumbering carts and narrow streets proved challenging for city dwellers:

> Though Expedition bids, yet never stray
> Where no rang'd Posts defend the rugged Way,
> Here laden Carts with thundering Waggons meet,
> Wheels clash with Wheels, and bar the narrow street

For Gay, picking through "the muddy Dangers of the Street" was the norm, while carriages and sedan chairs were the intruders:

> O happy Streets, to rumbling Wheels unknown,
> No Carts, no Coaches shake the floating Town!
> Thus was of old Britannia's City bless'd,
> E'er Pride and Luxury her Sons possess'd:
> Coaches and Chariots yet unfashion'd lay,
> Nor late-invented Chairs perplex'd the Way.

Gay didn't want to join those on wheels:

> May the proud Chariot never be my Fate,
> If purchas'd at so mean, so dear a Rate;
> O rather give me sweet Content on Foot,
> Wrapt in my Vertue, and a good Surtout!

One hundred and twenty years after Gay, the belief that slower users of the highway should get out of the way of the faster ones was used by Charles Dickens in *A Tale of Two Cities*. This has a famous beginning ("It was the best of times, it was the worst of times") and a memorable ending ("It is a far, far better thing that I do, than I have ever done …"), but it also has an interesting description of a road bully. The novel was written in 1859 but set in the years leading up to the French Revolution of 1789. The *ancien régime* is personified by the Marquis St. Evrémonde, an aristocrat who thinks peasants are "rats" and who feels the roads – *his* roads – should be free of obstructions so he can be driven through the streets of Paris at the greatest possible speed. When his carriage, horses driven wildly at his insistence, kills a child, St. Evrémonde's uncaring response leads an onlooker to stalk him, and stab him to death in his bed.

> With a wild rattle and clatter, and an inhuman abandonment of consideration [St. Evrémonde's] carriage dashed through streets and swept round corners, with women screaming before it, and men clutching each other and clutching children out of its way. At last, swooping at a street corner by a fountain, one of its wheels came to a sickening little jolt, and there was a loud cry from a number of voices, and the horses reared and plunged. But for the latter inconvenience, the carriage probably would not have stopped; carriages were often known to drive on, and leave their wounded behind … "It is extraordinary to me," said he, "that you people cannot take care of yourselves and your children. One or the other of you is for ever in the way. How do I know what injury you have done my horses."

Dickens may have been writing about pre-revolutionary France but the portrayal of a toff charging through crowded streets was behaviour he could have just as easily witnessed in London. English aristocrats frequently tore through London, and other cities, in their sleek, muscular carriages. Forty years later they would do so in primitive motor cars. The victim blaming displayed by the uncaring St. Evrémonde would be paralleled by many of the pioneer motorists, and what had been an aristocratic haughtiness became, by the 1930s, a mindset common to many motorised road users, intoxicated by their menacing power, lords of the road, whether their vehicles were luxurious or second-hand jalopies.

WHEELED TRAFFIC in the 17th and 18th centuries may have been unpopular with many existing users of the roads but, even though the new users of the road were rich and powerful and could therefore do as they pleased, historic "rights of way" trumped any concerns about novelty – in theory, if not always in practice. The same was true of the 19th century when cyclists played a key role in reshaping what streets were for. Legal battles in Britain – and America – saw highway rights extended to cyclists. The legal battles they fought – and won – helped motorists gain the same rights some years later, said urban historian Clay McShane: "Regulation of … bicycles … formed the basis for the later legal reaction to the internal combustion auto." He added that the bicycle also "led to a great upsurge in urban street traffic in the late nineteenth century and especially in the 1890s … New street traffic would lead to a series of changes in urban street design, in traffic regulation, and even in the definition of a street itself."

BRITISH CYCLISTS and motorists have the same "easement-like" rights as pedestrians and equestrians – the right to "pass and repass" over public highways, such as roads. This is the right of "passage". There's also a right of "carriage" – in other words the right to carry something while travelling. Up until late in the 19th century the word "carriage" meant the act of carrying and had nothing to do with a wheeled vehicle.

Unless prohibited by law, operators of vehicles (cyclists, in law, operate vehicles) are on British roads "by right," not "by permission."

"Rights of way" – the freedom to use public highways in Britain without let or hindrance – are considered "birthrights," and are held dear, partly because they are ancient, with the first English law text on the public use of the king's roads produced in the 12th century. In the 13th century Henry de Bracton wrote that the king's highway was "sacred" and that anyone who obstructed it "made an encroachment on the King himself." In 1757, the 1st Earl of Mansfield, highlighting the birthrights of those using the king's highway, referred back to a judgement of 1468: "The King has nothing but passage for himself and his people, but the freehold and all profits belong to the owner of the soil."

In other words, landowners own the soil below the "right of way" – in fact, quite a way below: ownership is down to the centre of the earth – but not a lot can stop folks exercising their king-given rights to passage over that soil.

British Lord Chief Justice Edward Ellenborough ruled in 1812 that "every unauthorised obstruction of a highway to the annoyance of the King's subjects is a nuisance." The free passage rights afforded to travellers was reconfirmed in an 1868 court case when Lord Justice Cairns said: "In truth a public road or highway is not an easement; it is a dedication to the public of the occupation of the surface of the land for the purpose of passing and re-passing."

Arcane, perhaps, but such dusty decisions have ramifications in the real world, including down to our own day. Eleven years after the judgment of Lord Justice Cairns, a new player on the roads gained legal recognition (and accelerated the belief that roads were for fast-moving wheeled traffic). An old man was knocked down by a cyclist who had been "riding furiously." The cyclist – a Mr. Taylor – had descended Muswell Hill in London when he narrowly missed an old lady, and most certainly bowled over an old man. His defence team argued that as a cycle wasn't defined as a carriage, in a law passed 45 years previously, before bicycles existed, there was no case to answer. Sneaky. The plea was disregarded, and Taylor was fined. But the case was appealed, and two judges ruled that cycles were henceforth to be considered carriages under the law. This was bad for Taylor, but good for cyclists in general. It meant that cycles, for the first time, had a legally defined status as "carriages," and cyclists would be able to pass and repass, albeit not furiously, over the highways of Britain. Thanks to *Taylor v Goodwin*, cyclists had gained some birthrights.

Sir John Mellor, one of the two justices involved in the Taylor case, was one of England's most eminent judges. He sat on the Queen's bench division of the High Court. According to *The Times*, Sir John was a champion of the highway rights of what are today known as "vulnerable road users." In 1869, complaining about the aggression from some drivers of horse-drawn carriages, he said he would hand down stiff penalties to those drivers brought before him and convicted of "reckless driving." An editorial in *The Times* agreed with such a tough stance. It's worthwhile quoting the editorial at length for it shows that, even before motorists came along, pedestrians were harassed on "their" roads by those with weight on their side:

> Jew and Gentile, Tory and Radical, patrician and plebeian, are all agreed as to the unpleasantness of having a cartwheel driven over the head or stomach, and all are more or less exposed to it ... Reckless drivers ... do not seem in the least to care ... whether they have knocked down a Duke or a dustman ... Mr. Justice Mellor ... thinks ... that accidents happen because the drivers do not believe, or, at any rate, will not admit, that "foot-passengers have as much right to cross a street or thoroughfare as persons driving have to pass along it." They hold, that is to say, that the pedestrian's proper sphere is the pavement, that when there he has a distinct right to consider himself safe from all vehicles whatsoever, and a just cause of complaint if they trespass on his rightful demesne; but that in the road, on the other hand, he is the trespasser, a fish out of water in fact, who ought to be thankful that he is tolerated there at all ...

> [Justice Mellor] considers there is "great and habitual recklessness in driving in the metropolis" and he threatens to inflict a "severe sentence" on any driver convicted before him of an offence so dangerous to the community ...

> Everybody who knows London knows how common criminally reckless driving is and yet, unless where it happens to be attended with very serious consequences, it very rarely meets with punishment, simply because ... nobody but the helpless sufferer feels any strong disposition to have it punished. We welcome Mr. Justice Mellor as an important exception to this rule, and have little doubt that, if a few of the "severe sentences" which he threatens are inflicted, there will be a marked diminution not only in actual injuries to life and limb, but also in the discomfort and inconvenience which timid pedestrians now experience from "the perils of the streets."

Justice Mellor's intercession made not the slightest difference. *The Spectator* was still complaining about the "perils of the streets" in 1894: "Every year the Moloch of vehicular traffic claims its tribute of victims in our London streets ... London crushes every day under its chariot wheels, five, or possibly ten, of its fellow-citizens ..."

Light, flighty hansom cabs, able to dart about the city, were of but little danger to pedestrians, reported the magazine. The heavier vehicles, even though slower, were by far the biggest worry:

> As a rule the carelessness of the driver varies somewhat in proportion to the invulnerability of the vehicle that he drives ... The private coachman and the driver of the tradesman's cart have far less compunction in teaching an old gentleman to get out of their way by running him down ... By far the worst offender is ... the driver of the hooded van ... Their own immunity from hurt makes them callous with regard to the injuries they inflict upon others. They are the leviathans of the street, to be avoided by all its smaller fry ...

But *The Spectator* had not yet "touched upon the vehicle that contributes more largely than any other to the perils of the street" – the bicycle!

> Strangely enough, it is the one that is itself the most easily damaged, and has the best cause of all to avoid collision. Cyclists are never tired of assuring us that it is more dangerous for them to run into the man on foot than it is for the latter to be run into.

In words that echo down to us today, the magazine added:

> The trusting wayfarer, who steps from the pavement into a perfectly silent and apparently empty road without taking the precaution of looking behind him, runs the risk of being knocked head over heels by a machine driven at the rate of twelve miles an hour ... twice the speed of any other conveyance in the street.

IN DECEMBER 2001, the "tech world's most-speculated-about secret" was a transportation device. The inventor said the device – codenamed Ginger, and which cost $100 million to develop – was to be "to the car what the car was to the horse and buggy."

Apple's Steve Jobs gushed: "If enough people see this machine, you won't have to convince them to architect cities around it; it'll just happen."

Ginger's inventor, a hugely rich, highly successful medical and robotics innovator, said:

"I would stake my reputation, my money and my time on the fact that 10 years from now, this will be the way many people in many places get around."

Dean Kamen's reputation is intact and he still has oodles of money but all the time he spent on his pet project didn't result in the creation of the Next Big Thing. Kamen's project was the Segway. The company still exists and the product still sells, but cars have not been displaced. Why did the Segway flop? There are precious few places to ride them. In the UK, Segways have no right of way on public highways such as roads, footways and footpaths. (In Canada, there are similar restrictions, and many US municipalities also ban the device from sidewalks.) In the UK Segways are not classified as "carriages" with rights on the "carriageway" parts of the public highway, but they are classified as "mechanically propelled vehicles."

The "birthright" to public highways doesn't extend to every proposed user. Fall on the wrong side of highway laws – as Dean Kamen found out – and you can kiss goodbye to your right to use the public highway.

In the UK, Segways cannot be used on public highways because they have not been included in the list of "carriages" that fall within the scope of the 1835 Highway Act:

> If any person shall wilfully ride upon any footpath or causeway by the side of any road made or set apart for the use or accommodation of foot passengers; or shall wilfully lead or drive any horse, ass, sheep, mule, swine, or cattle or carriage of any description, or any truck or sledge, upon any such footpath or causeway; or shall tether any horse, ass, mule, swine, or cattle, on any highway, so as to suffer or permit the tethered animal to be thereon; every person so offending in any of the cases aforesaid shall for each and every such offence forfeit and pay a [fine].

As this act appeared before the development of bicycles, there was no mention of bicycles and so, when they first took to the streets in the late 1860s, the users of bicycles feared they had no legal status, or legal right to be on either roads or sidewalks. To attain such rights was the avowed aim of the Cyclists' Touring Club. This was founded in 1878 to "secure a fair and equitable administration of Justice as regards the right of bicyclists to the public roads. To watch the course of any legislative proposals in Parliament or elsewhere affecting the interests of the bicycling public, and to make such representations on the subject as the occasion may demand."

When it went into battle in the *Taylor v Goodwin* case, the CTC did so knowing the stakes were high, but it hoped the principle of the "right of way" for bicycles, as "carriages," would, eventually, win through. The highway rights that the 1879 court case appeared to confirm were ephemeral, and a great many local by-laws were put in place to restrict the new-fangled bicycle. It wasn't until 1888, with the passing of the Local Government Act, that the "right" for cyclists, and their "carriages," to use the highway was clarified by Parliament. 1888 was "destined to be an ever memorable [year]," cyclists said at the time.

The CTC formed a committee to oversee the progress of the Local Government bill through Parliament. It was feared that if county councils were given powers to create their own by-laws these would be used to prohibit bicycles. The CTC had political clout: it asked one of its members – who just so happened to be an MP – to lodge an amendment to the bill. Sir John Donnington "won a brilliant victory for the Club," wrote James Lightwood, the author of a 1928 history of the CTC.

When the act – with the critical amendment – was duly passed, a writer in the *Law Journal* said the Local Government Act of 1888 was the "Magna Carta de Bicyclis."

Lightwood enthused:

> As a result there disappeared ... every enactment which gave to Courts of Sessions, Municipal Corporations and similar bodies in England and Wales power to resist and hamper the movements of cyclists as they might think fit. The new order of things established once and for all the status of the cycle.

The legal definition of bicycles as carriages allowed cycling to prosper. Without a clearly defined and nationwide legal status, it would have been easier for localities to ban the use of bicycles.

IT'S SOMETIMES stated that pedestrians and cyclists enjoy use of British roads by statute, but motorists are only allowed on by licence. This is almost right. Cars are not (yet) sentient; motor vehicles still have to be piloted by human operators and, since 1903, those human operators have required licences to pilot their motor vehicles on public roads. If you drive a car without a driving licence, you commit an offence. In theory, a driving licence can be removed from those motorists who prove themselves nuisances before the law. In practice, such licence revocation was – and is – rare. Why? The early motorists believed themselves to be "gentlemen," not "cads," and, today, magistrates and juries seem to think roughly the same, and also appear to operate on the principle of "there but for the Grace of God go I" when deciding whether to revoke driving licences, which are deemed so sacrosanct their removal is akin to amputating a limb, or perhaps two.

In a report published in 2002, Britain's Institution of Civil Engineers complained that the "right of way" – mostly for motorists – had prevailed over any sense of "right of place":

> Many activities that take place in the street are covered by weak, or non-existent, rights. There is no formal right to remain in a street. There is no right of public assembly. There is no right to have a party in a street – people must apply for a temporary closure at a cost of several hundred

pounds. A child has no right to play in the street. There is no right to play football in a street – even though 100 years ago this was a common practice. Individuals have no right to park their cars in the street. The rights of people living in or occupying property that fronts a street have also been relatively weak. They exercise a right to access their property but have no strong rights against the impact of increased traffic.

Despite what Professor Hass-Klau said about British egalitarianism, soon after gaining equal rights to the use of the road, some motorists set about extinguishing the road rights of others. Complaining about this "highway robbery," essayist and Cambridge University lecturer Goldsworthy Lowes Dickinson said:

> The citizen who does not motor has become a kind of outlaw on his own highways. He travels, whether on foot, by carriage, or by bicycle, under conditions which render enjoyment impossible, and safety of life and limb precarious … Motorists are the chartered tyrants of the road, and they use, or abuse, their privileged position with an inconsiderate insolence.

ROADS WERE not built for cars. Nor were they built for bicycles. They were not built for sulkies, or steam engines, or any form of wheeled vehicle. Roads were not built for horses, either. Roads were built for pedestrians. H. G. Wells pointed this out, from an urban perspective, in 1901: "The streets of all the mediæval towns, were not intended for any sort of wheeled traffic at all – [they] were designed primarily … for pedestrians." (Most medieval historians would dispute this, stating that towns and cities relied on the goods transported hither and thither by small carts.)

Wells highlighted the previous importance of pedestrians in order to make the point he felt they would not hold sway for much longer. A former leisure cyclist and, by 1901, an enthusiastic motorist, Wells predicted a future where the motor car would hold sway. As usual, he was ahead of his time. In 1901, the debate about the future of the street, of the road, had hardly begun. And by the time the debate was in full swing, motorists had already annexed – by speed and power – the great majority of roads, and some motorists were clamouring for "motor only" roads, too, either by imposing restrictions on who should now be allowed to use Britain's "ordinary" roads, or promoting new-builds.

William Joynson-Hicks, chairman of the Motor Union and a Tory MP, feared motoring would wither and die if, perchance, motor cars were allowed only on those roads set aside for their use. "I am totally and entirely opposed to taking the motorist and placing him on the heights of fame with a special road to himself," he worried in 1909. "Once allow us to be put on separate roads and there will be an increasing outcry to keep us to those roads and to forbid us access to the ordinary roads of the country."

Some years before this there had been parliamentary discussions about restricting the use of motor cars on the roads of Britain but, even before the majority of MPs were motorised, such restrictions would have been unthinkable because it would have encroached on historically resonant highway rights. When, in 1927, there was talk of restrictions being placed on the free movement of motor cars in English cities, arch-motorist Lord Montagu of Beaulieu played the liberty card: "If I am right in my opinion that the right to use the road, that wonderful emblem of liberty, is deeply ingrained in our history and character, such action will meet with the most stubborn opposition," he warned.

The motoring peer perhaps did not consider that the rights of motorists to go as fast as they damn well liked might have restricted the highway rights of road users *not* in fast-moving motor cars. This "negative liberty" – or freedom from interference by other people – was expressed by the 17th century English philosopher Thomas Hobbes when he wrote "a free man is he that in those things which by his strength and wit he is able to do is not hindered to do what he hath the will to do."

One man's freedom can be another's oppression. Who has the right to be on the road and with what purpose and with what accompaniments? Defining rights is usually done when there's either a threat to deny their existence, or when they come into conflict with other rights. The right of the motorist to speed conflicts with the pedestrian's right to free passage along the road without threat of death.

In theory, the public highway is a shared resource. This was made clear in a court case in 1933, when the judge said:

> No member of the public has an exclusive right to use the highway. He has merely a right to use it subject to the reasonable use of others ... The law ... recognises that there are ... competing public interests. The law relating to the user of highways is in truth the law of give and take. Those who use them must in doing so have reasonable regard to the convenience and comfort of others and must not themselves expect a degree of convenience only obtainable by disregarding that of other people.

Obstruction of free movement on the highway, say by speed limits imposed on motorists, may be seen by some as a loss of liberty but such restrictions lead to freedom for other users of the highway. Today, highway freedoms are not shared out equally. Society has allowed those with motors to gain more benefits from the road than those without motors. The "right of way" – the right to pass and repass along a public highway – tends to trump all other "rights," especially when the player exercising the right of way is faster, stronger and, due to the principle of "if you can't beat 'em, join 'em," present in greater numbers. The historic and long-standing rights of pedestrians, cyclists and others to use the Queen's highway no longer exist in reality, and the rights were made null and void from the early days of motoring.

John Elliot Burns, president of the Local Government Board and an MP, said in 1913 that the "public have a right to be protected from needless risk and intolerable danger ..." He urged motorists "to show, in the most sportsmanlike way, the spirit of the road ... that is, the inherent right of everyone to the road." Clearly not all motorists were aware of this, for Burns added that motor car owners ought to "[show] greater regard for some people than motorists are inclined to show." (Burns was a cyclist.)

TECHNOLOGY HISTORIAN Kurt Möser of the Karlsruhe Institute for Technology believes motorists became more aggressive as cars became faster and more powerful:

> Driving appeared to be a biologically determined activity, allowing motorists to perceive themselves as a higher species in evolutionary terms, better adapted to the new demands of the modern world, having faster reactions, more developed senses and a better intellect.

Pioneer motorists thought themselves "gentlemen," believing aggressive drivers were a small minority of "cads," but Möser disputes this, believing that "forms of collective automobile-based aggression are not aberrations from an ideal but an essential part of car culture, part of its inherent attraction and therefore at least partly responsible for its extraordinarily successful long-term distribution and acceptance."

WHILE CYCLISTS from the 1870s onwards had excited some debate about what roads were for – and who they were for (children shouldn't be allowed to play on roads, said some cyclists, anticipating the same views from motorists twenty years later) – the steady encroachment of the motor car in the early 1900s, becoming faster and more powerful month by month, led to a fundamental reappraisal of hundreds of years of highway "rights." Motorists were in a similar position as the rich land-grabbers 200 years ago, during the long period of the English "enclosures," when land in common use by the many, was fenced in and appropriated by the few. Access to these common lands had been restricted by the new land "owners," and, by dint of their speed, motorists were now restricting all other road users. In effect, motorists "privatised" the road network, for the benefit of their own kind alone. Was this to be allowed to continue? What were roads for? Can a road truly be a "public highway" when only those members of the public in motor cars had comfortable access to that highway? Who *really* owned the roads?

Ownership was complex. So, too, was expected use. Roads were not merely conduits for travel – all life was lived on the roads, on the streets (the definitions of these two terms were left legally vague). The road was deemed to be public space, not private property. Children played on the road, vendors sold from the road, people met and talked on the road. The road wasn't a fixed space, hemmed in by kerbs. Roads were fluid; they were more than just highways for "passing and re-passing," more than just about movement.

Prior to the 20th century there were few road rules, except against lewdness and vagrancy, or seeking to stop riding on the shafts of carts. There were no street signs in cities, and apart from the admonition to "keep moving," no traffic management. There were no white lines in the centre of the road, no law that stated which side of the road a traveller had to use. (It was only tradition to keep to the left; travellers could do as they wished, and often did so, leading to chaos.) In 1829, barrister Robert Wellbeloved codified for Parliament a *Treatise on the Law Relating to Highways*. This led to the 1829 Highways Act, which defined a highway as: "Any thoroughfare which is open to all the King's subjects. No distinction between carriage road, horse road, or mere footpath." Wellbeloved wrote that every right of way remained a "public easement," and although this easement required the consent of the property owner who owns the soil over which the highway runs, the consent was "presumed where the public have had a prescriptive possession." In other words, consent of the property owner for public right of way was presumed because of the long-standing traditional use by the public.

The 1829 act said that "no distinction can be found between footpaths and carriage roads: the right of the public is of exactly the same quality over one as over the other" and "any way which is common to all of the King's people, to be traversed by them, is a highway."

William Cunningham Glen, another barrister, added to common law as it pertained to highways by stating, in 1862, that:

> Every person, in every parish and hamlet, has an equal right to use the highways within it, at all times and seasons, for passing and re-passing, on purposes of lawful business or pleasure; and the law entitles every person to the enjoyment of that right without let or hindrance.

Not that cyclists of the period always appreciated the road rights of others. Pedestrians, complained "Nemo", a writer for mid-1890s high society cycling journal *The Cycle World Illustrated*, were "possessed of several sorts of devils" for daring to continue to exercise their right to walk in the middle of the road:

> There is no pleasing the creature, and what renders the situation so irritating is the fact the surly, selfish pedestrian is, in the eye of the law, just monarch of all he surveys, and can spread his obstructive body all over the road if it so pleases him, footpath or no footpath.

American illustrator Joseph Pennell, famed for the European cycle tours he did with his high-society wife Elizabeth, revealed his inner road hog when, in 1902, he talked about how pedestrians now had to get out of the way of those propelled by motors (he gave up pedalling and became a motor cyclist).

> The fact must be brought home to [the] imbecile at once that he has got to keep to his part of the highway, that is to the side path. The British belief that a man has the right to camp out in the middle of the road, or use it as a reading-room, because his grandfather did, must be knocked from his head, even if by sudden concussion … These are his last years, let him make the most of them … The motor is going to become the means of locomotion … It is the pedestrian and the horse that have got to give way.

BY THE early 1900s, the right of pedestrians to use the roads – their "birthright" – was becoming more academic than real. There was a great – but ultimately futile – flowering of books, articles and organisations concerned with the road rights of pedestrians, a concern that was international. The pedestrian provenance of roads formed the introduction to a 1930s comic novel *The Little Golden Calf* by Russian authors Ilya Ilf and Evgeny Petrov. (Think *Three Men in a Boat* set in post-revolutionary Soviet Russia.)

The novel starts: "You have to love pedestrians," and continues:

> Pedestrians make up the greater part of mankind. Not only that, the finer part. Pedestrians created the world. It was they who built towns, raised skyscrapers, installed drainage and plumbing, paved the streets and lit them with electric lights. It was they who spread culture all over the world, invented painting, thought up gunpowder, flung bridges across rivers, deciphered Egyptian hieroglyphics, introduced the safety razor, abolished slavery, and discovered that a hundred and fourteen tasty, wholesome dishes could be made from beans. And then, when everything was ready, when our planet had acquired a comparatively well-planned appearance, the motorists appeared … It should be noted that the motor car was also invented by pedestrians. But for some reason the motorists soon forgot about that. They began to run over the meek and mild, clever pedestrians. They took over the streets the pedestrians had created. The roads were doubled in width and the pavements were narrowed down to the size of a tobacco pouch. The pedestrians began to huddle against the walls of buildings in fear. … The ordinary automobile – designed by pedestrians for the transportation of goods and people – has taken on the terrifying outlines of a fratricidal missile.

The *Manchester Courier* reminded readers in 1902 that "carriageways", despite the name, had not been built for the exclusive use of carriages, or other wheeled vehicles. The pedestrian must not be designed out of the equation for "the carriageway exists primarily for him …"

In the same year, Albert R. Shattuck, president of the Automobile Club of America, told a meeting of the club that "good automobilists" despised those who drove their machines "furiously." Shattuck was applauded for this, "as well as when he said that a nurse pushing a baby carriage had far more right to the highway than the owner of an automobile."

THE IDEA that one sub-set of road users "owns the road" did not originate with motorists. It has an ancient history – failure to cede the "right of way" on the narrow, rutted road to Thebes in Ancient Greece was the cause of the fatal quarrel between the mother-marrying Oedipus and his father King Laius. Closer to our own day, motorists were once the underdogs – the drivers of horse-drawn hansom cabs felt the roads were theirs and wanted rid of the upstarts. In July 1896, Margate cab driver John Harlow urged on his horse to overtake one of the new-fangled motor cars, cutting in and ramming it. "The road belongs to us," shouted the cab driver at the pioneer motorist. "If you don't get out of the way I shall smash you up."

In America, 19th century teamsters felt they owned the road, and let "lesser" users know it. (A teamster was a person who drove a team of draft animals, usually pulling a wagon.) Cyclists reported being whipped by teamsters. Later, so did motorists.

British stagecoach drivers of the turnpike era had a similar superiority complex, especially those driving Royal Mail coaches. English essayist Thomas De Quincey, writing nostalgically and largely metaphorically, in 1850, enthused over the speed derived from "animal beauty and power." He said, "we heard our speed, we saw it, we felt it as thrilling." And this speed "was not the product of blind insensate agencies, that had no sympathy to give, but was incarnated in the fiery eyeballs of the noblest amongst brutes, in his dilated nostril, spasmodic muscles, and thunder-beating hoofs."

No one in their right mind would get in the way of horses driven in such a manner, and those that did could expect little sympathy:

> His Majesty's mail … would upset an apple-cart, a cart loaded with eggs … Huge was the affliction and dismay, awful was the smash … we had not time to laugh over them. Tied to post-office allowance in some cases of fifty minutes for eleven miles, could the royal mail pretend to undertake the offices of sympathy and condolence? Could it be expected to provide tears for the accidents of the road? If even it seemed to trample on humanity, it did so, I felt, in discharge of its own more peremptory duties.

This get-out-of-my-way mentality, trampling on humanity, extended to "lesser" stagecoaches. De Quincey remembered

> being on the box of the Holyhead mail, between Shrewsbury and Oswestry … when a tawdry thing from Birmingham, some "Tallyho" or "Highflyer," all flaunting with green and gold, came up alongside of us. What a contrast to our royal simplicity of form and colour in this plebeian wretch … But all at once a movement of the horses announced a desperate intention of leaving us behind. "Do you see that?" I said to the coachman. "I see," was his short answer … he slipped our royal horses like … hunting-leopards after the affrighted game. Passing them without an effort, as it seemed, we threw them into the rear with so lengthening an interval between us as proved in itself the bitterest mockery of their presumption; whilst our guard blew back a shattering blast of triumph that was really too painfully full of derision.

Other users of the road were "usurpers" and had to jump out of the way when they heard "the trumpet that … announced from afar the laurelled mail":

> Look at that long line of carts and carters ahead, audaciously usurping the very crest of the road. Ah! traitors, they do not hear us as yet; but, as soon as the dreadful blast of our horn reaches them with proclamation of our approach, see with what frenzy of trepidation they fly to their horses' heads, and deprecate our wrath by the precipitation of their crane-neck quarterings.

In the 19th century, the first cyclists were chastised by stone-throwing youths as well as by carriage owners. The former were doing it for fun (a game that tailed off once cyclists, for protection, started riding in packs) but carriage owners whipped and otherwise abused cyclists because the urban dandies on "silent steeds" were encroaching on "their" roads.

Riders of bicycles believed their mode of transport deserved space on the roads of Britain, and had first done so in the 1820s, during the "dandy horse" craze. Writing in 1869, the English barrister Joseph Bottomley Firth (author of a bicycle book, and who would later become a Liberal MP and an influential municipal reformer), was clear that bicycles should stick to roads, rather than encroach on the rights of pedestrians: "The progress of the Bicycle seems steady and sure … [but] it is perfectly certain that they must be kept off footpaths [so as not to] terrify peaceable people who are content to walk …"

Cyclists, the new highway users, were not welcomed with open arms by existing road users. Pioneer American cycle tourist Karl Kron, writing in 1887, complained about his "encounters with road hogs" and how the "mere act of purchasing a horse creates the curious hallucination [in the driver] that he simultaneously purchases an exclusive right to the public highways." And this belief, vigorously vouchsafed, was caused by the incursion of the newcomer: "The traits of this Hog can be satisfactorily studied only by a bicycler, for save in his inspiring presence the hallucination lies dormant."

"The Road Hog as he is …" and "The Road Hog as he should be," from a cycling magazine in 1891

According to the *Oxford English Dictionary*, Kron was the first to use the term "road hog." It's a term that was picked up by the cycling press, and used against carriage and wagon drivers, later becoming the term for a motorist "who 'hogs' the road, making overtaking difficult." To other motorists a road hog was whoever was in front of them, daring to block their way. To those not in cars a road hog was a speeding, uncaring motorist.

The pedestrian's best defence against harsh treatment on the roads was to give up being a pedestrian, and become a motorist. Such a conversion – a fictional amphibian conversion – was recounted by Kenneth Grahame in *The Wind in the Willows* of 1908. Toad, Rat and Mole were ambling along the road beside a horse-drawn gypsy caravan when "far behind them they heard a faint warning hum…"

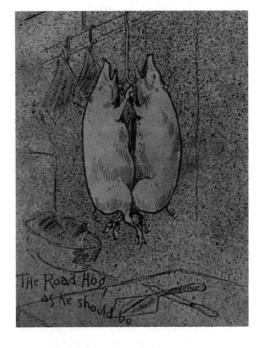

Glancing back, they saw a small cloud of dust, with a dark centre of energy, advancing on them at incredible speed, while from out the dust a faint "Poop-poop!" wailed like an uneasy animal in pain. [In] an instant … the peaceful scene was changed, and with a blast of wind and a whirl of sound that made them jump for the nearest ditch. It was on them! The "Poop-poop" rang with a brazen shout in their ears, they had a moment's glimpse of an interior of glittering plate-glass and rich morocco, and the magnificent motor-car … dwindled to a speck in the far distance … The Rat danced up and down in the road, simply transported with passion. "You villains!" he shouted, shaking both fists. "You scoundrels, you highwaymen, you – you – road-hogs!"

Being thrown into the ditch had a startling effect on Toad. He "stared fixedly in the direction of the disappearing motor-car. He breathed short, his face wore a placid, satisfied expression, and at intervals he murmured faintly "Poop-poop!"

"Glorious, stirring sight!" murmured Toad … "The poetry of motion! The *real* way to travel! The *only* way to travel! Villages skipped, towns and cities jumped – always somebody else's horizon! O bliss! O poop-poop! O my! O my!"

Toad could think of nothing else but to become a reckless road hog, too: "O what a flowery track lies spread before me, henceforth! What dust-clouds shall spring up behind me as I speed on my reckless way! What carts I shall fling carelessly into the ditch in the wake of my magnificent onset!"

The self-proclaimed "Terror of the highway" became a motorist and clung to the maxim that might was right:

[Mr. Toad] increased his pace, and as the car devoured the street and leapt forth on the high road through the open country, he was … Toad the terror, the traffic-queller, the Lord of the lone trail, before whom all must give way or be smitten into nothingness and everlasting night.

IN A long and detailed polemic in *The Nineteenth Century* magazine, barrister and early motorist Walter Bradford Woodgate argued in 1903 that British highways very much belonged to pedestrians. Motorists could use the highway by "privilege of statute" but not by "birthright," he said. Woodgate was writing months before the introduction of driving licences, which demonstrated vividly that, in theory, such "privileges" could be removed. (This was why the motoring organisations – libertarian when it came to such things – were opposed to the introduction of driving licences, as well as compulsory insurance and speed limits.)

The right of motorists to use the highway, said Woodgate, was a "pure creation of statute" and had "no independent existence at common law." The rights were, therefore, different to those long accorded to the "pedestrian, equestrian, and driver of any vehicle that is propelled by beast or man."

He stressed that "the non-motorist enjoys the use of the road as a birthright" and that it "does not seem that the motorist has any similar birthright to the road."

Woodgate was a staunch opponent of motorists who chose to use the public highway as a racetrack. He said such motorists were not desirous of A-to-B transport, but speed for speed's sake:

The pleasure [of motorists] appears to consist mainly in the exhilaration derived from velocity, and from rapid motion from one locality to another, paramount to any appreciation of scenery en route, or of any desire for hygiene in taking the air … The deduction from this observation is that any measure for licensing higher velocity will be in effect a statutable warranty for a moneyed minority to make public highways a playground for certain new toys, and a locality for pastime.

He pointed out that allowing toffs to "play" with their "toys" on the highway could be seen as unfair because children of the poor were often officially chastised for playing on the highway:

> Now, when children of the poor, whose facilities and locality of pastime are far more limited than those of the wealthy classes, desire to multiply hoops in thoroughfares, or to seek enjoyment at impromptu football or skittle-cricket on the macadam, they are promptly tabooed by the police; and local councils … enact by-laws against the dangers of children's hoops in the roadways … it seems … to be an anomaly to recognise a claim for pastime on the highway that may result in any curtailment of the enjoyment of that highway by the rest of the public, and which is inconsistent so long as use of the highway is refused to the toys of the children of the poor.

To protect the rights of pedestrians, the driving of motor cars on public highways should be fenced in with restrictive laws, said the barrister. There need be no additional restrictions placed on non-motorists: "If public opinion shall ever express itself that non-motor traffic is equal to motor traffic in production of peril, and in evasion of responsibility for injury, no doubt the Legislature will then provide accordingly."

Woodgate's long article chastised "plutocrat" motorists and said that if Parliament favoured motorists in forthcoming legislation it would be "legislating for the classes against the masses."

Numerous MPs had similar concerns. Going back to the debate over the Motor Car Bill of 1903 featured in chapter 1, it's illuminating to find so many MPs fretting that motorists, given free rein on British roads, would soon monopolise them, to the detriment of all other users.

"In order that these gentlemen may enjoy their rights, we are asked to turn our country roads into railway lines," Sir Ernest Soares, the Liberal MP for Barnstaple, complained. "We shall have to give up the use of the roads entirely to the motor fraternity."

Sir Charles Cripps, the Tory MP for Stroud, said:

> It is our birthright to have the common use of these roads, and, speaking as a countryman who lives in a district where the roads are narrow, I say without hesitation that we no longer have as our birthright the common use of these highways. We can no longer go out ourselves without danger; we are afraid to send out our children.

His suggested solution was radical: "If these motorists … are not kept in order they will have to leave our roads altogether."

He added "in the long run the people will never submit to the intolerable nuisance which has been created."

This point was echoed by William Burdett-Coutts, the Tory MP for Westminster, who warned: "No other class of invention in this country has ever had to rely upon conditions which sacrifice the public convenience to the privilege of the few."

Motorists, said Burdett-Coutts, had been given a right to use the roads "which in practice they have illegally seized upon, and which, as it is utterly inconsistent with popular rights, they should be summarily deprived of."

John Lawson Walton, Liberal MP for Leeds and later Britain's Attorney-General, pointed out that, on the contrary, motorists had every right to share the roads with other users:

> It has been assumed … that the motorist is an intruder on the highway, that he has no right there, that he has a precarious tenure obtained under certain statutes, that he is regulated by

previous measures ... Now it would be well ... to get rid of the notion that an ordinary passenger who uses the highway on foot ... has a higher right to the use of that highway than the motorist. The right and the obligation rest equally upon all who make use of the highway.

John Scott-Montagu, the Tory MP for the New Forest who later became the 2nd Baron Montagu of Beaulieu, argued that motorists simply wanted to exercise the same rights as other citizens, and had no desire to "monopolise" the roads: "[Motorists] only wish to be included as part of the public who have the right to use the roads ... No motorist has ever expressed a wish to monopolise the highways."

They had no need to wish, they merely had to command – and that command was done with power and speed. The concern that roads risked being monopolised by motorists was shared elsewhere. Baron Michael Pidoll, an Austrian Government official, wrote in 1912 that cars were taking over Vienna. Motorists, wrote Pidoll, thought pedestrians were "an annoying accessory of the street." He decried that motorists believe "the purpose and function of public ways and streets begin and end with traffic." He argued, streets were "more than mere thoroughfares. Rather, they belong to the whole layout of the city; they are the population's site of settlement; they form the surroundings of the buildings, the milieu in which the personal, social, and economic life of the city in no small part takes place ..."

Pidoll asked rhetorically, "Perhaps the public streets should be kept free of people?" and answered in the negative, arguing that allowing motorists to colonise roads went against basic rules of fairness. "From where does the car driver take the right to rule the street which does not belong to him but to everybody?"

IN THE 1870s, cyclists were very careful to stress that highway rights were very much for everybody and that cyclists wanted to share the commons, not rule them. Patent lawyer Charles Pratt, one of the first cycling journalists in America, wrote:

> Every person has an equal right to travel on the highways, either on foot or with his own conveyance, team, or vehicle. This right is older than our constitutions and statutes ... The supreme rule of the road is, Thou shalt use it so as to interfere as little as possible with the equal right of every other person to use it at the same time ...

Pratt wrote that in 1879, when cycling was still young, when not all wished to grant highway rights to the newcomers. Urban cyclists, on their expensive high-wheelers, were seen by many as highway interlopers. The freshness of the activity and the opposition from many quarters caused the new users of the road to group together. This "freemasonry of the wheel" had a strong gravitational pull and like-minded "cyclers" formed fraternal clubs. These clubs organised rides and socials – "smokers" were popular – but were too localised to have any clout nationally, and national clout would be needed if cyclists were to achieve their key objectives – better roads and the explicit right for cyclists to ride on those roads. American road surfaces often left a lot to be desired, and some localities passed ordinances restricting the use of the "birotate chariot" within town and city limits. In 1880, 130 or so cyclists founded the nationally-focussed League of American Wheelmen. Local cycling clubs continued organising rides and socials, while the new national body agitated for change.

The two most active parts of the national organisation were the Good Roads committee, and the Rights and Privileges committee. These committees were organised nationally and locally. The prime mover nationally was lawyer and club stalwart Isaac B. Potter. "The name of no man is more widely known in L.A.W. circles than is that of Isaac B. Potter," said an 1895 profile in the League's weekly, mass-circulation magazine. (Potter later went on to be a prime mover in automobile organisations, helping pioneer motorists win the same rights that he gained for cyclists.)

His chief success was the so-called "Liberty Bill," legislation passed in 1887 that, for the first time, gave cyclists explicit rights to be in the parks of New York City, and on the roads, too. What Potter called the "wheelman's Magna Charta" was the result of two years of expensive campaigning by himself and others. The campaigning was necessary to fight for cyclists' rights to be on the road. As Potter said:

> In Brooklyn an ordinance was passed … forbidding the use of bicycles on the public streets and several arrests followed. In New York, the Board of [Central] Park Commissioners adopted a regulation forbidding the use of bicycles within the Park limits … About 1885 it was determined to test the validity of this regulation.

Three members of the L.A.W. rode into Central Park – which had nine miles of carriage roads, set aside for posh carriages alone – and were arrested and thrown in jail after refusing to pay their fines. (Exactly the same tactic would later be used by motorists.) The L.A.W. leapt to the cyclists' defence but lost the case and appealed. In April 1887, the League took the case to Albany, the capital of New York state, and the "famous Liberty Bill" was introduced in the Assembly. In June, a public hearing was held before the Governor "and never before was a piece of legislation proposed which drew to the capital a larger gathering," said Potter.

"Wheelmen were present from all parts of the State: the Executive Chamber was crowded and the corridors of the hotels swarmed with cyclists who had come to Albany to witness the final struggle on their behalf."

Potter added: "For many days the fate of the bill was in doubt; but, finally, on the last day of grace a telegram came … which said: 'The Liberty Bill has been signed … It is therefore law.'"

In 1895, the League's magazine remembered: "From this splendid beginning the courts have established beyond question the right of the bicycle to use any road that is open to the horse-drawn vehicle." A league pamphlet told would-be members, "When the League was formed the bicycle had no legal recognition; now it is universally recognized as a carriage, and may travel with impunity wherever any carriage does."

The Liberty Bill wasn't national in scope, but most legislatures bowed to it. Those that didn't were tackled by the vigorous Potter and his associates, the tab for their time, effort and lodgings picked up by, among others, Colonel Albert Pope of the Pope Manufacturing Company. Potter wrote:

> In every contest for the establishment of wheelmen's rights, the League of American Wheelmen had been the militant and aggressive force … New members came to its aid … Among these [was] Albert A. Pope of Boston. Himself a wheelman, and a member of the League, brainy in make-up, broad in views, a fighter for principle, and endowed with the sinews of war, he supplied thousands of dollars in pushing the Central Park contest.

More money had to be supplied when the city of Topeka in Kansas arrested a Mr. Swift for riding across the Kansas River Bridge. Later, the Kansas Supreme Court reversed Swift's conviction, with the presiding judge commenting:

> Each citizen has the absolute right to choose for himself the mode of conveyance he desires, whether it be by wagon or carriage, by horse, motor or electric car, or by bicycle, or astride of a horse …

Perhaps the judge was a cyclist, for he said: "[Bicycles] are not an obstruction to, or an unreasonable use of, the public streets of a city, but rather a new and improved method of using the same ..."

Sterling Elliott would have very much agreed with that. In the 1890s he was a president of the L.A.W., and later a prominent motorist. In 1899, he wrote a front-page editorial in the *L.A.W. Bulletin*, asking "Who Owns the Roads?" His answer was the same as Charles Pratt's twenty years previously – everybody:

> The bicycle has opened, closed and settled the question of who owns the roads – they belong to the people; not the people who travel in some particular fashion, but to everybody. The humblest hobo who uses the road in tramping from house to house begging his bread has the same rights as has the millionaire who doesn't dodge his taxes.

Naturally, the hobo would be tramping on foot, and the millionaire would be in or on some form of conveyance, but still, the same principle applies: roads are part of the commons, goods belonging to all.

THERE ARE no records of Elliott's views on road ownership from when he became a keen motorist but there are many examples in early motoring literature that show how the right for all to travel on the road was morphing into a belief in superior rights for those who could travel fastest. Just one month after the Emancipation Run, the 1896 event that celebrated the granting of road rights to British motorists, *Punch* published a cartoon that alluded to a concern that motorists might one day wish to have British roads to themselves. The cartoon showed two "motists" passing each other. On the road there was a sign, said to be have been erected "by order, Motor Association." The sign stated, chillingly: "All trespassers on the high road will be prosecuted."

Punch wasn't predicting a motorway, it was predicting the erosion of ancient rights, a prediction that soon came true. The erosion would take the form of bans for slower road users. Despite freedom and birthright concerns the idea that the public highway ought to be apportioned to different users, started to go mainstream in the 1890s.

IN AN 1897 article in the Christmas number of *The Rambler*, a weekly cycling magazine created by *Daily Mail* founder Alfred Harmsworth, a writer asked, "Why Not Cycle Paths Everywhere?"

> Cycling is such an established institution now-a-days ... that it is quite time something was done towards providing special bicycle paths on our roads ... At present in this country there are over one million bicycles in use ... Thus a greater proportion of persons ride bicycles than use carriages or ride on horseback ... it is quite possible ... to lay an asphalte strip on main roads for the exclusive use of cyclists ...

Civil engineer Sir John Wolfe-Barry, the son of Houses of Parliament architect Sir Charles Barry, was very much in favour of such cycle paths. "No one who has lived in London can doubt that the pressure on the streets is getting yearly heavier and heavier, and becoming more and more unmanageable," he told a meeting at the Imperial Institute in Kensington, in his role as chairman of the Royal Society of Arts. His "Address On The Streets & Traffic of London", delivered in November 1898 and published as a popular pamphlet the following year, was one of many similar plans for fast-growing London, which was, long before the motor car, crippled by chronic congestion.

Wolfe-Barry, the person in charge of building London's now famous Tower Bridge, had an "interest in traffic problems." Sir John was "clear about two things: the immense pecuniary loss resulting from congestion and overcrowding, and the unwisdom of temporary makeshifts to alleviate those evils."

Wolfe-Barry's congestion-busting proposal was for London to build wide arterial thoroughfares, with separate "bicycle roads." In his address, he used the word "bicycles" eighteen times and mentioned motor cars not once. He recognised that the building of London's public transport network had done little to alleviate congestion. In fact, it had added to it, as more people started to make more and more journeys, which had a knock-on effect once people exited the stations.

"My plea then," urged Wolfe-Barry, "is that what is wanted to meet the requirements of the traffic of London is not so much additional railways, underground, or overground, traversing the town and connected with the suburbs, but rather wide arterial improvements of the streets themselves."

The builder of Tower Bridge had a soft spot for bicycles but thought that cycling – booming in the mid-1890s and largely the preserve of the upper and middle classes – was doomed unless it could be made safer, via separation:

> … the numbers of [bicycles] are only kept down in the metropolis by the dangers which their riders encounter in our streets … It is a form of vehicular traffic which should not be undervalued or lost sight of, but which is, practically speaking, impossible at present in Urban London … [Yet] one cannot but recognise that the bicycle, as a means of rapid and cheap locomotion, is a new endowment to mankind, and even now we can see what an advantage it would be to the bulk of Londoners if they could travel safely and at perhaps eight or ten miles an hour, on their bicycles from their homes to their work and back again.

Wolfe-Barry's proposed solution to the problem of congestion – and cyclist safety – was the creation of wide thoroughfares "about 120 feet wide, that is to say, as wide as Whitehall, opposite the Horse Guards." These thoroughfares ought to be segregated, thought Wolfe-Barry, with lumbering horse carriages and carts getting a "slow lane", faster trams taking over another portion of the carriageway, and speedy cyclists getting centrally-located "bicycle roads."

> All these new routes should have a raised or sunken road throughout for bicycles and [trams], so that these should not mix with either ordinary vehicular or pedestrian traffic. Communication between the streets and the sunken roads could be given by ramps at selected spots for bicycle access, and by steps, and stables for the bicycles could be provided at the level of the sunken road by excavations.

The proposal would be costly, admitted Wolfe-Barry but reminded listeners of the great costs spent on London's rail network:

> When one contemplates the cost of such a work as an arterial street 120 feet wide through the length and breadth of London, the prospect is, no doubt, somewhat alarming. A street of this kind four or five miles long, with side streets and the works of construction, must mean an expenditure of many millions of money, though the recoupment from the ground-rents of such a new street would be very important if no undue haste in their realisation were made. This, however, is the kind of undertaking required for the London of the future, and if foreign capitals can undertake [to build] great streets … why should we take such niggardly views of what is really important for the public good of our metropolis?

Seven years after this lecture, Wolfe-Barry was in a position to influence policy: he was appointed as consultant engineer to the Royal Commission to inquire into the Means of Locomotion and Transport in London. Bicycles did not get a single mention in the report from this committee, despite hearing from witnesses from the CTC and NCU. (Motor cars weren't mentioned much either, the report focusing instead on horse-pulled hackney carriages, trams and omnibuses.) Segregation of traffic was not advocated in the report.

While segregation of traffic did not become official policy in Britain, there were no qualms about using the technique in the Netherlands. Just one month after Wolfe-Barry's address to the Society of Arts, *The Spectator* reported that "On the route from the Hague to Scheveningen there lie parallel to each other a carriage road, a canal, a bicycle track, a light railway, side-paths regularly constructed ..."

Such separation of transport modes in the Netherlands wasn't new. *Harper's New Monthly* reported, in 1880, that "there is a little town in Holland in the streets of which no horse is ever allowed to come. Its cleanliness may be imagined, and its quiet repose."

Mode separation has ancient roots. Roman and Chinese roads were often segregated for different modes. In the modern era, Napoleon constructed some roads which were divided in three: a gravel lane for marching soldiers, a beaten earth lane for cavalry, and a setted lane for heavy artillery. This idea was also exported to French colonies: in 1809 Herman Daendels built a wide road in Java which had a lane "kept in prime order" for stagecoaches and another for "buffaloes and carts." In 1910, a 50 metre wide road was built between Lille and Tourcoing. This 12km road had a six metre wide macadam lane for heavy traffic, two 3.6 metre outer lanes for light vehicles, and separate paths for horse riders and cyclists.

The concept of mode separation was discussed in Britain in 1821. A proposal for segregated ways was proposed by Lewis Gompertz, an industrious Jewish inventor (thank him for the drill chuck bit). His radical vegetarianism led him to campaign against the mistreatment of the animals that were at the heart of Regency and later Victorian street transport: horses. Gompertz was one of the co-founder's of the Society for the Prevention of Cruelty to Animals, which later had the Royal added to the front, creating the RSPCA. He preferred walking to riding in a horse-drawn carriage in London and was, therefore, much taken with the velocipede, the German machine that meant "fast foot" in Latin.

The velocipede running machine – or hobbyhorse, a bicycle without cranks or pedals – was introduced to the world by Baron von Drais. He had created his contraption in 1817 as a horse-substitute because, it is now believed, the price of oats, and everything else, had soared after the planet was plunged into darkness after the 1815 volcanic eruption of Indonesia's Mount Tambora. 1816 was known as the Year Without a Summer. Horses starved because of lack of fodder. Later chronicles talked of "pferdesterben", horse agony, and the Draissine – or velocipede – was believed by many to be the perfect replacement for the horse. Velocipede riding became all the rage, including in Regency London, but use of the machines on sidewalks was banned. Gompertz believed the new machines should have been provided with their own paths, "allowing them three or four feet of the width of the roads for their sole use, and for that to be kept in good repair; this they deserve, and persons while using them would not be exposed to danger where there are many carriages and horses, nor be obliged to wade through mud ..."

Gompertz, ahead of his time, added "and it is only by this being adopted that mankind would reap the advantage from machines for this purpose, of being converted from one of the slowest animals in the creation, to one of great continued speed from his own salubrious exertions ..."

However, the "velocipede mania" was short-lived, and once Regency dandies had tired of it by 1820, velocipede riding was all but extinguished as a form of transport. Gompertz tried to rekindle interest in the velocipede with various improvements but he didn't progress with his mode separation idea.

SEPARATION WAS easier to achieve in the Netherlands because 19th century Dutch rural roads were not built to the same standards as many of those in France or Britain, and so the early Dutch cyclists lobbied for improved bicycling paths, away from the poorly-surfaced roads. The lobbying was done by the ANWB, the Royal Dutch Touring Club, now the main motoring organisation in the Netherlands but founded, in 1883, as a bicycling club. The ANWB's roads commission, established in 1898, called for the construction of a separate parallel network of cycle roads, which got built.

In 2011, sociologist Peter Cox said the cycling infrastructure provided for cyclists in the Netherlands in the early 1900s "played an important role in overcoming the unsuitability of the existing roads because as a policy it was a part of a clear intention to use the cycle roads system to raise the status of cycle users as citizens, indeed to prioritise them."

While cyclists were prioritised in the Netherlands, with the bicycle becoming a Dutch national symbol by the early 1900s, cyclists in other countries found their hard-won highway rights to be short-lived. Speed trumps highway rights, as cyclists and pedestrians found out when motor cars came along. And motorists were quick to realise they would be able to go faster if the slower users of the road were removed and placed on their own, separated routes. No highway rights were to be extinguished using this method of "separation," promised motoring magazines and organisations.

"IT WILL be a matter of the utmost importance to reserve for the motor-vehicle the road upon which it is to run, and to divert to other channels the animals and vehicles which may hamper it," argued America's *The Automobile* in 1900. Pedestrians were also to be diverted away from roads. "The provision of sidewalks for pedestrians has been one of the means of preventing a congestion of the traffic of large cities," said the magazine.

As Peter Norton has shown in his book about the erosion of pedestrians' rights in the early 20th century, motorists didn't monopolise the streets of American cities overnight, but had to fight to suppress the road rights of slower users, and this fight proved to be essential for the success of motoring. "The street," said Norton, "was a place to walk, a place to play. In this traditional construction of the city street, motorists could never escape suspicion as dangerous intruders. While this perception prevailed, the motor age could not come to the American city."

The main selling point of the car was speed, and if pedestrians (and trams and cyclists) remained on the road, cars would have to travel at the speed of the slowest user. Until the 1920s, the rights of all road users were defended by the mainstream press, the police and the judiciary.

"The streets of Chicago belong to the city," one judge explained, "not to the automobilists." A Philadelphia judge attacked motorists for usurping children's rights to the roads. "It won't be long before children won't have any rights at all in the streets," he complained.

It took a concerted effort by "motordom" to turn what had been streets for people into streets for automobiles alone. Traffic control professional Miller McClintock said that a new age justified new ways. "The old common law rule that every person, whether on foot or driving, has equal rights in all parts of the roadway must give way before the requirements of modern transportation," he told an American newspaper in 1925.

"The engineers of 1930 no longer conceived of the street as a public utility, regulated by the state in the name of street users collectively," said Norton, writing eighty years later. "The [new status quo] overturned pedestrians' ancient legal supremacy in the street."

New York City magistrate Bruce Cobb complained that the pedestrians of 1924 faced "superior force in the shape of the omnipresent motor car," and had been "compelled to forgo asserting [their] legal rights of substantial equality on the highway, as they have existed almost from time immemorial." The traffic court magistrate continued: "The motorist has won his contest for the use of the streets over the foot passengers, despite the best efforts of police, courts and motor vehicle authorities to regulate him and his kind. The motorist has inspired fear and the sort of respect that brute force inspires." The road rights of all were now the road rights of motorists alone. "Though he may hug these rights to his breast," said Cobb, "Mr. Average Citizen, his wife and children, cross the city streets or walk the country roads with much the same assurance that a luckless rabbit feels when chased by a pack of hounds."

Pedestrians were hounded from the roads of Britain, too. In 1947, the journalist J. S. Dean, head of the Pedestrians' Association, wrote a polemic calling for an end to "road slaughter," and an end to the view that highways were made for the exclusive use of motor cars:

> The private driver is … most strongly influenced by the sense of ownership of his car, and, as he often believes, of the road as well. It is "his" car to do with as he pleases, and, as he often believes, it is "his" road too, and the other road-users are merely intruders who are there at their own peril.

He added, when else in history has humanity lived with the "foul, strange and unnatural" belief that it should be "common custom to kill and maim people because they get in your way"?

The slaughter was so bad, motoring enthusiast Rudyard Kipling was moved to write:

> When men grew shy of hunting stag
> For fear the Law might try 'em,
> The Car put up an average bag
> Of twenty dead per diem.
> Then every road was made a rink
> For Coroners to sit on;
> And so began, in skid and stink,
> The real blood-sport of Britain!

THE CHANGING nature of road "ownership" has been preserved in a series of British maps. In 1898, Messrs Bartholomew of Edinburgh stole a march on its many competitors by partnering with the most powerful road interest of the day – the Cyclists' Touring Club and its 60,500 members. Crowd sourcing from touring cyclists enabled Bartholomew to update its maps every couple of years. In the early 1900s, the descriptions for roads remained quaint – poorly surfaced roads were labelled as "indifferent" – but then in the 1920s there was a shift in emphasis. Major through routes – routes that had very often been brought back to life by cyclists – started to be listed as "motoring roads." Nothing had changed on the ground, but everything had changed in the minds of motorists. Roads were now "owned" by motorists. Motoring was less than 25 years old, yet the perceived interloper on the ancient roads of Britain wasn't the motor car, but the pedestrian, the equestrian and the cyclist.

Today, in Britain, many roads are no-go areas for those without motors. Heavy, fast-moving motor traffic has been allowed to take over what are often *public* highways in name only. On A-roads and B-roads alike there's usually precious little provision for anything other than cars and trucks. The public highway – once open to all – is now genuinely open only to those with motors. Pedestrians, equestrians and cyclists have retreated to footpaths, bridleways and (dire) cycle paths, yet these make for an indirect and incomplete network, suitable for (only some) recreation, of limited use for everyday travel. Requests to local authorities to make roads into highways usable by all, say by installing a parallel protected cycle path or a footpath, usually fall on deaf ears. The "liberty of the subject," Britain's supposed love of egalitarianism, worked for the early motorists when they wanted to maintain their "right of way" on the country's ancient highways, but once roads became thought of as "motoring roads" there has been no desire from the (motor-besotted) powers-that-be to make sure non-motorised road users regain "uninterrupted possession" of *their* "right of way" birthrights.

CHAPTER FIVE

SPEED

Now there is nothing gives a man such spirits,
Leavening his blood as cayenne doth a curry,
As going at full speed – no matter where its
Direction be, so 'tis but in a hurry,
And merely for the sake of its own merits;
For the less cause there is for all this flurry...
LORD BYRON, DON JUAN

The chariots shall rage in the streets, they shall jostle one against
another in the broad ways: they shall seem like torches,
they shall run like the lightnings.
NAHUM 2:4

**19th century philosopher John Ruskin said travel was "dull in exact proportion to
its rapidity." This was a minority view, most of his contemporaries were dazzled by speed.
Rapid communication was found to be pleasurable. From scorching to today's Strava, speed sells.
However, the freedom for one road user to travel fast on public highways has
always reduced the freedom available to others.**

The world goes on at a smarter pace now than it did when I was a young fellow," said Mr. Deane to Tom Tulliver in George Eliot's *The Mill on the Floss*. "It's this steam, you see ... it drives on every wheel double pace."

In 1860, when Eliot was writing, the trains *were* fast, and getting faster, but the earliest steam locomotives were just a brisk walk faster than stagecoaches, although promoters were keen to demonstrate the *potential* speed of steam. Richard Trevithick's 1808 locomotive – his third – was called, teasingly, "Catch me who can." When it was displayed in London on a circular track, close to today's Euston Station, it was billed as "Mechanical Power Subduing Animal Speed." Top speed? 12 miles per hour.

Few thought such locomotives would be much more than a slightly faster way of transporting coal from pit to wharf. The idea that they would one day carry people at speeds of 50 miles per hour or more, and on a "Permanent way" from city to city, was little more than a fantasy, except for those post-Trevithick engineers who surmised that they could coax, with incremental improvements, greater and greater speeds from the steam engines they built. It did not take long. Locomotives were soon able to travel at 20 to 30 miles per hour. Moderns may consider such speeds risibly low, but the first railway travellers thought these velocities nothing short of amazing. Travelling, for long distances, at the hitherto heady 30 miles per hour, "annihilates time and space," exclaimed a well-travelled doctor in 1841. (This phrase appeared in hundreds of transport-related books and articles in the 19th century, including in the first paragraph of one of the world's earliest books on the new pastime of cycling.)

Nineteenth-century naysayers predicted that humans would pop should they travel at anything above 30 miles per hour. This was soon proven wrong – not only was such speed survivable, it was felt to be downright pleasurable. At a trial run undertaken before the 1830 opening of the first railway to connect two cities – the Liverpool and Manchester Railway – famous actress Fanny Kemble reported that George Stephenson's "snorting little animal", fed not with oats but with coal, was capable of pulling an open carriage at "delightful" speeds:

> The engine ... set off at its utmost speed, thirty-five miles an hour, swifter than a bird flies (for they tried the experiment with a snipe). You cannot conceive what that sensation of cutting the air was ... I stood up, and with my bonnet off drank the air before me. The wind ... absolutely weighed my eyelids down. When I closed my eyes this sensation of flying was quite delightful, and strange beyond description; yet strange as it was, I had a perfect sense of security, and not the slightest fear.

Others weren't so fearless. Thomas Creevy, a Liberal politician, joining a similar test run, fretted: "It is really flying, and it is impossible to divest yourself of the notion of instant death to all upon the least accident happening."

In the early days of rail travel there were many train crashes but, just as today people block out the startling daily death toll on the roads, Victorians explained away rail deaths as the price of progress. People were besotted with rail travel, and speed was very much at the heart of this love affair.

And little wonder. At the beginning of the railway era, the fastest passenger-carrying stagecoaches, on the best turnpike roads in summer, could, on a good day, achieve eight miles per hour. This was considered "an altogether exceptional speed," said a 1903 chronicler, and even an average of eight miles per hour was only accomplished by changing horses frequently. In 1888, to win a £1,000 bet, the coachman Jim Selby raced his famous coach "Old Times" from London to Brighton and back in under eight hours: it required 64 horses in sixteen Formula 1-style horse-changeovers.

Mail coaches – waved through turnpikes without stopping, and with change of horses taking less than a minute – were faster, but still struggled to average ten miles per hour. With horseflesh as the motive power, there was a natural limit to the speed attainable, even on the smoothest of the newly improved main roads. Horses can gallop for short distances only. (America's famous Pony Express mail delivery service of 1860–1 was not as *express* as might be imagined – the small, light riders, changing horses frequently, averaged only 12 miles per hour.)

In 1781, coaching entrepreneur Nicholas Rothwell advertised that his fast coaches could reduce the travel time betwixt Birmingham and London from a full three days to "two days and a half." However, his 44 miles-per-day service ran only from May to the end of summer. And providence might step in to delay the journey, for Rothwell warned that the improved times were only "if God permit."

Neverthless, Rothwell was providing what people craved: greater speed. With greater speed, even if still well below 20 miles per hour, came greater danger. In Elizabeth Turner's *Cautionary Rhymes* of the

1840s, children were warned to avoid turnpike roads:

> Miss Helen was always too giddy to heed
> What her mother had told her to shun,
> For frequently over the street in full speed
> She would cross where the carriages run.

Carriage drivers couldn't stop thundering horses, even if they wanted to. And not all wanted to – a point made by historian Professor W. T. Jackman in a classic 1916 treatise on the development of transport in England:

> While coaching upon fine smooth roads, with all the glitter and show of elegant equipage, had much to interest and to stimulate those who were thus rolled along, there were some features connected with it which lent a darker aspect to the otherwise bright picture. One of these was the recklessness of the drivers, which caused a great many accidents. In the intense competition which prevailed, speed was of prime consideration and the coach which could reach its destination in the shortest time usually attracted the greatest number of passengers. Certain coaches, such as the Shrewsbury *Wonder*, acquired a reputation for celerity which was an asset of much advantage … the speed mania overshadowed all considerations of prudence.

Boy racers are nothing new, showed Professor Jackman, and nor are deaths from "dangerous driving", with punishments, then as now, not in the least acting as a deterrent to transport transgressions:

> The violent manner in which this business was conducted caused considerable loss of life. Two coaches which started from the same place and were going in the same direction were often found to race their horses at break-neck speed, without paying any heed to the protests of the passengers who were in momentary danger of instant death through the overturning of the coaches. Even the imposition of the fine that the law authorized for this transgression was not sufficient to deter drivers from committing the same offence again, for when the proprietors had paid the fine they would tell the coachmen that as they had once beaten the opposition they could do so the next time.

A writer in 1816 complained that speeding stagecoaches were a mortal menace:

> Under the old state of roads and manners it was impossible that more than one death could happen at once; what, by any possibility, could take place analogous to a race betwixt two stage-coaches, in which the lives of thirty or forty distressed and helpless individuals are at the mercy of two intoxicated brutes?

Stagecoach journeys in America were just as perilous. A mother in 19th-century New England forbade her 18-year-old daughter from travelling: "Your papa would not trust your life in the stage. It is very unsafe … Many … [are] the cripples made by accidents in those vehicles."

Thanks to the road improvements of Metcalfe, Telford and – mostly – McAdam, stagecoach journeys were much accelerated. The journey between London and Edinburgh took 45 hours and 30 minutes in 1836, at an average speed of 9½ miles an hour – one-fifth of the journey time required in the 1750s. This acceleration of the journey was to no avail, however, as once rails were laid between the two capital

In the 1880s and 1890s bicycles were the fastest vehicles on the roads.

cities, locomotives would be able to complete the journey, summer and winter, in times unfathomably fast to someone born in the middle of the 18th century.

A newspaper advertisement of 1754 boasted: "However incredible it may appear, this coach will actually arrive in London four days after leaving Manchester." Within 30 years that journey took just two days.

The increased speed encouraged more journeys, with the number of stagecoach services between British cities increasing eightfold between 1790 and 1836. Not everybody welcomed the progress brought by road speed. Highwaymen, for instance, were put out of business by the faster coaches.

And it was the speed of railways that killed off stagecoaches. "The calamity of railways fell upon us," moaned the "colossus of roads," Sir James McAdam, the general superintendent of metropolitan roads in England and son of the man who, thanks to the crushed-stone technique of macadamisation, did more than any other to increase 18th- and 19th-century road speeds. It's unsurprising that a son of John Loudon McAdam should be biased against railways. But most others were amazed at the spectacle, and mightily pleased with the speed.

"The railway had an air of parade and display that dazzled," said Jackman. "Its general aspect was that of vitality, energy and efficiency: the large trains, their promptitude of arrival and departure and the speed of the engines were all subjects of admiration ..."

Speed became an obsession. Trains, to some 1830s observers, may have been "black monsters" with "trailing clouds of smoke, disfiguring the landscape, destroying the privacy and seclusion of [landed] estates" but speed trumped all objections, with parliament nodding through track-laying legislation which, in horse parlance, rode roughshod over (usually well-compensated) landowners, and flattened tenement blocks, with working people thrown out of their homes with little in the way of recompense.

To object to the building of a railway line was tantamount to forcing water uphill. Ebenezer, a Quaker, wrote a letter to a northern English newspaper in 1825, complaining of the horrors he expected soon to be his lot, all done in the name of progress and speed:

> On the very line of this [proposed] railway, I have built a comfortable house; it enjoys a pleasing view of the country. Now judge, my friend, of my mortification, whilst I am sitting comfortably at breakfast with my family, enjoying the purity of the summer air, in a moment my dwelling, once consecrated to peace and retirement, is filled with dense smoke or foetid gas; my homely, though cleanly, table covered with dirt; and the features of my wife and family almost obscured by a polluted atmosphere.

Such complaints were commonplace, but ignored. Speed was sacrosanct. Subsequently, cyclists and, even later, motorists would complain about the fixed schedules of railways, citing a lack of independence. But until cycles and motor cars came along, the promise of prompt, efficient rail travel – and, above all, *swift* rail travel – was the wonder of the age. Speed sold.

John Ruskin
sees a cyclist! *Kuklos*

WHEN HE complained about the frenetic pace of life brought forth by the "bellowing fire" of the train, social thinker John Ruskin was a voice in the wilderness. "A fool always wants to shorten space and time," he mused. "A wise man wants to lengthen both."

And he was very much against the spirit of the age when he wrote: "It does a bullet no good to go fast; and a man, if he be truly a man, no harm to go slow; for his glory is not all in going, but in being." Travel, said the Sage of Brantwood, was "dull in exact proportion to its rapidity."

The scorn Ruskin heaped upon the train he later aimed at the fastest thing on the roads of the 1880s, the bicycle:

> I not only object but am quite prepared to spend all my best *bad language* in reprobation of the bi-, tri-, and 4-, 5-, 6- or 7-cycles, and every other contrivance and invention for superseding human feet on God's ground. To walk, to run, to leap, and to dance are the virtues of the human body, and neither to stride on stilts, wiggle on wheels, or dangle on ropes … will ever supersede the appointed God's way of slow walking and hard working.

Again, speed trumped such concerns. Bicycles were faster than the stagecoaches of a generation before, faster than horses over medium to long distances, and always faster than horses in harness. Jim Selby's London–Brighton–London record set in 1888 by the 64 foaming-at-the-mouth horses was beaten by cyclists within months.

John D. Long, US President McKinley's Secretary of the Navy, declared in 1899 that: "The man who owns a bicycle … throws his dust in the face of the man in the carriage, so that it is no longer pleasant to ride in a coach and four." The bicycle was only beaten for speed by steam railway engines at full pelt.

The cover of Charles Spencer's *The Modern Bicycle* of 1877 shows a high-wheel rider outpacing both a galloping horse and a steam train. A hare lies by the roadside, clearly exhausted at its attempts to out-run a bicyclist.

The bicycle, said Dutch professor Wiebe Bijker in a well-known analysis of technological change, was transformational, a "socially constructed speed machine."

This speed, on country main roads bereft of the stagecoach trade, attracted "scorchers," cyclists with arched backs and grim "bicycle faces," who treated the Queen's Highway as their own – and woe betide anyone who got in their way. (Speeding was often an eye-of-the-beholder thing. A pre-1900 *Punch* cartoon showed two crinoline-clad matrons riding their bicycles at one and two miles per hour, with the slower of the two stately women shouting "Scorcher!" at the faster.)

While most of the injuries caused by speeding cyclists on the public highway were minor, there were fatalities, too. Most of the news stories in 19th-century newspapers about pedestrians killed by cyclists warranted just a scant few lines but, for shock value, the penny newspaper *The Illustrated Police News* included gory graphics. The bloodthirsty journal carried thousands of stories about scissor stabbings, eye gougings and other gruesome murders as well as a handful of stories about deaths caused by bicycle scorching.

An old woman killed by a cyclist going at "full speed" made the newspaper in May 1878. One of the two cyclists barrelling along a "narrow lane" ran over the woman's legs and the injuries "apparently of no very serious nature at first, assumed a grave aspect after" and she died four days later. She had been walking in the lane, not on the footway. The collision had been "inevitable," said the newspaper.

A "fatal accident through bicycle riding at Almondsbury" in August 1878 was illustrated with a graphic of a young rider on a high-wheeler hitting an elderly gentleman on a steep descent near Bristol. The man, William Baker, 77 years old and the village postman, died from his injuries the day after being hit. The cyclist, Thomas Barter, "a young gentleman from Bath," told the coroner at an inquest that he couldn't have avoided hitting Baker, as the gentleman – who, it turned out, was short-sighted and always walked in the road rather than on the footway – diverted into his path. Witnesses agreed with the cyclist, and Barter was freed by the jury. The coroner commended him for "having done all in his power to alleviate the sufferings of the injured man."

"Fatal accident through bicycle riding at Almondsbury," The Illustrated Police News, *August 24th, 1878*

Barter may have been a gentleman, but four young high-wheelers caught scorching in 1881 on Kensington High Street in London appeared to be anything but. A policeman estimated they were riding at 16 miles per hour, while the cyclists reckoned they were riding "at a speed at which it might take ten minutes to walk half a mile." The judge estimated this would be "under four miles an hour, rather slower than a person would walk," and duly fined the four accused.

In *The Art and Pastime of Cycling* of 1893, journalists R. J. Mecredy and A. J. "Faed" Wilson wrote that speed was pleasurable:

The faculty for enjoying rapid locomotion is one which is implanted in the human breast from earliest childhood, and the fact of one's unaided efforts being the active cause of this locomotion enhances the pleasures derived from it.

Zola depicted the bicycle's "rush of speed" in his novel *Paris*:

> The two let their machines carry them down the hill. And then this happy rush of speed overtook them, the dizzying sense of balance in the lightning like, breathtaking descent on wheels, while the grey path flew beneath their feet and the trees whisked past at either side like the slats of a fan as it unfolds ...

The sheer exhilaration of cycling was something that had been used to sell the activity from its early days. In 1878, Gerard Cobb, president of the Bicycle Union and a Fellow of Trinity College, Cambridge, wrote that cycling was "primarily of commercial importance" but was also of practical benefit:

> ... the ease with which a bicycle can be driven, the distance it enables its riders to cover, its speed ... added to its durability and comparative cheapness, render it by far the best form of road-locomotion for all to whom economy, whether of time or money, is object.

Cyclists who were particularly good at scorching had the ideal outlet: racing. Cycle racing was one of the most popular spectator sports of the 19th century. Huge crowds gathered in stadiums to watch cyclists complete dizzying numbers of circuits, with especially lightweight bicycles built to go faster and faster. Speed – and distance – records were also popular, on the track and on roads, and, in one famous example, on a specially constructed wooden track insert. This allowed American Charles Murphy to slipstream behind a train at over 60 miles per hour. In 1899, "mile-a-minute Murphy" was news the world over.

Cyclists who scorched on the public highway were detested by pedestrians as well as by fellow cyclists, as evidenced by a large number of anti-scorching letters and editorials in cycling journals, and newspapers with cycling columns. An up-market society journal warned that if a "cycle tax" were

Motorists soon used their speed to push other road users aside. From: The Graphic, 1902.

brought in by parliament in 1896 it would be due to the "reprehensible and scatter-brained antics of that minute minority, the scorching brigade." *The Bards and the Bicycle*, an 1897 compilation of 200 British and American cycling poems and ditties, contained 17 contributions parodying the heinous act of scorching, with titles such as "Couldn't Help Scorching," "The Scorcher's Soliloquy," "The Scorcher's Back" and, showing this wasn't a male preserve, "The Female Scorcher." And those were just the poems with "scorching" in the title – others featured scorching as a secondary subject. Clearly, scorching was of major concern in the Victorian age, although a writer for *Punch* tried to put it into perspective: "The scorcher and the road-hog are the least representative followers of the sports which their conduct brings into question, and it is very easy to over-estimate their importance." Nevertheless, given the repetition of "ting-a-ling" in these poems, and other onomatopoeic phrases for bicycle bells and horns, many of the prototype Mr. Toads, numerous or not, expected those in front of their bicycles to get the hell out of the way.

Scorching cyclists were tame in comparison to the next speeders on the scene: motorists, as parodied by *Punch*:

> What rushes through the crowded street
> With whirring noise and throbbing beat,
> Exhaling odours far from sweet?
> The motor-car.
>
> Whose wheels o'er greasy asphalte skim,
> Exacting toll of life and limb,
> (What is a corpse or so to *him*)?
> The motorist's.

Speeding on bicycles was a precursor to speeding in automobiles. It was individualised speed, different to the speed attained in a train, more personal, seemingly more controllable (and certainly more controllable than speed on a galloping horse). For author Jeffrey T. Schnapp, writing in 1999, the "administration of one's own speed" was a "sacrament of modern individualism."

Schnapp said there were "two concurrent yet distinct experiences of velocity," one that he called "thrill-based" and the other "commodity-based". The first is experienced in modes such bicycles, cars, and motorbikes. "Commodity-based" velocity was that attained second-hand, in train and buses piloted by others. The difference between the two is that thrill-based transportation occurs when the passenger "can envisage himself as the author of his velocity," while in what could also be labelled "public transport" the traveller is "shielded from the natural environment and the engine, and passively submits himself to velocity."

IT WAS a number of years before motorists were able to go faster than cyclists. Initially, the best the proto-motorists could hope for would be to keep up with cyclists, as evidenced by a correspondent to *The Engineer* of London, who said in 1894 "petroleum carriages can go as fast as an ordinary cyclist cares to travel."

By 1899, cyclists were no longer in charge of the fastest vehicles on the road. "Hitherto the cyclist has enjoyed the unquestionable advantage of having at call a higher degree of latent speed than any other road user," remarked cycling paper *The Hub* that year. "The motor has come to stay, and we should be the last to deprecate the fact. But with its arrival there has passed from the cyclist pure and simple the advantage of possessing the palm for speed."

However, busy streets, ill-defined roads and observant policemen prevented motorists from scorching too often through towns and cities. A cover for *Leslie's Weekly* of 1901 shows New York's supposed "Twentieth Century Boulevard" where a "startling variety of methods of conveyance … mingle in dangerous proximity to each other." A couple on a tandem, dressed to the nines, are shown besting a motor car, as well as a number of horse-drawn cabs and an electric trolley bus. Four years later, cyclists were still the fastest things on wheels in London, in congested areas at least. The Automobile Club of Great Britain and Ireland measured speeds in Piccadilly, one of the busiest thoroughfares in the capital. While motorists – in theory – were not allowed to travel above 10 miles per hour, cyclists were clocked doing 15.85 miles per hour, faster than the 13.55 of the flighty horse-drawn buggy.

Police speed traps notwithstanding, motorists routinely travelled at speeds well in excess of ten miles per hour. Many felt it perverse not to. The early cars had poor brakes, terrible roadholding characteristics, especially in the wet, and were often piloted by newbies. Motor cars may have been small in number but their potential for doing harm for those in and out of motor cars was immense. This new danger no doubt forced many cyclists from their bicycles, and many retreated into the trolley buses, or became car owners themselves.

The term "scorcher" transferred from cycling to motoring. Newspapers and magazines which had previously complained about scorchers on two wheels now complained about scorchers on four. Automobile magazines – some of which carried editorials calling for motor car speeds to be voluntarily reduced in order to prevent motoring becoming a despised and banned activity – published the same sort of warning poems carried earlier by bicycle magazines. Here's one – with a familiar title – from a 1902 edition of America's *The Automobile Magazine*:

THE SCORCHER

Hurry,
Scurry,
Off with a flurry,
Dodging the cable cars,
Pushing his way through the thoroughfare
With many a jolt that jars.

Speeding,
Impeding,
Others unheeding,
An oath for those who protest;
A laugh for the pedestrian he brushes aside,
And never a thought for the rest.

Dashing,
Splashing,
Nothing abashing,
Over streets all slippery with slime;
Then an extra spurt and a finishing jerk,
And he saves a minute of time.

"Privileged sport", Puck Magazine, *June 9th, 1909.*

Many of the motorists who became "scorchers" had had their go-faster appetites whetted through cycling. As can be seen in chapter 14, many of the first racing drivers came from the world of bicycle racing. There was a natural progression from going fast on the cycling track to going even faster on the motoring track.

But motorists didn't restrict their speeding to the off-road circuit – they believed the public birthright to the highway gave them the right to go at whatever speed they bally well liked on that public highway. The early motorists – rich and influential – fought tooth and nail to prevent the "unEnglish" imposition of speed limits.

While cyclists had, on occasion, killed pedestrians, and horses killed plenty of them, motorists seemed to kill with abandon. The chairman of the post-war Pedestrians' Association, channelling Shakespeare, in 1947 described the slaughter as "Murder Most Foul."

While "motor car" is first mentioned in the court proceedings of the Old Bailey, the central criminal court of England and Wales, in 1899, it was another seven years before a case of manslaughter was brought against a motorist. A year after that the trial of Robert Evrard took place and the court transcript reveals details of how motorists, from the very start, tried to wriggle out of blame for "accidents" caused by their speeding.

Evrard was a 21-year-old chauffeur who, "by wanton or furious driving," killed a young girl on Oxford Street in central London. Omnibus driver Robert Harewood told the court he saw Evrard's motor car "going at 18 to 20 miles an hour" before it hit two girls crossing the road in front of him.

"I noticed two little girls, a little to the west of the refuge, waiting to cross from the near to the off side of Oxford Street," said Harewood:

> I eased up to allow them to cross. I was then about 14 yards from them. There was a butcher's tricycle in front of me. The children, walking side by side, started to cross between me and the tricycle. I heard a shout from someone on an omnibus coming the other way ... I saw a motor car just level with my front wheel; in another second it had caught the two children; one was thrown on to the near side, and the other the car ran over ... The car did not slacken pace before the children were struck.

Ernest Gale, the driver of the other omnibus, said Evrard's car was "going 16 to 20 miles an hour; it did not slacken pace ..."

Fourteen-year-old May Smith died from her injuries. Evrard claimed his car was travelling at no more than 11 miles per hour when he struck the two girls, claiming he knew this because he had been driving it gingerly due to "defects" that would "diminish its speed." One of his passengers, a fellow chauffeur, said the statement he had given to police that Evrard had been driving at 15 to 20 miles per hour should be corrected because, he said – probably not very convincingly – "I meant 15 to 20 *kilometres* an hour."

Evrard claimed he did "everything I possibly could to avoid the accident" and that "I did not slow up as I was passing the 'bus; I was not going fast enough to slow up."

The jury did not believe him and he was found guilty of manslaughter. Mr. Justice Bray, passing sentence, said:

> The evidence showed that this car was driven along Oxford Street, one of the most crowded thoroughfares in London, at least 16 miles an hour ... [It] was the duty of persons driving in the streets of London to anticipate [pedestrians crossing on the road] and they must not go on blindly because they thought the road was clear in front of them, when there were obstacles in their way which prevented their seeing whether the road was clear or not.

The judge added "it must be thoroughly well-known that persons who drove motor vehicles in this way must be punished." Evrard received six months' hard labour.

He got off lightly. A Justice of the Peace in Middlesex believed speeding motorists were the "enemies of mankind" and joked that they should be shot. This particular JP was Sir W. S. Gilbert, half of Gilbert and Sullivan of comic opera fame. Gilbert owned a succession of motor cars but ordered the gloriously-named Hardy McDonald McHardy, his "gentleman-chauffeur," to drive below the speed limit at all times. Gilbert had a reputation for toughness with motorists who came up before him accused of speeding.

In a letter to *The Times* in 1903, Gilbert used gallows humour to argue that Britons should be able to take the law into their own hands:

> I am delighted with the suggestion made by your spirited correspondent Sir Ralph Payne-Gallwey that all pedestrians shall be legally empowered to discharge shotguns ... at all motorists who may appear to them to be driving to the common danger. Not only would this provide a speedy and effective punishment for the erring motorist, but it would also supply the dwellers on popular highroads with a comfortable increase of income. "Motor shooting for a single gun" would appeal strongly to the sporting instincts of the true Briton, and would provide ample compensation to the proprietors of eligible road-side properties for the intolerable annoyance caused by the enemies of mankind.

Gilbert's view was not shared by many of his fellow gentleman motorists. Speeding was not seen as sinful. Early motorists thought it absurd that they, leaders of the land, should be brought before magistrates. The law was meant to be exercised on the little people, not on the upper classes. *The Times* sniffed in 1902 that the speed limit was "seldom observed by even the most law-abiding citizens, and it is habitually disregarded by persons of high station and authority whose normal respect for the law is instinctive and unimpeachable."

In an argument still used today, motorists were said to be far better judges of acceptable motor car speeds than jumped-up police constables and their hated speed traps. In March 1905, music hall proprietor Walter Gibbons wrote to *Autocar* magazine suggesting a Motorists' Protection Association for the Prevention of Police Traps. Racing car driver Charles Jarrott replied, saying arrangements had been made to patrol the Brighton road to warn motorists of these traps.

The first patrols went out in April 1905 – on bicycles. Alfred Hunter, writing in *Bystander*, a tabloid magazine, said: "Eight cyclists, each carrying a red flag, patrol the Brighton road every Saturday and Sunday, warning motorists of police ambuscades."

At the beginning of June, Gibbons and Jarrott – and shipping magnate Charles Temperley – formed the Motorists' Mutual Association with a "special staff of cyclists." With funds from its gentleman backers the anti-speed trap organisation appointed a full-time secretary, Stenson Cooke. At the end of June the organisation changed its name: henceforth it would be known as the Automobile Association. (It still is.)

Stenson, with not a shred of shame, wrote to *The Times*:

> I have the pleasure to inform motorists that the heavily trapped part of the Portsmouth Road from Esher to the 19th milestone will henceforth be patrolled by our cyclist scouts on every day of the week. This is our first step towards that daily protection which it is the aim of our committee to establish … [and] continue on every important road until the time shall arrive when police traps cease from troubling and the stop watch is at rest.

The Automobile Association relied on cycle scouts for some years. The organisation's famous car badge was "introduced simply to help the scouts identify AA members." To the annoyance of the police, scouts would salute AA members to warn them of speed traps. One member clearly didn't get the memo and wrote to the AA asking why his car had not been properly saluted. The reply stated:

> Sir, be appraised, [the scout] failed to salute you because that is our secret signal a speed trap lies ahead.

Road users have always wanted to go as fast as they damn well liked – from mail coaches through to scorching cyclists – and motorists in the early 20th century were no different in this respect. The Earl of Portsmouth, while not a driver himself, owned a fleet of motor cars and wanted his chauffeurs to drive fast from London to his Hampshire seat, Hurstbourne Park. According to a 1903 motoring yearbook "the Earl does not like the present speed limit, and has sped – under Mr. S. F. Edge's skilful guidance – at fifty-six miles an hour along Hampshire roads."

Despite drivers openly admitting to breaching the speed limit – and the champion-cyclist-turned-racing-driver Selwyn Edge was clearly many times over the maximum there – journalist James Edmund Vincent of *The Times*, writing in a 1907 motoring travelogue, said the typical motorist was not a "ruthless speed maniac" and therefore "anti-motorists" should not be allowed to slow the march of progress:

> The anti-motorist will … [be] convinced that the motorist is a dust-raising, property-destroying, dog-killing, fowl-slaying, dangerous and ruthless speed maniac. But, of course, the anti-motorist is quite wrong. The rational motorist, who is in the overwhelming majority – but black sheep are sadly conspicuous amidst a white flock – passes through certain regular stages of evolution. At first he revels without thought, or without conscious thought, in the sheer ecstasy of motion. The road which seems to flow to meet him, white, tawny or grey as the case may be, and to open before him as if by magic, the pressure of the cool air on his face, even the tingling lash of the rain as he dashes against it, result in a feeling of undefinable, almost lyrical, exaltation.

This "lyrical exaltation" in the "sheer ecstasy of motion," combined with the belief that every Englishman had the inalienable right to unimpeded progress on the public highway, led many motorists to believe that roads should be turned over to new masters, those with raw power under their perfect control. Motoring promoter and MP John Scott Montagu wrote in 1904 that main roads had been built for high speeds:

> [It is a fallacy] that the main roads of this country are not suitable for high speeds … Exactly the reverse is the case. Take the main roads leading out of London for example, such as the Holyhead road, the Great North road, the Bath road, the Southampton road, the Portsmouth road; these and many other roads were in the old days expressly built for speed for the fast mail coaches…

(Remember, these roads had been designed for speeds of about 12 miles per hour, not contemporary motor car speeds of double that.) Speaking in the House of Lords in 1907, Earl Russell called the imposition of a speed limit "artificial" and, in an argument used by motorists from that day to this, said it wasn't speeding that was dangerous, it was "anti-social driving." Trapping motorists and fining them for speeding was, "a very profitable employment," he complained.

"There are many objections of the most serious character to an artificial speed limit quite apart from the objection of the motorist himself," argued Lord Russell (who, like many of his caste, had earlier been a pedalling peer):

> One objection is that it makes into a crime an act which may not be criminal or anti-social in its character … East Sussex has gone in for an elaborate electric timing apparatus, which has earned its original cost many times over; and this system of trapping is now being extended all over the country. The result is that careful and considerate motorists are constantly being trapped, and become indistinguishable from the reckless and careless motorists whose licences ought to be taken away.

To Montagu, the extraction of fines from motorists caught for speeding was tantamount to theft: "[speed traps] are manifestly absurd as a protection to the public, and they are used … as a means of extracting money from the passing traveller in a way which reminds one of the highwaymen of the Middle Ages."

In a book written in 1904, Montagu warned motorists fond of the "poetry of pace" to be wary in areas known to have "prejudiced" magistrates, eager to fine motorists for speeding: "Beware of the local Bench in the matter of speed. They may be sensible, and the policeman kind or blind, but all are not so. The poetry of pace generally leads to a payment before the prejudiced."

The "poetry of pace" was portrayed as palpably, throbbingly, romantic. Speed has long been promoted as sexy, and fast motoring especially so.

In 1906, a French motoring promoter declared in an American magazine:

> The automobile is the idol of the modern age ... The man who owns a motorcar gets for himself ... the adulation of the walking crowd, and the daring driver of a racing machine that bounds and rushes and disappears in the perspective in a thunder of explosions is a god to the women.

Some women were seduced by speed as well as by the go-faster gods. Miss Nellie Bacon, writing in 1900 in an American motor car magazine about what she called the "craze for speed," enthused: "Whirling at a high rate of speed with little or no exertion affords a pleasure of the most exalted nature." She said it was a "pure pleasure" speeding along "shady lanes surrounded by natural beauty." (Of course, Miss Bacon had earlier been a cyclist.)

Speed was a one-sided pleasure. There was little appreciation of the needs of slower folk on those "shady lanes." Whether they be pedestrian, cyclist or dozing farmer in his horse-drawn cart, all were obstructions. The public "right of way" on the King's Highway was, by the 1920s, a right in theory only. The lack of an internal combustion engine equalled fewer rights. The fast car, harnessing the power of many horses, muscled other road users aside.

"Our hereditary instincts are shocked at seeing anything on the road faster than the horse," wrote cyclist and motor pioneer Charles Rolls in 1902, adding, in all seriousness, "but as our senses become educated we shall recognise the fact that speed of itself is not dangerous but the inability to stop is dangerous."

ALEXANDER BELL Filson Young, author in 1904 of the best-selling *The Complete Motorist*, waxed lyrical over the wonders of speed. One of the most poetic of the early motoring writers (and, like many other pioneer motorists, still a keen cyclist), Young said traffic snarls were "entanglements" that didn't prevent "king" car coming "into the noble kingdom of which it has so lately captured the throne." He rhapsodised over the joys of fast motor-car travel:

> The miles, once the tyrants of the road, the oppressors of the traveller, are now humbly subject to its triumphant empire, falling away before it, ranking themselves behind it. The wand of its power has touched the winds to a greater energy, so that the very air it consumes is crushed upon it with a prodigal bounty, sweetened with all the mingled perfumes of the fields and the seasons.

Yet for all his love of speed Young raged against "motoring cads," who besmirched the good name of careful motorists. Motoring would be irreparably harmed, he argued, if motorists didn't put their house in order. Young's was a minority voice even among his friends and associates, many of whom were aristocrats and racing drivers and almost all of whom had large, powerful motor cars, and thought speed limits were wrong both in law and principle. He pleaded for "common decency and humanity to prevail," for "[the motorist has evolved] the most blatant, the most cruel, the most revolting kind of selfishness that has probably ever been allowed to go unpunished." Remember, this is in one of the top-selling motoring handbooks of the time, a book that went through numerous printings and made money for its author and publisher for more than ten years.

"The motoring cad is the real enemy of motoring," thundered Young. Whereas many other commentators at the time felt such "cads" couldn't possibly be gentlemen, and must be from the aspiring middle classes, Young didn't differentiate, lumping all "cads" together:

> No advice that I can give will abate the nuisance of these people; it is their nature to be offensive, and unhappily the motor-car endows them with almost unlimited opportunities of indulging themselves. But there are others in whom mere thoughtlessness and perhaps a little of the intoxication that, in some people, springs from the control of power and speed, have bred a disregard for other people that is only less unpleasant than the ways of the motor hooligan. To such people I would repeat what has been so often urged in other places: remember that you are not the only users of the road; remember that you did not always own a motor-car …

Two years after the publication of *The Complete Motorist*, Young produced a shorter book, *The Happy Motorist*. He revisited the theme of motoring misbehaviour. Like Ruskin before him, he said speed was much overrated:

> If one's object in life [is] to get from place to place as quickly as possible (and it would be hard to imagine a more insane ambition) the motor car will help. But fortunately we do not all want to commit this temporal suicide … if we suddenly become bitten with the craze to do everything at speed … surely it were only logical to put a revolver to our heads, and take the whole at one gulp. The motor car, which is so often said to be a saver of time, is too often a destroyer of it.

Most other motorists disagreed, and Ruskin's views on speed were also dismissed. A writer in an American automobile magazine of 1902, wondered:

> Just what Mr. Ruskin might have written after he had encountered a 60 horse power racing car driven at top speed by a crack brained scorcher, would, in view of his foregoing opinions of bicycles, have proven most interesting reading.

Commenting in 1913, the economists Sidney and Beatrice Webb complained about the "menace" and "aggression" of motor car drivers:

> [The] motor car, which habitually travelled at three or four times the speed of the bicycle, with a load ten or fifteen times as great, and with fifty times the momentum, came as a serious menace both to the highways and to their frequenters … [The] turning loose on our roads of tens of thousands of heavy vehicles, often travelling with the speed of an express train, amounted to a real aggression on the safety and comfort of all the other users of the roads … [The] King's Highway ceased to be a place in which people could saunter, or children play …

Pioneer racing driver Charles Jarrott recognised in 1906 that "there is no wonder that there is a certain feeling of resentment against the modern swift-moving vehicle," – resentment caused by speed:

> I have seen a gentle old man – almost a patriarch in appearance – incapable in ordinary life of

acting inconsiderately to any one; but who, when seated behind the wheel of a powerful car, seemed to be possessed by the concentrated energy of a thousand fiends, and regardless of everybody and everything on the road, he has dashed along having the sole idea in his mind of travelling faster and still faster. Men not possessing sufficient courage to enable them to climb a high ladder on the side of a house seem nevertheless to be able to drive a motor-car at a great speed without turning a hair, and without feeling that the performance is attendant with danger either to themselves or other users of the road.

Nevertheless, for Jarrott, and many other motorists then and since, roads were no longer for children, horses, cyclists, or anything slower than fast motor cars. Roads were to be for speedy transport alone, shorn of their ancient role as highways for all. Jarrott predicted that some time in the 20th century the fast motor car would be "accepted as the only possible means of travel, transit and transport over our English roads," throwing into the ditch hundreds of years of British history.

The speed of motor cars – not the only selling point, but one of the key ones – has proven to be something of a misnomer. When everybody has access to wide, space-hungry vehicles that can travel fast, nobody can do so with ease. True speed, consistent speed, rather than the fits and starts of speed common on crowded motorways, requires the "open road." But, except for the wee small hours, this open road largely ceased to exist in the 1930s. Today, cars in "rush hour" London creep along at 9 miles per hour, an average speed not much greater than capable of horse-drawn carriages in the 19th century. Some progress!

Lewis Mumford, writing in 1961, believed the "fallacy" of speed led to the creation of "motor roads" which "devour space and consume time with increasing friction and frustration." The supposedly speedy motor road "under the plausible pretext of increasing the range of speed and communication … actually obstructs it and denies the possibility of easy meetings and encounters by scattering the fragments of a city at random over a whole region." He added:

> At the bottom of this miscarriage of modern technics lies a fallacy that goes to the very heart of the whole underlying ideology: the notion that power and speed are desirable for their own sake, and that the latest fast-moving vehicle must replace every other form of locomotion. The fact is that speed in locomotion should be a function of human purpose. If one wants to meet and chat with people on an urban promenade, three miles an hour will be too fast; if a surgeon is being rushed to a patient a thousand miles away, three hundred miles an hour may be too slow.

What speed-fixated transport engineers didn't seem to realise, said Mumford, was that "an adequate transportation system cannot be created in terms of any single limited means of locomotion however fast its theoretic speed."

The solution to motoring as a time-sink was obvious to many (then and now) – widen the roads. If roads are made wider, thought many motorists, we'll be able to drive more quickly. Many roads *were* widened but the speed gains made were soon wiped out by an increase in the number of motor cars encouraged to drive more by the wider roads. Nevertheless, the wide road for speeding upon was thought to be a modern road. Except it was not terribly modern at all.

CHAPTER SIX

WIDTH

*[In London] the existing layout of roads and buildings means
that there is simply not enough space to provide segregated
cycle lanes without adversely impacting other users.*
BORIS JOHNSON, MAYOR OF LONDON, 2011

**Many roads have been wide for hundreds of years. They were widened
not for motor cars but to reduce congestion, to create better vistas, to prevent
insurrection or to create healthier, wealthier streets.**

Today's BMW-built Mini is much wider than the British Motor Corporation's 1959 original, and is
also taller and longer. Other famous car models – such as the VW Beetle and the Ford Fiesta – have
also increased markedly in size and weight. Modern cars are larger partly because of airbags, crumple
zones and air conditioning units, but also because consumers prefer larger motor vehicles – hence the
success of Sport Utility Vehicles (SUVs). The motor vehicle "arms race" is leading to calls for road lanes
to be widened and parking spaces to be enlarged. Roads in most British cities are becoming more and
more choked as wider motor cars struggle to squeeze past each other. There's an epidemic of pedestrian-
unfriendly "pavement parking" – wheels half up on the sidewalk – and tempers fray when wing mirrors
are bashed as porkier cars pass each other. Yet, even before motor cars became so bloated, there were
space issues on many British roads. Some can hardly accommodate the passage of two motor vehicles at
once. This is a vivid demonstration of how many roads were not originally designed for motor cars. But
not every road in Britain is narrow, and not every wide road was built for motor cars.

VIEWED THROUGH a windscreen, most wide roads look as though they were built for cars and trucks.
Britain's motorways, cloverleaf junctions and dual carriageways of the 1960s and 1970s seem to bear
this out, but such car-centric highways are, in terms of mileage, the exception, not the norm. For every
one mile of purpose-built "motor road" in Britain, there are 95 miles of roads conceived originally for
non-motorised traffic.

Among the novel, motor-specific highways in Britain are some stretches of the suburb-strangulating "ring roads," which grew like Topsy from bypasses started in the 1920s. Bypasses are perceived to be modern but building new roads as short cuts to avoid urban bottlenecks did not start in the 1920s, nor did such roads originate to facilitate motor traffic. Rudgate, a ten-mile-long road south of Boroughbridge, is a Roman bypass of York. The road from Ladycross to Clarghyll in Northumberland was John Loudon McAdam's 1823 bypass of the then bustling mineral town of Alston. The New Road in London, between Paddington and Islington, was constructed in the 1750s as a bypass of Holborn. It was built for the driving of animals to the Smithfield meat market in the City. The Act of Parliament that established the 60-foot-wide New Road in 1756 stipulated "no new buildings be erected within 50 feet of the carriageway."

Today, the former New Road – known since 1857 as the Marylebone, Euston and Pentonville roads – is rammed with private cars, buses, taxis and trucks. The former turnpike has always been wide, and was designed wide long before motor cars came on the scene. Transport for London's "Independent Roads Taskforce" is said to be undertaking a fundamental rethink of road use in the capital but, to date, has not announced any plans for Euston Road other than for it to remain a motor-choked part of London's "inner ring road." Those on foot wishing to cross the most throttled parts of the road are huddled into "refuges" in the centre of the road, penned in like the sheep and cattle for which the road was designed.

NOT ALL of London's wide roads were built to accommodate the running of livestock – one was built wide so as not to fall foul of a vista-promoting Act of Parliament. Portland Place, a wide road running south from Marylebone Road, has been wide since it was built in the 1770s. It is 125 feet wide (from building to building) today, as it was in the 18th century. It was built to the same width as a stately home. Foley House was the home of Lord Thomas Foley. It had wonderful views over to what is now Regent's Park and, as a parliamentarian, Lord Foley was able to get a law enacted that prevented the erection of any building that could block his view.

Architect Robert Adam built what was later described as "one of the architecturally finest streets in London" by making Portland Place the same width as Foley House, thereby sticking to the letter of the law by not blocking the vista from Lord Foley's pile. In 1878, historian Edward Walford wrote of Portland Place:

> Eastward of Harley Street and running parallel with it, is Portland Place, a thoroughfare remarkable for its width, being upwards of 100 feet wide, in respect of which it contrasts most agreeably with the narrow thoroughfares which prevail in most quarters of London, reminding us of the broad boulevards of Paris and other foreign cities …

Walford's description of "narrow thoroughfares which prevail in most quarters of London" flew in the face of actuality, but it was a much repeated claim. The belief that London's streets were "narrow and medieval" – true only of London's back streets such as the various "courts" or the blind alleys of Little Britain – proved persistent. Period illustrations and maps show that many of London's major roads have not been "narrow and medieval" for quite some time. John Rocque's 1746 map of London, the first trigonometry-based survey of the capital, provides an accurate depiction of the street widths in the mid-18th century, before the huge expansion of metropolitan London in the 19th century. The map shows that Holborn was as wide in 1746 as it is now. Cheapside, too, was wide. Cheap meant "market" in medieval English, and this road has long been wider than many other streets because it was once the location for a produce market. It stayed wide long after the market ceased to function – at the end of the 19th century, parts of it were widened even more. Charles Dickens, Jr., writing in his London dictionary of 1879, described Cheapside as the "greatest thoroughfare," but congested with traffic:

> Cheapside remains now what it was five centuries ago, the greatest thoroughfare in the City of London. Other localities have had their day, have risen, become fashionable, and have sunk into obscurity and neglect, but Cheapside has maintained its place, and may boast of being the busiest thoroughfare in the world … [The] great flow of traffic is constantly blocked and arrested …

The *perception* that London had narrow roads is due to this congestion. Congestion is not a new phenomenon. Describing a busy London road in 1726, *Robinson Crusoe* author Daniel Defoe said it was "exceedingly throng'd."

And streets can be "throng'd" when the vehicles that use them are wide. A great many pedestrians – or single-track bicycles – can fit into the space required for horse-drawn carriages (or motor cars), a point made as early as 1867. Writing about congestion-causing carriages – often conveying just one person – an editorial in the *New York Times* complained:

> Is it not absurd, is it not a disgrace to the inventive age we live in, to see a man obliged to employ, in order to get through the street, a great vehicle, as large almost as a house … which fills your eyes with ugly sounds, splatters you with mud, and obstructs the highway? In principle, nothing could jar more with the inventive age in which we live. So let us have the velocipedes …

"Narrow and medieval?"
Not Cheapside and Paternoster Row in 1873.

FROM THE 1750s onwards London expanded at a rate of knots, became the centre of a global empire, filled with people and was consequently phenomenally busy throughout the working day. You can't fit a quart into a pint pot. The City of London has plenty of genuinely narrow medieval back streets (on which motor cars can just about fit, such as Cloth Fair and the adjoining Middle Street) and a great many hidden alleyways and courts (where motor cars cannot fit) – but London's major thoroughfares are wide, and a great many have been wide for 250 years or more. Most of the rest of London's major roads were widened in the 19th century – before the advent of motor cars. Between 1855 and 1889, London demolished 14 hectares of buildings per year to make way for wider roads.

In the 1880s and 1890s Herbert Fry produced a London guidebook with twenty illustrations providing "Bird's-eye views of the principal streets." These demonstrate the great width of the main thoroughfares some years before the arrival of motor cars. *See illustration on p. 115.*

An 1873 guidebook to London also contained birds'-eye view illustrations of some of the main thoroughfares in the expanding metropolis. King William Street and Gracechurch Street were shown to be wide enough to cope with eight or nine carriages passing each other at the same time. Fleet Street could accommodate seven or eight carriages in its width, as could Cheapside. The guidebook said that New Cannon Street was a "spacious new thoroughfare" and that "sundry fine new streets" were being constructed:

> It is a matter of general complaint that there are so few great channels of communication through London both lengthwise and crosswise; for the inferior streets ... are much too narrow for regular traffic. But this grievance ... is in a fair way of abatement, thanks to sundry fine new streets, and to the Thames Embankment, which ... now furnishes a splendid thoroughfare ... by means of which the public are now enabled to arrive at the Mansion House by a wide street ...

The 70-foot-wide Thames Embankment was authorised by an Act of Parliament in 1862. The widening of Gray's Inn Road, from Clerkenwell Road to Rosebery Avenue, was completed in 1892. Coventry Street was widened in 1881. Charing Cross Road from Charing Cross to Tottenham Court Road was completed in 1887. Park Lane was widened at its Oxford Street end in 1871, and at the Knightsbridge end nine years later. Mare Street in Hackney was widened in 1879. Goswell Road, opposite the Angel at Islington, was widened in the same year.

The widened roads were at least 60 feet across – not wide by the standards of the main thoroughfares of Paris but wide enough for six or more carriages to fit comfortably in the road. By the second half of the 19th century, most of London's main roads were most definitely no longer "narrow and medieval."

However, this myth continued despite plenty of evidence to the contrary. Essayist Hilaire Belloc, writing in 1912, claimed that London "is to this day a labyrinth of little lanes," which suggests that Belloc's powers of observation – at least where road widths were concerned – were not terribly strong. Belloc added that "by a special Providence the curse of the Straight Street has never fallen" upon London. No straight streets in London? Piccadilly, Victoria Embankment, Whitehall, the Strand, and Pall Mall were all wide and straight, and were made so long before Belloc's time.

Modern commentators – such as Boris Johnson, the Mayor of London – continue to state that London's roads are narrow and medieval, and therefore there's only enough space to accommodate (non-medieval) motor vehicles. The City of London has a partial medieval street *pattern* – built over an earlier Roman grid – but there are very few roads with medieval *dimensions*. The majority of London's main roads are plenty wide enough to accommodate multiple uses, including the provision of, say, protected cycling infrastructure. However, there's opposition to providing for anything other than motor vehicles. In 2014, the British Beer and Pub Association told a committee of MPs that segregated cycle lanes posed a "risk" to kerbside alcohol deliveries: "... it may be desirable to separate road users to protect those considered more vulnerable [but] further restrictions could seriously hinder the ability to deliver to pubs." (Heineken doesn't seem to have a problem with beer deliveries across the cycleways in the Netherlands.) The Department for Transport agreed with the BBPA ...

> ... in urban environments space is often at a premium. Providing a broad, high quality cycle route segregated from motor traffic in these circumstances ... is not always practicable.

LONDON'S ROADS were widened extensively in the 18th and 19th centuries in an attempt to reduce congestion, but this was by no means the only, or perhaps even the leading, reason. Wider streets were felt to be healthier streets, with less chance for the build-up of so-called "miasma", or noxious air. Miasma didn't exist as such but, of course, sunshine makes the best disinfectant and wider streets were certainly brighter and, therefore, healthier streets. (Contrast that today with London's poisonous "street canyons" where high buildings block the circulation of air, leading to world-beating concentrations of nitrous oxides from motor vehicles.)

Historian and civil servant Sir Laurence Gomme, writing in 1898, said that wider streets …

> … have the effect of giving greater air space and of admitting light and air where very much needed. Every large street improvement must confer a great amount of benefit upon the people in consequence of the air space which a wide thoroughfare always provides.

Those Londoners thrown out of their homes by 19th-century road widenings – even if many of the homes *were* hovels – may not have felt that they shared in this "great amount of benefit." Aristocrats fared better. The wide Northumberland Avenue was built after the 1874 demolition of a fine mansion owned by the Duke of Northumberland. He was well compensated for his loss, partly because he fought the demolition in the courts.

The Victorian imperative to create wider roads in London had started early in Queen Victoria's reign. A parliamentary select committee appointed in February 1838 to consider plans for the improvement of London's streets urged the building of "great streams of public intercourse". These wide roads were built for the "freer circulation of air" upon the advice of the great public health reformers of the Victorian age. One of the greatest of them all was Sir Edwin Chadwick. In the 1870s and 1880s, through to his death in 1890, Chadwick extolled the virtues of cleanliness, fresh air, sanitation and tricycling. He introduced medical men to the three-wheel cycle, including his friend Sir Benjamin Ward Richardson, another important public health reformer. Chadwick's lobbying resulted in one of the greatest Victorian health innovations – city-wide public sewer systems. Above ground he also lobbied for wider roads and better sidewalks for pedestrians. Specifically, he wanted sidewalks paved with granite slabs (helpfully, he patented a number of paving methods). He also argued for better methods for spreading asphalte on the roads, and he predicted that tricycles would take the place of horses in cities, leading to the cleaner, healthier road surfaces he believed would need to go in tandem with wider, cleaner roads.

The *Oxford Dictionary of National Biography* entry for Chadwick says "his passion for the public good still impresses and his achievements live on in every home and under every street in Britain." And not just under. According to Dr. Richardson, Chadwick …

> … paid early attention to road administration and road construction. By his evidence before a committee of the House of Commons he did much to get an Act passed for removing the administration of roads from the parish to the union; and effected a material reduction of ignorant and corrupt administration … He proposed … a road construction with a hardened wheel track of asphalte for roads of much traffic, and of highly hardened concrete for roads of lesser traffic and for the horse footway … The footway to a road of this kind would be made of coal tar asphalte granulated, specimens of which footways may be found in good working order near to Nottingham.

Dr. Ward Richardson said that Chadwick used his role at the Royal Society of Health to make "an examination of the whole subject of laying out, paving, and cleansing the streets of great centres," and that tricycles ought to be employed instead of horses.

"From the first introduction of the tricycle, Mr. Chadwick has taken the greatest interest in the science and practice of cycling," said Dr. Richardson. "Not one of our youths interested in the race or the tour on the bicycle or tricycle, has shown more enthusiasm on this matter than he."

Ward Richardson was the founder of the Society of Cyclists, an association of middle- and upper-class cyclists interested in history, social progress and cycle touring. Presumably Chadwick was also a member of Ward Richardson's organisation; he certainly gave talks to the society.

At one of his talks, delivered in November 1886, Chadwick talked about his desires for road reform, and what cyclists could do to bring about these reforms:

> The sanitary benefits that cyclists … may achieve, would also accrue by their agitating … for the amendment of all our roads … so as to bring roads everywhere into the same uniform condition of solidity for saving of friction and consequent loss of power. The cycling fraternity, containing as it does so many thousand observers, must, I should assume, by this time have obtained a very accurate knowledge of the state of all the roads in the kingdom …

Dr. Ward Richardson claimed that the "sanitarians have seen nothing that gave so grand an impulse to the health movement as the cycling crusade, which … is one of the leading features of the century." Despite Dr. Ward Richardson's claims, it would be a stretch to suppose that upper-class tricyclists had a dominant impact on the provision of wider roads in London, but they were certainly a vociferous part of the general movement aiming for cleaner, healthier streets.

BUILDINGS WERE swept away to make for wider, brighter streets and many of the build-outs – such as urinals, pedestrian refuges and even statues – that constricted otherwise wide roads were removed, long before motor cars came along.

The "London-has-narrow-medieval-streets" meme has long been wheeled out by those who wanted to build even wider streets. In the 1930s, the meme was used to promote grandiose plans for the flattening of much of London to make way for urban motorways. In a 1939 promotional film to accompany his 1937 report on redesigning London for motor cars, civil engineer Sir Charles Bressey complained about London's "narrow, winding streets." As he did so, the camera panned over a succession of very wide London streets.

In the film, Bressey claimed that Sir Christopher Wren had been constrained by the forces of "conservatism" in not being allowed to carry out his plan of giving London a series of wide boulevards following the Great Fire of 1666.

Within five or six years of the fire, many of the razed buildings had been rebuilt, with wider roads and, for the first time, sidewalks for pedestrians. It's often believed – not just by Bressey – that Sir Christopher Wren's post-fire plans for London, with wide, straight boulevards and dramatic plazas, were thwarted by obstinate property owners and conservative aldermen.

The reality was different. Wren's plan was just one of many submitted, and it was not thwarted by "obstinate Adverseness of a great Part of the Citizens." None of the grand plans were actioned. Instead, there were two Acts for the "rebuilding the Citty of London"; an emergency one in 1666 and an "Additionall" one in 1670. There was no time to wait for a "grand plan" and no single owner for all the properties concerned; and not all owners could be identified. London was rebuilt, piecemeal and quickly, by the property owners themselves for the practical reason that rents couldn't be charged for charred ground and businesses could not be run from heaps of ash. A Fire Court – in session until 1672 – dealt with disputes between tenants and landlords, and decided what should be rebuilt. Only two new roads were laid out after the fire: Queen Street and King Street. The city fathers bought up some strips of land along some formerly narrow roads and fixed their widths so that two carriages could pass each other. Streets that were formerly "narrow and incommodious for Carriages and Passengers and prejudiciall to the Trade and Health of the Inhabitants" were "inlarged … for the Convenience as Ornament of the Citty." Fleet Street, later the home of the British press – and, at the end of the 19th century, the HQ of the Cyclists' Touring Club – was one of many roads so widened.

But not all of London's roads had been "narrow and incommodious" prior to 1666. A street map of London engraved in 1593 shows that some of London's roads were wider than is often believed. John Norden drew the west–east roads – the roads parallel to the Thames – wider than the north–south roads. Thoroughfares such as Cheapside and the roads beside the old town wall are shown to be widest of all. The Great North Road – or, as Norden calls it, "the Way to Ware" – was also shown to be wide. The roads of Tudor London were often narrower than those of today but not all were as narrow as many people envisage them. Some Tudor roads were extremely wide, especially those that retained their market functions.

Ogilby and Morgan's large-scale map of London shows the City ten years after the Great Fire. Roads that were wide before the fire were still wide after it. Holborn, for instance, is shown narrow in some parts but positively bulging in other parts, like a snake that has swallowed a monkey. The British Library website has a zoomable version of the 1676 Ogilby map, with a Google Maps layer showing the modern streets. Using the transparency slider tool it's possible to see which of today's wide roads were also wide in 1676. The "monkey bulge" parts of Holborn in 1676 are the same width, building to building, as the modern Holborn. On Google Maps, Holborn – or, less romantically, the A40 – is split into two carriageways, each with two lanes. On the 1676 map Holborn is shown as a single, very wide road. Those who think Holborn was widened for motorists should have a play with the digital version of Ogilby's map.

Just fifteen years after John Rocque published his Map of London in 1746 some of the roads he depicted had been transformed out of all recognition. An act of parliament in 1760 allowed for the demolition of the medieval gates in the City wall. The seven gates, some of Roman origin, were "pulled down, and the ground laid into the street." Minories was widened to 50 feet, Aldersgate Street became 40 feet wide, and the other "gate" streets – including Aldgate, Ludgate, Moorgate and Bishopsgate – were also "improved and enlarged" becoming "more open in places." Cripplegate was the only one of the former gates to remain as a narrow lane. The *Gentleman's Monthly Intelligencer* said at the time that the gate demolition and road widening was part of a "beautifying" process for London.

MANY OF today's main roads may be blacktopped, dashed with white thermoplastic paint and zoned with barriers, but such accoutrements are mostly cosmetic – ugly, but not permanent. When television and films want to portray a period scene, production crews hide road signs and spread straw over the blacktop. Most period dramas tend to show pre-20th-century roads as twisty and narrow, but the main ones were often far wider than this. Before the stagecoach era, a few stretches of the Great North Road were much wider than even the widest parts of the current M1 motorway. The road from Helmsley to Pickering in Yorkshire had to be maintained to a width of 200 feet, as laid down in Edward I's Statute of Winchester of 1285. The Flamborough Inclosure Act of 1765 required that "all publick Highways or Roads" in the County of York had to be 60 feet wide.

Not far from where I'm writing, in my hometown of Newcastle, there's a four-lane road that links with one of the city's disfiguring double-decker motorways. Many people assume the wide, straight road was widened and straightened for the convenience of motorists. It was not – Jesmond Road has been as wide as it is since 1835. Forty miles south there's another wide road that many assume was widened for

*Stockton High Street has been 230 feet wide for
hundreds of years – it was not widened for motor cars.*

motor vehicles. Stockton High Street is reputed to be the widest high street in England. In places, the one-mile-long road is 230 feet wide. The buildings that flank it are mostly from the Georgian era – 1714 to 1830 – but the plots beneath the buildings are pre-medieval, so the road has been 230 feet wide in parts for many hundreds of years.

Motorists may assume that Jesmond Road, Stockton High Street, London's Holborn, and thousands of wide roads like them all over Britain, were widened for motor use, but they are mistaken. There are hundreds, perhaps thousands, of examples of wide roads in British cities, and many were built wide, or widened, before mass motorisation. Today, many urban roads look narrower than in previous eras because of street furniture – usually motor-centric in purpose. Strip out the extras and measure building frontage to building frontage, and the surprising width of many of Britain's city roads is revealed.

WIDTH, OF course, is relative, and one person's wide road is another's narrow one. Nineteenth- and early-20th century English town planners were extremely envious of the width of roads in American and European cities. In the 19th century the major thoroughfares in many Continenal capitals were far wider, from building to building, than most of London's, and this rankled.

"To Paris belongs the honour of having been the unrivalled leader of European cities ineffectually transforming the labyrinthine tangle of narrow mediaeval streets into broad modern thoroughfares," trumpeted town planner Inigo Triggs in 1909. "What lessons might be learnt of the value of vistas and axial lines from a study of the plan of Paris!"

He wanted London to plan for wider streets (to accommodate motor traffic) and felt no sympathy for those whose buildings were deemed to be in the way. "Adequately wide streets for future generations is [*sic*] of infinitely more importance than the immediate convenience of building owners," he said.

Similar to town planners who would follow him, and who couldn't disguise their joy at streets being razed by the Luftwaffe, Triggs almost seemed to desire another 1666: "Great fires in cities, although they must be regarded as grievous afflictions, have sometimes offered peculiar opportunities for the correction of many faults in the original designs of a city," he believed. What today would be considered beautiful – a curving street packed with old buildings – was considered "faulty" by many 20th century town planners. They craved blank sheets on which to create super-wide, straight motor boulevards.

Triggs believed London's roads were too narrow. Four carriageways were not enough, he felt: "The normal width of a wagon loaded is 7 feet 6 inches, or with a safety margin say 8 feet; thus a double carriage way cannot be less than 16 feet and the four carriage roadway 32 feet."

He added: "In a business thoroughfare each [road] should be wide enough to take three streams of traffic and the road wide enough to take four, which would give a total width from building to building of at least 55 feet." Cheapside was already 60 feet wide, and the Embankment was 120 feet across. But this wasn't enough for Triggs, because he observed that every time a road was widened it quickly filled with traffic: "Every year for many years past a number of new streets have been provided in London, giving a temporary benefit, the effect of which seems to quickly disappear ... [In] spite of ... many ... improvements we still have the tremendous congestion of traffic."

Triggs blamed the congestion on horse-drawn vehicles. If "quick-going traffic" was catered for – meaning motor cars – congestion would decrease:

> The congestion of street traffic is principally due to the mixture of slow-going and quick-going traffic. There are very few roads which, except at crossings, would be insufficient for their traffic were it not for the mixture of slow with quick traffic ... There would be no struggle to pass, as the need for one vehicle to pass another was due to the difference in the pace of horses and the difference in the weight of their loads. With motor traction, light and heavy traffic, subject to a few exceptional loads, would go at the same rate and use the same track. In London we are not concerned with streets of ample width, where quick traffic could go its own pace ...

The solution, for Triggs, was separation. London should "divide the varying speeds into groups, by making provision for the separation of the slow and quick traffic and strictly confining them to distinct channels of progress ..."

TOWN PLANNERS' love of blank sheets of paper for laying out their "distinct channels of progress" is not new. English military surveyor Robert Hoddle – born in Westminister, London – had just such a *carte blanche* when, in 1837, he laid out the grid for what would become Melbourne in Australia. Red-neck motorists in this city may believe the wide downtown streets were made wide for them, but these roads have been wide since 1837. Hoddle laid out the width of Melbourne's principal streets with a Gunter's chain, an imperial-to-metric measuring device. This portable surveying instrument – 66 feet long and with 100 links – was designed in about 1610 by English clergyman and mathematician Edmund Gunter. The length of a cricket pitch is 66 feet, or exactly one chain.

While roads in most Australian towns were made one chain wide, Hoddle specified that Melbourne's main streets would be one and a half chains (99 feet) wide.

The streets of many American towns and cities were also laid out using Gunter's chains. The Land Ordinance of 1785 stipulated that new property boundaries had to accommodate 33-foot strips donated from each landowner so a 66-foot-wide right of way for the road could be laid out. Detroit's famous Woodward Avenue – the former Saginaw Trail and the road leading from the centre of the city to Ford

Motor Company's Model T factory – was widened to 66-ft in 1806. The Homestead Act of 1862, which opened up the American West, also used the 66-foot chain as a measuring instrument.

Joseph Smith, founder of the Latter Day Saint Movement, wanted the settlements he planned for his Mormon followers to have extremely wide streets. The City of Zion plan, which he prepared in 1833, used a grid pattern with the principal streets being 132 feet wide. Smith's plan was not divinely inspired, unless God measures with English cricket pitches: a 132-foot road is two chains wide.

When, in 1847, Brigham Young laid out the new Mormon settlement of Salt Lake City, he based his grid on Smith's 1833 plan. Famously, he ordered the streets built wide enough so that a wagon team could turn round without "resorting to profanity." Less famously, the width of Young's non-swearing streets was 132 feet. Such massively wide streets would later facilitate the growth of motoring, but Salt Lake City's roads, like many other wide roads around the world, were not created wide for motorists.

THE WIDE roads espoused by influential town planner Reinhard Baumeister in 19th-century Germany had military uses, but he mainly wanted them to be built wide to accommodate the growth in horse-carriage traffic. Writing from the 1870s through to the First World War, he also advocated road segregation, with wide roads for fast-moving vehicles and narrower, restricted roads for residential use, with protected zones for pedestrians. In the 1880s and 1890s, delegates from the United States visited Germany to see Baumeister's urban planning in action but his ideas for the segregation of traffic did not cross the Atlantic, and he remained ahead of his time.

That wide roads provided a military benefit was also one of the key reasons Baron Haussmann created the sweeping, majestic boulevards of Paris, starting in 1853, long before motor cars. However, the military benefit was to quell revolution rather than repel invaders. Acting under the instructions of Napoleon III, Haussmann flattened much of medieval and revolutionary Paris to create his wide, straight, long boulevards. Dramatic-looking, yes, but the widths and straightness were not provided for the pleasure of carriage drivers. Air circulation for health, and the desire to be grander than London, were part of the plan but crowd control was a major impetus. Narrow roads can be used for throwing up barricades. While much of the Champs Elysées is today surfaced with setts, the road was originally surfaced with macadam as were Haussmann's other boulevards. The use of compacted crushed stone instead of setts, or tarred-wooden blocks, reduced the availability of ready-made missiles and fire-starters.

Mark Twain said Haussmann's wide, straight roads were a sop to Napoleon's plans for his own safety:

> He is annihilating the crooked streets and building in their stead noble boulevards as straight as an arrow – avenues which a cannon ball could traverse from end to end without meeting an obstruction more irresistible than the flesh and bones of men – boulevards whose stately edifices will never afford refuges and plotting places for starving, discontented revolution breeders. The mobs used to riot there, but they must seek another rallying point in future. And this ingenious Napoleon paves the streets of his great cities with a smooth, compact composition of asphaltum and sand. No more barricades of flagstones – no more assaulting his majesty's troops with cobbles.

Much to Haussman's annoyance, his grandiose urban planning didn't stop the insurrection of 1871 that led to the Paris Commune, a socialistic government that briefly ruled Paris in the spring of that year. Haussmann's city makeover didn't stop this mini-revolution, partly because the street-widening plan was yet to be finished. Many roads were still narrow and surfaced with tarred wooden blocks, which the insurrectionists used as weapons, in bonfires and in barricades. Victor Hugo, chronicling the 1830 revolution in *Les Misérables*, wrote: "The barricade was built with setts ... Not a stone out of line ..."

The wide boulevards of Paris, designed before motor cars, may have had a military back-story, but they were undoubtedly grand and popular with drivers of horse-drawn carriages, and cyclists. Pedestrians, too, were catered for lavishly. Ninety-five kilometres of the new wide boulevards were created, and all had generous sidewalks.

The grand boulevards of Paris eventually became motor promenades. A trickle in the 1890s, the number of motor cars on Parisian boulevards became a scourge by the 1920s. One pedestrian, out for what he thought would be a pleasant evening stroll along the sidewalks of the Champs Elysées in the Indian summer of 1924, was so disgusted by speeding motor cars that it changed his life. And ours.

That pedestrian was Charles-Édouard Jeanneret-Gris. He's better known as Le Corbusier, the architect god of modernism. In 1925, he described a walk in Paris the preceding year that became a fight for survival. He was forced from the Champs Elysées by a throbbing stream of motor cars. "It was as if the world had gone mad," he complained. "The fury of the traffic grew and grew."

Comparing the maelstrom of motorised traffic with the more peaceful boulevards he had known before the Great War, he felt that as soon as he left his house, "we were in danger of being killed by the passing cars. I think back twenty years, when I was a student; the road belonged to us then; we sang in it, we argued in it, while the horse-bus flowed softly by."

The road belonged to us! – with "us" being people not in motor cars. Just as Mr. Toad was persuaded to own a motor car after being thrown into a ditch by one, Le Corbusier's solution to having to cower before power was to become one of the powerful. The result was modernism, with motorisation at its core: "I was assisting in the creation of a new phenomenon ... traffic. Cars, cars, fast, fast! One is seized, filled with enthusiasm, with joy ... the joy of power."

Le Corbusier and his acolytes helped transfer power to motorists, creating very wide, motor-only roads. "We must kill the street!" he said. The modern motorist needed "a new type of street," he believed, a wide street that could operate as a "machine for traffic." He wanted to bulldoze Paris and create a new city, ringed by wide "aerial superhighways." Cars would dominate on these wide roads; culture be damned: "Cafés and places of recreation will no longer be the fungus that eats up the pavements of Paris," promised Le Corbusier. Such comments inspired others to create infrastructure for motors and motors alone. So successful were Le Corbusier's ideas that wide roads are now thought to have been widened for motorists; history be damned.

CHINA, ONCE the land of the space-efficient bicycle, now experiences the world's worst traffic jams. A 60-mile jam in 2010 lasted for ten days – pedal-powered entrepreneurs sold food and water to the stranded drivers, with bicycles the only vehicles able to move. Despite the building of more and more roads, motorists around the world continue to use them in inefficient ways. Congestion – especially in cities – is accepted as normal; some libertarians think such blockages are a sign of economic virility.

In the 1890s and early 1900s, it was believed the motor car would be the cure for congestion. Motor cars were shorter than horse-drawn carriages, and faster, too. Moving to motors would transform cities, believed pioneer motorists – and town planners such as Triggs and Bressey. They weren't wrong about that. Motor cars led to the increased spread of urban sprawl – a phenomenon started, in a small way, by bicycles but accelerated by omnibuses and then trams.

Worby Beaumont, assistant editor of *The Engineer* in the 1890s, believed motor cars would "displace horses so as to save the space now occupied by them."

Beaumont was a leading member of the Cycle Engineers' Institute, later to become the Institution of

Automobile Engineers, and also a committee member of the Roads Improvement Association, created by two cycling organisations. In *Motoring*'s 1904 listing of the world's motorists, Beaumont said he didn't yet own a motor car and listed cycling as first among his hobbies. He was no fan of the horse and even less of the "road apples" deposited by horses. More motor cars, and fewer horses, would "avoid the spreading all over the streets of that which renders them dirty and unhealthy, and avoid the pounding to pieces to wood, asphalt and others of the best paving with the three-cwt hammer of iron-shod feet."

Inventor Thomas Edison believed that automobiles would cure the congestion caused by horse-drawn carriages in New York. If carriages "could be transformed into motor cars overnight," he said in 1908, it would "so relieve traffic as to make Manhattan Island resemble *The Deserted Village*."

H. G. WELLS believed fast motor cars would civilise cities by sidelining pedestrians, horses and cyclists. In his 1913 novel *The World Set Free* he imagined a city of 60 years in the future:

"The insanitary horse and the plebeian bicycle had been banished from the roadway," he wrote. Pedestrians would be second-class citizens: "The foot passenger was restricted to a narrow vestige of the ancient footpath on either side of the track and forbidden at the risk of a fine, if he survived, to cross the roadway."

Wells correctly predicted many things – such as war in the air, the European Union, tarmac roads, wind farms, tanks, motorways, sexual liberation and the internet – but he didn't predict traffic jams. His future was an extrapolation from emerging technologies. Motor cars of the early 1900s were for elites, and so for elites they would remain, imagined Wells. Where motor cars reigned, pedestrians were seen as misfits: "[The protagonist's] freedom to go as he pleased upon the roads may be taken as a mark of increasing social disorganisation and police embarrassment …"

Roads of the "plutocratic age" were "fenced with barbed wire against unpropertied people," said Wells, and "along the road swept the new traffic, light and swift and wonderful …"

Swift, that is, until car ownership was for the many, not just the few. For Wells, it wasn't long before the realisation started to set in that the motor car, and the wide road, would not be a cure for congestion. In fact, they both appeared to make congestion far worse. In a BBC radio programme broadcast in 1932, Wells said:

> See how unprepared our world was for the motor car. It was bound to … congest our towns with traffic. Did we do anything to work out any of these consequences of the motor car? No, we did not … In the case of the motor car, we have let consequence after consequence take us by surprise.

His solution was to build more roads.

When younger, Wells had been an ardent cyclist and his earlier works, while dreaming of a future where swift motor cars would be the norm, didn't marginalise cycling

In 1901 he wrote *Anticipations*, a futuristic vision of life 50 and 100 years thence. Wells could imagine a future of fast-moving trucks, buses and motor cars on super-wide "motorways." He predicted grade separation (i.e., roads that bridge other roads):

> Their traffic in opposite directions will probably be strictly separated … where their ways branch the streams of traffic will not cross at a level but by bridges. It is easily conceivable that once these tracks are in existence, cyclists and motors other than those of the constructing companies will be able to make use of them.

Wells believed that urban cycling – of benefit to shop assistants, his former occupation – should be encouraged, by reining back the horse:

> At present the streets of many larger towns, and especially of such old-established towns as London, whose central portions have the narrowest arteries, present a quite unprecedented state of congestion. When [a historian] comes to review our times ... he will be struck first of all by the omnipresence of mud, filthy mud, churned up by hoofs and wheels under the inclement skies, and perpetually defiled and added to by innumerable horses. "Just where the bicycle might have served its most useful purpose," he will write, "in affording a healthy daily ride to the innumerable clerks and such-like sedentary toilers of the central region, it was rendered impossible by the danger of side-slip in this vast ferocious traffic."

Cities of the future, thought the 1901 Wells, would be home to "soft-tired" motor cars, and a "torrent of cyclists." Travel between cities would be done on "new wide roads ... here cutting through a crest and there running like some colossal aqueduct across a valley, swarming always with a multitudinous traffic of bright, swift (and not necessarily ugly) mechanisms ..."

Four years later Wells could still imagine a strong future for cycling. "Cycle tracks will abound in Utopia," he said in 1905. The quote, a favourite of cyclists the world over, has long been taken out of context. In his 1905 vision of the future, the cycle tracks he talked about were more like scenic routes than the intra-urban expressways for bicycles that many people assume he meant. Motorways would be provided for cars but most high-speed travel would be on "double railways or monorails or what not."

In the countryside, "swift and shapely motor-cars" would have wide "motor roads." Pedestrians and cyclists would have separate routes: "Cycle tracks will abound in Utopia, sometimes following beside the great high roads, but oftener taking their own more agreeable line amidst woods and crops and pastures; and there will be a rich variety of footpaths and minor ways."

Of course, "swift cars" and their wide "motor roads" did not cure congestion. Far from it. While bypasses and a few new arterials could be – briefly – enjoyed by between-the-wars motorists, most urban roads, even wide ones widened yet again, remained as congested as ever. Spotting an opportunity to entice the elite out of cars and into aeroplanes the de Havilland Aircraft Company placed an advertisement in a 1930 edition of *The Motor* reminding readers, as if they needed reminding, that the golden days of motoring were already long gone and that flying was quicker than driving:

> Motoring today means nothing more than a bonnet-to-luggage-grid procession ... gone forever are the joys of the old open road ... the traffic congestion has reached such a pitch that to escape it successfully one must now travel in another dimension. The air offers you pleasant relief from the crowded and dangerous roads ...

ROADS IN cities have been congested for hundreds of years. Despite the building of "relief" roads in the 18th and 19th centuries, London still suffered from chronic traffic congestion, so it should have come as no surprise that when car ownership increased in the 1920s the potential for more regular occurrences of gridlock would increase too. During the 1926 General Strike in Britain a front cover of the *London Illustrated News* carried a full-page photo of the Thames Embankment jammed with scores of private motor cars. The newspaper marvelled that the "traffic was so congested that cars were practically touching each other." Such images were used to argue that building a great many new and wider roads would "cure" congestion. It did not. Almost without exception, once a new road is built it quickly fills with motor vehicles. This is known as "induced demand," and the theory is credited to J. J. Leeming, a British road-traffic engineer and county surveyor, writing in 1969.

That building more roads leads to increased congestion was discussed long before it was given a name. Writing in 1866, surveyor and engineer William J. Haywood, one of the builders of the Holborn Viaduct, said that the new thoroughfare would attract more travellers: the "facility of locomotion stimulates traffic of itself." His solution? Build more roads, of course. This was also the conclusion of Sir Charles Bressey's "Highway Development Survey" for London, published in 1937. In his report – penned with the great architect, Sir Edward Lutyens – Bressey wrote:

> As a typical instance may be quoted the new Great West Road which parallels and relieves the old Brentford High Street route. According to the Ministry's traffic census extracts … the new route as soon as it was opened carried four and a half times more vehicles than the old route was carrying. No diminution, however, occurred in the flow of traffic along the old route and from that day to this the number of vehicles on both routes has steadily increased … These figures serve to exemplify the remarkable manner in which new roads create new traffic.

Bressey's solution? Bizarrely, the same as Haywood's. Campaigners have a pithy phrase to describe induced demand: "Building more roads to prevent congestion is like a fat man loosening his belt to prevent obesity."

This phrase is based on a 1955 article by Lewis Mumford. Writing in *The New Yorker*, the great urban planning specialist suggested that "people … find it hard to believe that the cure for congestion is not more facilities for congestion."

> Most of the fancy cures that the experts have offered for New York's congestion are based on the innocent notion that the problem can be solved by increasing the capacity of the existing traffic routes, multiplying the number of ways of getting in and out of town, or providing more parking space for cars that should not have been lured into the city in the first place. Like the tailor's remedy for obesity – letting out the seams of the trousers and loosening the belt – this does nothing to curb the greedy appetite that [has] caused the fat to accumulate …

Despite having a great multitude of wide roads this greedy appetite is still with us.

CHAPTER SEVEN

HARDTOP HISTORY

... mud, mud, mud, deep in all the streets.
CHARLES DICKENS, GREAT EXPECTATIONS

Few things minister more to the health and pleasure of the people than an adequate system of well-maintained roads. The country will reward and posterity will acclaim the statesman who can succeed in covering England with a network of broad and dustless highways ...
WILLIAM REES JEFFREYS, 1906

Asphalt is a bitumen-and-aggregate carpeting that's so ubiquitous it's invisible. Blacktop has a long history but there was no inevitability about its mainstream adoption. It took many years of trial and error before the modern recipe was settled upon. In the meantime, many roads were capped with granite setts, dusty macadam and forgiving rubber. London's roads, like that of many other cities, were surfaced with Australian hardwoods.

According to British tabloid newspapers, potholes are the telltale signs of a country in decline. When recent cold winters accelerated the number of such pockmarks the mainstream media demanded that cash should be lavished on road mending. Potholes matter because they remind us that our civilisation relies on surface silkiness. Holes in the road can rip asunder a car's suspension, cause a cyclist to crash or hobble a pedestrian. When roads are resurfaced, we quickly forget about the previous imperfections. It's all too easy to become blasé about blacktop. Well-maintained roads are so smooth that they are potentially somnambulant and, at motorway junctions and the like, they have to be roughened with rumble strips to judder and jolt motorists into paying attention.

Highway smoothness is a relatively new phenomenon. Roads have been capped with a silvery-black crust for only the last 80 years or so. During an average lifetime, we've gone from a society with very few bitumenous roads to one that is deemed uncivilised without them. Just-in-time deliveries of everything from car parts to frozen prawns seemingly couldn't happen without hardtop. In 2003, author Jeffrey T. Schnapp called asphalt a "material of frictionlessness" that allows moderns to travel smoothly and swiftly, but not without consequences – the speed a hard road encourages leads to deaths. Despite its lethal potential, asphalt is a substance, believes Schnapp, that few ever think about – it's "relegated to the domain of the necessary but presupposed." Schnapp added that "... asphalt asserts itself as the era's invisible but ubiquitous support … The tarmac hovers beneath the perceived surface of the modern landscape like a hidden god."

IF TODAY'S road surfaces are sterile, those of the 19th century were anything but. In 1894, *The Times* estimated that by 1950 every street in London would be buried nine feet deep in horse manure. An American doom-monger of the 1890s concluded that, by 1930, the tide of manure in New York would rise to Manhattan's third-storey windows. The prediction was that cities wouldn't be able to cope with an increase in horses, or their waste products. It's often claimed that it was the motor car which rid cities of manure. This is not the case; cities got rid of manure, and did so before the end of the horse era. Unofficial dung-heaps may have been common in cities in the first half of the 19th century, but from the 1840s onwards sanitation campaigners such as Edwin Chadwick, spurred on by epidemics of cholera, typhus and other infectious diseases, were highly successful at cleaning up cities, with London in the vanguard. Chadwick – and officials with the new Boards of Health – closed cesspools, removed dung heaps and made plans for great sewers.

By the 1890s, urban corporations were very efficient at removing what was euphemistically known as "dust." Period maps show a great many "manure depots" dotted around most British towns and cities; manure no longer piled up in dung mountains on city streets. Some of it was trodden in to the road, of course, working its way into joints between setts or absorbed into those wooden blocks still made from softwood. In the later Victorian period, cities around the world repaved with Australian hard-woods, which absorbed less manure. Horse urine remained a problem, though: 40,000 gallons of the stuff was passed on the streets of New York each day, according to one commentator in 1880. Also writing that year, another source said Regent Streets's wooden block surfacing had to be replaced because "it had become so saturated with ammonia that the emanations tarnished the plate in silversmith's shops." Urine soaked away, leaving just a residue, while most manure was uplifted and ended up on farmers' fields. As roads were coated with urine, dust and more, most cities would "water" their streets. They were hosed down a number of times during the day, with horse-drawn watering carts or, in some cities, street-side hydrants. There was also a hosing down done during the early hours of the morning. This was facilitated by the lack of private property dumped on the streets overnight: all carriages were stored off-the-street. Cities were clogged with carriages during the day but, at night, there were no streets littered with parked motor cars.

Before the 1890s, urban manure was collected by street urchins, who cleaned crossings in the hope of tips. This system was formalised in London in the 1840s by social reformer Charles Cochrane, who created the National Philanthropic Association. This organisation formed military-style Street Orderly Brigades which gave wages – and uniforms – to those least likely to get a job any other way. Cochrane's street cleaners were trained to "dart out and remove animal excrement almost as soon as it plopped onto the carriageway." A French visitor in 1888 noted that horse manure would be on the streets for no longer than ten minutes before being swept up. Today's road workers can be spotted from afar thanks to hi-vis yellow jackets; Victorian street cleansers, in London at least, wore red jerseys for the same reason.

In New York, Colonel George E. Waring Jr. professionalised that city's street-sweeping service and his 1890s reforms were widely copied in other American cities.

During the glorious age of urban sanitation, sewers saved more lives than doctors. The clean-up was taken seriously. London's impressive Embankment wouldn't exist if it weren't for the fact that it stands on top of an expansive Victorian sewer. The Embankment's wide carriageways and generous sidewalks were a happy side-effect of the installation of a wide-bore sewer which, among other benefits, reduced the stench from the Thames, a long-running complaint from the occupants in the nearby Houses of

Parliament. It may have been conceived as a covering for much of London's crap, but the Embankment was laid out as a posh boulevard, with access restricted to high-class carriages and, later, bicycles.

Underground railways and electric trams on the streets reduced the need for horses, leading to health gains in addition to those brought by better sanitation. Fewer horses meant less airborne "dust", or pulverised manure. Tuberculosis was a leading cause of death in the 1890s and as the number of horses declined so did the spread of tuberculosis (infant mortality also reduced after 1890, although medical academics say there is little hard evidence that fewer horses equalled healthier people). Motor transport often gets the credit for the demise of the "unhygienic", "unsustainable" city horse, but the city horse was well on the way to displacement before motor cars came along.

Bicycles and motor cars could travel on the road surfaces preferred by horses but wheels – especially those shod with pneumatics – came into their own when surfaces became harder and smoother. Victorian cyclists were at the forefront of the clamour for these improved road surfaces – which were also easier to keep clean. This was niche activism at the time, with many interests opposed to the improvements being demanded. The surfacing trials that some cycling officials helped carry out – before motoring organisations did the same – eventually led to the agreed recipes for today's ubiquitous asphalt.

IN *THE Wheels of Chance* H. G. Wells wrote about the road surface concerns of turn-of-the-century cyclists. Out in the sticks they rode on macadam. Chris Hoopdriver, the bicycle-riding hero of Wells' social satire followed a wayward heroine by picking out her tyre tracks imprinted into road dust. According to Wells the road through Godalming was the "vilest in the world, a mere tumult of road metal, a way of peaks and precipices." In the same way that some Brits may greet each other with a comment on the weather, Wells' hero had a greeting that made plain what cyclists were most interested in: "A splendid morning and a fine surface," Hoopdriver said to a fellow cyclist.

In 1899, Wells wrote *When the Sleeper Wakes*, a novel set in the 22nd century. Wells believed the future would feature skyscrapers, mega-cities and – thanks to wide, high-speed highways – a depopulated rural hinterland. The roads of the future would be surfaced with "Eadhamite." The novel's hero had "made a big fortune speculating in roads – the first Eadhamite roads … His roads killed the railroads – the old things – in two dozen years; he bought up and Eadhamited the tracks."

Wells' first description of his fictional road covering – which predated modern manufactured asphalt by only eight years or so – had been in a magazine article in 1897. Eadhamite so transformed roads that "the railways, robbed of their rails, had become weedy ridges and ditches upon the face of the world …" Old roads – "strange barbaric tracks of flint and soil, hammered by hand or rolled by rough iron rollers, strewn with miscellaneous filth, and cut by iron hoofs and wheels into ruts and puddles often many inches deep" – were replaced with "patent tracks made of a substance called Eadhamite." Wells said that Eadhamite "ranks with the invention of printing and steam as one of the epoch-making discoveries of the world's history."

Eadhamite ways were built for fast motor cars, yes, but for bicycles, too. Wells imagined a future where cyclists had their own separate paths:

> These [Eadhamite] ways were made with longitudinal divisions. On the outer on either side went foot cyclists and conveyances travelling at a less speed than twenty-five miles an hour; in the middle, motors capable of speed up to a hundred; and the inner, [was] reserved for vehicles travelling at speeds of a hundred miles an hour and upward.

By the 1920s Wells' vision of an epoch-making solid running surface for roads had come to life, and modern manufactured asphalt was starting its rapid spread around the world. In 1926, Basque mining engineer Pedro Juan Larrañaga celebrated the wonder material. Before its dystopian aspects became all too clear, London-based Larrañaga eulogised asphalt as a "thing of beauty helping the road to attain a still higher destiny":

> A well-paved asphalt road is the greatest missionary of civilisation at our disposal to-day … Good roads mean healthy movement, and this in turn means Life. Their absence means stagnation, filthy festering and Death! With beauty, truth and sunshine, can we not truly say that modern asphalt paving drives the Devil away?

Asphalt roads were clean roads, and for Larrañaga cleanliness was not just next to godliness but was to be the bringer of democracy, with asphalt binding road users in a form of mutual understanding:

> The world today stands at the beginning of the Road Transport Era, with which is intimately linked an era of Hygienization. A clean weatherproof road surface becomes the channel of civilization, along which the other gifts can flow. This clean road will contribute more to education and to the raising of the standard of living than any other known channel. The clean road will be the meeting place of democracy; the Rolls-Royce limousine, the Ford tourer, the cycle and the donkey cart will learn to know and respect each other.

VICTORIAN AND Edwardian roads were experimentally topped with a mishmash of coverings, some more teeth-jarring than others. A turn-of-the-century cyclist in London would have had to bounce, dip, glide and swerve over roads topped with tarred wooden blocks, steel sheeting, rubber, macadam and, in a few high-status areas, viscous asphalte, nowhere near as solid as today's aggregate-studded asphalt. There were, however, some road surface treatments stiffer even than asphalt. In 1887, a British engineer developed an "iron pavement … for the construction of Cycle Ways" and American engineers had the same idea in the early 1900s, with "iron roads" trialled in some cities, although for motor cars alone.

Another decidedly solid road covering was that of granite setts (cobbles are bulbous river stones, setts are flat). Johnnie Dunlop's discomfort when riding over setts in Belfast on solid rubber bicycle tyres prompted his ageing father to introduce pneumatics, the tech innovation from cycling that eventually propelled motoring to world domination.

Victorian setts are frequently still visible a few centimetres beneath London's crumbling asphalt roads. Setts are thought to be ubiquitous beneath the blacktop. They're not – most of London's roads in the late Victorian era were covered with hardwoods imported from Australia. Wooden roads were quiet, deadening the noise of horses' hooves and iron-rimmed carriage wheels.

Let's go on a Victorian-era bicycle ride. We'll start at Charterhouse Square, close to London's Smithfield meat market, on the edge of the City. There has been a livestock market on this site for over 800 years, but today's market buildings were erected in the 1860s. And this is when Charterhouse Square's granite setts were installed. They are still open to the elements, having somehow escaped blanketing by asphalt (and as the setts are Grade II listed, they will remain uncovered). The five-sided Charterhouse Square is dotted with rose-coloured granite setts from Mountsorrel, north of Leicester. This granite was first quarried for roadstone in the 1820s when Scotsmen from the granite city of Aberdeen were charged with digging it out. Montsorrel granite was chosen for Charterhouse Square not because of its pleasing palette, but because of the Regent's Canal. This linked in to the River Soar navigation, which enabled barges to bring stone to London from Leicestershire. The likelihood of a road being surfaced with Mountsorrel granite decreased the greater the distance from the canal. Today, setts are specified for upmarket urban gentrification projects but setts tended not to be used in posh areas in Victorian Britain: the greatest concentration of setted roads in London, for instance, could be found in the impoverished East End, close to the terminus of the Regent's Canal.

Setts were later brought to London by rail. However, it remained expensive to move the granite away from railway stations so the types of granite used in different parts of London were still dictated by distance from the unloading point. Silvery Cornish granites were transported on the Great Western Railway and were used on those few West End streets that used setts. Darker granites from North Wales were transported via the London and North Western Railway.

In the Victorian era, most of the "posh" West End was surfaced with wooden blocks. Other forgiving road surfaces used in London from the 1890s until the 1930s included cork and rubber. For a correspondent in *The Bicycling World* of 1884, "A cyclist's paradise will consist of rubber roads ... like the twenty yards under the archway of the hotel in front of Euston Station. It is delicious. Try it and die." London's St. Pancras Station still had rubber road tiling in 1934.

Rubber roads allowed for soft landings, an attribute also of the cork road covering developed by the Cork Pavement Company of London. According to engineer Henry Percy Boulnois, this was made up of "ground cork pressed into a bituminous mixture ... It is claimed for it that it gives absolutely secure foothold for horses or pedestrians in any weather, and is durable, perfectly noiseless, and non-absorbent ..." It also prevented the "breaking of fragile articles falling upon it."

However, for Boulnois, a member of the British government's Road Board, nothing surpassed wood as a road surface. He was effusive about wood-block roads in an 1919 textbook on roads, even though recipes for asphalt were well on their way to being standardised:

> Wood blocks are now proving to be one of the most popular materials for street paving, not only in London, but all over the civilised world ... In wood paving we seem to have reached the *ne plus ultra* of road construction. I have seen cobble stones give way to water-bound macadam, which in turn was displaced for the old fashioned granite setts, and this was finally removed to make place for wood paving. Whether in the evolution of road making this description of paving will disappear in favour of more better [*sic*] material remains to be seen, but so far, there appears to be every indication that wood paving will hold its own for some years to come, as the most suitable pavement for streets in the cities and towns of this country.

Boulnois was a friend of author Sir Arthur Conan Doyle: "[We] often used to go to Doyle's house after dinner, and, in his smoking-room, discuss all sorts of subjects, from metaphysics to more mundane matters. How well can I remember those enjoyable evenings when we settled mighty problems to our own satisfaction."

Doyle was a great cyclist. In *Scientific American* in 1896, he was quoted as saying: "When the spirits are low, when the day appears dark, when work becomes monotonous, when hope hardly seems worth having, just mount a bicycle and go out for a spin down the road, without thought on anything but the ride you are taking." Doyle's detective hero didn't ride a bicycle, but Sherlock Holmes, like Hoopdriver, was supposed to have been able to identify bicycle tyre treads imprinted into the dusty macadam that covered most rural roads. "I am familiar with forty-two different impressions left by tyres," said Holmes in *The Adventure of the Priory School*.

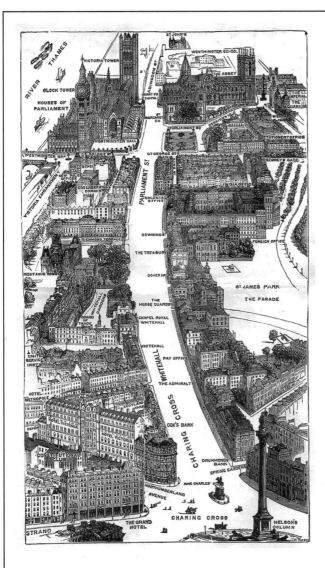

London, 1896

"We're nearing Millbank Penitentiary," said Sherlock Holmes. Dr. Watson, familiar with his friend's powers of deduction, nevertheless expressed his surprise. "How the deuce do you know that?" he said. "I can't even see the hand in front of my face!"

Holmes and Watson were in a Hansom cab, hurrying to the Palace of Westminster. The streets were blanketed with a "pea-souper" fog and, through the gloom, not even the gas lights could be discerned.

"It's elementary, my dear Watson," the great detective replied. "I have studied the different road surfaces of this grand metropolis of ours and, from the sound of the wheels on the road, I can tell which streets are covered in granite setts; which are made from compressed asphalte; those which are covered in timber blocks; and those made with indiarubber. As you can clearly hear from the distinctive crunching from beneath our wheels, right now we're on a macadam road. A few moments ago we were on a road covered with, if I am not mistaken, wooden blocks from our antipodean colonies, or more specifically, Jarrah. This particular Aboriginal hardwood has a density ten times that of the Swedish deal that covers some of our other streets. The sound of a cab's wheels on a Jarrah road makes a particular sound and, by estimating the speed of our horse, the number of turns it takes and the sound from the road,

I can work out our approximate location even in total darkness, give or take 25 yards."

Watson sat back, impressed.

"Come now, Watson," ejaculated Holmes. "We are here. Make ready your revolver and let us hurry in, a great crime is due to be committed here tonight and if we tarry I fear we will be too late to prevent it."

WOOD

If you think most of London's roads were covered in "cobbles" when Holmes and Watson solved tricky cases in the 1890s, that's just as fictional as Holmes and Watson themselves. There are plenty of setts poking through asphalt but they survive because they don't burn. When London's roads were resurfaced with asphalt most of the capital's wooden blocks were ripped out for firewood.

There were different kinds of wood on the roads of London. The posh streets were covered in creosote-soaked blocks of expensive Jarrah, an Australian hardwood. Workaday streets would have been paved with blocks of Swedish yellow deal, a softwood that detractors said absorbed horse urine and manure and, when pressed, would spray it back out.

During the journey to Parliament from their shared digs, Holmes and Watson would have travelled on wood-block roads (Baker Street, Oxford Street, Drury Lane and The Strand); macadamised crushed-stone roads (Constitution Hill and Millbank); and, via a detour thanks to a blockage I've concocted on Birdcage Walk, a short stretch of sheet asphalte road (Victoria Street). At no stage during this journey – which I imagined for this book; it's not in any of the Sherlock Holmes stories – would the detective and his sidekick have travelled on granite setts.

Sir Arthur Conan Doyle didn't include any of this detail in his novels. That roads were surfaced with timber would have been unremarkable to Victorians but today it's highly surprising to discover that London's roads were once not just a fire risk, but an Australian fire risk.

In the wet, London's timber roads were oily and smelly, and could be slippery for two-wheeled vehicles. Cyclists preferred sheet asphalte or well-maintained macadam.

In the dry, London's wooden roads could make for good riding. *The Times* reported in 1884 that:

> The cyclist … is everywhere to be seen … He comes in to his work down Oxford-street and Holborn; the long stretch of wood pavement that goes from Piccadilly Circus to Kensington is his delight.

Writing in 1890, an American cycle tourist reported that London's "wood block pavement is smooth enough to ride on."

He didn't comment on the smell, but others did. The surveyor to the Holborn Board of Works, wrote in 1895 about the "most sickening odour" given off by wooden roads:

> Wood pavement has one most serious disadvantage – it offends more than any other against public hygiene … Let anyone dwell, say, for twenty-four hours by the seaside or in the pure air of a rural district, and travel to town, alighting, for example, at the Victoria Station, the roadways of which, as you know, are paved with wood. What greets him on arrival? The most sickening odour given off by the pavement in question… [*Note: "pavement" here means the road surface, not the sidewalk.*]

W. H. Delano, general manager of the Compagnie Générale des Asphaltes de France, which supplied Paris with much of its natural asphalte, wrote in an 1893 book about bitumen that wood pavements were not "hygienic":

> As animals have not yet been trained to use water-closets and urinals the public highways are defiled with their dung and their urine; these, as well as other filth, are absorbed by the wood, and ferment in its fibres. Under a hot sun, morbid germs are drawn up into the atmosphere and inhaled by the inhabitants, stunting the growth of children and debilitating adults …

Delano – sticking the knife into his rival road-surfacing material – added that wood-block pavements had other disadvantages, too: "There is another danger, viz. that in case of riots the wood blocks smeared with petroleum and set alight, might aid the criminal design of incendiaries, as in the case of the Paris Commune in 1871."

The use of wooden blocks to cover the streets of London had started in the 1840s with the importation of Swedish softwoods, leading to a trade deficit with the Baltic region. But untreated yellow deal rotted and was quickly rutted by carriage wheels. Many of the wooden pavements laid in the 1840s were grubbed up within just a few years and usually not replaced. In 1867, American ordnance engineer Benjamin Berkley Hotchkiss patented an improved way of laying wooden pavements. He created the Paris Wood Paving Company and the London Wood Paving Company.

In 1872, Messrs. Mowlem and Company – founded in 1822 and still in existence today – took over the business and contracts of the London Wood Paving Company and created the Improved Wood Pavement Company. This company was still advertising its wooden road blocks in the 1920s.

The Mowlem offshoot was one of the companies that popularised the use of Australian hardwoods such as Jarrah and Karri Eucalyptus woods. These began to be used in London from 1888, and were longer-lasting than previously used woods.

Other British cities also paved some streets with Jarrah. This was mainly due to the success of a year-long lecture tour by Richard Watkins Richards, the city surveyor of Sydney. In a paper written in 1904, Richards claimed that Australian hardwoods – such as Blackbutt, Tallowwood, bluegum, red gum, turpentine and mahogany – were the "nearest to the perfection of an ideal carriageway pavement for all conditions, as traffic, climatic, meteorological, and constructional, that are met with in cities of all countries."

Many of London's most famous thoroughfares were still covered with wooden blocks until the 1920s. This can be seen on the Bartholomew's Road Surface Map of London from 1922 (first published in 1906). It confirms that most of London's roads, even into the 1930s, weren't covered in setts but surfaced with wood blocks.

Most histories say that just a few of London's roads were surfaced with wood, such as those outside hospitals, where a quiet running surface was vital. However, Bartholomew's map – frequently updated thanks to on-the-ground intelligence supplied by cyclists – shows that a great many of London's inner-city roads were surfaced with wood. (The map is included in the colour plates section of this book.)

Delano, writing in his bitumen book of 1893, listed the following roads as being surfaced with natural asphalte: King William Street, Gracechurch Street, Queen Victoria Street, Cheapside, Aldgate, Holborn Viaduct, Newgate Street, Moorgate Street and Cornhill. These roads are shown as asphalted on the Bartholomew map. There's further confirmation of the accuracy of the map from vestry reports, such as one from 1884 which stated that a number of London's most important thoroughfares were paved with wood. The Strand, Northumberland Avenue, Charing Cross Road, Trafalgar Square and Whitehall were all surfaced with wood.

Doyle's friend Boulnois, author of the splendidly titled *Dirty Dustbins and Sloppy Streets* of 1881, remarked that "the increased use of wood as a paving material, especially in London and the suburbs, has been remarkable during the last few years, the reason, no doubt, being its near approach to noiselessness without that slipperiness attributed to asphalte."

Boulnois also recommended continuity of road surfaces, a bugbear of both cyclists and those in charge of horses:

> … experience has shown that horses and drivers become more used to and confident upon continuous streets of the same paving. It is found that where a horse has to travel for a few

yards upon macadam, then upon stone setts, then upon wood, and, lastly, upon asphalte, or any combinations of these pavements, that accidents by falls are more likely to occur.

For shopping streets he recommended wooden roads:

> The class of property which abuts on a street should also to some extent guide the selection of the paving material. Stone setts may be very suitable for streets of warehouses, but would be inexpedient for residential streets, especially where there might be hospitals, schools, or places of worship. The fact of the greater part of the streets in the West-end of London being verged with shops has been the cause of so much wood pavement having been laid down.

As London had a wide variety of road administrations, organised via vestries, there was a wide variety of road surfaces. According to an 1895 book by Boulnois, Fulham had 100 yards of granite setts in the 1890s, and 4½ miles of wooden roads (deal, mostly). Westminster had three quarters of a mile of setts and 3½ miles of wood (deal, Jarrah and Karri). Islington had 12 miles of setts and just half a mile of wooden roads (mostly Jarrah and Karri). Chelsea had no granite setts but more than four miles of wooden roads, mostly deal, with some stretches of Karri.

Edinburgh's Princes Street was surfaced with creosoted beech. Many of Britain's wooden roads weren't ripped out until the 1950s. The creosoted blocks burnt well and were much in demand for home heating, as shown by Lord (Alan) Sugar's autobiography. The electronics entrepreneur – and born-again cyclist – got his first taste of business by chopping the discarded wooden blocks and selling them for use as fire-lighters:

> In the late fifties the roads in [Hackney] were being resurfaced … The removal of the old road surface uncovered a base layer of wooden blocks set into the ground in a herringbone pattern … It occurred to me that these discarded wooden blocks could be made into fire lighting sticks.

In America, many of the richer cities also had wooden road surfaces. The wooden roads in Chicago burnt vigorously in the Great Fire of 1871.

Indianapolis was the city with the most wood-block roads. New York had just one, said Brooklyn's city engineer in 1900, but the system ought to be used more widely, he felt:

> The only piece of wood pavement of this class which has been laid in this country … is on Twentieth Street, between Broadway and Fifth Avenue, in the Borough of Manhattan, where, in 1896, the Australian "Kari" wood was laid. The work was done with the greatest care, and the resulting pavement has proved quite satisfactory … Improved wood pavements are a luxury. They have many points of superiority over asphalt. They are so considered in London, where their use is continued, although they require renewal oftener than asphalt, and much more often than granite. They will undoubtedly be used more frequently in this country when the people are willing to pay the additional cost for the quiet and freedom from dust and from the somewhat disagreeable glare of asphalt.

ASPHALT

Asphalt caps most of today's roads, car parks and school playgrounds, and is assumed to be a modern material. In fact, it has been used on roads since antiquity. Babel Street, the processional road of ancient

Babylon, was made by Nebuchadnezzar's father for the glorification of Chaldean god Marduk. It had bricks grouted with pitch, the Biblical word for asphalt. This "glorious road ... on which no enemy ever trod ... glistened with asphalt."

Pitch, also known as bitumen, is the heaviest, most viscous part of petroleum, and was found in clumps by the Dead Sea and other parts of the ancient Middle East. The Roman name for the Dead Sea was the Lake of Asphaltites. The "slime pits" of the Bible – into which fell some of those fleeing from Sodom and Gomorrah – were pools of natural *asphaltum*. (Some Bible translations use the word "tar pits", which isn't correct as tar is a man-made distillate of coal.) Strictly speaking, asphalt is a mix of bitumen, sand and stone but, confusingly, the word is also used to describe bitumen without the additions. As well as its ancient use as a waterproof grout for ritual pools and vessels, bitumen was used for caulking the underside of boats, including, according to the authors of Genesis, Noah's Ark. Egyptian Royals – and their cats – were stuffed with many aromatic unguents, but the mummification was done with bitumen. The Persian word for bitumen is "mumiya", which is where we get the English word "mummy" for an embalmed corpse.

As well as the natural deposits by the Dead Sea there are sources of bitumen at the Pitch Lake in Trinidad, and Lake Guanoco in Venezuela. Bitumen from the Pitch Lake was used by Sir Walter Raleigh in 1595 to caulk his ships. Trinidadian bitumen was used on the streets of New York and Washington, D.C., in the Victorian era. In Europe, the main sources of bitumen were from Val de Travers in Switzerland and Seyssel in France. The first asphalt patent in Britain was lodged in 1834 by John Henry Cassell, operating from Cassell's Patent Lava Stone Works in Millwall, London.

Natural asphalte – with that extra "e" – and an improved stone mix was used for street paving in Paris in the 1850s. Threadneedle Street in London was given a free surfacing of asphalte in 1869 thanks to a demonstration by the Val de Travers Asphalte Company.

Nineteenth-century recipes for asphalt left much to be desired, with much of that spread on roads and sidewalks still quite viscous, as shown by *Little House on the Prairie* author Laura Ingalls Wilder. In the 1930s she wrote of her first encounter with an 1870s asphalt surface, in the city of Topeka in Kansas:

> In the very midst of the city, the ground was covered by some dark stuff that silenced all the wheels and muffled the sound of hoofs. It was like tar, but Papa was sure it was not tar, and it was something like rubber, but it could not be rubber because rubber cost too much. We saw ladies all in silks and carrying ruffled parasols, walking with their escorts across the street. Their heels dented the street, and while we watched, these dents slowly filled up and smoothed themselves out. It was as if that stuff were alive. It was like magic.

Horses, and their keepers, were less sure of the material's magical properties – horses slipped more on asphalt than any other surface. In 1878, America's *Manufacturer and Builder* magazine described the London horse-owners' campaign against the use of asphalt:

> In May, 1869, Threadneedle street was paved with compressed asphalt by the Val de Travers Company ... It is as smooth as marble slabs and not noisy, and the only objection to it comes from horse owners, members of the Society for the Prevention of Cruelty to Animals, and the horses themselves. Unfortunately, the horses cannot vote, or the asphalt would all be removed at once. The general public, who like to travel on a smooth roadway and object to noise, are very well suited with it ...

Bicycle-riding Victorians thought asphalt to be a wonderful wheeling surface. A writer in 1881 said that those roads in London surfaced with asphalt were crowded with cyclists:

> During the summer … in the heart of the city, when the business traffic of the day is done, and the streets are clear, an active scene may often be witnessed by gaslight. Under the shadow of the Bank and the Exchange, the asphalte thoroughfare is covered with a host of bicycle riders, performing a series of intricate evolutions on their iron steeds.

Like moths to a flame, American cyclists were attracted to asphalt, too – and, in the 1880s and 1890s American asphalt was the best in the world. Modern, manufactured asphalt took the best part of 50 years to evolve, and the person most responsible for its eventual success was a Belgian chemist. Edward J. De Smedt's "sheet asphalt pavement" was patented in 1870 while he was working on coal dust problems at Columbia University in New York City. On July 29th, 1870 the first sheet of Professor De Smedt's asphalt pavement was laid on William Street in Newark, New Jersey. The asphalt was made with native bitumen from West Virginia. The trial wasn't a success. Two years later, Battery Park and Fifth Avenue in New York City were carpeted with an improved mix, which fared better. Between 1876 and 1878, De Smedt used bitumen from both Lake Trinidad and Val de Travers to create two separate asphalt trials on the high-profile Pennsylvania Avenue in Washington, D.C. Cyclists flocked to the smooth, clean roads, not caring which country the bitumen came from.

De Smedt didn't have the market to himself, however. Others soon developed their own asphalt recipes for use in American cities. Civil War cavalry general William Woods Averell and businessman James L. Graham formed the Grahamite Asphalt Pavement Company to make Averell's "Improvement in Asphaltic Pavement," patented in 1878. The company won contracts in New York and Washington, D.C., leading to patent disputes with De Smedt. These were settled with the complex joint formation in 1880 of the American Asphalt Pavement Company. One of the executives of this new company was Amzi L. Barber, who, via yet another new company, went on to become America's leading supplier of asphalt. Barber knew which side his bread was buttered – alongside Colonel Pope, he was one of the main financial supporters of the League of American Wheelmen's Good Roads movement, which pushed for the widespread adoption of asphalt some years before motorists made the same call.

"The use of asphalt in American cities … has not yet acquired the wide popularity to which its excellent qualities entitle it," editorialised the L.A.W.'s *Good Roads* magazine in 1893:

> It is doubtful, indeed, if a better form of pavement has ever been devised … the experience of cities like Buffalo and Washington, where many miles of this pavement have been in use for several years, fully warrant the praise bestowed upon it by the people who know it best.

And the people who knew it best – apart from the manufacturers, of course – were cyclists. In 1895, when New York City proposed grubbing up its few short stretches of asphalt, cyclists started a successful campaign against its removal:

> The question of tearing up the asphalt pavement on Eighth Avenue from Thirteenth Street to Central Park is felt by the members of the Board of Trade to be a question of considerable importance to cycle riders … The Board set up a committee, consisting of city officials and members of the L.A.W. to "prevent the proposed taking up of the asphalt."

The Barber Company had largely perfected the recipe for "asphaltic cement" by 1905, although other manufacturers continued to experiment. Not until well into the 1920s were standard recipes agreed for the material we now take so much for granted. It took a further 20 years for asphalt to become the road-surfacing material of first choice. Meanwhile, at the beginning of the 20th century came the "invention" of tarmac.

TARMAC

Tarmac – the generic name for asphalt in the UK – did not originally contain any bitumen, so was not a true asphalt. As the name suggests, tarmac was made from tar, a man-made product. While it's also black and viscous, this extraction of coal does not have the same properties as bitumen. Tar plays little part in modern road-making. The original tarmac was a mixture of coal tar, stones and blast-furnace slag. It was made commercially available in 1903 after being "discovered" in 1901 near to today's Denby pottery outlet shop by Edgar Hooley, a county surveyor from Nottingham. In a 2009 profile, the BBC said that Hooley "invented" tarmac when he

> … noticed a smooth stretch of road close to an ironworks. He asked locals what had happened and was told a barrel of tar had fallen from a dray and burst open. Someone had poured waste slag from the nearby furnaces to cover up the mess. Hooley noticed this unintentional resurfacing had solidified the road – there was no rutting and no dust.

Hooley's "accidental discovery" bears all the hallmarks of a foundation myth. At least 13 similar "accidental" discoveries of solid road coverings have been recorded prior to Hooley's supposed light-bulb moment. The usual story is that a barrel of tar or natural asphalt falls from a wagon, mixes with iron-working slag and gravel, and is pounded to a solid sheet by passing wagons, after which a savant comes along, notices the hard road surface and exits stage left to produce their own version. From the 1860s onwards there are road-capping eureka examples from France, Australia, America and Mexico.

However, the Romans got there first: there's a 1st-century road in Sussex surfaced with a thick – and hard – mass of iron slag. No doubt a Roman centurion discovered the miracle surface after a barrel of pitch rolled from some local's cart. The surface was discovered in 1939 by wealthy antiquarian Ivan Margary, a self-taught expert on Roman roads. He called it "cinder concrete". In the 1930s and 1940s, Margary explored the countryside close to his home near Royal Tunbridge Wells, tracing the route of the hitherto unrecorded Roman road from Lewes to London. The course of this road passed many Roman iron-working sites, so the potential for barrels of pitch to roll from carts and be accidentally smothered with slag was great. Some of the "blooms" that would have capped the road are still visible in fields. The slag surface was not an accidental deposit, but manufactured – 12 inches thick in the centre of the road, reducing to 3 inches at its cambered sides.

Before bitumen-and-aggregates became the de facto road covering in the 20th century there were various road treatments in the 19th century, including spraying tar on macadam. A footpath on Margate Pier in Kent was constructed by this method in 1822. Unsurprisingly, the resulting surface came to be known as "tarmacadam". In 1840, Alexandre Happey coated stones with tar on a short stretch of the Lincoln road two miles outside Nottingham. Tarmacadam would have been a well-known road covering to a turn-of-the-century Nottingham-based surveyor such as Hooley. His patent was for an improved method of manufacturing tarmacadam, not the discovery of a new class of road covering.

In 1907, William Rees Jeffreys of the Roads Improvement Association organised a tar-spreading trial to combat the menace of dust. The trial, advertised in the motoring and cycling press, was conducted on the Hounslow–Staines road, and was won by Thomas Aitken of Cupar, Scotland, for the "Aitken's

Pneumatic Tar Sprayer."

The RIA's dust-abatement trial of 1907 wasn't the organisation's first experience of such experiments. "In 1902 I went to Geneva as the representative of the Cyclists' Touring Club," wrote Rees Jeffreys in his memoirs. "M. Charbonnier, Cantonal Engineer of Geneva, showed me an experiment he was making with hot tar on the road between Geneva and Lausanne."

Cycling organisations were key players in the improvement of Britain's roads, a subject I explore in the next chapter.

CHAPTER EIGHT

"WHAT THE BICYCLIST DID FOR ROADS"

*The Roads Improvement Association … founded by cyclists, and which has hitherto
consisted almost exclusively of cyclists, is calling motorists to join its ranks, seeing that they
are equally interested in the maintenance of the highways throughout the United Kingdom.*
LINCOLNSHIRE ECHO, 1901

**In 1886, ten years before the arrival of motor cars, a group of well-heeled individuals
created an influential organisation that lobbied for better road surfaces, and pushed for the
nationalisation of Britain's neglected highways. The trailblazing Roads Improvement Association
eventually became the cornerstone of the "motor lobby" but it was founded, funded and
originally run by cyclists.**

Perhaps the most important result of my bicycle-riding," Rookes Evelyn Bell Crompton wrote in his memoirs, "was to draw my attention forcibly to the state of our roads." Like many other highway reformers, Colonel Crompton developed his interest in road surfaces thanks to a formative time as a cyclist.

Between 1910 and 1919 Crompton was consultant engineer to the British government's Road Board, one of a number of former cyclists who sat on this forerunner to the Department for Transport. He was also one of the founding members of the Automobile Club, and became the body's vice-chairman. The Crimean War veteran may have been a pioneer motorist, but that didn't stop him cycling:

> I accompanied some of the members [of the Automobile Club] on a good many road tours – they driving their cars, I riding my bicycle … perhaps for a hundred miles in the day.

Crompton was also the first president of the Institution of Automobile Engineers. This organisation had been founded as the Institution of Cycle Engineers, and Crompton was one of many members of this cycling body who transferred seamlessly when it became a motoring one. Crompton had fond recollections of cycling:

> I took to bicycling [in 1895] on the persuasion of my friends as a remedy for the neuralgia from which I suffered a great deal … My neuralgia and other troubles entirely disappeared, and for some years I was an enthusiastic cyclist, and could do as much as two hundred miles in the day without being overtired.

We might, perhaps, take that last claim with a pinch of salt, but Crompton wasn't one to boast unnecessarily. He was one of the most successful electrical engineers of the age, with a thriving business. One of Crompton's friends was another electrical engineer of note. Sir David Salomons was a key motoring pioneer and, as has been noted already but is worth repeating because it's not in any automotive history books, he was also an official with the Cyclists' Touring Club and president of his local cycling club. Salomons worked with politicians and civil servants to help legalise motoring in Britain. Motoring was able to grow and prosper in Britain because of the country's relatively good road system. One of the reasons for the quality of this road system was the campaigning work done by cyclists from 1886 through to the early 1900s, a quarter of a century during which the funding provision for roads rose significantly. Pioneer motorists – like Crompton and Salomons, and many others who had also been keen and well-connected cyclists – benefited from the roads campaigning work of the cycling organisations.

Colonel Crompton.

BRITISH ROADS fell into disrepair after the arrival of railways and the collapse of the stagecoach trade. Some of the turnpike roads had been extremely well built and they would have been a massive improvement on the roads of just 30 years previously. The agriculturist and social commentator Arthur Young travelled widely in the second half of the 18th century and complained bitterly about the state of turnpike roads: "From Chepstow to the halfway house between Newport and Cardiff [the turnpike] continued as mere lanes of hugeous [*sic*] stones as big as one's horse, and abominable holes." The turnpike between Preston and Wigan in 1770 had ruts "four feet deep and floating with mud from a wet summer." A road "close to London" was the "worst of all the cursed roads that ever disgraced this Kingdom in the very ages of barbarism." And these were the trunk turnpikes – minor roads would have been even worse.

After the improvements of Telford, Metcalfe and McAdam road travel became easier and swifter. Hard-packed macadam created a solid surface but this relied upon frequent maintenance. Turnpikes at their peak were dotted with piles of roadstone for carrying out running repairs; post-railway turnpikes were left to rot and some returned to the conditions that had so exercised Young. But not all. There were a great many British roads which were kept in good order. In fact, without these good roads it might have been harder for cycling to become as popular as it did. The main roads radiating out of Coventry, for instance, were straight, flat and well-surfaced – they were used to test and refine the first high-wheel bicycles.

American cyclists were often full of praise for English roads. In 1889, a party of affluent American cycle tourists said the macadam roads surrounding Stratford upon Avon were, "Hard as asphalte, smooth as a billiard table, and clean as a well-swept floor." English cyclists did not always appreciate how good some of their roads were in comparison to those in other countries. However, diffuse "ownership" of roads led to widely differing surface conditions from parish to parish and what might be an exceedingly well-maintained road in one locality could become a morass of mud in another. Cycling road books of the 1880s and 1890s described highway conditions in great detail, and cycling magazines would devote many column inches to the condition of important roads. The "State of the Roads" column in *Bicycling*

News was especially good at keeping riders abreast of the latest highway conditions. Readers sent in detailed road reports, the "user-generated content" of the Victorian age. Here's a selection from 1886:

From Slough to Maidenhead, road very bad. Hounslow to Colnbrook, fair …

First six miles out of Chelmsford almost as good as a track, clear and splendid road conditions …

Good road to Haverhill, all clear, except on entering the town, where must dismount, macadam all over the road …

Roads to Ware, very good, no stones. Ware to Biggleswade, magnificent going, few stones …

P. Bernstein writes:- "I should very much like you to caution riders passing through Knightsbridge of the bad state of the wood. Returning from Ham Common on Sunday at a fair pace, my bicycle went into a deep rut, just outside Albert Hall, and I was shot out of the saddle with great force, escaping with a severe shaking, one or two bruises, and a broken bell …"

CARTS AND carriages did little damage to well-made macadam roads because the small angular stones used as a top layer knitted together to form an all-weather surface. Ironically, given the later history of cyclists as road improvers, some of the pioneers used high-wheel machines fitted with hooks that ripped into the seemingly solid surfaces:

> … a brake was made to dig a spike into the ground so that your progress was marked down any slope by a very palpable track. Perhaps the road authorities protested; at any rate this particular variety of brake, although undoubtedly efficient, did not last long.

Pioneer cyclists tended to be young, athletic, wealthy and time-rich. Their bicycles were rare, valuable and avant-garde. The trail-blazing of the bicycling pioneers is expertly described in a history of the CTC, written in 1928 by James Thomas Lightwood, himself a pioneer:

> No sooner had the bicycle become recognized as a new means of progress in this country than those who possessed them experienced a longing to get away from towns and streets and explore the countryside. This joy of the open road was a new experience, giving all the charm of novelty mingled with a spice of adventure and a modicum of risk … Roads were bad, maps indifferent good, sign-posts frequently illegible or misleading, wayside inns and country hotels were rarely prepared to receive guests … But those were the days of great adventure, and the first impulse of those who mastered the art of riding the bicycle was to go forth on voyages of discovery into the Great Unknown.

"The Great Unknown" is over-egging it but those early cyclists were among the first travellers in a generation to set out to explore Britain via its neglected trunk-road network. As long-distance transport had all but migrated to the rail network travelling on roads in the pursuit of leisure and not just A-to-B transport was largely an alien concept. The formerly busy coaching inns came to life again as watering holes for urban gentlemen on day cycle tours from the cities, or who rode from town to town on long-distance rural tours. Closer to the centre of towns, those interested in racing their machines sought out the flattest, best-surfaced roads to partake in organised "scorching".

Nationally, two clubs that aimed to stimulate and organise cycle touring and racing were formed within six months of each other. The Bicycle Union and the Bicycle Touring Club are still with us today as British Cycling and the Cyclists' Touring Club.

The Bicycle Touring Club was founded at the North of England Meet of high-wheel riders held on the Stray at Harrogate, Yorkshire, on August 5th, 1878. The club was the idea of three young blades: Stanley

Cotterell, an English medical student studying in Edinburgh, S. H. Ineson of the Bradford Bicycle Club and T. H. Holding of Banbury in Oxfordshire. Renamed in 1882 to accommodate the tricyclists who joined the club, the aims of the Cyclists' Touring Club were to

> … encourage and facilitate touring in all parts of the world. To protect its members against unprovoked assaults. To provide riding or touring companions. To secure and appoint at fixed and reduced rates hotel headquarters in all parts of the country. To enlist the co-operation of a leading wheelman, who should act as a Consul in every town, and who should render to his fellow members local information of every description.

Ten years after its first meet the CTC's membership reached 20,000, making it the largest athletic club in the world. And its members were influential:

> It not only includes in its roll many of the nobility and gentry in all parts of the land, it is supported by some of the highest dignitaries of the church, by members of the legal, medical, military, and naval professions, and indeed by amateur riders … who produce credentials showing that they belong to a respectable station in life.

Similarly, many of the first members of the Bicycle Union were also from the upper echelons of British society. What would later become the National Cyclists' Union was formally established at a meeting in the Guildhall Tavern, London on February 16th, 1878. The prime mover behind the formation of the Bicycle Union was Cambridge University music tutor Gerard Cobb, who was also the president of the Cambridge University Bicycle Club. Cobb was an enthusiastic rider and encouraged many of his fellow dons to ride, too. Cambridge's modern renown as a cycling city can be traced directly to Cobb's evangelism for his favourite form of transport and recreation.

While the NCU was formed to organise and represent cycle racing it was also an active lobbyist for cycling in general. Racing at this time took place on roads rather than on tracks or velodromes and so the national body for cycle racing naturally had a great interest in defending the road rights of cyclists. In fact, the stimulus for the original formation of the club was to put the interests of cyclists in front of Parliament. Late in 1877 there were concerns that Westminster wished to impose restrictions on cycling and would do so via a Highways Bill. In July 1878, Cobb joined with C.R. Hutchings, the club solicitor, and Coventry cycle manufacturer Nahum Salamon to press the cyclists' case before the president of the Local Government Board, which had part jurisdiction over the nation's roads. The NCU officials urged that the Highways Bill "should be so framed as not to make its operation toward bicycle riders oppressive." It was stressed that cyclists formed a large and influential body and that "any hasty or ill-conceived legislation with regard to them [would be] most undesirable."

The Local Government Board also received representations from the CTC. Touring cyclists wanted the same thing as racers – better roads. With no national highways administration, cyclists had to lobby locally for improved roads.

In Cambridge, Cobb became an active roads campaigner. He addressed the town's paving commissioners seeking highway improvements. Many 19th-century cyclists volunteered to sit on their local highway boards, although their work in improving roads is rarely if ever linked to their love of cycling. CTC book author James Thomas Lightwood was a member of Lytham's Board of Improvement Commissioners and was Chairman of the town's Streets Committee for four years. At the same time he was also the CTC's Chief Consul for Lancashire, and a member of the CTC's national Council.

In many regions cyclists raised money to help pay for the superior metalling they craved, stressing that the improvements they were willing to part-fund would be of benefit to all road users. The Midland Road Fund was one of a number of private pots of cash, raised by cyclists, that helped pay for road repairs, as reported by *The Birmingham Daily Post* in 1884:

> The state of the roads from their point of view as cyclists ought to be sufficient to make them join together for their improvement, but any benefits they secured for themselves in this direction would be shared by the general public, for it was not only cyclists that had to complain of the condition of the roads round Birmingham, but all who used wheeled vehicles …

The fund was also used to pay for court action against negligent surveyors. In August 1884, the NCU and the Midland Road Fund lodged a court case against the highway surveyors of four parishes in the Midlands for "neglecting to keep the main roads in a proper state of repair."

The lawyer for the NCU told Halesowen Police Court that the action was "the commencement of a crusade" by the cycling organisations, "with Lord Bury at their head." The court was told that the cycling organisations "numbered over 20,000 members" and "represented a body of cyclists who were to-day traversing the roads in this country in all directions."

The cycling organisations made it clear that this was not a crusade against individual highway officers but against "the system under which they were expected to work."

Thomas Codrington, a highways expert working for the cyclists, "presented a lengthy report on the [Halesowen] roads," which he "considered decidedly bad." Codrington had been the superintendent of the main roads of South Wales, and at the time of the court action by cyclists, was head of the highways department of the Local Government Board. (He later wrote a textbook on the maintenance of roads, as well as an influential early book on the Roman roads of Britain, the first to fully catalogue the extent of the Roman transport network.)

A cycling magazine reported that Codrington inspected the main road between Birmingham and Halesowen and found much of it to be in a poor state of repair. The surveyors "admitted that they knew nothing of road making or road repairing, and had not even heard of Telford or McAdam."

The Halesowen magistrates found in the cyclists' favour, an outcome that did not pass unnoticed elsewhere.

Wheeling magazine believed that

> … a new era has dawned for the dulled intelligences of our country road surveyors, and they are to find out that there is a public whose rights may no longer be laughed at; and there are

representatives of that public who, having the power, are determined to set this question about bad roads right.

An editorial in a London newspaper reported favourably on the victory:

> From the report of the case heard at the Halesowen police court, we are afraid that the highway boards throughout the kingdom will regard the cyclists as adding a new terror to existence. The public, however, will doubtless think otherwise, and will be inclined to applaud the action of the noble and ever increasing army of bicyclists, tricyclists, and other knights of the road.

The newspaper described cyclists as "self-constituted custodians of the ... highways." And cyclists thought of themselves in this way too – the lobbying for good roads was seen as a public good, as evidenced by an editorial in a cycling magazine in 1885:

> [The Birmingham] proceeding is, we may hope, only the first step in a great movement destined to be of equal advantage to the ratepayer, the driver of vehicles, and to the wheelist.

There were further court cases in Yorkshire, Lancashire and Bedfordshire, with the cyclists winning each time. Such cases were easy to win – all the cycling organisations had to do was supply proof that the roads in question were not repaired up to the standard required by the Highway Act of 1835. The mere threat of legal action by uppity cyclists was enough to get road gangs sent out on repair missions.

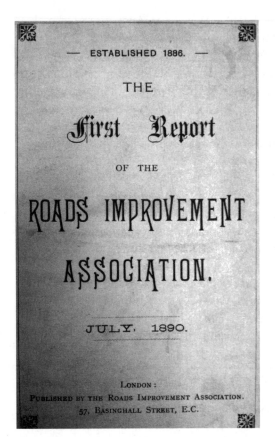

— ESTABLISHED 1886. —

THE

First Report

OF THE

ROADS IMPROVEMENT

ASSOCIATION.

JULY, 1890.

LONDON:
PUBLISHED BY THE ROADS IMPROVEMENT ASSOCIATION.
57, BASINGHALL STREET, E.C.

In 1888, the CTC persuaded the Corporation of Birmingham to compare its road-making methods with that recommended by the CTC's retained experts. The CTC's methods were found to be superior, and were consequently adopted by the Corporation.

As well as employing the threat of court action and conducting "road laying experiments", cyclists also enlisted the help of some of their prominent and well-connected members, applying pressure behind the scenes. One such member was Sir Alfred Frederick Bird, the elder son of the founder of Alfred Bird and Sons, the food business famous for its eggless custard powder. He was a champion tricyclist, and an "energetic member" of the CTC, representing Warwickshire on the club council.

Bird was part of a deputation that went to the Corporation of Birmingham to protest at the state of roads on behalf of cyclists, and he kept up a long correspondence with the body.

Other cyclists also used this middle-class way of pushing for change – like Bird, they wrote a great many letters. "The Roads Committee of the N.C.U. will emancipate the Metropolitan clubman from the thraldom of the road-making demon," reported a cycling magazine in 1886, and it would do so with the pen:

... it only required a polite letter from a member of the Roads Committee to bring forth a gang of men who promptly filled up the ruts and holes in the macadam ... In this matter ... persuasion would seem to be better than force.

If the act of writing one letter to a single surveyor could produce positive results, cyclists surmised that a great many communications could have an impact nationwide. The roads committees of the NCU and the CTC decided to pool resources and, in October 1886, they formed the Roads Improvement Association.

"This association has formed with the view of generally taking up the question of roads in the whole of the kingdom," wrote the new organisation's secretary in January the following year:

> The bad state of some roads ... is a disgrace to the authorities, and although the ratepayer is heavily taxed, the money expended is of little use through the employment of untrained men and their want of knowledge of the best and most economical system of repair. To the removal of this state of things the Roads Improvement Association will devote its best energies, undertaking ... prosecutions at law as a last resort when all other efforts have failed ... We are now issuing pamphlets fully dealing with the subject ...

Cannily, the Roads Improvement Association didn't advertise itself as a bicycle organisation – but it was clear who would benefit most from improved roads, a point made in the Badminton Library's 1887 book on cycling:

> ... the man who is dragged through ruts and over stones by the labour of his horse is not quite so keen in his appreciation of a bad road as the man who feels its effects in an aching spine and twisted muscles. So cycling roadsters, after a considerable amount of preliminary growling, have girded up their loins for action ...

The action consisted of pamphleting – the RIA built up a body of technical literature in order to emphasise the "scientific" methods of creating and improving roads. These books and pamphlets were sent in their hundreds of thousands to newspapers, highway surveyors and members of highway boards "showing them that by the adoption of a system such as is sketched out in the pamphlet, far better roads can be obtained at an expenditure of much less money than is at present spent upon the majority of our Highways."

The RIA had been seed-funded with cash from individual cyclists. Local cycling clubs also provided funding. The RIA's annual report of 1890 acknowledged this support from cyclists and their clubs, but pointed out that the "work of the Association is to secure better roads throughout the kingdom, not for Cyclists only, but for the general body of the Public ..."

The RIA's literature included *The Roads Improvement Association – Its Teaching Confirmed* by Thomas Codrington, the Roman-roads expert who had acted for cyclists in the Halesowen court case.

The RIA also produced 2-inch iron gauge rings, stamped with the name of the Association, which were supplied to surveyors and road men to measure stones for use in making macadam roads.

The first patrons of the RIA were aristocrats interested in cycling. Lord Thring was the First Parliamentary Counsel from 1869 to 1901, an innovator in the framing of legislation. Viscount Curzon was a Conservative politician who served as Treasurer of the Household between 1896 and 1900. The Duke of Fife was the Lord Lieutenant of Elginshire from 1872 to 1902 and married into the British Royal Family. The Earl of Albemarle was Under-Secretary of State for War between 1878 and 1880 and co-wrote the Badminton Library book on cycling. Earl Russell, the elder brother of the philosopher Bertrand Russell (who was another keen cyclist), was the largest individual donor to the RIA in its pre-motoring days.

The RIA had some early successes. In its annual report for 1891 it was said that

> ... various Roads in the Parishes of Greenwich, Lee, and Lewisham, Berkshire and West Riding of Yorkshire, have been repaired and improved through the efforts of the Association ... A Yorkshire correspondent writes as follows:- "The branch roads over the hills in the West Riding have been put into superb condition and are a treat to ride on."

The report for 1892 stated

> The bad condition of many of our roads and the rough way in which they are often repaired is a disgrace to the authorities, and although much good has already been done by the Association in an unobtrusive way, it still has much to do ...

This "unobtrusive way" lasted for some years but it was to be overhauled by two cycling officials who turned the RIA into a very effective political lobbying organisation – William Rees Jeffreys of the CTC and Robert Todd of the NCU.

"Automotor Journal" (Yellow Cover) Copyright Photo.

At the R.A.C. Norwich Meet.—The Hon. C. S. Rolls and Mr. Robert Todd watch the events from the "ropes."

Robert Todd was a pioneer motorist as well as a long-time official with a cycling organisation. Here he is with Rolls–Royce co-founder Charles Rolls at a motor meet.

TODAY, REES Jeffreys is known as an arch motorist, but he started his 50-year career in the improvement of what he called "despaired and neglected roads" as a cyclist. In 1900 he was elected a member of the Council of the Cyclists' Touring Club and was a representative on the Council of the RIA. By 1901 he was secretary of the RIA and – along with Robert Todd, president of the NCU and chairman of the RIA – argued that the organisation should rein back its pamphleting and should, instead, focus on political lobbying. Rees Jeffreys and Todd wanted the CTC, the NCU and the RIA to push for a "Central Highway Authority and a State grant for highway purposes."

In 1901, a deputation from the RIA and other bodies visited Walter Long, the President of the Local Government Board, to hand in their "proposals for certain administrative and legislative changes in the existing system of highway administration," said *The Times*. Those present were Todd and Rees Jeffreys as well as William Worby Beaumont, the RIA's vice-chairman and a former chairman of the Institution of Cycle Engineers; Ernest Shipton, secretary of the CTC; S. R. Noble, secretary of the NCU; Colonel Crompton; and O. E. Beatty, vice-chairman of the CTC. There were also two representatives from the Automobile Club – in 1901, the RIA was still mainly a bicycle-based organisation (although the cycling officials on the board were also now motorists). NCU president Todd would remain as RIA chairman until 1908.

In 1902, the RIA wrote to Prime Minister Arthur Balfour requesting an inquiry into highways administration. Balfour was a keen motorist but in the late 1890s he had been a keen cyclist – for a time he had been president of the NCU. Attached to the letter to Balfour were the names of MPs who were in favour of the inquiry. Many were motor-car-owning MPs but some were still cyclists.

Lord George Hamilton, Conservative MP for Ealing, supplied a first-person statement: "Lord Geo. Hamilton, as a cyclist, is also much interested in the state of the roads, and any proposal likely to improve their administration will have his sympathetic support."

Sir James Fortescue Flannery was both an MP and a member of the CTC. Regarding the inquiry, he told the *CTC Gazette*:

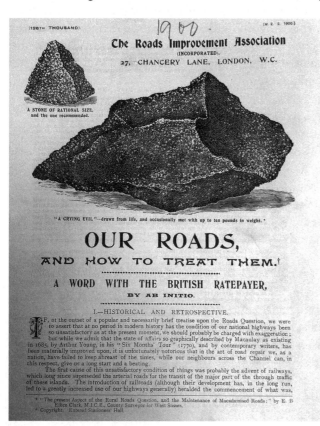

> The tendency of modern progress is in the greater use of highways, greater freedom for that use and greater efficiency of the highways themselves. The question has an important bearing … upon the comfort and convenience of cyclists, of whom I am one … I shall very cordially support the proposal for a full inquiry into the condition and possibilities of improvement of roadways.

The RIA's lobbying eventually paid off in 1903, with the Government starting an inquiry into the "Existing System of Highway Administration". The first witness before this inquiry was the RIA's Rees Jeffreys, who stated that his cycling credentials were superior to his motoring ones. Cycling bodies still provided most of the RIA's funding. As well as being led and funded by cycling officials, much of the practical work carried out by the RIA was done by cyclists. Technical data put before the 1903 parliamentary committee was provided by cyclists – they supplied information on road surfaces and the location of tramlines. Cyclists also mapped road stewardship, plotting which local authorities looked after which stretches of road.

In the *CTC Gazette*, Rees Jeffreys said the inquiry's terms of reference were "everything that could be desired from the cyclist's point of view."

He added: "To no class in the community are good roads so important as to cyclists."

Perhaps so, but Rees Jeffreys clearly had a different road user in mind when, in the inquiry, he pushed for the provision of a wide boulevard around London, and wide roads radiating out of all Britain's major cities. In the opinion of Rees Jeffreys – an opinion shared by other cycling organisation officials – the provision of wider, straighter roads for motorists would free up space for slower road users on the "ordinary" roads of Britain. This was a false hope because to restrict freedom of passage to motorists was never seriously considered by Parliament. Instead, in just a short space of time, cyclists – and pedestrians – became alien and undesirable users of British roads. Alien and undesirable to motorists, that is. Motoring may have been hand-cranked into life by cyclists but this contribution was all but forgotten by the 1920s as cycling morphed into a proletarian form of transport.

Earlier, the contribution was still fresh in the minds – of academics, at least. In 1913, highway-history experts Sidney and Beatrice Webb wrote that:

> It was the bicyclist who brought the road once more into popular use for pleasure riding; who made people aware both of the charm of the English highway and of the extraordinary local differences in the standards of road maintenance; and who caused us all to realise that the administration, even of local byways, was not a matter that concerned each locality only, but one in which the whole nation had an abiding interest.

The Webbs recounted that in the twelve years between 1890 and 1902,

> … when the traffic was still almost wholly made up of horse-drawn vehicles and pedal bicycles, the total expenditure on main roads in rural districts was nearly doubled, the mileage being greatly increased and the annual cost per mile rising from £43 to £66. The total expenditure in these years on main roads in urban districts was more than quadrupled, the annual cost per mile rising from £49 to £207 … The increase in the aggregate road expenditure in England and Wales, between 1890 and 1902, outside London and the County Boroughs, was no less than 86 per cent.

This huge increase in spending on the roads of Britain cannot be pinned solely on the campaigning efforts of cyclists, but their agitation would have had some effect. Historians tend to emphasise, instead, the creation in 1888 of county councils, which gained much jurisdiction for main roads, and levied a charge on ratepayers for upkeep of these highways. However, there were thousands of road boards spread throughout Britain – there was no single, overarching roads body. The cycling-based RIA supplied technical literature to the new county councils and wrote to all of the new county councillors spelling out their new powers – and duties – where roads were concerned.

If it's hard to pin the increased spending on the efforts of cyclists, one thing is certain: the funding increases came before motorists arrived on the scene.

The overarching roads body finally became a reality in 1909 with the creation of the Road Board, the first central authority for British roads since Roman times. The first secretary of the Road Board was former cycle tourist Rees Jeffreys, who resigned from the RIA to take up his new post. Rees Jeffreys had started campaigning for such a body while he was still an official at the CTC but the reality, when it came, was not all he had hoped for. The Road Board – funded by the Road Fund – was led by a railway executive, and made very few of the new roads Rees Jeffreys champed at the bit to get built. The bulk of the monies raised by the tax on motoring – or "road tax" – were spent on resurfacing work.

Such improvements to the roads definitely benefitted motorists. The CTC would remain part of the RIA until 1933 but, by then, cycling was considered working class and, even though cyclists were still the majority users of roads, the reorganised RIA became mainly interested in provision for motorists. Rees Jeffreys became one of the leading champions of motorways, but he didn't forget his cycling roots or that cyclists had been the first and most vociferous road reformers. In his 1949 autobiography he reminded readers that "Cyclists were the class first to take a national interest in the conditions of the roads."

CHAPTER NINE

"THE MECCA OF ALL GOOD CYCLISTS"

*Of all stretches of highway popular amongst cyclists, the Ripley Road, without dispute,
is by far and away the most famous ... The Ripley Road is known, at least by name, to
cyclists in every part of the globe; and particularly in the case of American wheeling
visitors ... a "run to Ripley" figures as surely on their programme, as
does a trip to Stratford upon Avon.*
THE HUB, 1896

**For the final 30 years of the 19th century, Ripley in Surrey – a short ride from London – was
the go-to destination for the smart set of the day. The 10 miles between the Angel Inn
at Thames Ditton and the Anchor Hotel at Ripley were world-famous, and busy with
cyclists on all manner of machines. Many of those who would go on to become influential motor
magnates cycled along the "Ripley Road" and, years later, would gather for nostalgic reunions.**

On Whit Sunday 1894, the police in Kingston upon Thames said that 20,000 cyclists had passed
through, en route to Ripley. An exaggeration perhaps, but an indication that Ripley was – according
to Viscount Bury in 1887 – the "Mecca of all good cyclists."

Thanks to the "votaries of the wheel," long-neglected roads came to life again. Certain roads became
famous, and none more so than the Ripley Road, part of the old Portsmouth Road, from London to
what was England's chief naval seaport. Twenty-three miles distant from Westminster Bridge, Ripley
was the perfect distance for a there-and-back ride for metropolitan "cracks" on their fast and trendy
high-wheeler bicycles.

Prior to the coming of the railways, 23 stagecoaches had raced along the macadamised London-to-
Portsmouth turnpike road each day. Many of the coaches carried sailors on leave. Ripley was a staging
post that catered to the passing trade – with pub names such as the Anchor, the Ship and the Jolly Sailor.

Portsmouth could be reached by rail from 1841, with Woking taking the place of Ripley as the
area's post town twenty years later. Trains were faster, cheaper and more comfortable than stagecoaches.
"Railway mania" killed off the stagecoach trade, with formerly important towns, such as Ripley, bypassed.

Bicycles changed this. Roads, including the Ripley Road, came to life once more. Coaching inns in
particular welcomed the new trade, as described in a *Daily Telegraph* editorial in 1880:

Not the worst thing that they have done, these knights of the road, has been to rehabilitate

The Anchor at Ripley. The gentleman on the tandem appears to be cycle racer Selwyn Edge who went on to become an executive in the motor industry. Owner Mrs. Dibble is the stern looking lady in the central group; her son, Alf, is on her left.

and set on their legs again many of our old posting-houses and decayed hostelries all over the country. Bicycles have … taken the place of coaches; they frequent all our great main roads, and gladded the hearts of innkeepers, who look out for the tinkling bells which herald the advent of a 'club' of wandering velocipedists, just as they anticipated of yore the gladsome tootling of the horn that bespoke the approach of the Enterprize, the Highflyer, or some other well-known conveyance of the old coaching days.

Most riders to Ripley were gentlemen, moneyed and with leisure time. A trickle of riders in 1869 became a steady flow in 1870 and a torrent by the late 1880s.

The undulating Ripley Road was fast in parts – a good "scorching" road. The flattest, fastest stretch was at Fair Mile Common, near Cobham.

But the Ripley Road was beloved by 19th-century cyclists for reasons other than its speed alone. The road was charming and beautiful, dotted with clumps of Surrey pines on deserted commons. And the road was romantic: it passed Regency pleasure grounds and had been a famous haunt of highwaymen in pre-turnpike days. But, perhaps most important of all, the road was loved because of a pub: the Anchor. This was a 16th-century almshouse later converted into an inn. Thirty years after the almost complete death of the coaching trade, hotels such as the Anchor were down on their luck. The Anchor, however, had a resourceful owner, a widow named Mrs. Dibble. Two of her daughters worked in the inn and they were, by all accounts, attractive.

Cyclists were the first through traffic on rural roads since stagecoaches, and Annie and Harriet, their brother Alf and Mrs. Dibble bent over backwards to please the new arrivals. Ripley's Anchor hotel became the honeypot location on a honeypot road, most especially on Sundays.

The Anchor was seen by cyclists as a beam-ceilinged throwback to simpler times. The early cyclists were the dominant users of the white Portsmouth Road, and thought themselves in a rural idyll, a far cry from their life in a city of grime. (Thanks to soot, even London's mud was black.)

Cycles were machines of escape; they offered independent means of locomotion out of overcrowded cities and, importantly, away from villages and towns being enlarged and "improved" by railways. A jaunt into the countryside appealed to upper- and middle-class Victorians, who had a rosy, romantic view of agrarian "old England", which was disappearing before their eyes. The rural aesthetic – promoted by thinkers such as John Ruskin – inspired many Victorians. Watercolour artist Myles Birket Foster painted arcadian scenes of smock-wearing yokels in front of tumbledown cottages – Cadbury's used his paintings on their packaging, his was a genuine "chocolate box" style. He lived in Witley, just off the Portsmouth Road, ten miles from Ripley, and many of his sentimentalised portraits of the English countryside featured (a largely fictitious) Surrey.

Victorians were keen to experience Birket Foster's "untouched" and "natural" countryside for themselves. The birth of the weekend – when middle-class Victorians had time for play – saw an explosion in recreational activities, such as sightseeing and taking part in sports. Not coincidentally, cycling combined these two passions.

The Popular Recreator of 1873 had a section on cycling. Writer Charles E. Innes described a social ride he had undertaken along the Portsmouth Road:

> Before descending the hill leading from Ockham Common, let us rest a few minutes to enjoy the glorious sunset over Bolder Mere, with its dark background of firs, and the surrounding gorse lit up a sea of gold, for we may travel many a mile on our way ere we view a lovelier scene.

Bolder Mere is still there, albeit much reduced, and many of the commons that would have been familiar to Victorian cyclists are still there too, although it's now necessary to tune-out the traffic noise from the six-lane A3 that today forms part of the "between the Houses" route from the Angel to the Anchor. The A3 is a motorway in all but name and London's tarmac tourniquet – the M25 – is another intrusion on the landscape described by Innes.

Many other authors of the day waxed lyrical about the scenic wonders of the countryside along the Ripley Road, creating a romantic legend – the "cult of the Ripley road" – that attracted cyclists to the road until they were squeezed off by motorists.

In *Coaching Days, Coaching Ways* in 1888, W. Oustram Tristram said back in the coaching days there had been a "constant throb of traffic on the direct Portsmouth Road." In 1888 there was "not much throb of traffic about … now."

The villages and towns on the old Portsmouth Road were now "suggestive of laudanum, mandragora, poppies, hop-pillows, and other sedatives."

The Portsmouth Road was also noted for its aristocratic pleasure grounds. These were not open to most of the passing cyclists – the National Trust wasn't founded until 1895 – but they would have been familiar landmarks to middle-class cyclists, and no doubt many unofficial visits were facilitated by the new means of locomotion. The pleasure grounds at Claremont, a country house close to Esher and bordering the Portsmouth Road, were an early example of English landscape gardens and had been worked upon by Sir John Vanbrugh and Lancelot "Capability" Brown. In 1726, the gardens were described as "the noblest of any in Europe."

The estate had once been owned by Robert Clive, one of the key instigators of Britain's Indian Empire. Claremont later passed into royal hands. Queen Victoria was a frequent visitor, both as a child and as an adult, and she bought the house and its grounds. In 1877, she presented nearby Esher with a drinking fountain and this would have been a favourite stopping point for cyclists doing a "run to Ripley." Sightings of Queen Victoria on the Ripley Road would have been relatively common. In July 1884, riders from the Holborn Cycling Club reported seeing the Queen on the Ripley Road at Claremont. She was in an open landau drawn by two horses. The cyclists were on the way back to London after tea at the Anchor and, upon seeing the Queen, they drew up in a line and saluted her. She "gracefully bowed her acknowledgements."

Another estate that bordered the Portsmouth Road was Painshill, which was visited by the likes of William Gilpin, the artist and author who popularised the "picturesque" landscape ethic; and John Adams and Thomas Jefferson, two of America's founding fathers, the second and third presidents of the USA.

Viscount Bury – president of the National Cyclists' Union – called Ripley "the Mecca of all good cyclists."

Painshill was created by the Hon. Charles Hamilton, an 18th-century gentleman MP who transformed the "accursed hill" into an internationally famous, naturally landscaped pleasure ground, and one that was planned to have a hermit.

There's no hermit at Painshill today but the gardens have been restored to their former glory. Another garden of note, just to the north of Ripley, is the world-renowned Royal Horticultural Society Gardens at Wisley. This was an experimental garden in the 1890s – it was owned by a treasurer of the RHS – and would have been known to green-fingered cyclists, some of whom no doubt stopped for a tour before lunching at the Anchor.

THE 30-YEAR use of the Ripley Road by cyclists was largely recreational but the first riders on the road had been racers. A party led by champion racer John Keen – a builder of high-wheel bicycles – is the first recorded use of the road by cyclists. Keen had started racing as early as 1869. He used the flat Fair Mile Common stretch of road in 1870 for a one-mile challenge match against a rider from Kensington. The 1884 visitor book for the Anchor has an entry by Keen, saying he had been frequenting the pub since 1870. But he wasn't attached to a single pub. In 1873 Keen and other riders met to discuss cycling matters in the Hut hotel, an alehouse overlooking Bolder Mere.

One of these matters was no doubt the state of the roads, including the once well-surfaced Portsmouth turnpike. The stretch between Claremont and Guildford was "copiously stoned", wrote friends of Keen in 1877, a reference to a lack of maintenance of the Ripley Road.

Road maintenance was done – or, usually, not done – by parishes and local ratepayers. In the 1890s, some of the cyclists who rode on the Ripley Road collected monies for "Road Menders' feeds", hot suppers for the old men who worked on the road between the Angel and the Anchor. The dinners were held from 1890 to 1908, with hundreds of road menders entertained, plied with tobacco and given half a pound of tea each.

Keen and his friends were interested in breaking records, so they needed the smoothest surface possible. They soon gravitated towards purpose-built cinder and wooden tracks. Recreational cyclists were more than happy with the surface of the Ripley Road. According to *The Boy's Own Paper*, the 1870s roads out of London towards Portsmouth were "rough" but the Ripley Road wasn't:

> Starting from Westminster Bridge, along the Albert Embankment, through Wandsworth, over Wimbledon Common, to Kingston, the road is all macadam, and rather rough riding. From Kingston to Esher the road improves, and chance through Cobham to Ripley, twenty-three miles from London, is very good, but rather hilly. Ripley is a delightful country place, six miles from a railway station, consequently free from excursionists. From Ripley to Guildford the road is splendid – six miles of the best roadway in England.

"Riding the Ripley Road" was so popular that it came in for criticism in some quarters. In 1885, *Wheel World* sniffed: "The Ripley Road craze is positively harmful to cyclists; men would be infinitely better in all respects for varying the direction of their journeyings."

This fell on deaf ears – the Ripley Road and the Anchor inn were key components in 19th-century cycling, in popular imagination, in the press and even indoor recreation – *Wheeling*, the board game, went through a number of editions from 1896, and featured the Anchor hotel as the game's destination.

The Anchor also inspired pedalling poets. E. S. Ward of the Zephyr Bicycle Club of Maida Vale penned this ditty, which he inscribed in the Anchor's visitors book in 1881.

> Whenever I take my rides abroad
> For this I'll allus hanker,
> That I'll be guided by the Lord
> to Ripley's famous Anchor.

A party of "20 or so" high-profile American cycle tourists – including journalists and politicians – rode the "historical ground of the far-famed Ripley Road" in June 1889. At least 100 English cyclists rode with them from London, with another 100 meeting them at the Angel at Thames Ditton, "and so into Ripley where 200 or 300 more cyclists were waiting our coming. In all there must have been 500 wheelmen present …" At the "flag-bedecked Anchor we pulled up our flying steeds" and the cyclists were hosted to a meal given by the Ripley Road Club "and then all repaired to the cyclists' church near by …"

JUST AS all roads once led to Rome, so most of the wheel marks on the Ripley Road – "the Appian Way of cycling," wrote American author Elizabeth Pennell in *Harper's Magazine* in 1897 – would once have led to the timber-framed Anchor inn. The metropolitan riders had to ride past other pubs to reach the smaller, cosier Anchor. The Talbot was run by elderly proprietors, so tended to attract a more sober crowd. The Hut at Bolder Mere was scenic but quiet. The Hautboy at nearby Ockham was popular for

The Anchor's Annie Dibble was "as comely as of yore".
Here she is serving at a cycling club dinner

raucous musical parties, but it was the Anchor that attracted the majority of cyclists.

Henry Sturmey's *The Cyclist*, first published in 1879, wrote of the Anchor's charm which "brought more cyclists to its portals than any other [bicycling hostelry]." The Dibble family were "as obliging a family to their customers as were ever collected together …" They had a "never-failing disposition to oblige with meals at all sorts of unearthly hours, and a wonderful patience to the noisiness of athletically-trained youths in general."

This out-of-hours service – which was meant to be offered to all by innkeepers, who, it was thought by travellers, ought to be happy to be dragged from their beds – was famous among local cyclists, one of whom wrote in 1877:

> I pulled up at the Anchor … and asked what I could eat. Answered the fair Annie "Cold ham, cold mutton, cold beef." "Anything hot?" asked I. "Mustard," said she, and scored one.

Annie, then 22, was the prettier of the two Dibble sisters. In an 1880 article in *The Wheel World*, racer Harry J. Swindley wrote about bowing "at the throne of beauty" – thought to be a reference to Annie. She was raved about by the riders ("… as comely as of yore" and "divine fair") but Annie never married,

139

perhaps kept too busy catering to the hundreds of cyclists who descended on the hotel at the weekend. Historian Les Bowerman, author of *The Romance of the Ripley Road*, has researched the Dibble family and has often wondered why Annie Dibble wasn't married off to one of the many rich young gentlemen who sang her praises:

> They were a strange old lot, those Victorians, with their class distinctions. I guess it was a question of amateur gentlemen as opposed to ladies in trade. On one occasion, at Christmas, a bit of "squeezing" was recorded, but that seems to have been as far as it went. Generally speaking, they seem to have kept to their allotted roles.

Charles Harper, author of a nostalgic series of 1890s road history books, said that the Ripley Road was the "most frequented by cyclists of any road in England … an almost inconceivable number take a journey down these twenty-three miles from London, and back again in the evening", but he disapproved of club cyclists, and women in Rational dress:

> The Ripley Road … is the stalking-ground of self-advertising long-distance riders, of cliquey and boisterous club-men, and of the immodest women who wear breeches awheel.

Riding in a long skirt was difficult. The Rational Dress Society promoted knickerbocker suits, deemed too masculine by some. But *Cycling* reported in 1895 that "Rational dress is winning the battle between convention and comfort on the Surrey roads."

In 1898, Viscountess Harberton, president of the Western Women's Rational Dress Association, was refused luncheon in the coffee-room at the Hautboy & Fiddle in Ockham, close to the Ripley Road, because she had arrived on her bicycle wearing "exceedingly baggy knickerbockers reaching below the knee." Lady Harberton left the hotel in a huff and lodged a complaint with the Cyclists' Touring Club, which listed the Hautboy as one of the rider-recommended hostelries of the area. The CTC took legal action against the landlady of the Hautboy, Mrs. Martha Sprague, and a trial took place in 1899. Mrs. Sprague was acquitted. The CTC lost this particular case (in law books it is known as *Regina v Sprague*) but the fight for women's rights went on – woods close to the Ripley Road were later the destination for rides to support the suffragette movement.

Part of the fight for women's rights was featured in H. G. Wells' *The Wheels of Chance*. The novel's hero was Hoopdriver, an upwardly-mobile cycle tourist, who falls for Jessie, a young lady wearing "Rational dress". The two ride together on the Ripley Road:

> Mr. Hoopdriver … rode on in the direction of Ripley, along an excellent but undulating road. He was pleased to find his command over his machine already sensibly increased …

As Hoopdriver rode "swaggering along the Ripley road", he came to the Anchor inn (Wells renamed it the Unicorn for the novel) and "after propping his machine outside the door" he talked to the barmaid about the "weather, of the distance from London, and of the excellence of the Ripley Road."

Ripley later appeared in H. G. Wells' more famous novel, *The War of the Worlds*, an epic about a Martian invasion of Earth:

> It was this howling and firing of the guns at Ripley and St. George's Hill that we had heard at Upper Halliford. The Ripley gunners … fired one wild, premature, ineffectual volley, and bolted … through the deserted village, while the Martian, without using his Heat-Ray,
> walked

The start of the "between the Houses" ride (with the "Houses" being public houses, i.e., pubs) was the Angel Inn in Thames Ditton. Note the workshop on the right – it's the bicycle manufacturing premises of former cycle racer John Keen. The photograph was taken in the mid-1890s yet some riders are still using penny farthings, ten or so years after the introduction of the Safety bicycle.

serenely over their guns, stepped gingerly among them, passed in front of them, and so came unexpectedly upon the guns in Painshill Park, which he destroyed.

Did H. G. Wells, who often rode in the area, flatten Painshill Park because he hated the climb?

The War of the Worlds was first published in serial form in *Pearson's Magazine* in 1897. This was the peak year for cycling on the Ripley Road. The boom years of 1896 and 1897 were followed by a market crash, and cycling slowly withered. This fading to grey wasn't caused by the arrival of motor cars, but motor cars certainly made the Ripley Road – and all other roads in England – less inviting to cyclists.

By 1909, motor traffic was well on the way to strangulating Ripley, as described by Eric Parker in *Highways and Byways in Surrey*: "The Ripley road, for the two days in the week when it is most used, is a place to avoid … Ripley itself, but for the traffic, would be the prettiest village on the road …"

Dust – thrown up by speeding cars – stayed in the air longer and longer as more and more motorised vehicles used the road. Jessie Pope, a humorist and long-time contributor to *Punch*, found little humour in the coming of the motor car. Her 1904 poem "Motor Martyrdom" did not hide her disgust:

> I never have clung to a motor car,
> Or crouched on a motor bike.
> Worry and scurry, clank and jar
> I cordially dislike.
> I do not care for grimy hair,

For engines that explode,
But of one and all I've the put and call,
For I live on the Ripley Road.

I drank the country breeze at first,
Unsoiled by fetid fumes,
But now I am cursed with a constant thirst
That parches and consumes.
I am choked and hit with smoke and grit
When I venture from my abode;
My pets are maimed and my eyes inflamed,
For I live on the Ripley Road.

Motorists were not just guilty of creating dust clouds – they also forced riders from their bicycles, as attested by this report from a cycling club newsletter in 1912: "Sal turned up to tea, cursing motors in general and with great particularity those which had driven him into the gutter."

Another cyclist wrote of seeing, near Wisley Hut, "a motor wreck – no uncommon sight on the Portsmouth Road these days."

Use of the phrase Portsmouth Road, and not Ripley Road, is instructive. By 1914, Ripley was no longer a destination, but rather a dusty bottle-neck on what would be named, in the 1920s, the A3 between London and Portsmouth.

By the 1970s, the congestion was so bad that a bypass was built and Ripley became a backwater again. Six miles of today's "between the Houses" route would be largely recognisable by the cyclists of the 1890s, but the Hut at Bolder Mere was swept away in 1976 by builders of the bypass. This obliterates much of the route to Esher 1890s cyclists would have known. Today's cyclists have to make do with a narrow, poorly-maintained, fits-and-starts cycleway.

CHAPTER TEN

GOOD ROADS FOR AMERICA

Good roads is what I'm wishin' for,
An' me and many a pard
Is allus keepin' on the stir
To wear 'em smooth and hard.
BICYCLING WORLD & L.A.W. BULLETIN, 1897

The push to pave America was started in the 1880s by cyclists who wanted smooth roads. The "Goods Roads" movement snowballed before the introduction of motor cars.

On May 26th, 1927 Henry Ford watched the 15 millionth Model T trundle off the assembly line at his factory in Highland Park, on the outskirts of Detroit. This "everyman automobile" had made Ford into one of America's wealthiest men. With him on that spring day – as well as a throng of pressmen – was his son Edsel, president of the Ford Motor Company since 1919. In a stage-managed move, Edsel drove the car and his domineering father to the front of the world's largest factory. The Model T was lined up for a photograph next to Henry Ford's first motor car, the bicycle-based Quadricycle of 1896.

A statement released to the press present at the photo-shoot lauded the Model T as the "pioneer" automobile, and claimed there had been "no conscious public need of motor cars when we first conceived it." The statement stressed that the "Ford car ... started the movement for good roads."

All three of these claims were false. In truth, the Model T was one of *many* pioneer motor cars; the market for motor cars existed long before the Model T's launch in 1908; and the movement for Good Roads certainly did *not* start with Henry Ford, his Model T or, for that matter, any automobile. The movement for Good Roads had been started by cyclists some years before the first motor car on American soil coughed into life.

The Ford Motor Company's press officers and advertising copywriters – working from interviews with Henry, and with copy approval from Edsel – had rewritten history, not just glossing over cycling's contribution to America's fast-improving road network, but deliberately and cynically obliterating all mention of the heavy lifting done by cyclists.

Production of the mythological Model T was ended the day after the Ford photo-shoot. A $1.3-million advertising campaign was rolled out on the following day to prepare the ground for a new car. The advert on May 28th was placed simultaneously in hundreds of American newspapers. Word for word, it repeated the false claims from the press statement.

In the days after Henry Ford's advertisement appeared in national papers, the false claims were restated by Ford dealers across the land in regional newspaper stories, including the *Hartford Courant* in Connecticut. This newspaper, like all the others, repeated the line that the Model T had "started the movement for good roads". Of all the newspapers to repeat the lie, this was the one that should have known better. The original Good Roads movement had been largely seed-funded from Hartford, as it was the home city of the Columbia-brand bicycle, produced in the factories owned by Colonel Albert Pope, the most committed supporter of Good Roads literature and promotions.

The Ford Motor Company wasn't the only automobile manufacturer to make false claims about the Good Roads movement. Five years before Ford's advert, John Jakob Raskob, the chief accountant at General Motors claimed:

> The automobile was born into a roadless world ... In [the Good Road] movement the automobile has been the most powerful missionary, emphasizing as nothing else has done the universal advantage to be derived from highways.

In 1954, PhD student Phillip Mason interviewed Christy Borth, director of the Automobile Manufacturers' Association and a highways historian of some note. Borth stated, yes, he was aware that cyclists *claimed* they had started the Good Roads movement but, he said, this claim was bunkum. The push for Good Roads had originated with the early automobile clubs, Borth stated categorically, predating the claims in Ford's advertisement.

In 1927, Ford's claims had met with little dissent. Richie G. Betts, editor of *Bicycling World* in the 1890s, was one of the few to offer a counterpoint. He complained to *The New York Times*:

> In the announcements heralding his new car, Henry Ford asserts that his famous Model T started the good roads movement in this country. In the interests of accuracy it is well to recall ... that the good roads movement arose not from the Model T or any other motor car, but from the bicycle ... The movement ... was started, sponsored and aggressively pushed by the once powerful League of American Wheelmen, which ... had good roads committees in practically every State in the Union, which published a good roads magazine, which was responsible for unlimited propaganda and for not a few laws ...

Just over a week later, *The New York Times* printed a response from the writer Frank Parker Stockbridge. He agreed that Henry Ford was not the "Father of Good Roads." Stockbridge said the real originator was Amos G. Batchelder, the long-time executive secretary of the American Automobile Association:

> Mr. Batchelder decided to launch a movement for Federal aid for good roads. Late in 1911 he asked me to assist him ... The first Federal appropriation for road building since the 1840's was passed by the Congress then in session ...

This was partly true but what Stockbridge failed to disclose was that Batchelder had earlier been an official with the League of American Wheelmen. Stockbridge, too, was yet another wheelman-turned-motorist.

A quarter of a century earlier, motorists had no qualms about crediting cyclists for the rapidly improving roads. George E. Walsh, a regular contributor to America's *The Automobile* magazine wrote, in 1902: "The effect of the bicycle on road improvement has been ... phenomenal in the past 10 and 15 years ..." and added,

> Directly and indirectly the bicycle has been the means of interesting capital in road building

Henry Ford and his son Edsel lean on the 15th millionth Model T as they stare at the bicycle-based Quadricycle.

to the extent of millions of dollars, and of spreading abroad more accurate and scientific data concerning road construction than was ever before done in so short a time. The bicycle practically paved the way for automobiling.

THERE WAS one claim in the Ford advert that *was* true: many American roads prior to 1905 had, indeed, been bad. Some were so bad they were described as:

Wholly unclassable,
Almost impassable,
Scarcely jackassable.

Journeys on such roads could be pitifully slow. Charles Paullin's 1932 *Atlas of the Historical Geography of the United States* plotted the time it took to travel on roads from New York in 1800 and in 1830. A journey to Detroit would have taken a month in 1800. After road improvements prior to the 1830s the journey time was halved. Paullin also plotted the journey times in 1857, by which point the US had developed the makings of a coast-to-coast rail network – the trip to Detroit now took just over a day. Paullin didn't include a map of road travel after 1857 but travel time fell backwards because, for long-distance travel, going by rail was by far the preferred and quickest option. Many of those roads built, or reasonably well-maintained, during the American turnpike- and plank-road eras were allowed to decline.

However, not every American road was dire. The author of a 1900 book that took a nostalgic look at New England's stagecoach days said: "… roads in the northern provinces, on the whole, were excellent. [The] great use of pleasure carriages [was] proof of good roads; in 1753 Massachusetts had about seven such carriages to every thousand persons. English carriages were very heavy. In America we adopted the light-weight continental carriages – because our roads were good."

From the chatter of American cyclists in cycling journals of the late 1870s and early 1880s, it's clear that many areas had excellent roads, praised as exemplars to other areas.

Lawyer, author and early cycling promoter Charles E. Pratt, writing in 1879, listed those cities that were perfectly suited to the "birotate chariot", his rather lovely phrase for a bicycle:

> I can say that most of the roads in the New England States, and especially about the principal cities and villages, and also the streets about Philadelphia, Wilmington, Washington, St. Louis, Cleveland, Buffalo, Albany, New York, Brooklyn, Newark, and their suburbs, are well suited for bicycling travel; and I am informed that Denver, Detroit, Chicago, Toronto, Sacramento, San Francisco, and many other cities, with their surrounding towns, offer good running for the birotate chariot.

Wheelmen of the 1880s loved Washington, D.C.'s asphalte streets and wanted other American cities to emulate them. In 1889, prospective delegates to a national meeting of the League of American Wheelmen were told that Hagerstown, Maryland had roads of a "very superior character", which made for a "cyclers' paradise":

> … eight superb limestone pikes radiate from Hagerstown … while intersecting pikes and cross roads form a network of thoroughfares for wheelmen that realizes the stereotyped phrase of cyclers' paradise. These pikes are of that smooth sand-papered kind that entrance the wheelman, while his surroundings of scenery and sweet odors from nature's garden make his runs veritable trips through fairy land …

However, these were exceptions and most late 19th-century American roads were poorly maintained, and often not very well made in the first place. Writing in 1891, the L.A.W.'s Isaac B. Potter complained that roads were guilty of

> … dissolving in the rains of April, baking and pulverizing beneath the rays of the midsummer sun, drifting and disappearing in the whirlwinds of November, and presenting at all times but little more than a roughened streak of soil to serve as a land highway …

The "depravity of … American roads" did not deter everybody, as was demonstrated by a group of hardy cyclists who undertook a relay ride from Chicago to New York in 1892. They managed to average almost ten miles per hour, even though "there were places in Ohio where the mud and mire actually reached to the knees, compelling the boys to carry their wheels on their backs," commented a bicycle magazine, adding …

> This long ride through such knee deep mud-roads as the plucky riders had to contend with, ought to be the incentive power to arouse the legislators of our country and the average

countryman to the crying demand of civilization for better roads … It has also shown the metallic courage and endurance that "bicycle dudes" are made up of … This ride may have the effect of setting legislators and farmers to thinking.

"Bicycle dudes" had long been painfully aware of highway shortcomings, as shown by this 1884 ditty about a hapless high-wheeler:

> He went for a peaceable roll;
> His wheel took a piece of a hole,
> And it soon came to pass
> That a requiem mass
> Was sung for the peace of his soul.

At least that fictional cyclist had a surface of sorts, even if it was a rough and lethal one. Rural roads in the winter were sometimes so glutinous that wagons couldn't hope to progress along them and many farmers retreated into enforced hibernation, unable to move until the mud was made solid by the cold. (Freezing temperatures resulted in other challenges, of course.) Horse riders may have been able to fight their way through muddy roads that cyclists and wagons could not, but the mud was sometimes so deep that even horses couldn't get through. Many major cross-country roads were little better in Victorian times than in the days of the Founding Fathers. One tale – obviously apocryphal because it appears in a variety of forms in a number of US states and from different periods – poked fun at the amount of mud that travellers might be expected to meet:

> Several strangers … started out on the road from Detroit to Pontiac and were winding their way over bogs and around stumps, and in constant danger of being swallowed up in the mire. One of the men, a little in advance of the rest of them, discovered what he thought to be a good beaver-hat lying on the road. He ventured to secure the hat by wading out, more than knee deep, to the spot. He seized the hat and, to his surprise, discovered a live man's head under it. The stranger in the mire declined assistance saying, "Just leave me alone. I have a good horse under me and have just struck bottom. Go on, sir, and leave me alone."

Horatio "Good Roads" Earle, Michigan's first highway commissioner, made it his mission to dethrone this "mighty monarch mud, who rules the road to the exclusion of everyone." Earle had earlier been President of the League of American Wheelmen. For any Gilded Age individual with an abiding interest in improving American roads the best organisation to join was the L.A.W.

THE LEAGUE of American Wheelmen was formed on May 31st, 1880 in the resort of Newport, Rhode Island, the epicentre of Gilded Age high society. The three prime movers were high-wheel bicycle importer Frank Weston and patent attorney Charles E. Pratt, both of Boston, and Kirk Munroe, a New York writer, adventurer and conservationist. Before the meeting Pratt wrote that the gathering of 31 club representatives at Newport "would offer a suitable occasion for organising a Wheelmen's Protective League, which should combine the best points of the Bicycle and Tricycle Touring Club in England."
The L.A.W. was extensively modelled on the Cyclists' Touring Club. (The traffic wasn't all one way – later the CTC's winged wheel logo with medieval-style lettering was a blatant copy of the L.A.W. logo.)
From the very beginning, the League was a supremely well-organised political body, not just a

The L.A.W. BULLETIN.

A Journal devoted to the interests of Cycling in America.   Published weekly.

THE OFFICIAL ORGAN OF THE LEAGUE OF AMERICAN WHEELMEN.

$1.00 A YEAR.
3 CENTS PER COPY.

Philadelphia, July 2, 1885.

VOLUME
NUMBER

fraternal club-of-clubs. Pratt was elected the organisation's first president. There was also a vice-president, a commander, corresponding and recording secretaries, a treasurer and two representatives from each state. This structure was closely replicated at the state and city levels – the interconnectedness allowed the L.A.W. to communicate swiftly to its large and influential membership. When the occasion demanded it, legislators could be bombarded with letters and telegrams in much the same way as today's cycle advocacy groups can summon a deluge of emails and tweets.

The original L.A.W. constitution stated that its "objects shall be to promote the general interests of cycling; to ascertain, defend and protect the rights of wheelmen; to facilitate touring ..." In 1888, two years after the CTC and the NCU of Britain created the Roads Improvement Association, the L.A.W.'s constitution was amended so that wheelmen now also pledged "to secure improvement in the condition of the public roads and highways ..."

The desire to "secure improvement in the condition of the public roads" would have been a concern shared by almost all of the earliest L.A.W. members, but the first to go on record was Lewis J. Bates of Michigan, editor of the Detroit *Post and Tribune.* He introduced the topic at the second annual meeting of the league, held in Boston in 1881. Bates described the bicycle as "one of the great benefits conferred on this country in that it educated young men to know the difference between a good road and a bad one ..." He urged the L.A.W. to create a good-roads campaign. Committee members and the members-at-large agreed with his sentiments but preferred, initially, to argue only for the right of cyclists to use public roads. Bates kept prodding – he wrote two good-roads polemics in *The Wheelman* in 1882, predicting that the political influence of cyclists would grow and that the L.A.W. would be the leader of a great national movement. He penned an article for the mainstream magazine *Outing* in 1884, urging cyclists to impress upon political candidates the importance of improved highways.

Between 1884 and 1886 the L.A.W.'s house journal carried hundreds of letters responding to Bates' ideas on a good-roads campaign. In 1887, league officials recommended such a campaign should be afforded equal status to that of securing cyclists' rights, and the organisation of races. Finally, after a vote in 1888, members agreed unanimously to create and fund a standalone committee, the National Committee for Highway Improvement.

This committee, which was the nucleus of the later Good Roads movement, included individuals who were upstanding members of their local communities. Junius Emery Beal of Ann Arbor, Michigan, was publisher of the town's newspaper, and also later a state legislator in the Michigan House of

Representatives. Dr. Charles S. Butler of Buffalo was the committee's chairman until 1893. In 1902, he was a committee member for a commemoration of the assassination of President McKinley at the Pan-American Exposition of 1901 in Buffalo.

One of the first tasks of the Highway Improvement Committee was the publication of a textbook, *Making and Mending Good Roads & Nature and Use of Asphalt for Paving*. 15,000 copies were printed. It was intended as a "text book upon road construction … designed for distribution among Legislators, Town, County and City officials."

The committee also had the "desirability of interesting", via letters, "bicycle manufacturers and dealers, roads construction companies, pavement companies, and steam roller … manufacturers in what we are doing."

There was an "immediate reply" from the president of the Barber Asphalt Paving Co. of New York, who "expressed very great interest in our work and a desire to contribute towards the expense." Amzi Barber donated $100. The International Pavement Co. of Baltimore also sent an "encouraging reply," and $50. However, bicycle-maker Gormully & Jeffery of Chicago (manufacturer of Rambler bicycles and, later, Rambler motor cars) "declined to give any assistance to the work … thus failing utterly to appreciate the work of the League in endeavoring to bring about an improved condition of the Public highways of our country."

In June 1889, Dr. Butler visited Colonel Pope in Boston. It was like pushing at an open door, with Pope supplying an immediate cash donation of $350 and the promise of a blank cheque for the future. "Go ahead with the work," Pope advanced, "and we will pay the whole or any part of the expense you desire."

CYCLISTS HAD launched their national crusade for improved roads for reasons of comfort and convenience. Lewis J. Bates wrote in 1882,

> the moment any person becomes a wheelman he is instantly and ardently convinced of the necessity for improved highways. Both his vote and his voice can be depended on … to support legislation to secure better roads and streets.

The intimate awareness of the quality of the running surface beneath their wheels meant that cyclists were ideally suited to surveying roads, a point made by Harvard geologist Nathaniel Southgate Shaler in his 1896 book on highway construction:

> … inspection of roads has of late become much easier because of the invention of the bicycle. This instrument not only provides swift transportation, but by its motion it indicates to the rider in a very effective manner the condition of the way it traverses.

ALMOST FROM the founding of the United States, there had been a lack of clarity over the subject of highway construction and maintenance, and whether roads should be paid for by the federal government, the states, counties, towns or individuals. Government, it was felt, must be kept small and limited, or it would become dangerous to liberty and to the people's welfare. To modern eyes it seems obvious that roads are nationally important – or at least that the strategically important highways ought to be considered so. But this was a minority view in the 19th century. Today's libertarians feel that transport matters should devolve to the states, counties and towns, but in the 19th century the majority of local and national legislators felt transport was the responsibility only of counties and towns. All roads were deemed to be local, not national, and, after the 1840s, when railways – a network that had been largely privately funded – were the most important means of long-distance communication, almost no federal money was spent on either building or repairing roads.

Cyclists were instrumental in starting the clamour to reverse this situation – they called for state and federal aid for roads, a radical platform for the time. In 1896, *Forum* magazine stressed that "good roads are inevitable ... and they are coming because the bicycle is creating an irresistible demand for them."

But not all cyclists were in favour of federal funding for roads. E. J. Shriver, an L.A.W. member and treasurer of the New York Bicycle Club in the late 1880s and early 1890s, believed that national funding for roads was "unconstitutional."

In an October 1889 issue of the L.A.W.'s weekly journal he lodged his opposition to the "new field of action of the League in ... urging upon Congress national improvement of highways."

He was also opposed to the idea, floated by other L.A.W. members, that unemployed men could be given gainful employment by working on roads:

> Should the League support the expenditure of ... money for the sake of giving employment, it must commit its members to the Socialistic doctrine that it is the business of the State to direct industry.

In the following week's journal, Albert Mott, Chief Consul of L.A.W.'s Maryland division, politely but cuttingly disagreed:

> Members of the L.A.W. advocating the building and maintenance of national roads ... is not in the least Socialistic ... that argument appears to be extremely far-fetched ... and is entirely unworthy of Mr. Shriver's bright intelligence, and very likely written without sufficient thought ... There is nothing political or partisan ... about [wishing for good roads].

Mott added that it was "good and patriotic policy" for the L.A.W. to mount a campaign to gain "internal improvements", such as federally funded roads.

But this was a largely urban view. Out in the countryside, most farmers thought differently. As there was no federal or state control of roads, their maintenance devolved to counties and towns – highways were deemed to be owned by those who lived beside them, and it was they who had to maintain them. Rural roads were therefore "owned" and maintained by farmers, who were deeply suspicious of outsiders using "their" roads, especially those "peacocks" on fancy bicycles riding out from the cities. (During the agricultural depression of 1893–4, farmers blamed their woes partly on urban elites and modern technology – the bicycle was emblematic of both.) As county roads traversed the properties of many farmers, their maintenance was shared. And where property is shared the "tragedy of the commons" often plays out. This is an economic theory according to which self-interested individuals behave contrary to a group's long-term best interests by depleting, overusing or neglecting a common resource. As English MP and enclosures specialist John Hales believed in 1581, "that which is possessed of manie in common is neglected by all." Or, as Colonel Pope put it three centuries later, "what's everybody's business is nobody's."

Pope believed this traditional and mostly rural view of roads stewardship ought to be overhauled. Farmers needed to be shown that it was in their economic best interests to have "their" roads in good shape year-round. Naturally, better rural roads would also benefit cyclists, and therefore Pope's business interests. Of all those entrepreneurs who funded the Good Roads movement over the years, Pope was the most consistent. He was also the most vocal, putting his mouth where his money was. For more than 30 years he toured the land, giving speeches about Good Roads, appearing before legislative committees and writing articles on the subject. Pope also endowed the first chair of civil engineering at the Massachusetts Institute of Technology, which was ground-breaking in more ways than one.

Private papers show that Pope believed he was influential within the League of American Wheelmen – money talks, after all – but at this remove it's unclear exactly how influential. The L.A.W. certainly became more active on Pope's favourite subject, but the betterment of roads was a shared concern. In 1889, the L.A.W.'s highway improvement committee drafted uniform legislation calling for the creation of state highway commissions, general taxation to pay for rural roads, and the development of highway surveys and plans. The legislation was put to the vote in nine states, and voted down in each one. "The farmers must bear the expense while bicyclists and pleasure-riding citizens will reap the larger benefits," pooh-poohed a Michigan farmers' organisation. The L.A.W.'s focus switched from draft legislation that could be construed to be only in the cyclists' interest to broader campaigning. "We must concentrate first on education, then agitation, and finally legislation," believed L.A.W. president James R. Dunn of Massillon, Ohio.

Under Dunn's presidency the league created, in 1891, the Roads Improvement Bureau. This became a powerhouse of information distribution – it published and mailed five million pamphlets, and secured the publication of scores of Good Roads articles in the leading magazines and newspapers of the day. Sterling Elliott, president of L.A.W. in the late 1890s, invented a labelling machine to speed up the mailings, and as discussed in chapter 14, behind the scenes, deals were done for the wheelmen to distribute their roads literature using the official government frank, lending their campaign legitimacy in the eyes of farmers. In 1892, with cash support from bicycle barons Pope and Albert Overman (both of whom later diversified into making motor cars) and George Bidwell, the League created the magazine, *Good Roads*. This "Illustrated Monthly Magazine Devoted to the Public Roads and Streets" was later merged with the weekly *L.A.W. Bulletin* and, at its peak in 1895, it had a monthly circulation of 75,000 and a sphere of influence many times this. The magazine was sent to L.A.W. members as well as surveyors, government officials, libraries, carriage-builders and farmers' organisations. In 1899, such was the clamour from newspapers for information on road reform that the L.A.W. created a National Press Committee composed of "practical newspaper men" throughout the US. The committee issued weekly bulletins on the League's Good Roads campaign to national and regional newspapers.

The L.A.W. spent a great deal of money and time trying to bring farmers on side, rather clumsily at first. League president Potter's 1891 polemic *Gospel of Good Roads* was well received in urban areas but less so in the countryside – it was patronising to farmers who were said to be "countryside bumpkins" fearful of technological change. Far more to the farmers' liking was *Must the Farmer Pay for Good Roads?* of 1898, in which Otto Dorner, the then chairman of the L.A.W.'s Highways Improvement committee (*see left*), advocated state aid for roads specifically to benefit farmers. "It is time to do away with the cruel injustice which places upon farmers … the entire burden of building highways for the whole people," he argued.

Dorner's 41-page booklet was mailed to farmers and others by the Department of Agriculture's Office of Road Inquiry. The first print run was 300,000 copies, but many more would be distributed over time. "The average farmer is inclined to resent any attempt to interfere with his road-building methods, which he considers peculiarly his own affair," wrote Dorner in *The Forum* magazine. "No reform, therefore, can be forced upon him."

However, thanks in part to Dorner's booklet,

> … the farmers of the United States are beginning to thoroughly appreciate the need [for] better highways; and the work of the League of American Wheelmen in the direction of State aid is receiving much support from the more progressive among them … The Farmers' National Congress … [commended] the efforts of the League of American Wheelmen to bring about the general introduction of the State Aid system.

The L.A.W's New York division – led by Potter – was successful in achieving an ambitious state aid programme for New York State's roads in 1898. This led to a rapid improvement of the state's highways – in the early 1900s New York State had the highest per-capita ownership of motor cars in America, due in no small part to the excellence of its newly improved highways, lobbied for by cyclists. Deputy State Engineer William Judson applauded the role of wheelmen at the meeting of the Third Annual Good Roads Convention, held in Albany in 1902. He said the L.A.W. was the

> … organization which began the good-roads movement in New York State, it being a matter of history that the original campaign for good roads was started in this state by the members of this organisation, and that the law under which we are working was passed by their influence.

As well as seeking state aid, the L.A.W. also officially adopted the position of seeking federal aid for America's roads. Starting in 1902, measures providing federal aid to roads were introduced at each session of Congress, culminating with the Federal-aid programme of 1916. The rudimentary Federal Aid Road Act was signed into law by cycle tourist and former L.A.W. member US President Woodrow Wilson.

WHILE COLONEL Pope part-funded and supported the L.A.W's work he had his own agenda. In 1889, he told a carriage-maker's convention that

> … the high point to be aimed at, is the recognition of the importance of the whole situation by the national government, and the establishment by Congress of a national system.

He then appealed to the carriage-builders' pecuniary interests:

> The farmer enjoying good roads will be a richer man on account of them, and have more money to buy your carriages, running into higher value (while his sons and daughters can have their bicycles and tricycles at less expense).

He rammed the point home: "Good roads mean for you and me better business." Join with us, he urged:

> We, who manufacture bicycles, feel that we have a right to fraternize with you … I feel that our interests in good roadways are equal and identical …

Wistfully, he then looked to the future:

> I hope to live to see the time when all over our land, our cities, towns and villages shall be connected by as good roads as can be found in the civilized world, and if we shall have been instrumental in bringing about this result, then indeed shall our children have cause to bless us.

Welcoming Pope's address to the carriage-builders, an editorial in the L.A.W.'s house journal reminded readers that members of the League – of whom there were 12,000 in 1889 – were no longer mere striplings: "The wheelmen of twelve years ago were many of them young men then, but they are middle aged men now, and they are in positions that give them influence."

However, Pope's call for carriage-makers to "divert a small percentage of [resources] … toward helping along in the good work" fell on deaf ears. They did not fund the Good Roads movement in any meaningful way. Pope pushed on without them. Throughout the 1890s he called in favours from powerful allies, including congressmen, governors and the Postmaster General – who wanted good "post roads" so that mail delivery could be expanded to even the most isolated of farms.

In 1895, *The New York Times* stated: "Already we owe very much to the wheelmen in improving roads both in town and in country … "

POPE'S 1889 idea for federal aids for roads and the creation of a national highway commission was not L.A.W. policy at the time – the organisation was still mostly working at the state level. The idea for national control of roads was borrowed from Britain's Roads Improvement Association and was fleshed out in speeches that Pope had printed and sent out to newspaper editors, politicians and eminent citizens.

In 1890, the cycle manufacturer George Bidwell introduced Pope to civil engineer General Roy Stone, who had studied at France's *École Nationale des Ponts et Chaussées* (National School of Bridges and Highways). Stone, too, believed that the Federal government should be responsible for the nation's roads. Stone and Pope initially got on like a house on fire, although their relationship cooled when Stone eventually landed the government highways promotional role that Pope may have been angling for all along. This role was given to Stone partly because of agitation organised by Pope. Stone preferred to work behind the scenes, while Pope was a populiser.

Through most of the 1880s and 1890s Pope was one of the key public faces associated with the demand for better roads administration. To Stone's annoyance, in 1892 Pope paid for and organised a petition requesting the creation of a federal Roads Department, among other things. 150,000 signatories appeared on Pope's petition (although it's clear from text on the petition form itself that Pope had been hoping for a million) and more than 1,000 newspapers endorsed it. Names were collected on individual sheets of paper printed by Pope and distributed by bicycle shops, newspapers, the L.A.W. and other

Pope's oversize petition is housed in the U.S. National Archives in Washington, D.C.

interested parties. These sheets were sent for collation to Pope's bicycle business in Hartford, Connecticut and combined into two rolls. The 1,400 yards of paper were coiled around two oak spools, and the giant petition was dramatically rolled into the Senate. The petition still exists, stored deep in the vaults of the National Archives in Washington, D.C. I've seen it – it's gloriously imposing.

Pope's petition was signed by the US Chief Justice and State Governors, and was endorsed by banks, large corporations, boards of trade, labour organisations and a future US president – but Pope's request for a Road Department was only partially granted.

A clause in an agriculture bill in 1893 created the Office of Road Inquiry and granted it funds. $10,000 wouldn't pay for building any roads, but it did pay for road research. The ORI's first chief was General Stone. His organisation, largely willed into being by cyclists, constructed short stretches of "object lesson" roads to show that excellence was possible. Despite the ORI being a federal department, the L.A.W. subsidised many of its activities and paid for some of its officials to attend Good Roads conferences and the like. (The ORI was founded six months before bicycle mechanic brothers Charles and Frank Duryea built the first American gasoline-powered motor car.)

While Pope did not – at first – succeed in getting a separate Roads Department, or federal aid for roads, a precedent had been set. The Office of Road Inquiry would eventually grow to become the Federal Highway Administration – roads were now lodged on the national, political agenda. The work of Pope and the L.A.W. helped to put the first federal mechanisms in place that would be used in the 1920s by the motor-dominated roads lobby to push for wider roads and, eventually, the Interstate highway system.

Writing about Pope's petition in 1894, Nathaniel Shaler wrote in *Harper's* magazine:

> The presentation of the great petition to Congress marks the last step in the effort of a number of men, of whom the most efficient has been Col. A. Pope, of Boston, to arouse the people to an understanding of the burden which their ill-conditioned highways impose upon them.

POPE'S PETITION wasn't the only one – the year after his, there was a "Petition of Boots". This was a proletarian protest march urging America's politicians to put unemployed men to work on federally funded roads. This was the first-ever protest march on Washington, D. C. and took place March to May 1894, organised by Jacob Sechler Coxey, a rich quarry owner from the same home town as the L.A.W.'s

James Dunn. There's no report of the two Massillon residents ever having met but, given their shared interest in road reform, such a meeting would have been likely.

"General" Coxey created the short-lived Good Roads Association of the United States. He told existing Good Roads advocates – mostly cyclists, of course – that instead of a Pope-style paper petition, he would organise something far more dramatic. His roads, he said, should be built by those put out of work by the "Panic" of 1893. This was a radical plan and not one likely to appeal to taxpayers or federal and state legislators. For a start, a great deal of what labour was expended on roads at that time was "free" – either statute "sweat equity" labour by farmers or manacled, slave-style labour by convicts in "chain gangs".

Coxey's grandiose plan would have swallowed the entire federal budget of the United States. (There's another fantasy element to Coxey's plan – one of those who observed the march was Lyman Frank Baum, the author of *The Wonderful Wizard of Oz* of 1900, and there's a theory that his movie-inspiring book is an allegory of Coxey's march.)

"Coxey's Army", a 500-strong group of unemployed men that the newly religious Coxey billed as the "Army of the Commonweal of Christ", walked 700 miles from Massillon to Washington, D.C. (Some rode bicycles; Coxey preferred his carriage.)

District of Columbia police, egged on by politicians, arrested Coxey and his lieutenant, Carl Browne (ostensibly for walking on the grass of the US Capitol) and dispersed the marchers.

The march generated a great deal of newspaper coverage, hardly any of it favourable. The most positive article on the march was written by one of Britain's leading political commentators, William Thomas Stead. His 1894 sketch of "Coxeyism and Its Commonwealers" in his *Review of Reviews* painted a vivid picture of the "sandwich men of Poverty".

"I met Browne at Chicago," wrote Stead. "I liked the man."

Browne told Stead about the plan for Good Roads:

> He discoursed to me copiously and energetically upon the importance of employing the unemployed in making good roads … I heartily agreed with him as to the desirability of utilising the wasted labour of the community in opening up the country by the construction of passable roads.

There's little surprise Stead would have been in favour of "passable roads" – back in Britain he was a very keen cyclist, and founder in 1893 of the Mowbray House Cycling Association, a high-society cycling club (see chapter 12). Stead's *Review of Reviews*, published in London, also carried articles on the L.A.W.'s Good Roads movement.

COXEY'S MONTH-LONG incarceration took the wind out of his sails – his march on Washington had achieved little but bad headlines. On the other hand, the slow-burn agitation by influential and persistent cyclists, while not as dramatic or confrontational as a well-publicised march, had a longer-lasting effect. Motoring interests, such as Ford and others, eventually took the credit for creating the Good Roads movement, but the real groundwork had been laid by cyclists, many of whom were "men of affairs, occupying high places in social and business life and exerting a wide influence in the several communities where they reside," claimed a writer in *Good Roads* in 1892.

> They command the respect of the entire country and are widely known, not only for their splendid services in the cause of road reform, but for the distinctive personal worth of which

their social and professional positions give evidence. They stand at the head of an organization, the largest, most active and most influential ever maintained for accomplishing a material improvement within the [nation] ...

In 1893, J. W. Stockwell, a farming lecturer at the Massachusetts State Grange, praised the L.A.W's hard work:

> To the cyclists belongs the honor of introducing the first bill for a radical change in road management. They had one object in view, better roads for the "wheel"; they had money and talent at their command ... they were courteous, and, in the truest sense of the term, gentlemen. It was delightful to meet men who, desiring legislation favorable to themselves, desired equal benefit to all and injury to none.

Putting such public-spiritedness into action, prominent members of the L.A.W. became board members of newly created state highway commissions. These bodies started to appear in the early 1890s, thanks in great part to the L.A.W.'s lobbying. The first was that of New Jersey, in 1891. The Massachusetts Highway Commission, founded in 1893, was led by cyclists. The first commissioner appointed was George A. Perkins, a member of one of the long-established and wealthy New England families. He later became Chairman of the Commission, in a position to implement many of the road policies he espoused when he was Chief Consul of the Massachusetts Division of the L.A.W. Perkins also gave lectures on road legislation to students in the Pope-funded Department of Civil Engineering at the Massachusetts Institute of Technology.

In 1893, Perkins wrote:

> Massachusetts has begun a movement which other states are sure to follow, and as in all great reforms she is bound to be in the van. All desire good roads, and they hope that the time is not far distant when the roads of Massachusetts and the other states, shall be as good as those of England and the European countries. [The L.A.W.] includes some of the most prominent public men of the nation ... For years it has carried on the agitation of the question of improved roads ...

The other two original members of the commission – Harvard's Nathaniel Shaler and road engineer William E. McClintock – were also L.A.W. members. In time the Massachusetts Highway Commission became the Massachusetts Department of Transportation. It was not the only embryonic state highway department to be initially dominated by League members. Michigan's first Highway Commissioner was L.A.W. president Horatio Earle. As mentioned earlier, Earle created the State Highway Department in 1905 when he was a State Senator (it is now the Michigan Department of Transportation). He was appointed as Highway Commissioner by Michigan's Governor, Colonel Aaron T. Bliss, yet another member of the L.A.W.

Earle was in charge of Michigan's roads during the early growth of motor manufacturing in Detroit. When he retired at the end of the 1920s, few knew he had started his highly productive roads career as an official with the L.A.W. When he had been made Highway Commissioner in 1905, the role of cyclists in highway history was already fading from memory. This had not been the case five years earlier. In 1900, the debt owed to cyclists was more obvious, and the early motorists – many of whom had been officials in the L.A.W. – relied on the innovations put in place by lovers of the birotate chariot. Road signs, maps, recommended hotels, improved highway surfaces and even motor cars themselves would not have been available to motorists in quite the same way without the pioneering work of cyclists.

George Isham Scott, writing in *The Automobile* magazine in 1900, described a motor-car trip from "New York to Washington and Back" that showed how motorists relied on the touring infrastructure left by cyclists:

> Leaving the ferry-boat we rolled through the streets of Jersey City, holding our first consultation with L.A.W. directions. A turn to the left on a long line of asphalt led us to the Boulevard and to the Plank Road, on which we rode to Newark … [Then] New Brunswick was reached, where an L.A.W. road-house offered hospitality.

In a 1903 article in *Munsey's Magazine*, Colonel Pope wrote that the bicycle had "attracted notice" to the "woeful condition of the public highways in this country."

Echoing almost exactly what he wrote when the bicycle was in the ascendancy some ten and more years previously, he opined: "The American who buys an automobile finds himself confronted with this great difficulty. He has nowhere to use it."

The solution in 1903 was the same solution he had proposed for bicycles in the 1880s and 1890s: "If the automobile is ever to become popular … it must first be provided with decent highways on which to run."

Tellingly, he added that the "representatives of automobiling have been content to take a secondary place in the agitation [for good roads]."

This did not last.

THE LEAGUE of American Wheelmen founded the Good Roads movement, but the cyclists' organisation had been canny enough to build relationships with others. In the 1890s it had assembled a coalition of interests to show that better roads would be of benefit to all. This coalition eventually included farmers, the postal service, railroad companies and, finally, fledgling automobile manufacturers, many of which had started life as bicycle manufacturers.

In 1905, the Office of Road Inquiry became the Office of Public Roads. Geologist Logan Waller Page became the body's first director. To bring together the disparate interests in the Good Roads movement, Page founded the American Association for Highway Improvement at a Good Roads Convention held in St. Louis, Missouri, in 1901. At this convention the L.A.W.'s long-time secretary Abbot Bassett presented a paper on the "history of the birth of the Good Roads movement, for which credit must be given to the wheelmen in general and the L.A.W. in particular."

By 1910, the L.A.W. had all but ceased to exist although Bassett would carry on publishing a monthly club journal into the 1920s. This became a magazine for cycling old-timers, wallowing in nostalgia. Bassett's talk at the Good Roads convention was the last time cyclists were given credit for starting the Good Roads movement.

"It gave the cause a start that nothing could restrain," said Bassett, adding that "other people have taken up the work, all profiting by the start given to it by the wheelmen of the eighties." This barb was clearly aimed at motoring interests (although Bassett was also a motorist at this time).

> Our first steps were in the line of education and agitation. We went into politics and the wheelmen's vote was large enough to be seen by the politician without the aid of glasses. The States, led by Massachusetts, took hold of the work and Highway Commissions were formed. The Government at Washington annexed the Bureau of Road Inquiry to the Agricultural

Department. Soon nearly every State had a Highway Department … We gave good roads, fitted to our purposes, to the country … our roads led the way to your roads and we are with you, hand and glove, in the movement to supply the highways that are demanded. For your roads shall be our roads and wheresoever you shall go you will find us close behind.

In 1911, Page and the American Association for Highway Improvement organised the American Road Congress in Richmond, Virginia, and pointedly called it the *First* American Road Congress. Bassett wasn't invited to give a talk. Instead, there were presentations from road engineers and automobile interests. Major W. W. Crosby, chief Engineer of the Maryland Roads Commission, expressed the hopes of many when he told the congress:

> Most of us who do not possess [a motor car] are looking forward to the day when we may, and most of those who already are fortunate enough to own one are anticipating the possession of two or of more.

The 1911 congress heard nothing about the long history of the Good Roads movement although Hugh Chalmers, president of Chalmers Motor Company of Detroit, made an oblique reference to L.A.W's pioneering work:

> Every improvement that was ever accomplished in this country has to go through the three stages of agitation, education and organization. We have been going through the agitating part of this program and also the educating part of it, and now we are up to the organization, and it is through this organization and similar organizations that we hope finally to accomplish the thing we want.

With the L.A.W. now moribund the Good Roads movement was taken over by automobile interests. In the 1920s state Good Roads associations – now almost wholly composed of motoring, asphalt and concrete interests – pushed for the comprehensive paving of America, smoothing the way for the hegemony of the automobile. Page and his American Association for Highway Improvement professionalised the study and promotion of roads, leading to their steady improvement.

One of the game changers for roads came in December 1914 with the founding of the American Association of State Highway Officials. This national association brought together the commissioners and engineers of the state highway departments that had been created in the 1890s thanks to the lobbying of cyclists. The AASHO became a highly influential part of the US "roads lobby". It played the leading role in drafting what became the Federal Aid Road Act of 1916 which led on, inexorably, to the road improvement programmes of the 1920s and 1930s, and eventually the 1950s.

The Dwight D. Eisenhower National System of Interstate and Defense Highways, enabled by the Federal Aid Highway Act of 1956, grew to today's 47,714-mile network of US motoring roads. The construction of this network occurred only after the advent of the automobile, but the importance of the highways agitation and education work done by cyclists prior to 1905 should not be dismissed. Henry Ford's 1927 version of history, with motorists as the sole originators of good roads, is demonstrably not true. It's very much worth repeating the words of Horatio "Good Roads" Earle who, in his memoirs of 1929, stressed:

> I often hear … the automobile instigated good roads; that the automobile is the parent of good roads. Well, the truth is, the bicycle is the father of the good roads movement in this country.

CHAPTER ELEVEN

AMERICA'S FORGOTTEN TRANSPORT NETWORK

No fact is brought more forcibly or more frequently to our attention than
the extent to which bicycles are now employed as a means of conveyance … They have,
to a large extent, superseded the ordinary methods of travel.
JUSTICES OF THE NEW YORK SUPREME COURT, 1899

**America was once mad for the bicycle. Many high-society types of the 1890s would
be seen on nothing else. Indoor track racing at venues such as New York City's
Madison Square Garden attracted sell-out crowds, and professional riders were the sporting
superstars of their day. Theatres, tobacconists, watch-makers, tailors and other
tradespeople reported reduced takings because people were out bicycling instead.
And, for a few brief years, the intense interest in cycling from American progressives
led to the creation of the world's best facilities for what was felt to be the
urban transport mode of the future.**

In 1890s New York there was a wildly popular bicycle-specific "pleasure route" from downtown Brooklyn to the happening resort of Coney Island. On the West Coast there was an ambitious cycle path on timber trestles, a road-in-the-sky for cycle commuters between Los Angeles and Pasadena. Elsewhere in America, Good Roads activists – frustrated by the continued poor quality of the nation's rural roads – took matters into their own hands and built "wheelways" for use by cyclists. These cycle paths – also known as "sidepaths" – were long-distance demonstrations of how Good Roads *could* be built. "The paths are being built from city to city and from town to town … and [are] proving invaluable object lessons in the good roads movement," claimed a newspaper in 1900:

> A farmer travelling along an almost impassable road with a dry, smooth and durable cycle path alongside does not need to be told the advantages of good roads.

The object-lesson roads built by the Office of Road Inquiry in the mid-1890s were short. Cycle paths were narrower but just as soundly constructed, and there were thousands of miles of them. Today, this forgotten cycle path network lies hidden beneath modern roads. In some regions, the cycle path network was dense. *Outing* magazine claimed in 1900 that "over one hundred and twenty-five miles of excellent wheelways, perhaps the best in the world, gridiron the territory about Rochester, N. Y." Some of America's first cycle paths were utilitarian, built ruler-straight from city-to-city, such as the 15.2-mile Albany–Schenectady path in New York State, which became the modern State Route 5. Others were meandering and scenic, such as the 41-mile path around Chautauqua Lake, also in New York State. There were plans to connect many of the city to city paths into long-distance routes. In 1900, *The New York Times* reported on the proposed 968-mile "trunk line" cycle path between New York and Chicago. "Work will begin in the near future ..." to connect those cycle paths which had "already been constructed."

Cyclists paid for these cycle paths themselves, paving the way, as it were, for the later taxes on motorists which helped pay for the interstate roads that, ironically, poured asphalt over the cycle paths, wiping them from the map, and memory.

As EARLY as the 1860s, Charles Anderson Dana, the velocipede-riding editor of the *New York Sun*, advocated the building of "an elevated railway from Harlem to the Battery – from one end of New York to the other – for the use of riders of velocipedes only." This was "to be thirty feet wide, on an iron framework, and the flooring of hard pine."

The structure remained a dream but 30 years later the call for dedicated cycling infrastructure had become louder and more insistent. An elevated bike path between Harlem and the Battery was again considered, with cyclists dreaming of a "delightful tour" on a midsummer night "catching glimpses of the Hudson at the cross streets, until the moonlit bay bursts upon the view in all its silvery glory!" (Of course, the reality would have been far different, with cyclists in close proximity to dirty, smelly trains, and facing the not inconsiderable difficulty of how to get a bicycle onto a trestle without long, shallow and space-hungry ramps.) There were also proposals for cross-country cycle-path trestles. In 1895, one newspaper reported that "it is proposed to construct an elevated cycle roadway, 16ft wide, of wood paved with asphalt, between Chicago and Milwaukee, a distance of 85 miles ..."

During the Klondike Gold Rush of 1896–9 an American entrepreneur proposed building the "greatest bicycle roadway in the world" in order to help those would-be prospectors setting out to reach Canada's Yukon region on bicycles. Many miners-to-be set off from Seattle on beefed-up "Klondike-special" bicycles but they never got the "Klondike bicycle track."

These particular elevated bicycle roadways literally never got off the ground, but simpler, cheaper ones did get built. Today, the concept of a city-to-city grid of bicycle paths would be considered for recreational use only (outside of the Netherlands, that is). In the 1890s, city-to-city bicycle paths were built for day-to-day use. A significant number of cycle paths were created in upstate New York, Denver, Minneapolis, Portland and California. In 1900, cyclists believed long-distance cycle paths would enable them to "go from New York to any point in Maine, Florida or California on smooth roads made especially for them."

While bicycle-only paths were the fervent desire of many cyclists (to get away from pesky teamsters, and at least have a well-surfaced path, even if it was a narrow one), this desire was not shared by all. The building of bicycle-specific routes became a divisive issue for the cyclists of the day. There were arguments over whether or not the provision of paths diverted attention from the need to improve roads for *all* users. Officials in the League of American Wheelmen were torn – some felt that their 20-year push for Good Roads had achieved little in the way of tangible improvements and that, despite a great deal of cajoling, it had been shown that farmers had no real interest in joining with them in demanding better highways; others believed victory was in sight and that to create bicycle-only routes would detract from the we-are-all-in-this-together message. The widest and grandest path of them all – the Coney Island Cycle Path in New York – was loved by many cyclists, but not all. Some refused to ride on it, believing such dedicated routes, while superior to the rutted roads of the day, would become the only ways open to cyclists. They feared being restricted to a small number of recreational bicycle ways, and banned from all other roads. Many in the wider Good Roads movement wanted cyclists to keep fighting for the improvement of all roads, and not be diverted by improvements to just *part* of the highway.

However, an editorial in the L.A.W.'s house magazine in 1895 showed which way the wind was blowing: "The time is getting ripe for wheelmen to demand separate roads or cycle tracks of their own along the leading highways and such plans should be made and provided for in the new systems of roads which are being planned and built."

Isaac B. Potter.

Chief Consul Isaac B. Potter expressed a change of L.A.W. strategy in newspaper interviews and was condemned for it by many members of the organisation he led. An editorial in *The New York Times* in 1896 was also dismissive, hoping that Potter would "consider, on more mature reflection, that his suggestion was a mistake." For the wheelmen to seek provision of their own cycle paths would be a "public calamity," thundered the newspaper, adding:

> What is needed is to convince the rural public that good roads are economical, so economical that they cannot afford to have bad roads. Even if the wheelmen were to agree that, so long as a cinder path was provided for them, they would not object to the rest of the road being by turns a mud-wallow and a dust-heap, they would defeat their own purpose, for the full and combined force of all the elements enlisted in favor of good roads is necessary to produce good roads, and has not yet availed for that purpose.

Potter refused to budge. In a follow-up article, he wrote:

> It is perhaps unfair to say that the public roads should be improved at great expense because bicyclists alone should seem to demand it, but it is not unreasonable to ask that a narrow wheelway should be improved at moderate expense on many country roads, which would otherwise be impassable to the great body of cyclists who have occasion to pass over them.

Perfecting just a slice of the public highway smacked of elitism, worried *The New York Times*:

> More or less talk is now heard concerning special paths for cycling. Money is being raised, too, in some sections to cover the cost of building them – some by contributions, some by taxation, the wheelmen only being levied upon for the necessary sums. [It] is doubted to be wise by many wheelmen to promote the building of pedal paths. It is better, they argue, to have good roads, which are a benefit alike to all classes, not to … merely those who ride bicycles … It has been the aim of the leading officials of the League of American Wheelmen to impress upon the minds of the members that no special path favors were desired, only good macadam roads …

That cyclists could one day find themselves confined exclusively to "their" part of the highway was felt by many to be a slippery slope and for some it was "class legislation," a big no-no.

The author of an article on the "Gossip of the Cyclers" page in *The New York Times* – a weekly page in 1896 – reported that the construction of cycle paths was "assuming large proportions," and that:

> The wheelmen have for years been anxious to assist in the improvement of country highways, but since others who use the roads have not been as enthusiastic, the wheelmen have preferred to avoid further delays and secure what they might on their own account.

However, on the same page on the same day, the civil engineer General Roy Stone – who was not a wheelman – urged cyclists to stay within the wider Good Roads movement rather than go it alone:

> The general movement for improved highways in the State of New-York through the action of the existing legislative commission has taken such promising shape that I earnestly hope the influence of the wheelmen of the State will not be diverted in the direction of constructing separate cycle paths. Their help will be greatly needed in bringing about the general improvement of highways in the State, and such combined movement ... will be of great value in its effect on the Legislature and upon public sentiment generally. If the bill for State aid which will be offered by the State legislative commission prevails, you will see many hundred miles of good roads built in the State of New-York ...

This plea from General Stone went unheeded, in some quarters at least. Many cyclists had seen the future and it would be one of separation from the inferior road network, with superior provision for those riding bicycles. Even the powers-that-be, it seemed, were often in favour of what detractors thought was pandering to pedallers. In 1895, Charles Schieren, the Mayor of Brooklyn, said:

> ... the cyclers rightfully demand good roads or paths for their accommodation. We must therefore plan additional facilities and build practicable roads for the exclusive use of the wheel ... We must ... set aside a portion of the roadway for the exclusive use of bicycles, or make additional paths for them ... Good streets and roads will attract many people to a city or town which has them ... Brooklyn is now seriously considering a plan for building a system of good roads and cycling paths ... which will give from twenty to thirty miles of excellent paths to the lovers of the wheel, and will prove a great attraction.

In later years, cyclists demanded cycle paths as a form of protection from motor cars, and motorists were staunch supporters of cycle paths because this would remove cyclists from "motoring roads"; but in the 1890s, those pushing for separate cycle paths were doing so to provide cyclists with a superior running surface.

Potter was not originally a supporter of cycle paths. He had long advocated "Good Roads for all." His 1891 *Gospel of Good Roads* was a widely-distributed L.A.W. pamphlet that demonstrated with hard numbers how good roads would benefit farmers economically. It encouraged them to join with cyclists to call for a radical overhaul of the antiquated system of building and maintaining roads. (The pamphlet was also condescending and patronising: Potter included made-up conversations with the dim and stubborn "Hubmire", a "typical representative of the farming class".) Conservative, stick-in-the-mud farmers, suffering from an agricultural depression in the early 1890s, would have no truck with radical ideas, especially those espoused by "them bicycle fellars." Most bristled at the idea of having to pay taxes for the making of good roads – at that time they were still "paying" for roads with annual statute labour, a form of sweat equity. Farmers also feared that all-weather roads would be of most benefit to the urban elites on their recreational machines.

Potter despaired of this rural stubbornness and, by 1896, he was arguing in favour of cycle paths, in tandem with the provision of good roads. "I do not for a moment admit that this work for cycle paths can be substituted for the wheelman's agitation for better roads," he wrote, "but rather do I regard it as a valued auxiliary for the greater cause, which seems to have taken new impetuous [*sic*] in those sections where cycle paths have been put down."

In 1898, Potter published *Cycle Paths*, an 86-page booklet which claimed that:

> Every cyclepath is a protest against bad roads, a sort of public notice that the public wagon ways are unfit for public travel, a wit sharpener to every highway officer who has seven holes in his head, and a splendid example of the charming relations which the [bicycle] and the roadway may be made to sustain each other.

Potter wrote that cyclists paid "heavily to maintain a wasteful system of mere mudways and whose every effort for improvement is opposed by the 'old settler,'" – by which he meant farmers – "who insists that the road is good enough." He added that the farmer was "not easily converted, and we may wait for centuries before he or his ilk will shout for better roads."

Other wheelmen went further. "Why should the bicyclist carry the farmer like a millstone around his neck?" complained a cyclist in 1896, asking: "What has the farmer, the man most interested, done for good roads when left to himself?" Another wrote:

> … we gladly welcome every law which tends to give us better roads. But while we are waiting for the action of the State, and the County Board of Supervisors, and the farmers we are quietly building some good roads of our own, which we call "side paths" …

These sidepaths were to be examples to spread the Good Roads message, wrote Potter in *Cycle Paths*:

> The bicycle path is a great object lesson for good roads and should be encouraged instead of frowned upon … It is a declaration of independence which for the time being lifts the bicycle out of the mud and puts the wheelman on a firmer ground of argument for good roads, takes from his critics the charge that the cyclist's warfare is a selfish one and supplies to every traveller an impressive exhibition of the value of a good wheelway.

Before the building of cycle paths, cyclists had created short stretches of object lesson roads in towns and cities, with the L.A.W. advocating such methods from 1891. In 1894, the L.A.W.'s Sterling Elliott – editor of the organisation's *Good Roads* magazine – was the first to push for the construction of short stretches of rural roads in order to "impress upon the farmer the value of such roads," but it was the network of cycle paths in rural areas that were the first long-distance model roads. By 1897 the creation of "object lesson roads" had become the most important activity of the Office of Road Inquiry.

IN ITS day, the Coney Island Cycle Path was the finest bicycle path in the world. Petitioned for from 1892 and finally built in 1894, it extended from Prospect Park in Brooklyn to the popular resort of Coney Island, a distance of 5½ miles. It was an addition to the 1870s Ocean Boulevard, a "pleasure parkway" from "the City of Churches" to the Atlantic Ocean. Opened in mid-summer, the Cycle Path was an instant success – so successful, in fact, that the path's crushed limestone surface had to be repaired within a month of opening. A year later, three feet were added to the original width of 14 feet.

Those who owned stalls, rides and eateries at the Coney Island pleasure beach thrived from the increase in business brought by the cyclists following their "straight run to the sea."

In June 1896, a return path was built on the opposite side of the boulevard. This was opened with a gala parade organised by the L.A.W., attended by 10,000 cyclists and upwards of 100,000 spectators. *The New York Times* reported:

> Attired in holiday garb and colors, the throng presented a picture pretty to look upon. That nearly every person in it was a cyclist or wanted to be was very apparent … Every public house on the boulevard was decked in flags and bunting, and many private residences were prettily decorated for the occasion … [a] juvenile rider had on a snow white Fauntleroy waist and red stockings with shoes to match. He was a cute little fellow, and somebody named him the 'Red Spider' … The bloomer girls received much attention, as usual. One plump lassie startled the reviewing stand with her green bloomers, but she didn't mind.

The Coney Island Cycle Path was "for the exclusive use of the silent steed" – carriages used the macadam road, and equestrians were provided with a soft, sand path. The bike route was paid for in part by cyclists. The L.A.W. paid $3,500 of the $50,000 necessary for its creation. Monies were raised by individual contributions, by newspaper campaigns (the *Brooklyn Daily Eagle* stumped up $50) and by fund-raising events such as theatre productions.

An appeal in *The New York Times* in August 1894 spelled out the advantages of cyclists part-paying for the proposed cycle path: "It is now within your power to have the most delightful and attractive wheelway ever provided for the exclusive use of cyclists: a smooth, clean continuous wheelway …"

The cycle path was "the first path in the world devoted exclusively to bicycles," crowed the *Brooklyn Daily Eagle*. "No wheelman who has ridden on it has complained, as the completed sections are so perfect that it is not possible to find fault with them."

City authorities liked the path because it got cyclists off the road, away from pleasure carriages and horse-wagons. According to *The New York Times*, "the path is looked upon as an improvement [because] wheelmen do not interfere with driving at all, as the large driveway is now used exclusively by the lovers of horses and carriages."

Brooklyn's Transport Commissioner "had two roads constructed on the Ocean Parkway entrance so that the bicyclists may enter or leave the Park without danger of collision with vehicles … At the Plaza entrance, he has had Flatbush Avenue asphalted, so that the bicyclists may cross the [tram] tracks safely, and this path has been carried through one of the walks in Reservoir Point Park, so as to enable the bicyclists to reach the Eastern Parkway cycle path without danger."

By and large, the Coney Island Cycle Path was for leisure rather than being a practical route, a point made snootily by *Referee* magazine in 1895:

> Did you ever hear of the Coney Island Cycle Path? Never? Then you have not been in Brooklyn this season, for no cyclist can step his foot into that sleepy town and draw a full breath before he gets this shot at him: "Seen our Cycle Path? No? You should do so at once. Finest thing in the country. Just grand, sir; perfectly GRAND." There is nothing like the Path. It is the favorite haunt of [the] boulevardier and is thronged each afternoon by crowds of these butterfly riders, who meander up and down its level stretches and call that cycling.

As Brooklyn had an estimated 80,000 cyclists it was perfectly natural to cater to the needs of a large, politicised and active group of citizens. With numbers and the support of high society, creating bicycle infrastructure was a given. New York City's Park Commissioner Timothy L. Woodruff was a wheelman. It was he who led the parade of 10,000 cyclists that celebrated the opening of the return Coney Island Cycle Path. In a speech to the cyclists, he said:

> I am prepared, in my official position ... to do everything within the limits of my powers as such to care for and advance the interests of the wheelmen of Brooklyn. I am anxious to do this not that I may cater to the comforts of a certain class of citizens, not because I am actuated by personal devotion to wheeling, but because I believe the safety bicycle is the most beneficial instrumentality of this wonderful age.

THE CYCLE paths that came to national prominence in the late 1890s had been metaphorically built on the foundations laid by Charles T. Raymond of the canal city of Lockport, close to Niagara Falls, New York State. "When our numbers were few, the road was good enough," Raymond wrote in 1894, "but now our number is myriad and we need a road of our own which shall always be dry, smooth and hard, and may be used as comfortably in rainy weather as in dry." For some reason, Raymond didn't like the term "cycle path," preferring "side path". He had been the founder of the Niagara County Side Path League, founded in 1890, and which used club subscriptions to pay for short stretches of urban cycleways. (His organisation also received cash from the Pope Manufacturing Company and the Overman Wheel Company.) Raymond became convinced that cyclists would pay directly for improved rural paths, and he "adopted and promulgated the doctrine that 'what all use, all should pay for.'"

Sidepaths were cheaper to build than improved roads – "Good sidepaths can be constructed at a cost of $100 to $300 per mile, while good roads cost from $2,000 to $5,000 per mile" he wrote in 1898 – and "every mile we build makes the wheelmen hungry for more." In 1896 he helped to draft a county law allowing Niagara to tax bicycle owners and build cycle paths with the proceeds. Naturally, not all bicycle owners welcomed this general tax and, when there was a proposal for the tax to be extended state-wide, the Niagara chapter of the L.A.W. came out in opposition urging "all wheelmen to strenuously oppose the passage of any such bills."

Newspaper claims that the "sidepath movement" was "growing with irresistible momentum" were threatened when cyclists mustered to block further taxation on their activity. Cyclists in the city of Rochester in Monroe County, New York – "the greatest bicycle town in the country," claimed the local newspaper in 1895 – argued against a tax on bicycle ownership. Urging the state governor to veto the bill, the editor of the *Rochester Post Express* railed against the "vicious principle" of "class taxation". He wrote that "there is no more reason why the bicyclists should be taxed for cinder paths than that owners of vehicles should be taxed for the construction of better highways."

Raymond pushed on and, following a sidepath convention held in Rochester in 1898, he helped to draft state legislation that encouraged localities nationwide to build cycle paths funded not by taxation on all cyclists but only on cycle-path users. New York's General Sidepath Act of 1899 allowed a county judge, "upon the petition of fifty wheelmen of the county," to appoint a commission of five people, "each of whom shall be a cyclist," to represent the cities and towns of the county. These commissioners were "authorized to construct and maintain sidepaths along any public road, or street." Those cyclists who chose to use cycle paths had to attach "sidepath badges" to their bicycles. "Spotters" stationed themselves on cycle paths, checking which bicycles sported up-to-date "tags".

Paying for cycling facilities was not an alien concept. Cyclists in Denver funded a 50-mile cycle path to Palmer Lake entirely by subscription. And in 1895, in the Twin Cities of Minneapolis–St. Paul, Minnesota, city workers built six miles of urban cycle paths paid for by cyclists, with the St. Paul Cycle Path Association stumping up the majority funding for another 14 miles of cycle paths in 1897 and 1898.

Payment for a cycle path "bicycle tag" was, in effect, an annual user fee, and was to be the only money raised for building and maintaining cycle paths. Central Point, a small city in Jackson County, Oregon, passed a law in 1901 providing for the construction of "bicycle paths on either or both sides of all public highways of the state for the use of pedestrians and bicycles." Cyclists – but not pedestrians – had to pay an annual tax of $1, for which they received a tag which, the law decreed, "must be securely fastened to the seat post of each and every bicycle."

The "object and intent" of the law, the legislature said, was "to provide for a highway separate from that used by teams and wagons." A similar law in Jacksonville, six miles from Central Point, said: "It is made unlawful for any person to ride a bicycle upon a bicycle path without having paid the license tax." This "provides a license for riding and [was] not a tax upon the bicycle."

Portland, Oregon, had a turn-of-the-century network of 59 miles of six-foot-wide cycle paths, paid for by a cyclists' user fee.

Many American states had no legal mechanisms for raising taxes to pay for road improvements. Cycle-path taxes helped to usher in funding regimes that would be later used very successfully to raise money from motorists.

In 1949, an Oregon newspaper reminded readers that the "road tax" levied on cyclists was "the precedent for and the granddad of the present system of automotive licenses, gasoline taxes, fines and penalties which were established … and dedicated to the task of constructing the state highway system."

However, there was a major difference, as revealed in 2012 by American historian Christopher W. Wells. He showed that the Interstate highway network was successful because of the invisibility of its financing, hiding the cost from end-users and not allowing the funds raised to be used for anything other than building yet more highways, a self-perpetuating system.

NOT EVERYBODY was in favour of setting aside a portion of the public highway for bicyclists. Court cases in 1900 halted the construction of a number of cycle paths. In Spokane, Washington State, property owners secured injunctions against a proposed cycle path, claiming – as many anti-bike-path campaigners do today – that such a path would be "an obstruction of the street … that it shortens the width of a highway already none too wide … that it is a menace to children … and prevents owners of vehicles from reaching their conveyances with ease." Authorities countered by saying the path would be an "ornament to the street" and that the "path is desired by the thousands of wheelmen in the city." (4,000 of the 17,000 adult population of Spokane at the time were cyclists.)

A "wealthy resident of West Islip, [Long Island]" argued that the building of a cycle path in front of his house was "unconstitutional." All of the court cases were lost, and county Sidepath Commissions felt emboldened to extend both urban and rural cycle paths. For two years there was a frenzy of cycle-path construction. Abbot Bassett, editor of *L.A.W. Magazine and Good Roads*, wrote in 1900 that cycle paths were "spreading with unexampled rapidity" and that they would form a "network of passageways for bicycle riders the continent over." He asserted that "no other feature of cycling life … has a greater hold upon the hearts of American cyclists." Cycle paths were the "very thing essential to their happiness," and cycle paths "defeated bad roads in a manner not foreseen by those foes of progress who decried the cause of improved highways."

While he admitted that cycle paths "[benefited] none but wheelmen," he wrote that it was "bosh" to

Coney Island Cycle Path, New York.

The California Cycleway, Pasadena.

claim that their provision amounted to "class legislation":

> When the first sidewalk was legally constructed, the law took into consideration a difference existing between pedestrians and [horse carriage] drivers … If pedestrians are by law entitled to a portion of the highway set aside for their exclusive use, why are wheelmen, when they exist in numbers sufficient for the law to take recognition of them, not entitled to a portion of the highway for their exclusive use?

Cycle paths were segregated both from the adjoining highway and from sidewalks, and were for bicycles only – other traffic could be fined for using them (and this use was tempting because cycle paths, while narrow, were far better surfaced than the adjoining roads).

Many cyclists – especially long-time riders, who were older and tended to be richer – were heartily in favour of cycle paths. They even had their own magazine, *Sidepaths*, published in Rochester, New York.

However, as localities quickly found out, not all cyclists took kindly to being charged for using cycle paths, and avoidance of the "bicycle tax" was rampant. Even if every cyclist in a town paid the annual $1 fee for a "bicycle tag", this wasn't enough to pay for a dense network of cycle paths, or to maintain the existing ones.

When the town of Hoquiam in Washington State tried to prosecute a tag-free cyclist, the action was overturned by the state Supreme Court, with justices ruling that the "streets of the town are … public highways, common to all the citizens of the state," and that access could not be denied to unlicensed cyclists.

Many bicycle advocates had long argued that local and national government ought to fund infrastructure projects out of general taxation rather than user fees. Historian James Longhurst wrote in 2013 that

> … voluntary funding streams were insufficient for the construction and maintenance of serious infrastructure … Like roads, sewers and water works, the sidepath project required large-scale physical infrastructure demanding a steady and long-term investment. Voluntary funding was neither of these things. … Weak, partial funding for infrastructure might as well be no funding at all.

America's most ambitious turn-of-the-century cycle infrastructure aimed to secure a more regular funding stream – the elevated California Cycle Way was a toll-road, barred to all but ticket-holders.

THE FIRST elevated highway between the cities of Pasadena and Los Angeles was built by one of the region's richest residents, and paid for with tram-style journey tickets. In the first year of the 20th century this grade-separated highway towered over train tracks, road junctions and slow-poke users of the rutted roads beneath. The wooden trestle was billed as a "speedway" and was to provide a flat, fast scenic route for Pasadena's thousands of cyclists, who could fly 50 feet high over the deepest section of the oak-studded Arroyo Seco river valley. The "ingenious scheme" was to be an uninterrupted "paradise for wheelmen."

The reality for the California Cycle Way turned out to be far different. Only the first mile-and-a-bit was erected, which wasn't long enough to attract sufficient paying customers. Within just months of opening, the cycleway had become a loss-making stub of a route rather than a profitable commuter cycling road for Pasadena's wealthy cyclists. Had it been built to length the year after it was first proposed, the cycleway might have turned a profit, and could have become the "splendid nine-mile track" that, in 1901, *Pearson's Magazine* (falsely) claimed it was.

Built with pine imported from Oregon, and painted green, the would-be superhighway had a lot going for it. For a start, it had high-society support: it was constructed for a company controlled by Horace Murrell Dobbins, Pasadena's millionaire mayor, and the investors included a recent former governor of California, as well as Pasadena's leading bicycle-shop owner.

The California Cycle Way was first mooted in 1896. "The idea was originated by Horace Dobbins ... who is himself a wheelman," said the *Los Angeles Herald*.

The cycleway was meant to run for nine miles from the upmarket Hotel Green in Pasadena down to the centre of Los Angeles. The first 1¼-mile stretch opened to great fanfare on New Year's Day, 1900 as part of the route of that year's Tournament of the Roses Parade. 350 bicycles, decorated with floral displays, took part in the main parade and no doubt many of them were ridden down the wooden track by some of the 600 cyclists who took part in the cycleway's inaugural ride.

In 1899, *Scientific American* called Dobbins' route an "elaborate wheelway" where "cyclists will ... be permitted to view the beautiful scenery without having to look out for ruts in the road."

Wide enough for four cyclists to ride side by side, with another nine feet available alongside to plank another lane, the great wooden cycleway made news around the world. In Britain, it featured on the front cover of a number of national and regional newspapers, including the *Dundee Post* in July 1900. The newspaper called it a "Curious cycleway" but remarked that similar cycleways ought to be constructed for Britain's "vast army of cyclists":

> Why should not proper cycleways be built between towns of common interest where the roads are bad or the strain of traffic makes riding a burden? If ... local authorities ... would take a leaf out of the books of railway companies and construct a proper track they would build up a profitable source of revenue from that vast army of cyclists that increases hugely every year ... The experiment has been tried in Southern California ... and gives promise of a high degree of success.

This promise of success did not materialise, however – the cycleway was scuppered, in part thanks to rights-of-way objections lodged by a railroad magnate. Henry E. Huntington didn't want speedy competition for his growing streetcar network. (The competition would be cheaper, too – a trolley-car ride from Pasadena to downtown Los Angeles cost 25 cents, while the cycleway cost 10 cents one way and 15 cents for all-day use.) Dobbins and Huntington's Pacific Electric Railroad company would continue to fight over the rights-of-way for the cycleway long after the cycleway had ceased to exist as a route for cyclists. The California Cycle Way Company secured an injunction against plans for new lines from Pacific Electric and, in turn, Pacific Electric tried to condemn that part of the cycleway that it wanted to cross. It wasn't until November 1902 that the two companies agreed to compromise.

By this time, cycling was on the wane in Pasadena and Los Angeles. The future, it seemed, was in fast public transit, with the building of streetcar lines the sensible thing for speculators to invest in.

A local newspaper reminisced in the 1950s: "Many Pasadena old-timers have happy memories of moonlight rides up and down that historic strip ... the Cycleway was Pasadena's pride and joy."

Pride and joy it may have been but as a usable route it was a short-lived. By August 1900 a local newspaper reported the "Cycleway will do no more work now ..."

Because the truncated cycleway wasn't terribly long, didn't go where people wanted to go and didn't have enough entry and exit points, it was of little practical value, and hence not used and not profitable.

A built-to-length cycleway would have had an income of approximately $20,000 a month "if half of the wheelmen in two cities patronize the road once a month," the company's prospectus had claimed. Most of the period photographs of the cycleway show it empty. This wasn't because there were no cyclists in Pasadena. The small city had 15 bicycle shops in 1900 and, according to the *Los Angeles Herald*, in 1898 the city's 9,000 residents owned 4,000 bicycles, with the Los Angeles area having "fully forty thousand bicycles." Pasadena's many cyclists shunned the cycleway because its enforced short length made it more of a fairground attraction for hotel guests than a transportation option for locals.

Had the full nine miles been built in 1897, the cycleway would have been the quickest, slickest way to get from upper Pasadena to downtown Los Angeles (the plan was to also offer one-way rental of bicycles). Dobbins also imagined that it would be used at the weekend as a fast, flat way of getting from downtown Los Angeles to the foothills of the Sierra Madre and San Gabriel mountains.

The plans for the cycleway had been ambitious. The idea was for it to be grade-separated, to fly over the rutted dirt roads of the city and to soar over the Arroyo Seco river. Its incandescent lamps, at 50-foot intervals, would make the curving cycleway visible at night down in Los Angeles. There were also plans for the cycleway to snake past a lavish casino to be built in the Moorish style, complete with "a Swiss dairy ... for the refreshment of the thirsty." Neither the casino nor the Swiss dairy ever got off the drawing board.

The cycleway's shortcomings would have been painfully obvious to Dobbins. Originally from Philadelphia and comfortably off thanks to having a rich father (Richard Dobbins constructed the buildings for Philadelphia's 1876 Centennial celebrations), Dobbins had holidayed in Pasadena with his parents since 1888. The family later moved to Pasadena, and Dobbins Jr. bought real estate, some of which he developed and profited from. In the 1890s Pasadena attracted wealthy vacationers from America's Eastern seaboard, many of whom relocated and became passionate about their adopted city. They were attracted to Pasadena's warm winter climate, horticultural delights (including citrus fruits and exotic winter flowers) and grand hotels. Pasadena's Valley Hunt Club was founded by wealthy industrialists from the East Coast and Mid-West, who in 1890, created the Tournament of Roses Parade, soon to be world-famous and still America's premier New Year's Day celebration. Dobbins was a Valley Hunt Club member, and was one of the directors of the committee that organised parades in the 1890s.

In 1895 Dobbins and his wife bought one of the mansions on Orange Grove Boulevard, Pasadena's "Millionaire's Row." At this prestigious address he would have rubbed shoulders with brewing magnate Adolphus Busch, David and Mary Gamble of Procter & Gamble fame (and fortune), and chewing-gum king William Wrigley Jr.

Dobbins had begun acquiring the rights of way down the Arroyo Seco valley at the height of the bicycling boom in 1896. He incorporated the California Cycle Way Company on August 23rd, 1897. The company prospectus said that the route would be open to "bicycles or other horseless vehicles" (motor bicycles, rather than motor cars).

Dobbins was company president and majority stockholder. Other investors included Henry Markham, who had been Governor of California two years previously; Ed Braley, owner of Pasadena's biggest and oldest bike shop, the Braley Bicycle Emporium (now a Scientology church) and "Professor" Thaddeus Lowe, a Civil War balloonist who, in 1891, had helped create the Pasadena & Mount Wilson Railroad Company, which ran a steep-incline railway to the top of Mount Wilson.

From 1900 to 1901, Dobbins was chairman of Pasadena's Board of Supervisors (precursor to the City Council – hence he was mayor in all but name) but, despite this leading role, and earlier elevated positions in the city's administration, he had been initially unable to secure permission for his cycleway during the first year of his company's incorporation. It took another city vote in 1898 before he got the required licence, a costly delay. Erection of the structure didn't start until November 1899. The

Patton and Davies Lumber Company of Pasadena supplied the Oregon pine, and builders erected the first stretch of cycleway in just three months (grading cuts through the foothills had taken place in the preceding two years). On the first day of construction, the *Pasadena Daily Evening Star* said the "first section" of the cycleway would be "rushed to completion."

The cycleway ran downhill from the luxurious Hotel Green, adjacent to the Sante Fe railroad station, to The Raymond, a resort hotel with its own nine-hole golf course. Pasadena was not yet friendly to "autocarists." Arthur Raymond, owner of The Raymond, didn't much like the first vacationing motorists. A sign outside his hotel read "Automobiles are positively not allowed on these grounds."

Another sign outside the hotel pointed the way to the Dobbins' Cycleway, which is how the route was known locally. To the outside world it was the Great California Cycleway and it was claimed to be a rip-roaring success. In September 1901 the mass-circulation *Pearson's Magazine* devoted three pages to the cycleway.

"On this splendid track cyclists may now enjoy the very poetry of wheeling," puffed T. D. Denham.

> At Pasadena they may mount their cycles and sail down to Los Angeles without so much as touching the pedals, even though the gradient is extremely slight. The way lies for the most part along the east bank of the Arroyo Seco, giving a fine view of this wooded stream, and skirting the foot of the neighboring oak-covered hills. The surface is perfectly free from all dust and mud, and nervous cyclists find the track safer than the widest roads, for there are no horses to avoid, no trains or trolley-cars, no stray dogs or wandering children.

Denham claimed that "industrial activity will be so quickened [by this splendid track] that the country will enjoy such prosperity as it has never known."

His article stated that the California Cycleway was nine miles long, as did most of the other press reports about the structure. Given that the cycleway had closed for business a year before, it's rather strange that *Pearson's Magazine* printed such a misleading piece – the magazine also reported as fact the supposed existence of the casino and the Swiss dairy.

Pearson's wasn't totally wrong – the cycleway *did* exist in September 1901 and it was probably still used. (The moonlight trips mentioned in the 1950s newspaper article may have been illicit rides – and dangerous, too: "A Mexican boy took hold of a live electric wire on the cycleway and received a shock which made him unconscious," reported the *Los Angeles Herald* in 1906.)

In March 1901 a local newspaper reported that the cycleway was "to come down from Central Park tract" and that Dobbins "agrees to turn his franchise back to the city free of cost – to be paid only what that section of the structure cost."

In October 1900 Dobbins told the *Los Angeles Times*: "I have concluded that we are a little ahead of time on this cycleway. Wheelmen have not evidenced enough interest in it ..."

There are photos of the cycleway still standing in 1905, although by 1906 a newspaper said that it was "an eyesore to some people." The following year the *Los Angeles Herald* said the "old wooden trestle" was "objectionable" and that Dobbins had applied for it to be pulled down. Permission for the demolition wasn't granted because the Board of Supervisors believed Dobbins "desires to use the old right of way for other purposes." He did – he wanted to build a rail-road.

While at least parts of the structure may have been extant in 1919, most of it was pulled down in stages, and the lumber sold off. Some of those parts of the right of way owned by the city were used for a curving, scenic motor road. In December 1940, at the opening ceremony for the Arroyo Seco Parkway, Governor of California Culbert L. Olson declared it to be the "first freeway in the West." The 45-mph Parkway used short stretches of the former cycling route. Today, there's a modern cycleway that follows some of the flood-control channels down the Arroyo Seco and this also uses a few short stretches of the Dobbins' Cycleway route.

In 1958, Pasadena mayor Harrison R. Baker said that Dobbins was "way out in front of all of us" in dreaming up what would become, in part, the main asphalt route between Pasadena and Los Angeles.

An urban myth has since grown up around the California Cycleway. Newspapers and blogs claim that the cycleway was killed off by the motor car. "The horseless carriage … caused the demise of the bikeway," wrote the Public Information Officer for the City of Pasadena on her blog in 2009. In 2005, a feature for the *Pasadena Star News* claimed that "Automobiles spelled doom for the cycleway."

Numerous online mentions of the cycleway have trotted out the same angle. In January 2014, the architecture correspondent for Britain's *Guardian* newspaper even claimed that the structure, abandoned in 1900, was "destroyed by the rise of the Model T Ford," a car not introduced until 1908.

There's no proof that the advent of the automobile had anything whatsoever to do with the financial collapse of the cycleway. In 1900, motor cars were still fresh on the scene and very few people thought they had a certain future, and even fewer thought they had an all-dominant future. It was another 15 years before automobiles started to dominate in the Los Angeles area. In the eight years from 1914 to 1922 the number of vehicle registrations in Los Angeles County quadrupled to 172,313. Until well into the 1920s, Pasadena was not as auto-centric as Los Angeles, and the city still had an efficient public transit network in the 1920s and into the 1930s.

Ironically, there's a photograph from 1900 showing Dobbins on the cycleway in his steam-powered Locomobile motor car. He told the *Los Angeles Times* that "we will lie still for a time and use [the cycleway] for automobile service," but this would have been 14 years too early and it would have also needed a great deal of modification. A short pleasure track for automobiles would have been just as pointless as a short hotel-to-hotel cycleway.

As part of a deal, Dobbins transferred ownership of some of the cycleway's rights of way to the City of Pasadena in August 1902, in return for adjoining rights-of-way, yet there were no plans, at that time, to turn any of these into a prototype freeway. All eyes – including Dobbins' – were on turning the route into a rail-road. In 1909 Dobbins incorporated the Rapid Transit Company in order to create a fast streetcar line into Los Angeles. Via newspaper reports, Dobbins told Pasadena residents:

> The Pasadena Rapid Transit railroad to Los Angeles will be built, and it is my honest belief that this road will be built and the cars running between Pasadena and Los Angeles inside of eighteen months. [By road, Dobbins meant rail-road; and by car, Dobbins meant trolley-car]. The right of way is ours absolutely. We own every inch of it … It is absolutely the shortest line between the centers of population in Pasadena and Los Angeles, and always will be.

The Rapid Transit Company's one-stop streetcar line to Los Angeles – like the full length of the earlier cycleway – was to remain a dream. In 1917, the City of Pasadena bought out Dobbins' interest in the Arroyo Seco route, and parts of his company's rights of way became motoring roads, including stretches of the Arroyo Seco Parkway.

Dobbins lived in Pasadena until his death in 1962, at the ripe old age of 94. No doubt he drove along the Arroyo Seco Parkway a great many times, and it's not too fanciful to imagine that he did so with an intimate and ironic appreciation of what might have been.

If the California Cycleway *had* been built to plan in 1897, it might have had a successful life but it would have been a brief one: the automobile may not have killed Dobbins' dream in 1900 – that bubble was burst by the streetcar and the waning popularity of cycling – but the Southern Californian love of motor cars would have killed off a nine-mile cycleway soon enough.

CHAPTER TWELVE

PEDAL POWER

*If wheelmen secure us the good roads for which they are so
zealously working, [the] body deserves a medal in recognition of its philanthropy.*
BENJAMIN HARRISON, US PRESIDENT, JULY 1892

**In the 1890s, American cyclists were a force to be reckoned with.
They voted for candidates in favour of Good Roads, and could decide local and
national elections. Behind the scenes, officials from the League of American Wheelmen
were cogs in the Federal government machine.**

On the evening of Saturday July 25th, 1896, a parade in downtown San Francisco attracted 5,000
cyclists. The torchlit parade was watched by "fully one hundred thousand spectators," reported the
local newspaper. Its lavishly-illustrated article was headlined, "San Francisco bicycle riders as disciples
of progress." Many of the cyclists were in costume – the political parade was dressed up as a rolling
party. The "Enthusiastic Outpouring of Devotees of the Wheel ... Are Determined On Improving the
City's Thoroughfares," said the *San Francisco Call*, predicting that "the wheelmen's vote would be a
potent factor in determining future municipal administration."

Politics would be decided by the "pedal-turners," reported the newspaper: "The turnout last night
was ... a test of the political strength of the wheelmen, and it showed how great that strength really is."

The parade had a kiss-the-baby aspect: it was led out by the daughter of a bicycle-shop owner,
four-year-old Valentine Conwell, "with beaming eyes ... and winning smile." But for those municipal
politicians who failed to do what the wheelmen wanted, there was a threatening aspect, too: "The San
Francisco Road Club has a float of gruesome form ... pregnant with suggestion." It was a gallows, from
which hung a dummy representing "the first man who will vote against good [roads]."

The parade was part of a well-organised political campaign to persuade the city authorities to improve
more of the main business roads in the Mission District. Folsom Street had already been "bitumenized"
and was "a perpetual delight to wheelmen." The two-wheel agitators now wanted more streets to be
paved with asphalt to give safer passage over the intersecting tram-tracks – "slots" – that bisected the
city. "Repave Market Street," was the cyclists' demand.

> Placards of every size and color and glaring transparencies reiterated the laconic demand
> for street improvement ... And few of the thousands of spectators who witnessed the great
> demonstration last night failed to realize that this war cry is going to be one of the great slogans
> of the coming municipal campaign.

Within months, Market Street *was* repaved, and in celebration another well-drilled parade rolled out, this time over a smooth road surface. One of the key reasons for the campaign's success was the political support the L.A.W. could command. The organising committee for the first parade consisted not just of shopkeepers and L.A.W. members, but also politicians, including the Mayor of San Francisco, two Congressmen, two Senators and a number of the City Supervisors. The Gilded Age was a bicycle age: cyclists had political clout.

HIGHLY ORGANISED, tightly knit and mostly middle class – with campaign dollars to spend and thousands of block votes to cast for the favoured candidates in any election – cyclists in cities across America were a force to be reckoned with. The *New York Times* reported that the L.A.W. in 1894 decided that "the time is ripe for concerted action … on political lines." The organisation would urge cyclists to vote only for a politician if he was in favour of Good Roads. "If he is favorable to them, they will work hard to elect him; if opposed to their views, then they will do their best to defeat him."

L.A.W. president Charles H. Luscomb wrote to members urging them to secure political consensus on the need for Good Roads:

> The League of American Wheelmen is bound to secure better roads and you, as a wheelman, are expected to assist at the polls … Whatever your politics may be, you must see to it that the good roads interest is well looked after … Don't vote for a candidate opposed to good roads …

In Chicago, a bicycle-friendly administration bent over backwards for bicyclists. "Windy City" wheelmen were thick on the ground, and could sway elections. In 1896, the *Chicago Times Herald* reported that cyclists were persistent single-issue lobbyists:

> The cycling organizations of Chicago … are sending out letters to the various candidates for the legislature … for the purpose of ascertaining their sentiments on the question of Good Roads … Nearly all candidates for office are in favor of good roads nowadays, when the wheelmen constitute such a considerable factor in the voting strength of the cities.

Carter Henry Harrison IV – former co-owner of the *Chicago Times* and a relative of US President Benjamin Harrison, quoted at the head of the chapter – was elected mayor of Chicago in 1897, swept into power on a pro-bicycle ticket. His campaign had circulated posters and lapel badges with the slogan "Not the Champion Cyclist, but the Cyclists' Champion."

This wasn't just good politics. Harrison was an active wheelman for some years before his 1897 campaign. In 1892 he was a guest speaker at a white-tie banquet in Chicago organised by the L.A.W. He was introduced as the "cyclists' lifelong friend." *The Sporting Life* reported: "Carter Harrison claims to have been the first person to have made the assertion that THE BICYCLE WOULD BE THE CAUSE OF GOOD ROADS." (This was a strange claim to make, considering that Colonel Albert Pope was also one of the guest speakers.)

Up against the athletic John M. Harlan, a former American footballer, Harrison racked up a number of century rides on a bicycle equipped with "handlebars of the scorchiest type" and publicised the fact. He had "a brilliant thought," for attracting further votes:

> … why not utilize my cycling record as an offset to the Harlan football boasting? My brother-in-law, Heaton Owsley, with his twin brother, Harry B., were owners of the St. Nicholas Manufacturing Company, makers of the Hibbard bicycle. I had joined the Century Road Club,

was entitled to wear its badge with eighteen pendant bars each engraved with the date of the particular run it represented. It made a brave show. Shortly after the nominations I had the Owsley brothers send a brand-new wheel with scorcher handlebars of the scorchiest type to the Morrison photograph gallery in West Madison Street ... I then betook myself to the gallery with my riding togs to be photographed head-on, body bent double over the scorcher bars, an attitude that always gave a fiendish expression even to the mildest of faces! What with the rakish cap, the old gray sweater and the string of eighteen pendant bars, I looked like a professional; a picture which I knew would carry weight with the vast army of Chicago wheelmen.

After winning the election, Mayor Harrison repaid the vast army of wheelmen by killing off a tram-track down the centre of Jackson Street ("Jackson Street Must Be Boulevarded!" the cyclists had petitioned, covering the city with yellow ribbons emblazoned with the slogan). He ordered that water trucks that patrolled the city's roads to dampen the dust had to leave "a space of four feet on each side of thoroughfares next to the curb," so that cyclists didn't have to ride through mud. "This unsprinkled space is intended for the especial use of bicyclists," he promised. He also created a cycle path from Edgewater to Evanston along the north–south Sheridan Road. The upmarket Edgewater neighbourhood was home to the city's Saddle and Cycle Club, opened in May 1895, an upper-middle-class retreat for equestrians and cyclists. The *Chicago Tribune* counted 48 cycling clubs in 1892, with 6,000 members. Many of these clubs built and owned their own buildings, some with bicycle valets and indoor gymnasiums. The Old Park Cycling Club spent $50,000 on its headquarters, all raised from the deep pockets of its high-society members. In 1895 there were fewer clubs – 33 – but 4,000 more members than three years previously. Cyclists ruled the roads of Chicago, and had the run of the city's 40 miles of boulevards, which were off-limits to "teamster" wagons.

Edith Ogden Harrison, Chicago's First Lady in 1897 and a famous children's author in the early 20th century, would later write approvingly of these pre-automobile days:

> Everyone was supposed to ride a bicycle and one was not what they called "in the swim" unless you mastered the wheel ... Especially during the lovely summer evenings, before every ... home on our block, one could see the trim bicycles awaiting the cessation of an early dinner for the owners inside the houses, for it was a foregone conclusion that everyone took a ride after dinner in the cool of the evening ... Almost at its very appearance, the riders numbered in the hundreds. [The] traffic in this really expensive sport became a thing of wonder.

Cyclists weren't influential in the 1890s merely because there were lots of them. They were influential because many prominent individuals – from business, high society, politics and more – were keen cyclists. The "freemasonry of the wheel" was real. Politicians who weren't cyclists knew not to cross them. In 1897, Charles P. Weaver was elected mayor of Louisville, Kentucky, after he promised the city's 20,000 cyclists that he would pave Broadway "from First Street to Ninth," and that he would prevent abutters from sprinkling the roads in front of their houses with so much water they turned them into a "perfect loblolly" of mud. Robert A. Van Wyck, the first mayor of New York City after the consolidation of the five boroughs into the City of Greater New York in 1898, had run on a ticket that, in part, courted the cyclist vote.

In 1898, as part of his election campaign, Van Wyck wrote: "I deem it proper to make special mention ... of the pressing necessity for proper bicycle paths, and to add that, if elected, I shall make it my duty to have them constructed."

New York was the city that built the world's finest bicycle path of the time, the Coney Island Cycle

Path. It was also a city where politicians were officials with the L.A.W. Lawyer and politician William Travers Jerome worked on the successful 1894 campaign of William L. Strong for mayor of New York City. He later became New York County District Attorney. In the 1890s, he was on the Board of Consuls for the New York chapter of the L.A.W.

The L.A.W. was strictly non-partisan. It favoured candidates who were most in tune with the demand for Good Roads, and it had been politically aware since the formation of its campaign in the 1880s. L.A.W. membership eventually rose to over 100,000 but its reach was far wider than this. Even those cyclists who weren't members would have been aware of the organisation's Good Roads literature and its political campaigning. Cyclists were no shrinking violets. They would gather in their hundreds at political meetings, their voting intentions made clear with bunting, badges and decorated bicycles.

In 1881, L.A.W. president Charles E. Pratt had urged the "laying aside all differences of party politics" in locations where members lobbied municipal governments, so that they could "combine, and use their earnest organized efforts to defeat and kill off politically any alderman, mayor, or other official who should attempt to deny their just rights."

Two years later, the president of the National Association of Amateur Athletics of America – who wasn't yet a cyclist but, to cheers, promised that he would become so – told gathered wheelmen at a banquet in New York:

> I think that if we make a little deal with the politicians it wouldn't be very long ... before you will have both the Republicans and Democrats running after the "wheel" votes.

By the end of the 1890s, L.A.W. president Sterling Elliott was predicting that cyclists might one day hold the balance of power, "so that even the president of the United States could be elected or defeated by the united forces of bicycle riders." This was far from fanciful. In the 1896 election campaign for US President, the L.A.W. had its own room in the campaign headquarters of the Republican Party.

In October 1896, 300 Indiana cyclists boarded a chartered train to Canton, Ohio. They mustered in front of the house of Governor William McKinley and presented him with a bicycle. The Republican politician was in the running for President of the United States, and cyclists wanted to remind him of their block voting power. "Major McKinley is not a bicyclist," reported the *Indianapolis News*, "but has frequently expressed his admiration for the sport, and no one will be surprised to see him at one of the cycle schools with his new [bicycle] in the near future."

Governor McKinley's "admiration" for cycling was no doubt coloured by the fact that earlier in the month his house had been the staging point for a demonstration by 3,000 cyclists, one of whom told a newspaper that they represented "no particular section of the country, but all sections; no particular occupation, but all occupations; no particular interests, but all interests; no particular rank in life, but all ranks." The "no particular interests" claim was false – cyclists were solely interested in Good Roads. And this laser-like focus – and the fact that politically motivated wheelmen were active in all parts of the nation – attracted McKinley's campaign manager, Mark Hanna of Cleveland, Ohio. Hanna was chairman of the Republican National Committee, and the ace political manipulator – and fundraiser – of his age. (George W. Bush's adviser Karl Rove was likened to Hanna in the 1990s.)

Hanna and McKinley may have been in cahoots with large business interests – the "trusts" – but they couldn't ignore the swing-vote influence of the cyclists, especially as the Democratic candidate for the presidency had launched an unheralded, and seemingly popular, campaign tour of the nation. Most historians believe the idea of McKinley giving speeches from his lawn was suggested by Hanna as a counter to the tour conducted by William Jennings Bryan, which personalised politics at a time when Americans tended to vote for parties rather than individuals.

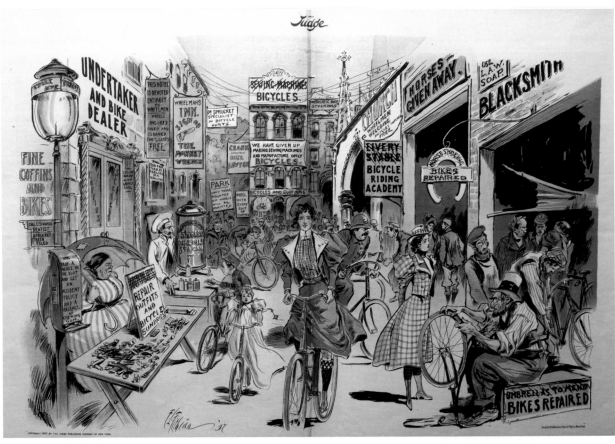

For all I care a speedy cure
This Season may you find,
And, in your 'Sportive Ventures', your
TURN-OVER to your mind!

Bertram Hope.

Are you ready to be scandalised? (And, no, it's worse than just the placement of a poorly drawn 1870s bicycle on an 1890s post-card.) All is – nearly – revealed on plate xv.

FARMER BIGOSH (*to Miss Biker*)—"Well, I'll be gol-durned! I knowed you city doods wus big babies, but I swar ef i tho't one 'ud cry like a gal ef he tore his breeches!"

JUDGE'S FASHION DESIGN.
The wheel-costume for female bicyclist.

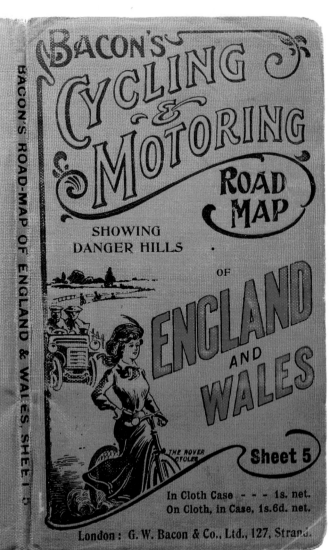

THE PASSING OF THE HORSE.

CYCLING IN ENGLAND—DOWN THE RIPLEY ROAD.—Drawn by Joseph Pennell.—[See Page 768.]

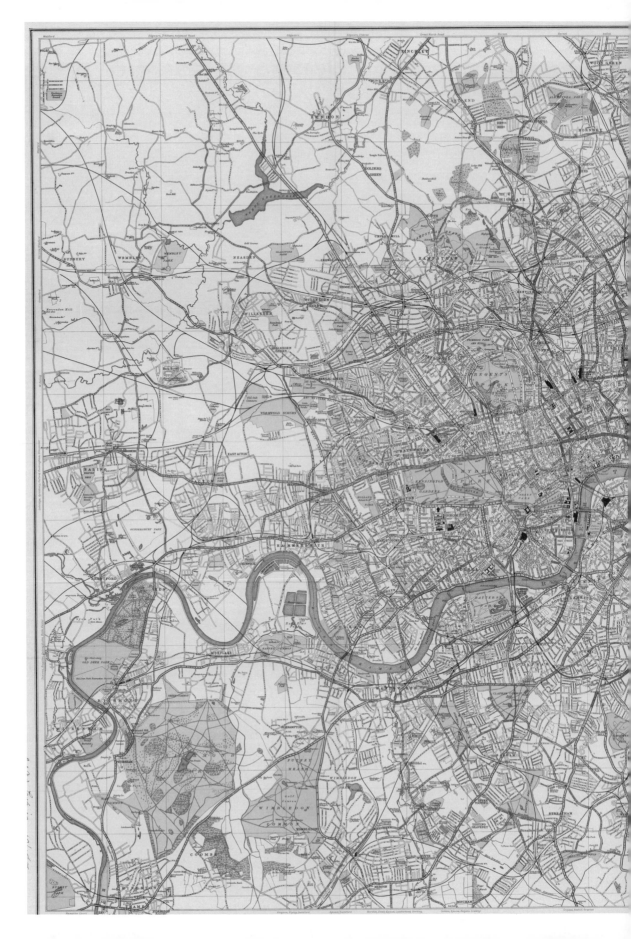

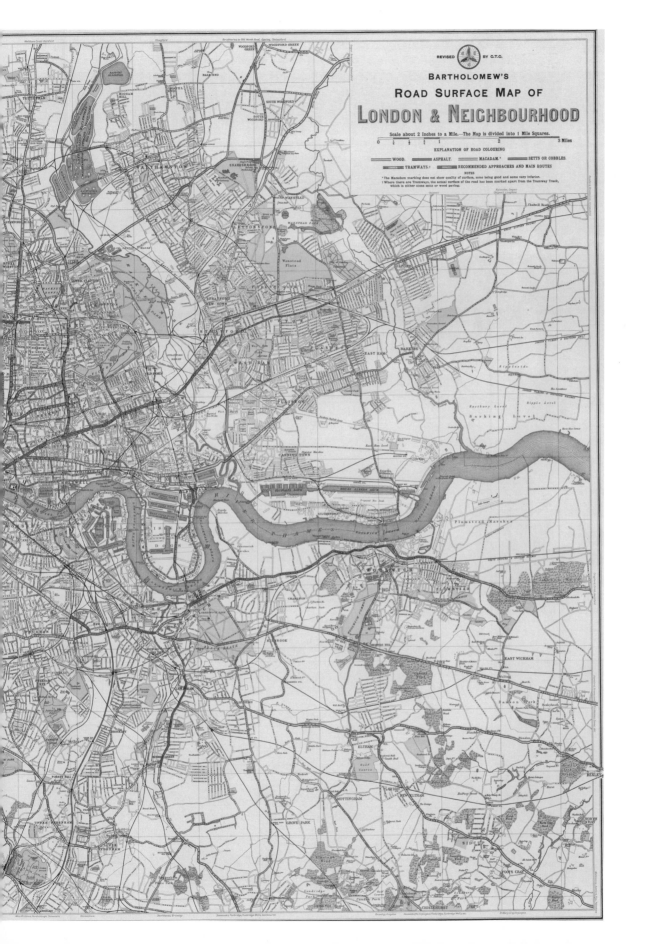

REVISED BY C.T.C.

BARTHOLOMEW'S

ROAD SURFACE MAP OF

LONDON & NEIGHBOURHOOD

Scale about 2 Inches to a Mile.—The Map is divided into 1 Mile Squares.

0   ¼   ½   ¾   1   2   3 Miles

EXPLANATION OF ROAD COLOURING

WOOD.   ASPHALT.   MACADAM.*   SETTS OR COBBLES.

TRAMWAYS.   RECOMMENDED APPROACHES AND MAIN ROUTES

NOTES

* The Macadam marking does not show quality of surface, some being good and some very inferior.
† Where there are Tramways, the actual surface of the road has been marked apart from the Tramway Track, which is either stone setts or wood paving.

CYCLISTS' TOURING CLUB

MEMBERSHIP CERTIFICATE

No. 7316

W. T. Pearson

Hanover Works

Leyburn

E. R. Shipton

SECRETARY.

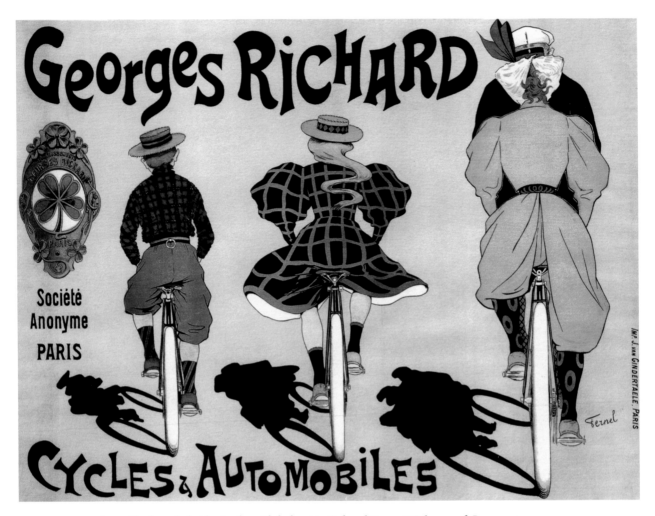

i. The bearded rider in the pith helmet is Colonel Pope. © Library of Congress.

ii. Road scene by seascape artist Seth Arca Whipple, the winning entry in an 1897 competition organised by the League of American Wheelmen. © Detroit Historical Society.

iii. Belle Époque poster advertising Cycles Gladiator. Signed "LW". Printed by G. Massias of Paris, 1895. And close-ups of the Whipple painting.

iv. Portion of "North Country Mails at the Peacock, Islington" by James Pollard. Note how the small boy has to jump out of the way of the "laurelled mail." And, the livery trade at risk in "A Modern Street Scene," *Judge* magazine, USA, 1897.

v. Sir Weetman Dickinson Pearson and the later Lady Pearson on bicycles, part of the stucco frieze panels at Paddockhurst House in Sussex by artist Walter Crane, 1897. Courtesy of Worth Abbey. And a risqué English Victorian greetings card – note the watering cart.

vi. Two cartoons poking fun at cycle fashion for women, *Judge* magazine, May 1896. And Bacon's Cycling and Motoring Map. c. 1899, with a back cover advertisement for the Rover Cycle Co, which would soon go on to produce the Rover motor car.

vii. "The passing of the horse." *Puck*, April 26th, 1899. And the Ripley Road from *Harper's Weekly*, 1897. Drawing by Joseph Pennell, an American cycle tourist who lived for much of his life in England and who was intimately involved with cycling organisations (and later motoring ones, too) on both sides of the Atlantic.

For all dull care a speedy cure
This Season may you find,
And, in your 'Sportive Ventures', your
TURN – OVER to your mind!

Bertram Hope.

"COO, LOOK—THERE'S A CYCLIST!"

McKinley gave speeches from his front lawn to a great many interest groups and, as with politicians today, he told them what they wanted to hear. But bicyclists were different. They were well-travelled and diffuse and could spread a political message far and wide. Part of McKinley's well-funded campaign involved the use of bicycle imagery. A number of different badges were produced showing McKinley astride his bicycle. "To the White House," said one of them. In 1896, riding a bicycle was a metaphor for success. Bicycles were progressive, McKinley told the 3,000 cyclists that gathered on his lawn:

> In the category of inventions I doubt if any vehicle or means of locomotion was ever so favorably received. Its use is long since out of the realm of romance and song and belongs to one of the greatest and most wonderful inventions of the time … The Americans are eminently a practical people, and were quick to see both the convenience and utility of this beautiful machine, so simple and perfect in every part …

The cyclists, "radiant in costumes of gray and with brilliant pennants", had come from "Pittsburgh, Cleveland, Buffalo, Chicago, Cincinnati and other points." McKinley welcomed them to his home and said that "political clubs on wheels are novel in political contests and are truly American." The arrival of cyclists on the national scene "marks a new era in campaign work," and he could see that cyclists were now a "mighty force in American politics."

To tap into this force, the Republicans created the National Wheelmen's McKinley and Hobart club. (Garret A. Hobart was McKinley's running mate.) This club, said a newspaper, was to

> … do active work during the campaign and on election day. In the next six weeks there will be many parades and other demonstrations, in which the wheelmen's companies will take part. It will be a new feature in political parades, but will be one that will add wonderfully to their effectiveness. One of the pleasant duties will be to escort the distinguished speakers who may come to this city during the campaign.

The *Chicago Tribune* said the newly formed club would attract opinion formers:

> These men, when they see their companions joining the National Republican Wheelmen's club, will join "just to be with the crowd" … The Republican leaders have recognized the wheel as an important factor …

A campaign organiser in San Antonio, Texas, received a note from Republican headquarters in Chicago:

> … you are requested to promote the immediate organization of McKinley and Hobart Wheelmen's clubs in every precinct in your county … Kindly send us the names of one or two prominent business men who ride the bicycle, in each town in your county, who may be commissioned to organize these clubs … Wheelmen's clubs will be an important factor in this campaign.

A great many of these political wheelmen's clubs were duly created. 1,500 wheelmen paraded down Michigan Avenue to Washington Park on October 1st. In Indianapolis at the end of the same month 100 Republican wheelmen rode to former President Benjamin Harrison's home to escort him to the railway station as he set out on a speaking tour in support of McKinley.

The Republican bicycle club in Terre Haute, Indiana, had 850 members. Membership was open to "all wheelmen who are interested in sound money, steady work and good roads."

The Democrats, by comparison, made little effort to woo the cyclist vote. In November 1896 McKinley won the election, becoming the 25th President of the United States. It's uncertain how big a part the cycling vote played in McKinley's victory but the Republicans certainly thought it had been worth chasing. McKinley learnt of his victory thanks to William K. Bellis of the Bellis Cycle Company of Indianapolis who arranged for a relay of cyclists to carry the news from Indianapolis to Canton, Ohio "in order that a cyclist might have the distinction of informing the president-elect of his victory ..."

ALTHOUGH ONE writer claimed in 1895 that "We may yet see cyclists turning a general election – if any party is indiscreet enough to offend them," there was no such thing as the cycling vote in Britain. Nevertheless, individuals very keen on cycling were in positions of influence, both in politics and in the media. Many of these individuals later transferred their loyalties to motoring. William Plowden, in his classic 1970s book about politics and motoring, wrote that, "Among the prominent and habitual breakers of the [speed] limit [in 1903] was the Prime Minister A. J. Balfour." Prior to his conversion to motoring, Balfour was president of the National Cyclists' Union, and developed his love for speed on a bicycle.

Hugh Oakeley Arnold-Forster, Balfour's Secretary of State for War from 1903 to 1905, was a touring cyclist, who submitted much of the information in an 1897 book on cycling in Ireland.

According to the *Pall Mall Gazette* in 1898, there was a "passion for wheeling" in Parliament, with MPs not yet as keen on motoring as they would become:

> In popularity with members of Parliament the bicycle can give many points to the motor car and yet beat that mechanical atrocity hollow ... Mr. Healy's partiality for the cycle led him to defend the privileges of its riders with quite remarkable vigour in the House the other day.

Herbert Gladstone, the Home Secretary from 1905 to 1910, and the youngest son of Prime Minister William Ewart Gladstone, was a keen cyclist in the 1890s, and also used his influence in Parliament to secure measures favourable to cycling, claimed *The Hub* magazine in 1899:

> Cycling has quite won Mr. [Herbert] Gladstone over, and he is among the staunchest friends of the pastime ... It was he who, as First Commissioner of Works, took the initiative in tackling authorities with a view to the opening of Hyde Park for cycle riding during certain hours of the day ... Mr. Gladstone's excursions have included town as well as country riding ... He is keen upon the subject of street paving ... and upon road maintenance generally.

Herbert, 1st Viscount Gladstone was a Liberal statesman, but cycling crossed the political divide. In the 1890s, vice-presidents of the Pioneer Cycling Club of London included politicians of all stripes, including Percy Thornton, the Conservative MP for Clapham and prospective Conservative MP, W. M. Chinnery, who was beaten in the 1892 General Election by the Independent Labour Party's John Elliot Burns. When journalist Harold Spender wanted to interview Burns in 1900, he did so from the saddle of a bicycle:

> Anxious to see Battersea on the eve of the greatest struggle in its history, I had ridden southwest to the silver Thames, crossed that beautiful park, with its smooth roads, its ample playing fields, and large calm waters, and had emerged in the Battersea Road. The thoughts of a bicyclist

are wonderfully calmed by a smooth road, and I had begun to think pleasantly of Battersea. But the city is the man; you cannot think of Battersea without thinking of Burns. His energy is writ large on every corner of this pleasant city – on the park, the public buildings, the cottages, the very roads. He has sweetened Battersea by the ceaseless infusion of ideas, and so it has become his city, the one poor suburb of London that has sweetness and light. So I was thinking when I looked up, and there was the man himself. He was riding towards me on his bicycle, the handlebars decked with a bunch of blue and white ribbons; alert, robust, radiant with confident strength.

Sir John Aird, a civil-engineering contractor and the Conservative MP for Paddington North from 1887 to 1906, was for many years the president of the Bath Road Club, one of London's pre-eminent cycling clubs.

John Douglas, the 9th Marquess of Queensberry, most famous today for the boxing rules which he endorsed and for the part he played in Oscar Wilde's downfall, was a controversial parliamentarian in the 1880s and also a keen cyclist, "frequenting the Ripley Road almost daily".

The most prominent pedalling politician of the Victorian age – and who used his influence to further the cause of cycling – was William Coutts Keppel, 7th Earl of Albemarle. He was a long-time president of the National Cyclists' Union and the Civil Service Bicycle Club. Also known as Lord Bury, he was the co-author of an 1887 book on cycling for the aristocratic Badminton Library of Sports and Pastimes. Lord Bury was an influential chap. A former soldier, he entered parliament in 1857, serving as Treasurer of the Household (a Deputy Chief Whip) between 1859 and 1866. Between 1878 and 1880, and then 1885 and 1886, he was Parliamentary Under-Secretary of State for War. He wrote his cycling book the year after leaving office.

As president of the NCU from 1883 – a post he held while a parliamentarian – he was well able to fulfil the obligation to "watch the course of any legislative proposals in Parliament or elsewhere affecting the interests of the bicycling public, and to make such representations on the subject as the occasion may demand," a founding aim of the NCU.

Before he became a politician in the 1880s, barrister Joseph Firth Bottomley Firth was the author of one of the first books on cycling. *The Velocipede – Its Past, Its Present & Its Future* was published in 1869. Like other pioneer cyclists, Firth was intensely interested in roads. In his book – deliciously sub-titled "Straddle a Saddle, then Paddle and Skedaddle," – he wrote:

> When the Dandy-horse was in the heyday of its popularity it was modestly proposed by one enthusiastic rider, that one half of the king's highway should be given up to the machine … perhaps we should have the same demand again; if indeed some ambitious M.P. did not introduce a new Highway Act, to provide roads on purpose.

Firth became the Liberal MP for Chelsea in 1880. He did not introduce a Highway Act to provide roads for cyclists but he did become a municipal reformer, involved in improving living conditions for all Londoners, and that included reform of roads, sanitation and other matters that interested cyclists.

While MPs may feel they wield the ultimate influence, the Victorian age saw the rise of the media as a power in the land. One of the most dominant of the newspapermen who made up the late-Victorian "Fourth Estate" was William Thomas Stead, who had deep connections to cycling. BBC interviewer and historian of the Victorian era Jeremy Paxman put Stead third in a list of the top ten eminent Victorians, calling him "one of the greatest newspaper editors of all time." Lord Esher said in the 1890s that Stead was so influential that he "came nearer to ruling the British Empire than any living man." In 2012, the British Library described him as a "towering presence in the cultural life of late Victorian and Edwardian society."

Stead was no ordinary journalist. He is known as the father of New Journalism, and creator of the tabloid reporting style. (He shares this accolade with Alfred Harmsworth, founder of the *Daily Mail* in 1896 and editor of *Bicycling News* in the 1880s, when he developed his tabloid style.). Stead was editor of the *Pall Mall Gazette* in the 1880s and founder and editor of the *Review of Reviews* in the 1890s. He said the Victorian press had the power to get "Ministers driven into retirement, laws repealed, great social reforms initiated, Bills transformed, estimates remodelled, Acts passed, generals nominated, governors appointed, armies sent hither and thither, war proclaimed and war averted."

This highly influential journalist was noted for his love of cycling. He founded a society women's bicycle club, the Mowbray House Cycling Association. Established in May 1893, the association was a cycling club for high-society ladies who, when not riding, raised money to pay for bicycles to supply to working women. The organisation's president was Lady Henry Somerset, and one of the club's most prominent supporters was Frances Evelyn "Daisy" Greville, the Countess of Warwick, mistress of the Prince of Wales. (She's supposed to be the Daisy in Harry Dacre's 1892 comic song "Daisy Bell", the music-hall favourite, with the famous bicycle made for two.)

The Mowbray House Cycling Association was run by Miss Nellie Bacon, Stead's personal secretary and a long-time cyclist. A New Woman, she would later become a motoring writer and a suffragette. In an article for *The Automobile* in 1900 she said she had been a cyclist for seventeen years. In 1894 she told a woman's emancipation magazine that "... an ordinary girl like myself can do sixty or seventy miles per day quite easily."

Bacon was a cycle tourist and perhaps it was she who persuaded Stead to allow fellow cycle tourists to avail themselves of his "acre of garden, with a lawn tennis ground, a gymnasium, and a swimming bath, under the shade of oaks and elms." These facilities were offered to touring cyclists at no cost, although they had to give at least two days' notice. Stead asked his society friends to offer similar facilities and those that did so included Lady Henry Somerset and the Countess of Warwick.

Stead's children were also keen on cycling. Two of his young sons went on a bicycle tour of Europe in 1893 and, judging from the effusive praise Stead heaped upon the Humber bicycles used on the tour, it's possible that they were gifted by Humber, a company noted for its eagerness to get famous folk on its machines. (A Humber ad from 1905 showed "A few riders of Humber Cycles," made up of 62 members of royalty, nobility and high society, including "HM King Edward VII, HRH Prince of Wales, General Baden Powell, Rt Hon A. J. Balfour ...)"

When interviewing famous characters, Stead would steer the conversation round to cycling. In 1897 he talked bicycles with Mark Twain: "I asked if he ever cycled. He said yes, he had ... He was all for a bicycle; a tricycle he thought, was a miserable compromise."

Stead went down with the Titanic. He died alongside Colonel John Jacob Astor IV, the American socialite who became known for his collection of motor cars and his financial support of the nascent Automobile Club of America but who had earlier been a member of the L.A.W. and who had patented a bicycle brake in 1889.

DESPITE HAVING numerous cycling MPs and bicycle-friendly media moguls, Britain never experienced L.A.W.-style block voting from cyclists. America's political system was more conducive to lobbying of all forms, whether that was behind the scenes or via block voting. It had been that way since the 18th century, although special-interest pleading increased markedly in the second half of the 19th century. The use of committees as primary drivers of legislation in America was well suited to the advancement of interest groups, whether commercial – such as the demand for railroad subsidies – or of a non-pecuniary nature, such as the wheelmen's demand for Good Roads. Britain didn't have an equivalent of "pork barrel" politics – the practice of politicians securing public funds for the support of particular projects within their electoral constituency or personal interests. Overt political lobbying in Britain didn't start until the 1930s.

There *was* a pre-1914 political campaigning group in Britain that used bicycles but this was for practical reasons rather than for furthering the cycling cause. The Women's Social and Political Union, founded in 1903 as a radical offshoot from the genteel suffragette movement, used bicycles as campaign vehicles. The WSPU Cycling Scouts were formed in 1907 as a means of quickly and efficiently spreading the suffrage mission. Suffragettes dressed in the purple, white and green of the union, and with bicycles draped in the same colours, would sally forth from Sloane Square for destinations on the outskirts of London. "The Saturday bicycle meetings of the Suffragette scouts are proving a great success," said the WSPU campaign newspaper in 1908. WSPU branches around Britain formed their own brigades of Cycling Scouts. Growing impatient at a lack of political progress, WSPU members became increasingly more radical, using bicycles to blockade MPs in their cars and then, eventually, smashing shop windows, setting postboxes alight and even fire-bombing public buildings (no doubt using bicycles as getaway vehicles).

THE VIOLENCE of the radical suffragettes was a sure sign that they had no behind-the-scenes influence. Special interests, then and now, that wield influence do not need to campaign publicly. Historians often claim that the L.A.W's special pleading failed and that when the agitation of the 1880s and early 1890s faded away in the mid-1890s the L.A.W. was a spent force. This is not the case. The L.A.W. went quiet because it had gained a position of influence *inside* the federal government. L.A.W.'s top national officials no longer needed to throw their weight around in public.

Thanks to years of agitation and also Colonel Pope's mammoth petition mentioned in chapter 10, wheelmen caused the creation in 1893 of the Office of Road Inquiry, a bureau within the federal government's Department of Agriculture. Because of the expertise of L.A.W. officials many became unofficial consultants to the nascent ORI – others obtained paid freelance jobs with the bureau. It was a symbiotic relationship. In return for lobbying for increased appropriations for the ORI, League officials gained significant benefits from the government department they were boosting. The key benefit was the postal franking privilege – the L.A.W. was able to send out its Good Roads literature without cost and with the government's stamp of approval. This was financially beneficial but also of extreme importance in persuading farmers that the Good Roads message, long espoused by "them bicycle fellars", was favoured by the Department of Agriculture.

"The farmers now understand our aims much better than they did a few years ago, and … they can safely hob-nob with us, as it were," wrote Otto Dorner, chairman of the L.A.W.'s National Committee for Highway Improvement, to the ORI director in 1898.

The ORI appointed volunteer "Public Roads Correspondents" to monitor the condition of roads throughout the country – many of the appointees were wheelmen. These agents were issued official certificates by the government and were provided with stationery, maps and other information, as well as use of the government frank.

Lawyer Gregory C. Lisa wrote in 1995 that the L.A.W "captured" the ORI in several ways:

> First, the Bureau owed its existence, as well as subsequent appropriations increases, in large part to the lobbying efforts of the League. Second, numerous unofficial contacts and favors by

the Wheelmen caused Bureau officials to become further indebted to the League. Finally, the League served as an invaluable source of information, model legislation, political pressure on congressional representatives, and publicity.

The League was also allowed to fund the ORI's work: E. G. Harrison, a "Special Agent" for the ORI, often had his expenses paid by the L.A.W. Inviting him to a Good Roads meeting, L.A.W. president Isaac Potter assured Harrison that "of course your expenses will be paid by the L.A.W."

Sterling Elliott, the league president after Potter, made the following offer to the head of the ORI, General Roy Stone:

> It would be of the greatest assistance to us in our work to have it officially understood that we were in some sort of co-operation with your department. We can certainly be of great assistance to each other and to the cause which we are both working for. We shall be in a position to spend some money for printing. I understand that is your weak point.

The League also provided the government department with detailed maps, a 300,000-name mailing list, and technical guidance. Cyclists had been the instigators of the Good Roads movement and were the natural "go-to" experts for a newly created department. L.A.W. officials also drafted model legislation for the ORI – all behind closed doors.

General Stone knew who he could rely on to bolster his young department. In an address to a Good Roads banquet in 1897, he said: "Every wheelman is a preacher, a worker, and a fighter for good roads."

In a letter to Stone in 1900, Dorner expressed his optimism: "It seems to me that the prospects for good roads are brighter than ever before, and nothing will please me better than to see your office put upon a strong basis."

The ORI's budget was increased year on year, partly because of the lobbying work done by wheelmen. What was good for the ORI was good for the L.A.W., and vice versa. At times, the two organisations seemed as one. The most widely distributed ORI publication was *Must the Farmer Pay for Good Roads?*, written by Dorner in 1898. It was a L.A.W. publication, but distributed in its millions by the ORI.

The ORI eventually morphed into today's Federal Highway Administration. For the first seven years or so of its life, the organisation relied on the behind-the-scenes work, expertise and funding of the L.A.W. That cyclists were secretly influential at a critical point in American highway history was obscured by the fact that many L.A.W. officials later moved sideways into motoring organisations. The quiet contribution of cyclists was glossed over. That cyclists were once powerful is now almost totally forgotten.

CHAPTER THIRTEEN

MOTORING'S BICYCLING BEGINNINGS

If it wasn't for bicycles, there would be no cars.
GEORGE DRAGONE, 2007

**The motorists and cyclists of the 1890s and early 1900s were not from different sections
of society – they were frequently the exact same people. If you could go back in time
and quiz a pioneer motorist you'd discover, more times than not, he was a cyclist before
he donned the automobilist's fur-lined, floor-length motoring coat. The first motorists
often came from the ranks of champion cyclists, some of whom were aristocrats. Or they
were owners of bicycle manufacturing companies. Or they were cycling journalists.
Many of motoring's key pioneers were officials in cycling organisations. Motoring
pioneers originally celebrated their cycling credentials. By the end of the 1920s,
with the development of its proletarian image, cycling's vital contribution to the
development of motoring was deliberately suppressed.**

Bicycles, in the form we know them today, had only the merest head start over motor cars. John
Kemp Starley's Rover Safety bicycle was unveiled in a marquee next to London's Blackfriars Bridge
in January 1885 at Britain's main annual bicycle exhibition. Later the same year, in Germany, Carl Benz
used cycle technology developed by John Kemp Starley's uncle to make the world's first motor car.
"The early efforts of the German inventors, Gottlieb Daimler and Karl Benz, are in reality a part of
cycle history," said a historian from the Smithsonian Institution in Washington, D.C., in 1953. "Directly
and indirectly the bicycle had a decided influence on the introduction and ready acceptance of the
automobile."

Just as the motor car and the cycle overlapped, so too did those intimately involved in motoring and
cycling. Those interested in road locomotion in the 20 or so years before the First World War had very
often developed that interest on bicycles and tricycles. Tricycles, especially, were vehicles for moneyed
individuals, unwieldy vehicles requiring stabling and sometimes even specific servants. Ownership of
such expensive status symbols invariably later led to ownership of motor cars, which were even more

Hon. Charles Rolls on the front of a Cambridge University racing quad.

expensive and status driven. "Bicyclists ... were the very first to become ... votaries [for motoring]," *Scientific American* told readers in 1899, adding "it was through them that the automobile was first introduced to the public."

Automobile retailer Thomas F. Dunn, president of the Pennsylvania Automotive Association, reminisced that 1899 was the kick-off year for US motor car sales and that many of these sales were to cyclists: "The year 1899 was the real beginning of this great industry ... Sales this year were mostly to the wealthy and to bicycle enthusiasts."

Many historians, even eminent ones, have ignored the role of cycling in the gestation of motoring, making the mistaken assumption that motorists of the 1890s were from a higher class than cyclists. Asa Briggs, the leading specialist in Victorian social history, wrote of bicycles that those who "bought them ... came from different sections of society" to those who bought automobiles, and that "by contrast, the first motor car owners were plutocratic." The first motor car owners were, indeed, plutocratic – motor cars were luxury items and purchasers were *de facto* wealthy – but pioneer motorists were *not* from a different class to cyclists.

"Motorists [after 1896 were] richer and more influential than the cycling lobby," claimed history professor Stephen Inwood. In fact, cycling lobbyists were important and influential members of the nascent motor lobby. The organiser of British motoring's keystone event – the Emancipation Run of 1896 – was Harry Lawson, a long-time cycling promoter and bicycle designer in the 1870s. Frederick Simms, an employee of Lawson's who became known as the "Father of British motoring," was a member of the Cyclists' Touring Club in his youth. Simms founded the ultra-exclusive Automobile Club of Great Britain and Ireland, later to become the Royal Automobile Club. Another founder of this Club was Ernest Richard Shipton, secretary of the Cyclists' Touring Club from 1883 to 1907. He was also one of the Automobile Club's 1890s board members. Many of the organising stalwarts of the first American automobile organisations had originally been key officials in bicycling organisations. The majority of pioneering motoring journalists – in America, France, Austria and England – started as writers for cycling magazines.

The Self-Propelled Traffic Association, one of the world's first motoring organisations, was founded in London in 1895 by Sir David Lionel Salomons, a trustee and life-member of the Cyclists' Touring Club. In 1895, this particular bicycling baronet was also an active president of his local bicycle club and a member of the National Cyclists' Union. In 1899, he paid for his children to become life-members of the CTC, and some of them were still keen cyclists six years later. Salomons was one of the staunchest promoters of motoring in Britain and well known as such abroad. Salomons was also one of the founding members of the Automobile Club de France. This, the oldest motoring club in the world, was later led by stalwarts such as Chevalier René de Knyff. He was one of a number of the founders who had been cyclists first: de Knyff had been a racing cycling manager in the 1890s before becoming one of the world's first racing drivers.

Salomon's Self-Propelled Traffic Association later merged with Britain's Automobile Club, a prestigious gentleman's club to begin with, not originally a road rescue organisation. It had a posh, central London clubhouse, and posh members. Many of the founder members had been famous racing cyclists: Selwyn Edge had been a champion racing cyclist before he became a racing driver; the Hon. Charles Rolls, aristocrat, playboy, daredevil and co-founder of Rolls-Royce, received his first rush of road speed on the fastest vehicle of the day, the bicycle, and he too had been a bicycle racer, captaining the Cambridge University cycling team. In 1897, at the same time as Rolls was racing for Cambridge University, the wealthy Lionel Martin was racing bicycles for Oxford University. He later co-founded Aston Martin.

The apparent ignorance among social historians of the elite status of many Victorian cyclists can also be found in William Plowden's otherwise reliable 1970s classic about the politics of the car, which is very strong on Victorian motoring. Plowden claimed that early motor cars were "owned by people of considerably higher social status" than cyclists. This was true of the cyclists and motorists in the 1930s, when cycling had morphed into "poor man's transport," but it certainly wasn't true of the 1890s. Cycling was, briefly, the preserve of royalty and the aristocracy, and for a longer time of professors, surgeons, doctors, factory owners, lawyers and others from the aspiring middle classes, but not yet the working man.

The prolific motor historian Timothy Nicholson claimed Victorian cyclists were a separate body to motorists. He wrote that "cyclists were not men of substance." Again, this is a characterisation true of cyclists in the 1930s, but not the 1890s. "Although very numerous, [cyclists] lacked political muscle," said Nicholson, ignoring the fact that those early motorists – such as Salomons – successfully lobbied to overturn legislation oppressive towards motor cars, and remained active in cycling organisations.

In America, officials from the League of American Wheelmen had influence behind the scenes in the precursor to the Federal Highway Administration, influence they kept as they morphed into motorists.

MANY HISTORIANS appear to rely not on facts but on prejudice that took off from the 1920s. Far too many have downplayed the role of cycling in the history of highways and motoring. It's easy to see why: many of the early advocates of motoring developed selective memories where their own cycling was concerned – especially some years later, when cycling had developed into a proletarian pursuit.

Pulitzer Prize-winning American novelist Edith Wharton, author of biting novels about the New York high society into which she was born, wrote a motoring travelogue in 1908. Missing out the vital contribution of cycling to *fin de siécle* mobility, it started thus:

> The motor-car has restored the romance of travel. Freeing us from all the compulsions and contacts of the railway, the bondage to fixed hours and the beaten track … it has given us back the wonder, the adventure and the novelty which enlivened the way of our posting grand-parents.

Wharton had developed her love of motoring in Europe, buying a Panhard–Levassor automobile in 1904. At her American home, a grand house in Lenox, Massachusetts, she kept a Pope-Hartford touring car, a petrol-powered automobile from one of America's top marques of the day – a firm with deep cycling roots.

However, this wasn't Wharton's only link to bicycling. She had once been a cyclist, and proud of it. She started cycling in summer 1883 in the exclusive resort town of Bar Harbor in Maine, then famous for the opportunities it provided for unchaperoned outdoor activities for women from the leisured elite. Walking, cycling and canoeing were all popular in the resort towns favoured by the Gilded Age elite – towns such as Newport, Rhode Island, where Wharton summered, and where she set her Pulitzer-winning novel *The Age of Innocence*. In 1889, Wharton and her husband purchased a town house on Fourth Avenue at 78th Street in New York. This was a neighbourhood not then as fashionable as it would become. Why this particular location? In a letter to an architect friend, Wharton said she chose this particular town house "on account of the bicycling" in nearby Central Park. Wharton, like others of her class, had once been deeply attached to cycling, an attachment that became shameful once cycling developed into transport for the masses.

The peak of cycling's popularity with America's moneyed elite was in 1897. In the 1930s, Wharton made a great deal of her love for motoring but her memoirs made only dismissive references to cycling. They were written at a time when cycling was no longer something that an American president, say, would do.

It's LONG been said that Thomas Woodrow Wilson, President of the United States during and for three years after the First World War, was a huge fan of the automobile. "No more ardent motorist ever occupied the White House than President Wilson," wrote an American motoring magazine in 1916. This was the year President Wilson signed the Federal Aid Road Act, the law that saw national money starting to pave America.

What history books (apart from this one) ignore is that Wilson had been an ardent cycle tourist. He spent long vacations cycling around Europe. It's almost certain that Wilson's interest in Good Roads started when he was a cyclist, before and during his time as a law and politics professor at Princeton University.

Wilson, whose mother was born in Carlisle, spent many vacations cycle-touring in northern England, including in the Lake District. England's rural roads of the late 1890s, especially the main ones, were far superior to the roads Wilson would have endured as a cyclist in America. Wilson was definitely an avowed advocate of good roads. He compiled the Democratic Party's policy on Good Roads for the 1916 presidential election campaign: "The happiness, comfort and prosperity of rural life, and the development of the city are alike conserved by the construction of public highways," he wrote.

"We, therefore, favor national aid in the construction of post roads and roads for military purposes." This had been the campaigning platform of American cycling organisations since the late 1880s.

MANY MOTORING pioneers came to regard cycling as little more than a pre-motoring stepping stone and were only too glad to swap legwork for condensed horse-power. However, not all motoring pioneers rejected or stopped cycling when they became hooked on automobiles. In *Motoring Illustrated*'s yearbook for 1904 – a listing of the world's most significant motorists, and therefore a listing of almost all of the motorists then known – many of those who submitted entries listed cycling as an interest, as well as shooting, yachting and other typical pursuits of the moneyed.

Sir Alfred Bird MP, a food magnate and one of the founding members of the Automobile Club, "loved the sport of cycling for its own sake and rode consistently from 1869 to his end in 1922." Other motoring pioneers who kept on pedalling included Lionel Martin, the co-founder of Aston Martin, who carried on cycling to his dying day. Quite literally: he died after being knocked from his tricycle by a motorist.

Henry Sturmey, founder and first editor of *The Autocar*, was a cyclist his whole adult life as well as being one of the key motoring pioneers. Today, he's better known as the designer of the Sturmey–Archer cycle gearing system.

Montague Napier, designer and builder of the world-beating Napier racing cars, and the up-market car brand of the same name, not only didn't stop cycling when his motoring career took off, he rode a high-wheeler, despite it being dated. Friend, fellow racing cyclist and business partner Selwyn Edge, Britain's most celebrated early racing driver, said Napier would "go for a ride on his high ordinary cycle which is to-day commonly known as the penny-farthing," and he did this "well after the turn of the century." According to Edge, Napier did this for pleasure: "he did not do it for the sake of mere eccentricity or cheap notoriety for he was a man who never sought the limelight." (Like Martin, Napier and Edge were members of the Bath Road Club, a cycling club.)

Frank Shorland, a champion racing cyclist of the 1890s who became an executive at Raleigh before becoming a motor mogul (while still in the cycle trade he was one of the few to drive in the London–Brighton Emancipation Run of 1896), had a "short abstention from active cycling" before acquiring a Swift Club Tourist bicycle in 1925. "A friend tells me that he received a great shock the other Sunday," reported a journalist for *Motor Trader*. "He came across Frank Shorland on a bicycle. Time was … when Frank was a champion rider … and history records how his prowess in this direction led him first into the cycle trade and through it to the motor trade industry, with which he has long been connected."

Henry Ford was the most famous motoring pioneer to cycle into his old age. The young Ford cycled to work on his prized lightweight bicycle when, in 1893, he was an engineer for the Edison Illuminating Company, and he still cycled to work when he was making his first motor cars. Ford's 1890s lightweight bicycle would have been an antique in 1940 when the 77-year-old carmaker, still with an eye for the latest tech, rode three miles every evening on an English sports bicycle claimed to weigh a svelte 12 lbs.

MANY OF the first "how to" books on motoring used cycling analogies to help motor car novices get the hang of things. In Lord Harmsworth's *Motors and Motor-driving* of 1904, motoring experts referred to cycling many times. In the section on tyres and punctures, journalist Charles Lincoln Freeston wrote: "While it is probable that most automobilists will have previously become acquainted with a cycle-tyre, it is desirable to describe the repair process throughout."

Freeston also described how to brake on hills by referring to braking on Alpine cycling tours.

Early motorists who took their cars on Alpine journeys had often made the same journeys on bicycles some years previously. Freeston certainly had: in 1900 he wrote a cycling guidebook to the Alps and dedicated it to "my fellow members of the Cyclists' Touring Club." Freeston's other contributions in Lord Harmsworth's book (Harmsworth was proprietor of the *Daily Mail* and other newspapers, and got his break in journalism, in the 1880s, by editing *Bicycling News*) were on car lighting and a history of automobile clubs.

Motoring was originally for moneyed elites but, even when driving a motor vehicle became part of an occupation, there were good reasons for recruiting cyclists. Cyclists had excellent road sense. *Motor Trader*, in 1925, said:

> We have always maintained that … cyclists make the most skilful drivers. Well-known drivers, such as Edge, Jarrott, Instone, Stocks, first learned their road lessons on the humble bicycle. Shorland, who was perhaps the finest cyclist the country has ever seen, belongs to this class. He possesses road sense, is a fine judge of speed, has that sound instinct, combined with unerring judgement …

Cyclists also tended to have good mechanical skills, something of a vital requirement if you wanted to be a turn-of-the-century chauffeur. Before he became a famous racing driver, and before lending his name to an automobile company, Louis Chevrolet had been a chauffeur, and before that a racing cyclist and bicycle maker.

When, in 1899, the Motoring Manufacturing Company of London advertised for "young men … willing to give some little time to be perfected in driving," the firm knew who would make the best chauffeurs – "cyclists preferred," it stated.

Costume de chauffeur en 1900.

As WILL be amply demonstrated in this and the next chapter, pioneer motorists and cyclists were part of the same tight clique. Those few who shaped cycling in the 1880s and 1890s moved seamlessly across to the similarly niche world of motoring. There's a tangled web of connections between many of the leading players, including those famous today as pioneer motorists. Many of the famous early motorists already knew each other because they had socialised together as cyclists.

There's more to this interconnectedness than people; there's also spatial geography. For instance, before it became Motown – or Motortown – Detroit was a Biketown, a centre for bicycle production, and a hotbed for incubating leaders of the Good Roads movement. Similarly, in England, the motor manufacturing industry was concentrated in the Midlands because that's where the bulk of the cycle manufacturing industry had been based, clustered around Coventry thanks to the pioneers of English cycling who had congregated there, in the late 1860s, to make the first high-wheeler bicycles.

Cycle manufacturers became automobile manufacturers in France, Germany, America and in most other countries where motor cars were made. In England, before the stock market crash of 1929, there were 200 separate manufacturers of British cars, many of which had first been bicycle manufacturers. Very few survived into the 1930s, mainly because of the market dominance of Detroit's most famous cyclist, Henry Ford.

The Ford Motor Company (Henry Ford's third stab at the auto business) was incorporated in 1903. In 1911, the company opened a car factory in Manchester, England. By 1913, the factory was making 7,310 cars each year. The next biggest car marques were all former (or current) bicycle makers. Wolseley produced 3,000 cars in 1913; Humber 2,500; Rover 1,800; and Sunbeam 1,700. By 1929, Morris – a firm that sprang from a bicycle shop – accounted for half of all the cars made in Britain.

William Morris – later ennobled as Lord Nuffield for his philanthropy and contribution to the British economy – had been a successful racing cyclist in his youth. Despite being one of the richest men in Britain in the 1930–50s, he didn't flaunt his wealth. His office was decorated plainly, the only ostentation being a cabinet containing his most prized possessions: his cycling trophies. He remained proud of his cycling roots and, at the time, it was well known that Britain's most successful motor magnate had funded his automotive empire from the profits generated by his three Oxford bicycle shops.

Writing in 1934, Detroit-based technology historian Arthur Pound said:

> In showmanship, as well as in mechanics, the automobile trade owes a considerable part of its early momentum to the bicycle trade. By an easy transition firms making bicycles and bicycle parts began to make automobiles and parts … Hundreds of the most effective of the early automobile salesmen came directly into the new field from the bicycle trades.

Frank and Charles Duryea – bicycle mechanic brothers – produced the first automobile for sale in America. Colonel Albert Pope's company made electric cars, and many New York taxi cabs in the late 1890s and early 1900s were electric Columbia cars. At this time, Pope's Columbia was still America's leading bicycle manufacturing company, and had been making bicycles since the high-wheeler era. Alexander Winton of Cleveland was the leading manufacturer of gasoline-powered vehicles in 1900: he had earlier manufactured his own brand of bicycle.

Other industrialists who became big in automobiles from bicycle beginnings included Thomas B. Jeffery, John N. Willys, and John and Horace Dodge. The Dodge brothers operated the Evans and Dodge Bicycle Company in the 1890s. As well as their own brand, they sold car parts to Henry Ford (they also took an important, and lucrative, stake in the fledgling Ford Motor Company). Bicycle salesman Willys made motor cars in the former Pope bicycle plant in Toledo: this plant would later make the Jeep, America's archetypal military off-roader. Jeffery's Rambler motor car started life as the Rambler bicycle.

Another bicycle man – George N. Pierce of Buffalo – produced the Pierce-Arrow, America's leading luxury motor car marque of the 1920s and 1930s.

Greater detail on these characters, and many others, can be found in the appendix, where I list more than sixty motor marques with bicycling beginnings.

CHAPTER FOURTEEN

WITHOUT BICYCLES MOTORING MIGHT NOT EXIST

*The invention which had the most immediate
influence on the early history of the automobile was the bicycle.*
RUDI VOLTI, 2006

**The first automobiles contained more cycle DNA than horse-drawn carriage DNA.
In the late 1890s and early 1900s there was a seamless transfer of technology, personnel,
and finance between bicycle and motor car companies. Pioneer racing drivers,
motoring journalists and automobile event organisers tended
to have cut their teeth in the world of cycling. Officials in the early motoring
bodies often kept on working for cycling organisations.**

Writing in his 1988 social history *The Automobile Age*, motoring historian James J. Flink made a brief, little noticed claim:

> No preceding technological innovation – not even the internal combustion engine – was as important to the development of the automobile as the bicycle.

Engage reverse gear. Not even the internal combustion engine! Quite some claim. Flink didn't back up his claim with pages of evidence. I shall now do so.

Motor car manufacturers benefitted from products, production techniques, materials, innovations and tooling either developed specifically for cycles, or perfected for them. "Cycles" rather than "bicycles" because some of the technological developments used on the first motor cars – such as differential gearing – were lifted from tricycles. And, in the late 1880s, from a quadricycle came the knuckle-bone axle, a key development used on many of the early motor cars, and which, before the patent ran out in 1907, made Sterling Elliott a wealthy man. Elliott, whom Thomas Edison called a "genius," was a bicycle magazine publisher and, in 1896, the president of the League of American Wheelmen. Elliott's knuckle-bone concept was developed for a four-wheel cycle designed for his wife.

Some of the developments adopted by the automobile industry from the cycle industry were much smaller than knuckle-bone heads. Ball bearings, for instance. Tungsten steels, developed in the 1870s, were used by the new and innovative cycle industry, creating stronger, more precisely engineered ball bearings. Cycle companies didn't invent bearings, balled or otherwise, but their use on cycles led to great advances in the technology.

The internal combustion engine is one of the few advances that wasn't developed first in the cycle industry. Many of the other key innovations – from electric resistance welding to steel-frame tubing, and from pneumatic tyres to metal-stamping technology – were perfected by cycle companies before being adopted by emerging automobile companies (many of which were cycle companies).

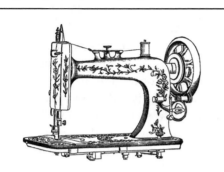

IT COULD be argued that sewing machines influenced motor-car technology, via bicycles. Many cycle companies started life as sewing machine concerns, from Coventry Machinists and Howe Machine Co. in England, to Dürkopp and Opel of Germany. And when Colonel Pope needed a factory to build the bicycles he imported from the (sewing-machine) factories of England, he turned to the Weed Sewing Machine Company of Hartford, Connecticut. As well as a transfer of technology – including manufacturing methods – there was a transfer of personnel, capital and know-how.

Cycle industry experimentation in machining, steel hardening, manufacturing with aluminium, and achieving fine tolerances would prove to be transformational for the emerging automobile industry which, thanks to widespread cross-pollination between companies and engineers, allowed for a swift, seamless transfer of technologies from the innovative and then still profitable cycle industry to the fledgling, not-at-all-profitable automobile industry.

🕭 MOTORING TECHNOLOGY

The motor car was not "invented," or based on any single scientific breakthrough, but was, rather, an amalgam of earlier innovations – and a great many of the critical ones came from the cycle industry. Had there been no cycle industry to spring from, the automobile industry might have never achieved critical mass. Companies in the horse-drawn carriage industry, apart from a few notable exceptions, were not terribly innovative, and most were dismissive of the upstart automobile industry. Critically, carriages were made from wood, while many early automobiles – like bicycles – were made from steel and, later, aluminium.

Henry Duncan, owner of upmarket carriage-maker Brewster & Company, admitted in the 1920s that the bicycle industry had a key advantage over the carriage industry: "The metal construction of the bicycle brought it more closely in touch with the all metal automobile," he said.

Automobiles may have been "dismissed by horse-drawn vehicle manufacturers as a passing fad," as carriage historian Thomas A. Kinney said, but they eventually snuffed out the carriage-making industry. Not that the motor car killed off carriages alone – the horseflesh business was at risk of extinction some years before the automobile came along. This threat came in the shape of Frank J. Sprague's electric streetcar system, installed in 1888 in Richmond, Virginia. By 1902, the US had 15,000 miles of track, and 97 percent of urban street railway systems were electric. This swift form of urban locomotion reshaped cities, as did the similar development of urban railways underground in cities such as London. Suburbs weren't created by cars – merely accelerated by them. Had it not been preceded by the cycle industry, the automobile industry might not have been nimble enough to see off the competition from urban rail. Luckily for those who love automobiles, the cycle industry *did* exist and it was the ideal launch platform for motor cars.

Today, bicycles may be viewed by some as old-fashioned relics of a less technologically advanced era but bicycles were at the cutting edge of industrial design in the last quarter of the 19th century. In the ten years before 1900, a third of all new patent applications at the US Patent Office were cycle-related; in Britain more than half of the 28,000 patents filed in 1896 were for improvements in cycles.

Due to the employment of stronger steel alloys, and improvements in steel tube manufacturing, the weight of an average Safety bicycle fell from 42 pounds in 1890 to 22 pounds by 1895. The constant innovation made cycling very attractive, with frequent launches of new products that improved – or claimed to improve – on earlier models, making them lighter and faster. Yet these particular consumer durables weren't designed to be as long-lasting as were many of the manufactured products of the time, not so much in durability (bicycles were built tough) as in terms of fashion. It was the bicycle industry and not, as is usually claimed, the automobile industry that popularised the concept of planned obsolescence, the policy of designing a product with a limited useful life, so it will become obsolete or unfashionable after a period of time, leading to the purchase of "new, improved" models, year after year.

Henry Ford decried such methods, preferring to build cars "so … no one ought ever to have to buy a second one," a concept that probably very few in his company or the wider automobile industry, shared – which Ford complained about in his 1922 autobiography:

> My associates were not convinced that it was possible to restrict our cars to a single model. The automobile trade was following the old bicycle trade, in which every manufacturer thought it necessary to bring out a new model each year and to make it so unlike all previous models that those who had bought the former models would want to get rid of the old and buy the new.

Assembly-line manufacturing, another concept popularly thought to have been introduced by Henry Ford, was used by cycle factories first. The Pope Manufacturing Company organised the production of bicycles – and, later, electric cars – by assigning individuals to single, repetitive tasks. A reporter from the *Scottish Cyclist*, given a tour of Pope's American factories in 1893, reported:

> From there I went to several great flats where lathes, drills etc were to be numbered by the hundred, the most striking feature being the remarkable adaptations of machinery for labour saving purposes. Everywhere, automatic machinery abounded.

Colonel Pope anticipated Ford in better pay for workers. During a lecture he gave in 1892, Colonel Pope remarked "everyone should sympathize with the workingman, for the better his wages, the more he has to purchase the goods of the merchant and the manufacturer."

Pope was also ahead of Ford on another matter. Pope's best employee was not a factory worker but "he is the most faithful fellow in the world," claimed the Colonel:

> He has been in my employ for seventeen years, yet he has never even asked for a holiday. He works both day and night, is never asleep or intoxicated, and though I pay him more than $250,000 a year, I consider that he costs me nothing. His name is Advertisement.

While the US automobile industry later dominated advertising expenditure in the American press, the first industry to dominate had been the cycle industry. Cycle company advertisers were also innovative and, in France, highly progressive, helping to support poster artists such as Henri de Toulouse-Lautrec, who was later to find fame as a post-impressionist painter. Leonetto Cappiello, the Italian-born Paris-based illustrator considered the father of modern advertising, also produced iconic posters for cycle manufacturers, right through until the end of the 1920s.

A number of historians of advertising claim that cycling's mass-market promotions stimulated advertising in other sectors. David Hounsell, a professor of technology and social change, credits the cycle industry with the development of "slick mass-marketing practices" to fuel and sustain the mid-1890s bicycle boom. Cycling entrepreneurs also innovated in direct marketing. Sterling Elliott, he of the knuckle-bone steering, created a punchcard machine that automated the address labelling system for the 120,000-circulation weekly magazine for the League of American Wheelmen.

According to historian Ross Petty, the cycle industry was responsible for creating a great deal of modern advertising and marketing:

> The bicycle advanced the practice of advertising by developing competitive advertising content, image advertising in posters, research techniques to determine advertising effectiveness, and support for the new media, magazines. The industry also developed new promotional techniques including … obtaining celebrity endorsements. It perfected the trade show and annual model changes. Most significantly, the bicycle of the late 1800s was marketed using segmentation techniques that have been thought to have been developed more recently.

Those engineers and innovators who transferred from cycling to motoring kept on innovating and usually did so with no further contribution from the world of cycling. Technological developments that were crucial for the first motor cars – such as wire wheels and tubular steel frames – were quickly superseded by technologies better suited to motor cars as they became faster and more powerful. Cycling and motoring – once joined at the hip – became separated and went their different ways. Today's motor car has evolved to look nothing whatsoever like the bicycles and tricycles whence, in part, it sprang but the cycling DNA is present and important nonetheless.

ASSEMBLY-LINE MANUFACTURING

Henry Ford usually gets all the credit for introducing parts standardisation and the moving assembly line ("the way to make automobiles … is to make them all alike … just like one pin is like another pin when it comes from the pin factory") but many industrialists were there before him, including bicycle builders – such as the Western Wheel Works of Chicago where, in the 1890s, machinists remained seated and runners brought materials to them. These builders also borrowed from other industries, including meat-packing factories – progress is often about evolution rather than revolution.

Henry Ford didn't introduce assembly-line manufacturing into his own factories – company engineer Clarence Avery did that – but Ford was well aware of the benefits on offer from such techniques. He was aware of this because he visited American bicycle factories and saw an earlier form of the method at close quarters.

Colonel Pope's mammoth factories churned out hundreds of thousands of Columbia-marque cycles every year for most of the final quarter of the 19th century. Pope's factories were equipped with modern machine tools, and the manufacturing methods were progressive too, including standardisation of parts.

Pope was making bicycles with interchangeable parts as early as 1881. A factory visitor reported that Columbia high-wheel bicycles were made on "the truly American scale; that is, they started with a view to making every part of the bicycle by machinery, so that the parts should be interchangeable." The visitor described the drafting room, the forge shop, a number of specialised welding shops, the polishing room, the lathe room and the paint shop.

Pope had identified the importance of interchangeable parts on a research trip to Coventry bicycle factories in 1878, and he "proceeded to manufacture on a large scale and according to the best methods on the interchangeable plan."

He wasn't the first American industrialist to use interchangeable parts, but he expanded the process. According to geographer Glen Norcliffe, Pope created a system that "involved advances in specialization and vertical integration, considerable technological innovation, major advances in the interchangeability of parts, innovative use of advertising and promotion of mass consumption, and the development of a corporate culture that sustained the system."

By the end of the bicycle boom in 1897, Pope owned one of the largest vertically-integrated industrial complexes in the world.

Henry Ford "visited and admired" Pope's bicycle factories in Hartford before he started to manufacture cars, said Pope's great-great grandson.

When Pope started making automobiles, factory supervisor Harold Hayden Eames organised work gangs to carry out assembly-line-style jobs. The automobile industry inherited extremely high standards of precision and accuracy from machine shop owner Henry M. Leland, famous in the 1890s for his precisely machined bicycle parts. He later went on to create the Cadillac car. Alfred P. Sloan, president and chairman of General Motors, which later absorbed the Cadillac brand, considered Leland to be "one of those mainly responsible for bringing the technique of interchangeable parts into automobile manufacturing."

The employee at the Ford Motor Company most responsible for the adoption of the moving assembly line was William S. Knudsen. In his native Denmark Knudsen had been a mechanic at his brother's bicycle shop and, in 1898, he worked for a bicycle import business. In 1900, at 21 years of age, he left Copenhagen for a new life in America, working first as a riveter. By 1902 he was back in the business of bicycles, working for cycle manufacturer John R. Keim Mills of Buffalo, New York. Ford inherited Knudsen from a takeover of the Keim Mills, where Knudsen had risen to plant superintendent. Knudsen was partly responsible, in 1904, for turning Keim Mills from a bicycle-making factory into a steel-stamping factory. The company made parts for Ford but couldn't keep up with demand.

"When Henry Ford bought the Keim Mills in 1911, Knudsen found himself, like many another oldtime bicycle man, in the stripling automobile industry," said *Time* in 1937.

The assembly-line production of Ford cars started in 1913, kickstarted by Knudsen.

"As Mr. Ford's production manager in his great expansion period, Motorman Knudsen had a prime hand in creating modern mass production," reported *Time*. Output jumped from 8,000 in 1907 to a quarter of a million in 1914, with almost everything made in-house at one of the Ford plants.

Knudsen went on to work for Chevrolet from 1937 to 1940 and was president of General Motors where he "remained as friendly and democratic as he had been when a bicycle plant manager."

BALL BEARINGS

The rotating parts in automobile engines require extensive use of ball bearings. So important are these polished steel spheres that one famous motor car brand was named after the smooth ride made possible by them. In Latin, Volvo means "I roll", a reference to ball bearings. Volvo sprang, in 1915, from SKF, a Swedish ball-bearing manufacturer. Modern ball bearings are largely the product of a cycle-based technological feeding frenzy in the 1870s and 1880s. Cycle companies fought to produce the smoothest and strongest means of reducing friction between rotating parts. Even though Philip Vaughan, a Welsh ironmaster, patented a ball-bearing assembly in 1794, most technology historians agree it was the cycle industry that forged modern ball bearings. "The ball bearing industry is an outgrowth of the bicycle industry," said a 1950s technical treatise on ball bearing use.

In 1869, Parisian bicycle mechanic Jules Pierre Suriray patented a method for making steel ball bearings. The advantage of riding with a bicycle equipped with Suriray's ball bearings was demonstrated later the same year by Englishman James Moore by winning the world's first bicycle road race. Moore rode the 80 miles between Paris and Rouen on a bicycle with an oversized front wheel with ball bearings in the hub.

Joseph Henry Hughes of Birmingham gained a patent for improved ball bearings in 1877. *The Times*, in 1896, said of Hughes' work: "The perfection of the invention is shown by the fact that the bearing has never been modified since it was originally introduced; and so highly is it valued that it is now being adapted to carriages and many forms of machinery."

Never been modified? Other patent holders would have disputed that, and many did, some going to court to defend their patented improvements to these small steel balls and their races. Hughes' patent of 1877 was, in fact, filed jointly with William Bown, and "Bown's bearings" were ubiquitous on high-wheelers and tricycles in the 1870s and 1880s. Friction is the enemy of smooth forward motion on a bicycle – the cycle innovators knew that fortunes would be made by those who could reduce this friction. Bown and Hughes made their bearing assemblies in the Aeolus Works in Birmingham. Aeolus was the Greek god of the four winds. Bown and Hughes clearly wanted to demonstrate that a cyclist who used Aeolus bearings would always ride friction-free, as though they had the wind at their back. Races were won by riders using the latest and smoothest ball bearings. Ball-bearing technology was once so cutting edge that cycle companies promoted the use of the latest ball bearings in much the same way that today a bicycle company might crow that it equips its machines with the latest Shimano parts. Between 1877 and the mid-1880s there was an international ball-bearing arms race, with cycle innovators filing competing patents. The first patents were filed in England but there were also key innovations made in America and Germany, and, via SKF, Sweden.

In America, Colonel Pope's Columbia bicycles were fitted with ball bearings "machined down to exact size, case hardened to diamond density on its surface, and then polished." These were made for Pope in Ohio by the Cleveland Machine Screw Company. (Every inch a verticalist, he bought the company in 1894.) In Germany, bicycle mechanic Friedrich Fischer of Schweinfurt started a quest in 1875 to produce better ball bearings for the cycles he produced in the cycle shop he had opened three years earlier. Importing balls from England was expensive and in 1883 he produced his first ball-grinding machine. By 1887, the six ball-grinding machines in his First Automatic Cast Steel Ball Factory were mass-producing geometrically perfect balls for bearing races. In 1896, "Ball-Fischer" sold his bicycle shop. By now, his expanded factory was producing five million balls each week. His company became Fischer AG, or FAG – it's still one of the world's major producers of ball bearings – and, thanks to the demand from the bicycle industry, it was in a perfect position to supply the nascent automobile industry, which relied heavily on these tiny steel balls.

CHAINS

Roller chains can be found in the gearing system for raising and lowering the Thames Flood Barrier, and in the vector thrust nozzles of Harrier jump jets. Roller chains – among the most efficient means of power transmission known – were also used in the first motor cars, and beefy ones are still used for motorbikes. The use of chains in automobiles was a direct transfer of technology from the cycle industry. The bush roller chain was developed in the 1870s in England by Swiss-born Hans Renold, a naturalised Briton.

Chains have been used since antiquity but Renold's innovation was to add a cylindrical tube, or "bushing", over chain pins, aiding the movement of the chain over toothed sprockets.

A year after Renold died in 1943, Professor Dempster Smith wrote a eulogy in the *Proceedings* of the Institution of Mechanical Engineers: "Few realise how extensive is the influence of Renold's inventiveness on both civil and industrial life throughout the world." Professor Smith continued:

> Virtually every form of modern transport, by road, sea, or air, employs or depends on chain. Millions are bicycle-conscious without necessarily being chain-conscious. Likewise the automobile has at all stages of its development been one of the major industries utilising chain as an essential feature of design; in fact, there is hardly a phase of any industry or public works in which the chain is not to be found making an obscure but vital contribution to our welfare.

Renold left his native Switzerland at the age of 21, settling in the industrial boom town of Manchester in 1873. Within five years the engineer had bought into a chain-making company, James Slater, which made chains for cotton factories. Renold, accurately but unimaginatively, changed the name of this company to the Hans Renold Company. In 1880, Renold introduced – and patented – the bushing, adding to the roller that had been part of the James Slater product. Tricycles had been using chains since the 1870s, including the Morgan chain, "composed of links made from round steel wire alternating with tubular steel rollers," said Victorian cycle engineer Archibald Sharp in his masterful 1896 book on the science and mechanics of cycling. By the mid-1880s, cycle companies were using a number of different chains (Humber, single-link and pivot chains) but were settling on bush roller chains which, when paired with sprockets and gears, allowed the large front wheel of the high-wheeler to be reduced in size, and eventually opened the way for the Safety bicycle of 1884–5. Renold became rich from the rapidly expanding cycle business. He called his large Manchester factory, constructed in 1889, Progress Works. It was funded wholly out of profits.

Renold allowed much of his technology to be used free of licences, greatly expanding the use of bush roller chains all over the world. In America, bush roller bicycle chains would be used to transmit power on Henry Ford's 1896 Quadricycle and seven were used on the Wright Brothers' 1903 aeroplane. We even know the brand of chain used: Diamond. The Wright Brothers stocked Diamond chains in their bicycle shop.

By 1904, two-thirds of the bicycle chains made in America were Diamond chains. The Diamond Chain Company still exists. It was founded on Christmas Eve 1890 as the Indianapolis Chain and Stamping Co. By 1895, thanks to the bicycle boom, the company had 500 employees. Henry Ford bought his Diamond-marque chain on May 28th, 1896 (he kept all his receipts).

The company was co-founded by Arthur C. Newby, later known for his work with the National Motor & Vehicle Company of Indianapolis, founded in 1900. National was a group of engineers, draftsmen – and motor car racers.

Newby was also a co-founder of the Indianapolis Motor Speedway. One of the others was Carl Fisher, creator of the coast-to-coast Lincoln Highway. Newby and Fisher knew each other because they were cyclists, and members of the Zig Zag Cycle Club, founded by Newby.

Newby was also a local official in the League of American Wheelmen. In 1898 he built the Newby Oval, a 20,000-seat velodrome stadium, in order to attract the national convention of the L.A.W.

L.A.W.'s 19th annual meet was held at the Newby Oval during August 1898. One of the track riders who raced during the meet was Indianapolis native Marshall "Major" Taylor, the world-beating

African-American cyclist. Another racer at the meet was Barney Oldfield, who would go on to become America's top motor car racer. Bicycle racing on the Newby Oval soon waned and it was demolished early in the 20th century.

Newby died in 1933, a very wealthy man. His obituary said he was a "pioneer bicycle and automobile man and widely-known philanthropist." The *Indianapolis News* added: "Mr. Newby belonged to the world famous Indianapolis group of pioneers in personal transportation who followed mechanical progress from bicycles to automobiles."

DIFFERENTIAL GEARING

Differential gearing has an ancient history (Chinese, mainly), but chain-driven differential gearing for cycles was invented by James Starley, "father of the cycle industry." Differential gears are essential for automobiles. The rack-and-pinion gears on a differential axle, attached to a driveshaft, allow each of the powered wheels to rotate free of the other, while providing power to both. In 1821, French watchmaker Onésiphore Pecqueur had created the first differential for a road-going vehicle, but Starley didn't know of his work and was able to gain a patent for his own design. It was Starley's design that transferred to the automobile, not Pecqueur's.

In 1877, Starley made a "Sociable" four-wheeled cycle for two riders, seated side by side. Each rider could pedal independently, which brought the problem that, when cornering, the stronger rider could cause the four-wheeler to skip and slide.

"It was while riding this machine with his son that the need for a differential gear became manifest [to Starley]," said bicycle collector and friend-to-the-inventors Horace William Bartleet in 1931:

> They were going uphill, and Starley senior adjured [his son, Bill] to "wire in." This the hefty youth did, but as the power applied was only effective to his own driving wheel, it tended to push the steering round. In half a minute Starley said: "Get off. I have it." They pushed the machine to the top of the hill, had tea at a village, and returned. That was on a Saturday ... On Monday his father called William to get up, while he went to a brass founders, and within an hour Bill was working on the castings – two bevel wheels and one pinion ... Starley caught the 8 a.m. train to London to see his patent agent, and the invention was protected forthwith. Thus was evolved the differential gear, used to-day on practically ... every motor car.

Carl Benz's Patent-Motorwagen used a belt-driven bevel-gear differential, a transfer of technology from tricycles to the new world of motor cars.

A 1937 infotainment film by Chevrolet explained the workings of differential gears and featured historical flashbacks to pioneer motor cars. However, it didn't explain that the differential technology used by the early automobile manufacturers was originally developed for cycles.

PNEUMATIC TYRES

Of all the technological breakthroughs developed and shaped in the white heat of the intensely innovative cycle industry perhaps the most transformative was the pneumatic tyre. As shown in chapter 2, the success of pneumatics was by means a certainty. Dublin cycle racer Harvey Du Cros had to graft to create and nurture what eventually became a world-reshaping industry. Pneumatic tyres didn't just give the world comfort they also allowed for speed, first on bicycles, later on automobiles. The first motor cars, like the first bicycles, had solid tyres. Air-cushioned tyres quickly proved themselves in late-1880s bicycle races, and the technology transferred across to motor cars in the mid-1890s.

An influential motoring book said in 1905: "It is not too much to say that the motor-car in its present form and in its present state of efficiency would be impossible if the pneumatic tyre had not been invented."

HORNS AND LAMPS

The very first motor cars – such as Henry Ford's Quadricycle – didn't just use bicycle wheels and bicycle chains, but also used bicycle lamps and other brass accessories, including bicycle horns. A typical bicycle horn had a rubber bulb bellow on the end for squeezing out a satisfying "honk, honk." Motorists took to them like ducks to water – or like amphibians, at least: Mr. Toad definitely liked the "Poop-poop!" of the bicycle horn on his motor car. He knew it meant "get out of the way, I'm more important than you!" Cyclists used horns – and bells and whistles – to warn pedestrians of their presence but had once used bugles, especially for group messaging purposes. In the early days of cycling, high-wheeler clubs would ride with at least one bugler, who would pass on instructions from the club captain aurally.

The first bicycle clubs were masculine and militaristic, with uniforms, codes of conduct, and ranks. Cyclists didn't use standard military bugles but rather had special ones made, triple-coiled in order to make them more portable. Club buglers would carry these often highly decorated bugles on their hips, ready for action.

Many modern automobiles have an embossed bugle on the steering wheel to signify the horn. It would be impossible to prove but is at least theoretically possible that this stylised horn is, in fact, the bicycle bugle from the 1870s and 1880s. Early motorists didn't use orchestra horns as warning devices, they used bicycle horns.

They also used bicycle lamps, including, in America, the Solar from Badger Brass of Kenosha, Wisconsin. Badger was founded in 1898 and by 1917 the firm had an annual output of 100,000 bicycle lamps and 400,000 motor car lamps. Solar Lamps – so named because of their brightness – were adopted as standard equipment by the Cycle Division of the Dutch Army. As well as American car brands such as the Jeffrey Rambler – also made in Kenosha – the auto lamps were standard on cars by Lancia of Italy and Berliet of France. Acetylene lamps were very bright (imagine the flame of a cutting torch). The Solar Lamp had jewelled side panels, throwing out red to port and green to starboard sides of the bicycle lamp.

In England, the bicycle lamp of choice was the "King of the Road" lamp from Lucas of Birmingham. Lucas later adapted its lamps for motor use and added "Motoralities" – horns, pumps and lamps – to its selection of "Cyclealities."

Lucas still exists as a car electrics accessory brand and, in 2013, reintroduced its "King of the Road"-brand lights for bicycles (as LED lights). Founded by Joseph Lucas in the 1860s as a dealer in paraffin, Lucas also sold lamps for ships. Joseph's eldest son Harry was a keen cyclist and Lucas branched out into bicycle-lamp manufacturing in 1878. The King of the Road lamp was the leading acetylene lamp brand of the day, fitted to the front hubs of many high-wheel bicycles, including American ones. By 1888 Lucas was employing 50 people and 700 by 1896 at the height of the bicycle boom, including Walter Chamberlain, youngest son of Joseph Chamberlain, MP for Birmingham West and the Secretary of State for the Colonies.

BADGES

Bonnet badges – such as those for Mercedes-Benz, BMW and other marques – are well known the world over. Motor cars weren't the first to use such insignia. Historian Hans-Erhard Lessing of Germany believes motor car manufacturers developed bonnet badges as a result of similar badges made earlier for cycles.

Pressed and etched badges for use on cycle head tubes enabled manufacturers to differentiate their products. These badges have a long history. The first was used on the pre-1820s *Laufsmachine* by Baron Von Drais. These wooden "running machines" were decorated with Drais's coat of arms on a silver platelet nailed to the tiller. The platelet indicated that a licence of one Carolin had been paid (the cost to have a *Draisine* built was given as four Carolin).

In the 1860s, when pedals were attached to the early velocipedes, the machines had marque badges attached to them. Many early high wheelers had builder's badges on the backbone. Later the badge migrated to the front, on the head tube, and motor car manufacturers adopted the same practice.

KNUCKLE-BONE AXLE

Buggies and carriages are steered with reins: pull on the left and the horse turns to the left and vice versa. Now imagine steering a motor car with reins. It would be possible at slow speeds but very much not possible at moderate or high speeds. One of the key innovations that allowed motor vehicles to be operated, and steered, at both low and high speeds was the tie-rod steering mechanism developed in the 1880s by racing cyclist and cycle-builder Sterling Elliott, once a president of the League of American Wheelmen. To permit automobile wheels to be turned by the steering gear, the steering spindle and steering knuckle assemblies are hinged on the end of an axle. The pin that forms the pivot of this hinge is known as the king-pin or steering knuckle pin.

Elliott developed the steering knuckle assembly for his Quadricycle, a four-wheel cycle he built for his wife in 1886 (*see right*). The Quadricycle featured the non-turning front axle, a differential rear axle, independent vertical action of all four wheels, and self-equalizing brakes. Many of the earliest US motor car manufacturers paid royalties to Elliott in order to use his cycle axle. The patent expired in 1907.

Born on a farm in rural Michigan in 1852, Elliott moved to Boston in 1875, opening a small machine shop. Seven years later he expanded into larger premises and opened a cycle factory. Witty adverts for his wooden bicycle wheels and unusual cycles appeared in the US cycle press for many years.

Along the road from Elliott's small cycle factory was a photography business owned by the Stanley brothers, identical twins Francis and Freeland. The three became friends. The Stanley brothers became motoring pioneers, basing their steam car on Elliott's Quadricycle and using his knuckle-bone axle. The plans for the Stanley Steamer were bought by John B. Walker, editor and publisher of *The Cosmopolitan*, and he and asphalt contractor Amzi L. Barber (a financial supporter of the L.A.W.'s Good Roads movement) created the Locomobile Company in 1899. In the first years of the 20th century, the Locomobile steam car, based on a number of Elliott's innovations, was America's top-selling automobile.

Sterling Elliott

Elliott was an inveterate inventor. The modern and airy Elliott Museum in Florida contains a selection of his inventions, including a knot-tying machine used in bookbinding. In recognition for inventing this magazine stitcher, Thomas Edison invited Elliott to his Menlo Park home and called him a "genius." Elliott also patented postal machines which, long before the computer age, could update mailing addresses, automating the labelling of subscription-based magazines. For some years Elliott's business had the contract to sort and send (and, from 1895, to publish) the L.A.W.'s official weekly journal, which in the 1890s, also included *Good Roads* magazine. In 1885 the League had fewer than 5,000 members: eight years later it had more than 100,000. Elliott's labelling and mailing machine – sold to mailing houses and publishers around the world – helped the L.A.W. manage this huge growth in members. *Bicycling World and the L.A.W. Bulletin* was one of the highest-circulation weekly magazines in America in the 1890s. Elliott was in charge of the L.A.W.'s racing committee for some time and, in 1895, he became chairman of the committee on highway improvement. The Elliott Addressing Machine Company carried out mailings for the US Government and businesses around America.

Elliott died in 1922, a very wealthy man, with a winter "cottage" in Florida, a yacht big enough to hold one of his motor cars, and a fleet of other cars, including luxury English marques, such as Rolls-Royce. The company was continued by his son, also a prolific inventor. The company later became part of Dymo Industries, which today produces labelling printers for home and office use.

SHAFT-DRIVES

Bicycle shaft-drive technology flopped. But the bicycle's loss was the automobile's gain. Patented in the early 1890s, and made to very fine tolerances by bicycle companies, shaft-drives were taken up with gusto by automobile and motorbike companies. Shaft-drives don't require chains, using instead, in effect, a pole attached to a small bevel gear to transmit power from the pedals to the rear wheel. Shaft-drives are 86 percent efficient at transmitting power; chains are 98 percent efficient. The main advantage of a shaft-drive is cleanliness: chains are oily.

Professor Archibald Sharp, an eminent Victorian cycle engineer, wrote in 1896 that "if bevel-wheels could be accurately and cheaply cut by machinery, it is possible that gears of this description might supplant, to a great extent, the chain-drive gear; but the fact that the teeth of the bevel-wheels cannot be accurately milled is a serious obstacle to their practical success."

The obstacle to their practical success was not accurate milling – that problem was solved by cycle engineers, which later benefitted the automobile industry. The main problem was price. Shaft-drive arrived in the late 1890s, at a time when low prices sold bicycles, not the latest tech. Shaft-drive bicycles were more expensive than chain-drive models partly because of massive investment in the very latest in fine-tolerance machining. Sales of shaft-drive bicycles were never better than tepid, especially as the easiest solution to an oily chain was not to remove it but to hide it out of reach, within a chain-case.

The Pope Manufacturing Company introduced a shaft-drive bicycle in 1898. It could machine the bevel gear to tolerances of 1/2,000 inch whereas, even as late as 1903, Henry Ford had to be content with tolerances of 1/64 inch for his motor cars. Pope achieved such accuracy thanks to his investment in machining technology and bicycle testing techniques, and by employing metallurgical experts.

Other bicycle brands to fit shaft-drives included Pierce-Arrow and Winton. These two companies, along with Columbia, moved into making automobiles, taking shaft-drive technology with them.

In a 1913 book on steel manufacturing, Edward Russell Markham, who had worked for a number of bicycle companies in the 1890s, said that bicycle companies invested a great deal of money and effort into perfecting shaft-drive technology:

> Hardening bevel gears for bevel gear chainless bicycles caused a great many anxious moments in shops where it was attempted. One prominent manufacturing concern lost at one time 75 per cent, of all gears hardened, according to their own statement.

One of the lead innovators in cycle shaft-drive technology was Henry Martyn Leland of Detroit machine shop Leland and Faulconer, which specialised in cycling. Towards the end of the 1890s, Leland and Faulconer started making shaft-drive machine tools for the Pope Manufacturing Company, using ultra-fine tolerance methods developed by Leland and Frank E. Ferris, one of his engineers. L&F sold ten gear-grinding machines to Pope, and others to the George N. Pierce Company. L&F also made shaft-drive parts for other companies.

When Leland created the Cadillac automobile he used shaft-drive and gear-grinding technology. The George N. Pierce Company went on to make America's most luxurious automobiles, yet was still making bicycles until 1915.

TUBING

The automobile industry benefitted hugely from the developments in steel and aluminium manufacturing wrought by the cycle industry. Case hardening, swaging, annealing, electric welding, and die-making, as well as stamping and pressing, were all significantly improved for use on cycles – which reduced dramatically in weight. New techniques for stretching and thinning lightweight steel tubing made bicycles stronger *and* lighter.

Tricycle- and bicycle-based automobiles, such as the Patent-Motorwagen by Carl Benz and the Quadricycle by Henry Ford, were constructed from lightweight seamless steel tubing, which had been developed for the manufacture of cycles.

Rifles used tubes, too, but gun barrels were machined from solid billets of steel. Cycle manufacturers commissioned new ways of making lightweight steel tubes, first for high-wheeler bicycles, the red Ferraris of their day. Gunmaker William Charles Stiff of Birmingham formed the Credenda Cold-drawn Seamless Steel Tube Company to market his bicycle tubing. Stiff had perfected his process by 1882, with a US patent granted in 1886. He stretched steel billets into long, thin-walled tubes that could be cut and welded into frames for cycles.

High-wheelers made from such expensive, technologically advanced tubes became lighter, and so faster. Colonel Albert Pope's Pope Manufacturing Company of Hartford, Connecticut used Credenda tubes from England for the high-wheeler used by Thomas Stevens on his circumnavigation of the world between 1884 and 1886. Stevens – "perched on a lofty wheel, as if riding on a soap-bubble" – was the first cyclist to "girdle the globe." He had been born in England in 1854 but emigrated to the US in 1871. His derring-do exploits gripped the Victorian world. His travels showed that self-propelled, independent international travel, while exotic, was possible. And Stevens's journey had been made possible with lightweight, cold-drawn steel. His 50-inch Columbia, with English tubing, was light enough to hoist over a railway bridge to escape a passing train, with Stevens "letting the bicycle hang over."

"Globe girdler" Thomas Stevens.

Colonel Pope didn't use Credenda's superior tubes for long. He created his own tube-making plant, run by Harold Hayden Eames, a former naval lieutenant commander who was a pioneer of modern management. The factory was "one of the industrial wonders of New England." In 1892, the Pope Manufacturing Company created a metallurgy laboratory and testing centre, led by engineer Henry Souther. His insistence on the introduction of nickel to steel led to lighter and stronger tubes. A new tube factory was built in 1896 on Hamilton Street, Hartford, and at the time this was "one of the most innovative industrial buildings in the country." (It's still standing and still used as a factory.)

The Pope tube factory had a technologically advanced testing laboratory, as did other bicycle factories. Many of the steel-testing procedures that were later vital in the automobile industry had been developed by and for cycle manufacturers. Throughout the 1890s, the American Iron and Steel Institute published tests for various bicycle parts. These tests would later be used in the automobile industry. The Pope factory had advanced testing rigs for evaluating the endurance of frames and wheels. This type of rig was later transferred for use on motor cars.

The Pope Manufacturing Company's experience in fashioning cycle frames out of lightweight steel tubes was used in the mid-1890s when America's leading bicycle company started to produce motor cars. "Comparative lightness with great strength are the striking characteristics of the Pope vehicle," said E. P. Ingersoll, the editor of *The Horseless Age.*

> The steel frame upon which the body of the carriage rests is made of the Pope Tube Company's well-known .50 carbon steel and selected in dimensions that enable it to be used in the annealed state. As a result a better alignment of bearings can be insured. Everything about the carriage is made on a bicycle basis and ball bearings are freely used throughout.

In 1897 *Automotor* magazine carried a review of a cycle manufacturing book, pointing out that such a book would be of use to automobile manufacturers. "Much of the matter will be of as much use and interest to those concerned in automotors as it is to bicyclists," said the review, especially the chapter "relating to repairs, the sections, construction, and method of holding together the various parts constructed of tubes." The book, said the motoring magazine, "will be found to be of great practical utility to all interested in the design or manufacture of motor-carriages."

In *Motors and Motor-Driving* of 1904, William Worby Beaumont, assistant editor of *Engineer* and one of the key English automotive engineers of the early 1900s wrote that car frames were "made cycle fashion – of round tubes brazed together …"

As cars developed in power and speed, cycle-style lightweight steel tubing was replaced by heavier, cheaper u-channel frames, first used by Benz at the turn of the 20th century.

ALUMINIUM

In the 1870s, a bar of aluminium was worth more than a bar of silver. Scientists knew how to extract the wonder metal from bauxite, but not how to extract it cheaply. The puzzle was solved, almost simultaneously, in France and America, with Frenchman Paul Héroult beaten to the punch by Charles Martin Hall of Pittsburgh, who patented his process in 1886. Within just three years *Bicycling World* of America was reporting that it had "heard … of aluminium bicycles … it will weigh but one third of what the present day, steel cycle does."

The Hall–Héroult process enabled the eventual mass-market use of aluminum (the missing "i" was a hand-bill error by Hill that eventually caught on; *Bicycling World* was still using the second "i" in 1889). With metallurgist Alfred E. Hunt, Hall and others formed the Reduction Company of Pittsburgh (this became the Aluminum Company of America, or ALCOA, in 1907), which opened the world's first large-scale aluminium production plant. The Reduction Company had a small space at the sixth annual Pittsburgh Exposition in 1894. Booth number 41, opposite Horne and Ward's Millinery and Trimmings, displayed a one-off aluminium-framed bicycle next to a standard steel-framed model, and invited show visitors to take the classic lifting-the-bicycle test.

The bicycle industry was the first transport sector to use aluminium, and those bicycle designers and manufacturers who became automobile and aircraft designers and manufacturers understood the usefulness of aluminium.

Napier car engines, and later Napier aeroplane engines, were made partly from aluminium, starting with a cast aluminium crankcase in the 1899 Napier, the first car produced by Edge, Du Cros and Napier, three former racing cyclists.

Another bicycle-based threesome used aluminium. The Wright Brothers and their machinist Charlie Taylor used aluminium on parts for the first engine to fly. Wilbur and Orville Wright's aviation experiments were funded by the profits generated from their bicycle shop. The Wright Cycle Company was started in 1892 and was making hand-crafted, bespoke bicycles by 1896 (the bike shop closed in 1909). In 1901, Charlie Taylor was taken on by the brothers. He was a machinist who had worked for local firm which made farm equipment and bicycles, and who later started his own machine shop (which made bicycle parts) before being employed by the Wrights.

Taylor was tasked with making the lightweight, gasoline engine that would power the Wright Flyer. According to the Smithsonian's National Air and Space Museum, the "Wrights contracted a local Dayton foundry, the Buckeye Iron and Brass Works, to cast the aluminum crankcase. Buckeye acquired their raw aluminum from the nearby Pittsburgh Reduction Company."

In Britain, the first mainstream cycle company to use aluminium for frame tubing was Humber, in 1898. Humber had started making bicycles in 1868. A manager at the company's Wolverhampton factory designed a motor car in 1896 and the company went on to become one of Britain's biggest automobile manufacturers.

🦿 MOTORING PRESS

A great many of the first motoring journalists cut their teeth on cycling journals. And, similarly, many of the first motoring magazines had bicycling back-stories. Ditto for motoring books. *Motor Carriages: The Vehicles of the Future* by "Vagabond", the cycling editor of Newcastle upon Tyne's *Daily Chronicle*, was written in 1896 and was one of the first English-language books about motoring.

Motoring writer C. L. Freeston wrote a chapter on Alpine motor touring in the Badminton Library's 1904 book on motoring, lead-authored by the former *Bicycling News* editor Lord Harmsworth. Freeston had done the same Alpine journeys, on bicycles, some years previously. In 1900 Freeston had written a cycling guidebook to the Alps, and dedicated it to "my fellow members of the Cyclists' Touring Club." Freeston was later chief sub-editor of *The Observer* and, later still, *The Sunday Times*. He was also editor of *The Car Illustrated* and *The Motor-Owner*.

In America, many of those connected with automotive publishing in the 1920s had worked first on cycling magazines. Richard Schell, publisher of *Motor West*, was the former Philadelphia correspondent of cycle trade journal *The Referee*; motoring writer Louis Bergere was formerly associate editor of bicycle magazine *Bearings*; Ed Spooner, the motoring editor of *The Detroit Free Press* was also previously at *Bearings*; Charles P. Root of *Motor Age* was formerly editor of *The Referee*; and John C. Wetmore, motoring editor of the *New York Evening Mail* had first been "Jonah" of *The Wheel* and New York correspondent of both *The Referee* and *Cycle Age*.

While cycling journalists were at the forefront of promoting motoring, carriage journalists were more aloof. William N. FitzGerald, editor of carriage trade journal *The Hub*, wrote a speech for his publisher W. B. Templeton that poured scorn on the prospects for the motor car. The speech, delivered to the Carriage Builders National Association, urged its members to cast "to the winds all fear of the passing of the horse or the rejection of the carriage." The association thanked Templeton for presenting such an "able and timely and conservative address."

ALLGEMEINE AUTOMOBIL-ZEITUNG

Allgemeine Automobil-Zeitung – the official newspaper of the Österreichischen Automobil-Club, the Austrian Automobile Club – was founded in 1900 by Felix Sterne and Adolf Schmal. Writing under the name "Filius", Schmal also wrote a 1904 handbook for motorists, *Ohne Chauffeur*. This was Austria's most popular "how to" book on motoring, republished many times until 1930. Schmal took part in Austrian motor-car races, having developed a penchant for speed in an earlier career – he was a former champion racing cyclist, and Austria's first gold medal winner at the 1896 Olympic Games in Athens.

In the 1913 edition of *Ohne Chauffeur*, the former track racer complained about how motoring made monsters of some:

> I know kind, well-bred, and considerate people who, as soon as they feel the steering wheel in their hands and the gas pedal under their foot, are seized by an automotive frenzy. It seems as if everything we normally call good breeding is suddenly extinguished in them ... I have often asked myself what might be hidden in an automobile that would, in an instant, turn a well-bred and considerate person into a lout.

THE AUTOCAR

The Autocar wasn't the world's first motoring magazine – that was *La Locomotion Automobile*, a French monthly launched in 1894 – but *The Autocar* was the first weekly. And it's still published. Launched in 1895 and produced by Iliffe and Son of Coventry, the magazine helped popularise motoring.

Its first editor was inventor and pioneer motorist Henry Sturmey. He had been a pioneer cycling journalist while Iliffe was a pioneer cycling magazine publisher.

Iliffe was a long-established printer, stationer and wallpaper manufacturer working from two sites in Coventry. Printers can wait for commissions to come their way or they can keep the presses running with their own imprints. William Isaac Iliffe, joining his father's printing business in 1864, saw the merits of becoming a publisher. He published local newspapers and in 1878, at the start of the first bicycling boom, launched *The Cyclist*. Six years later he expanded the stable by acquiring *Bicycling News*. The young Alfred Harmsworth, later Lord Northcliffe, was invited to manage the title.

The Autocar was launched on November 2nd, 1895, "in the interests of the mechanically propelled road carriage." The use of the singular here is almost literally appropriate, as there were just a handful of cars in Britain in 1895 – perhaps as few as six. Iliffe and Sturmey were going out a limb, but as publishers of cycling titles they would know that providing the market with an enthusiasts' publication can stimulate sales of the product at the centre of the enthusiasm.

Despite there being no motor trade to speak of, the magazine prospered thanks to advertising booked by Harry Lawson, a motoring promoter who had earlier been a cycling promoter and inventor. Lawson expected his money to talk, and Sturmey didn't disappoint – the magazine was largely a mouthpiece for Lawson's company promotions. However, it was also an organ that did much to overturn the then crippling legislation preventing the take-up of motoring.

In its early days *The Autocar* carried cycling book reviews, ran cycle company advertising and made frequent mentions of cycling.

"The analogy between the early days of cycling and those of the motor car is strikingly great," wrote Sturmey in the magazine in 1897.

> And those who, like ourselves, were among the pioneers of cycling a quarter of a century back find an almost exact recurrence of events in connection with the new pastime ... Who does not remember the glory, long departed, of the great Hampton Court meets of cyclists, which were annually held in May, and of other similar gatherings held in different parts of the country?

Sturmey remained as editor of *The Autocar* until 1901. Although known best today for Sturmey–Archer cycle gears, he designed other cycle gear systems, and did so long after becoming a motorist. Sturmey remained a keen cyclist until his death in 1930.

DE KAMPIOEN

The Champion, magazine of the ANWB, the Royal Touring Club of the Netherlands, was founded in 1883. "The Champion" as in champion cyclist. *See "ANWB" in Motoring Organisations in this chapter.*

ALFRED HARMSWORTH

Press baron Lord Beaverbrook described Alfred Harmsworth as the "greatest figure who ever strode down Fleet Street." It might have been more accurate if Beaverbrook had said "rode down Fleet Street" for Harmsworth was an enthusiastic cyclist, familiar with the Cyclists' Touring Club and its 1880s headquarters at 139-140 Fleet Street. Harmsworth is best known for founding the *Daily Mail* in 1896 but he got his break in journalism thanks to his love of cycling. Later to become the first great press baron as Viscount Northcliffe, the lanky Harmsworth rode a penny-farthing and started his career in publishing by submitting freelance articles for the burgeoning cycle press of the 1880s. He believed the swift, daring bicycle would "revolutionise modern life." Like other pioneer cyclists, entranced by the possibilities of self-propulsion (human at first, mechanical later), Harmsworth went on to become a highly influential motorist ("perhaps the largest private owner of motor-cars in the world," it was said in 1903) and promoter of early aviation.

His first cycling articles were published in 1880 in *The Cyclist* and *Wheeling*. By the following year, the 16-year-old was also writing squibs for the London-based, publican-owned *Bicycling News*. In 1882, in an episode that a modern *Daily Mail* would have been all over like a rash, Harmsworth made a servant pregnant, forcing him to leave the family home and take lodgings.

His cycling didn't suffer, however, and nor did his freelance cycle journalism. He wrote more and more pieces for *Bicycling News*. When this weekly magazine was bought by Coventry printers Iliffe &

Son, Harmsworth continued to submit freelance pieces, including on the travel potential cycling gave the middle- and upper-class riders of the day. A typical ride for Harmsworth would be to leave his home in St. John's Wood, London at midnight and, with a friend, ride 75 miles to Eastbourne for breakfast. However, on a long-distance ride from Bristol, he caught pneumonia and, on doctor's orders, was told to leave London and its filthy air. Harmsworth moved to Coventry in 1885 and took a full-time job with Iliffe and Son.

Bicycling News was edited by racing cyclist and author George Lacy Hillier, working from London. Iliffe had an office on Fleet Street but the magazine was published and printed in the home of the British cycle industry. Harmsworth's introduction of the "brief, pithy paragraph" into *Bicycling News* ("its chatty articles will soothe your troubled hours") raised sales eightfold in just a few months. The short, incisive style would go on to influence mainstream publications, creating a less stultifying style of journalism,

Alfred Harmsworth is on the far right (as is, today, the newspaper he founded).

and signifying the start of a more readable, tabloid-style press.

According to the 1930s *Bartleet's Bicycle Book*, Harmsworth was deputy editor of *Bicycling News*. But in effect he was the editor of the magazine, with his boss Lacy Hillier providing leaders and racing reports but not having day-to-day editorial control.

Harmsworth stayed in Coventry and edited *Bicycling News* until 1888. Iliffe Senior offered Harmsworth a partnership in the business, praising him for his "self-reliance, ambition and abounding energy" – but the young blade wanted to set up for himself. With £1,000 saved from his time as a cycling journalist, he and his brother Harold (later Viscount Rothermere, whose family still owns the *Daily Mail*) embarked on a publishing career that would see them create the *Daily Mail* and the *Daily Mirror*, as well as buying *The Times*.

Harmsworth's first venture into publishing on his own account was with a *Titbits* rival called *Answers to Correspondents On Every Subject Under the Sun*, printed at first by Iliffe. (*Bicycling News* had had an "Answers to correspondents" column.) Early issues of *Answers* had articles on "What the Queen Eats," "How Madmen Write" and "Why Jews Don't Ride Bicycles." Within four years, *Answers* was selling over a million copies a week.

In the mid-1890s, Harmsworth returned to his roots and published *The Rambler*, a weekly magazine about the booming activity of cycling.

The Harmsworth brothers created the *Daily Mail* in 1896 and Alfred started the *Daily Mirror* in 1903. In 1904, Alfred became the youngest-ever peer of the realm, as Viscount Northcliffe, and in 1908 acquired *The Times*, owning it until his death in 1922. Quite an achievement for a former bicycle journalist.

MOTOR NEWS

R. J. Mecredy – known to friends and family as Arjay – was a "pioneer among pressmen," according to the baronet son of the Dunlop company's founder, Arthur Du Cros. Mecredy, a tall and gangling figure, founded and edited the Irish automobile journal *Motor News* in 1900 after being introduced to motoring by former cycle racing champion Selwyn Edge. The following year Mecredy published

"Arjay" Mecredy.

De Dion Bouton Cars and How to Drive Them, a book that the French manufacturer adopted as its official handbook. He was one of the co-founders of the Irish Automobile Club in 1901 and was its first secretary. Mecredy also secured for Ireland the 1903 Gordon Bennett Cup race, one of motorsport's pivotal (and most controversial) early races. He published *The Motor Book* of 1902 for the Irish market and it was taken up by Iliffe and Son for the world market. The curator of the Royal Irish Automobile Club Archive described Mecredy as "the Father of Irish Motoring."

Mecredy had been a cyclist first – and a very fast one. He was a champion on the tricycle and on the new Safety bicycle, in England as well as Ireland, creating world records in the process. In 1890, he won all four National Cyclists' Union cycling championships, held in London. He raced on a Humber Safety bicycle fitted with Dunlop pneumatic tyres.

Back in 1889, Mecredy was one of the first ever to ride on a cycle equipped with pneumatic tyres. He rode a tricycle from Dublin to Coventry, the first long-distance test of pneumatic tyres. Later he became one of four directors of the original Dunlop tyre company, established to exploit John Boyd Dunlop's innovation. According to *Cycle and Motor World*, Mecredy made a "handsome fortune" after the Dunlop company was sold to Terah Hooley in 1896.

Mecredy was a prolific writer, owning and editing the *Irish Cyclist* from 1886, and writing books such as *The Art and Pastime of Cycling* (1890). *Cycle and Motor World* said he was "the most enthusiastic every-day road rider in the three kingdoms."

He also invented bicycle polo, only 20 years after the official rules of equestrian polo had been fixed.

The first game of bicycle polo was played in 1891 in Ireland between the Rathclaren Rovers and the Ohne Hast Cycling Club. Mecredy's wife Catherine, also a cyclist, was "almost as phenomenally expert as he," reported *Cycle and Motor World*. "Their friends are all cyclists, and they are never happy except when out wheeling."

Mecredy's *Road Book of Ireland* was a popular cycle touring guidebook, first published in 1892, the year he retired from racing.

The Irish Cyclist became the *Irish Cyclist and Motor Cyclist* in 1913, as a sister title to Mecredy's *Motor News*. Mecredy used his early interest in cycle touring to push for motor touring in Ireland. He persuaded a consortium of investors, including Thomas Cook & Son and the (Irish) Great Southern and Western Railway, to improve an important rural road. His interest in roads was formed when he was a cyclist. In April 1897, while not yet a motorist, Mecredy helped form the Irish Roads Improvement Association. An Irish newspaper said that this association, which was modelled on England's Roads Improvement Association "should meet with all practicable sympathy and support," even though it encouraged increased taxation.

Mecredy had five children, one of whom was also a fast cyclist. Dr. Ralph Mecredy competed in the 1912 Olympic Games in Stockholm, riding for Great Britain. From 1913 to 1915, Dr. Mecredy studied at the Battle Creek Sanitarium in Michigan, where the Kellogg brothers had made flaked cereals in the 1890s, creating the Battle Creek Toasted Corn Flake Company in 1906. This grew into the Kellogg Company. W. K. Kellogg, founder of the company, was a life member of the League of American Wheelmen and perhaps Mecredy Jnr. and Will Kellogg discussed cycling together?

THE MOTOR

The Motor was published in 1902 by Temple Press, initially as *Motorcycling and Motor*. Temple Press became the great rival to Iliffe and Son, publisher of *The Autocar*. This rivalry didn't start in 1902 – the two companies had been at each other's throats for years. Temple Press had started life as a cycle-magazine publisher.

The editors of *The Motor* were Edmund Dangerfield and Walter Groves, both of whom had bicycling backgrounds. Just as Henry Sturmey made frequent references to cycling in *The Autocar*, so did Dangerfield and Groves in their motoring magazine, including in an editorial in the first issue:

> The majority of cyclists have followed the motor movement from its inception, and wherever motor events take place one will always find present the inevitable little crowd of interested cyclists …

Dangerfield was the son of a London printer, the owner of the Dangerfield Printing Company. Much to his father's annoyance, Dangerfield Jnr. spent his wages on cycling. He was one of the leading riders of the day, winning club time trials, including London's Bath Road Century in 1890. Sensing a gap for a racing paper, Dangerfield launched *Cycling* in 1891. It was a weekly, populist title, and is still published as *Cycling Weekly* (in 1900 it was briefly renamed as *Cycling and Moting*). After a dispute with his brothers, who were happy to remain under the thumb of an oppressive Victorian father, Dangerfield left the family firm and, in 1894, created Temple Press. *Cycling* was at the vanguard of the popular press, a chatty title. "It was bright, it was readable, it bubbled with enthusiasm and nothing like it had been seen before," enthused a former editor.

As well as *Cycling*, Dangerfield's fledgling company published *Cycle Manufacturer and Dealers'*

Edmund Dangerfield.

Review. Motor Cycling and Motoring would have been a natural addition for the company: the title was changed to *The Motor* in 1903.

Dangerfield remained a cyclist his whole life and saw no conflict with his interest in motoring. He opened a motor museum in Oxford Street, London in 1912, Britain's first.

In 1905, Dangerfield founded truck-trade magazine, *Commercial Motor*, another magazine still published today. This was edited for some years by George F. Laundy Sharp, a journalist who entered the world of motoring via his interests in cycling. Sharp had earlier been an assistant editor on *Cycling*. He was a keen racing cyclist and contributed to Essex Cycling Union's *Cycling Echoes* before landing the job on *Cycling*. The club cyclist was "an observer of, and commentator on, nearly all the car trials, hill-climbs and other early competitions which contributed to the building of the foundations of the motor movement in this country."

For many years Sharp – like cyclists before him – was also a member of the general committee of the Royal Automobile Club.

OMNIA

Introduced in 1906, French automobile magazine *Omnia* was published until the end of the 1930s and became famous for its beautifully painted covers showing large cars in glamorous and idealised locations. It was founded and edited by motoring promoter Louis Baudry, one of the earliest French motoring journalists (and who, with the cheeky addition of de Saunier, elevated himself to nobility). Baudry's first motoring article was published in *L'Illustration* in May 1895. He was the author of early motoring books such as *Theoretical and Practical Automobile* in 1897 and *The Art of Driving* in 1906.

These book titles would have been familiar to Baudry's audience for they deliberately harked back to his earlier books, *Theoretical and Practical Cycling* (1892) and *The Art of Cycling* (1894).

In the *Art of Cycling* Baudry wrote: "The cyclist is a man half made of flesh and half of steel that only our century of science and iron could have spawned."

WHEELMAN AND MOTORCAR WEEKLY

Wheelman and Motorcar Weekly was a short-lived motoring title created by Harry Lawson in May 1896 and edited by Harry Hewitt Griffin, a cycling writer since the 1870s. Griffin wrote an annual that gave "full descriptions of all the principal makes of bicycles and improvements introduced this season."

Griffin had also once been an editor of *Bicycling News*.

Wheelman and Motorcar Weekly incorporated *English Sports* and *Amateur Wheelman*. The motorcar content took the form of a supplement at the back of the magazine, its editorial content seemingly directed by Lawson. Sir David Salomons contributed an article to its first issue, but provided no further material.

Griffin had spoken at the launch of the Self-Propelled Transport Association in December 1895, and was also a director of Lawson's New Beeston Cycle Company.

❧ MOTOR RACING DRIVERS

With its lightweight frame and pneumatic tyres, a bicycle was the fastest thing on the roads in the Victoria era, especially over long distances. Descending hills on a well-surfaced road was a thrill for "scorchers" and, when artificial propulsion became available, speed-addicted cyclists were among the first to use engines to go even faster. They already had the skill to hold a racing line and were fearless (indeed, some were reckless). In America and in Europe, it was a natural and normal progression for racing cyclists to become racing drivers.

Herbert Duncan, one of early motoring's most flamboyant pioneer promoters, and a former bicycle racing world champion, said,

> ... many men in the early cycling days, who started to ride a bicycle as a sporting hobby, soon took up racing either upon the tracks or in road events and often developed into prominent champions, and they were sooner or later automatically launched into the cycle trade and eventually into the motor industry. Many of these men made considerable commercial progress and a few enjoy fortunes or enviable positions as well-known members of the motor industry.

Many of the earliest motor-racing organisers learned their trade organising cycle races. The majority of the first official timers at motoring events had first been timers for cycling events. The first-ever motor race was staged by a cycling promoter. On April 28th, 1887, cycling journalist Paul Faussier, publisher of *Le Vélocipède Illustré*, organised the first race of "horseless carriages," between Neuilly-sur-Seine and Versailles. It wasn't a terribly long race: Neuilly and Versailles are just over a mile apart.

FERNAND CHARRON
In 1900 *The Automobile* called Fernand Charron, the "First Chauffeur of France," a reference to his premier position as a professional racing driver: "chauffeur" did not yet have its modern meaning.

Charron, winner of the 1900 Gordon Bennett Cup, was a former champion racing cyclist. When he became a motor-racing pioneer he raced against other former cyclists such as Chevalier René de Knyff of Belgium and Alexander Winton, the Scottish-born American motorcar manufacturer who had earlier made bicycles. Charron had also raced his bicycle against the likes of England's Selywn Edge.

Motor racing pioneer Chevalier René de Knyff can be seen here third from the left, standing next to G. P. Mills, winner of the first Bordeaux–Paris cycle race. Herbert Duncan, a cycle racer who became a motor executive, is standing third from right. M. D. Rucker, sitting on the floor, also became a top motoring executive.

CHEVALIER RENÉ DE KNYFF

Chevalier René de Knyff was a Belgian-born pioneer of motor racing. He won early races such as Paris–Bordeaux in 1898; Spa–Bastogne–Spa in 1899, and Nice–Marseille–Nice in 1900. After his racing career was over he rose to become the president of the predecessor of the Fédération Internationale de l'Automobile (FIA), the world governing body for most motor-car racing events, including Formula 1. Back in 1895, he was also one of the founding members of the Automobile Club de France, the world's oldest motoring organisation, for which he was a roving ambassador.

Knyff was originally a bicycle-racing manager. His brother, Gaetan, was a champion cyclist, and later also became a motor-racing driver. In the early 1890s, Knyff associated with cyclists such as Herbert Duncan, Martin Rucker and Fernand Charron and others who would also transfer to the world of motoring.

TOM COOPER

Henry Ford promoted his cars by demonstrating how fast they could go. Tom Cooper of Detroit was one of his earliest racing-car drivers, alongside his friend, Barney Oldfield. Famous racing drivers such as Cooper earned huge purses at promotional events, including at State Fairs and the "barnstorming" circuits. Cooper's celebrity had been gained before becoming a racing driver: in the late 1890s he was the star of Detroit Athletic Club's bicycle-racing team, winning the US National Championships in 1899.

Cooper was a professional bicycle racer for six years, including racing in Europe in 1900. His last bicycle race was at Detroit's first major automobile race, held on October 10th, 1901. He and Barney Oldfield raced a motorised tandem bicycle against the clock.

GIOSUÈ GIUPPONE

Giosuè Giuppone was a France-based Italian racing driver, a professional for Lion-Peugeot. Before becoming a racing driver he was a track cycling champion, winning the Italian national championships for tandem-paced racing in both 1903 and 1904. He died in 1910 while practising for a road race for lightweight cars, the Coupe des Voiturettes, held on the Circuit de Boulogne in France. Giuppone was driving a powerful but unstable Lion-Peugeot and crashed after braking to avoid two cyclists who crossed the road in front of him on the descent through the village of Wirwignes. He was travelling at 60 miles per hour. One of the cyclists was hit, and thrown into a ditch, amazingly only slightly injured. The car spun and rolled over multiple times before Giuppone was thrown from the car. He died from head injuries.

CARL GRAHAM FISHER

Racing-car driver Carl Fisher, erstwhile holder of the automobile world speed record over two miles, is most famous today for proposing, in 1912, the Lincoln Highway, a 3,400-mile road from Times Square in New York City to Lincoln Park in San Francisco. This was kick-started via public donations. By 1915 there was enough money to start paving short sections of the road, originally called the Coast-to-Coast Rock Highway.

Fisher developed his interest in Good Roads first as a bicycle rider, then as a racer and then a bike shop owner. He had opened an Indianapolis bicycle repair shop in 1891 with his two brothers, Rollo and Earle. By 1893, with stock at cost from Columbia's Colonel Albert Pope and credit-free financing from bicycle maker George Erland of Columbus, Ohio, Fisher had the largest bicycle shop in Indianapolis, employing 12 mechanics.

Library of Congress

His bicycle racing helped him advertise his bike shop: "I never was a champion," admitted Fisher later, "although I've taken the dust of the best of them, Eddie Bald, Earl Cooper, Fred Titus and Arthur Zimmerman. I was only a second-rater but I made money at the game and designed, manufactured and sold the wheel that I rode."

Fisher's store later became one of the first automobile dealerships in America. Fisher told his fellow bicycle racer, Barney Oldfield: "I don't see why the automobile can't be made to do everything the bicycle has done."

Fisher was an ace publicist – one stunt to promote his bicycle store involved dropping an old Columbia bicycle from the roof of the tallest building in Indianapolis. The first person to retrieve it and drag it into Fisher's shop would win a new one. He also rode a bicycle on a high wire strung between the roof of his building and the next (he may have been a daredevil – the "Bart Simpson of the Belle Époque," said a biographer in 2011 – but he was held by ropes and wore a padded suit, just in case) and pedalled around town on a shop-built 20-foot Eiffel-Tower tall-bike, startling people at second-floor windows.

Fisher's Cycles had an attached riding school attracting the cream of Indianapolis high-society folk, eager to learn cycling from the famous Carl Fisher.

Thanks to his bicycle-racing experience (Fisher had been part of a barnstorming race team led by Barney Oldfield) Fisher became a record-breaking racing-car driver in the early 1900s. How he was able to race is a wonder, as he had severe astigmatism. Today he would be classified as legally blind. He crashed often, as he had done on bicycles – his childhood nicknames alternated between "Crazy Carl" and, thanks to the injuries from running and cycling falls, "Crip." At an auto race in Zanesville, Ohio, he skidded off the track, injuring a number of spectators, and killing security guard John Goodwin, "a Civil War veteran and a prominent member of secret societies." Goodwin wasn't the last to die from this smash. "They were dying for two years," remembered Fisher, with the auto racer's penchant for uncaring aplomb.

Undeterred, Fisher was one of the principal investors in building the Indianapolis Motor Speedway racing track. The other major investors were Arthur C. Newby and James Ashbury Allison. All three had been members of the Zig Zag Cycling Club, based at Fisher's Cycles.

This bicycle business had given Fisher the funds to invest in the innovation that would make his fortune. With Allison, he produced carbide-gas headlights used on many early cars, an improvement on the bicycle lights used up to that point. The compressed gas used in the lamps was highly explosive and Fisher and Allison's US factories would detonate so often that the company principals had telegraph message code-names for each plant's propensity to blow so as not to alert authorities to the expected regularity of the conflagrations. The Indianapolis plant was situated next to a food production facility. When it exploded, a large and unscheduled helping of sauerkraut was deposited on an adjoining hospital. Fisher and Allison sold the Prest-O-Lite business to Union Carbide in 1911 for $9m.

Fisher also turned a mangrove swamp into Miami Beach, making another fortune. He lost this one in the Wall Street Crash of 1929.

His 1912 idea for a transcontinental highway was not new: bicyclists had been calling for one since the 1890s, and it's probable that Fisher based the concept of his Lincoln Highway on these proposed long-distance bicycle roads. Fisher had been a member of the League of American Wheelmen and therefore a recipient of the organisation's *Good Roads* magazine, started the year after Fisher had opened his bicycle store.

The public subscription model for the building of roads had also been first used for bicycle roads or, more specifically, for "side paths."

Fisher's Lincoln Highway Association would have never been able to raise enough money to pave the whole 3,400-mile cross-country automobile route but it did what bicycle organisations had earlier done – improve short sections of road as promotional tools.

Fisher died, almost penniless, in a cottage provided by the burghers of Miami Beach.

BERNA ELI "BARNEY" OLDFIELD

Speed record-breaking motor-car racer Barney Oldfield was famous on the auto-racing barnstorming circuit in the early 1900s. His earlier career helped – he had been famous on the bicycle-racing barnstorming circuit. By the age of 18, Oldfield was racing professionally for the New York-based Stearns bicycle factory team, and was friends with Tom Cooper.

Oldfield and Cooper's story is intertwined with that of pre-Ford Motor Company Henry Ford. In April 1902, Ford asked professional bicycle racer Cooper to help build and race a car that could be entered in the Manufacturers' Challenge Cup that would take place at Grosse Pointe, Michigan in October. Two cars were built – the 999 and the Arrow. The 100-horsepower cars – about eight times as powerful as a conventional car at that time – were dangerous to drive. "The roar of those cylinders alone was enough to half kill a man!" Ford said.

After a test run, Ford refused to drive the car. Cooper also baulked. The former bicycle racer wired his barnstorming friend Oldfield and asked if he'd like to give it a go. Despite never having driven even a sedate and sensible motor car, Oldfield would pilot the 999 to victory against another bicycle man, the millionaire bicycle-and-later-automobile manufacturer Alexander Winton.

"I never really thought much of racing, but following the bicycle idea, the manufacturers had the notion that winning a race on a track told the public something about the merits of an automobile," remembered Ford in his 1922 autobiography: "The "999" did what it was intended to do: It advertised the fact that I could build a fast motorcar."

Ford milked the publicity, which helped promote his third – and final – automobile business but, unbeknownst to most, the 999 was no longer Ford's: he had sold it to Cooper. The 999 became America's most famous automobile of the time, earning Cooper and Oldfield a fortune over the next few months as they took it to barnstorming events all over the US. By 1903, Oldfield was America's leading racing driver.

Oldfield later raced for Alexander Winton and later still for Peerless. On the barnstorming circuit his Peerless Green Dragon always won races against "local" drivers. These drivers were on his payroll, all travelling together in Oldfield's private railway carriage. Such chicanery had been common on the bicycle barnstorming circuit, where races were invariably won by the celebrity rider rather than the supposed "locals."

JOHN WILLIAM STOCKS

J. W. Stocks of Hull started his career as a racing driver in 1897, competing in major European events, including the Gordon Bennett Cup. He also took part in the 1,000-Mile Trial of 1900, a key event in British motoring history. In 1902 he started to manage the De Dion-Bouton motor agency in Britain and in the 1920s operated J. W. Stocks Limited of Broad Street, Birmingham, selling Renault cars. Champion racing driver – and former champion racing cyclist – Selwyn Edge thought his friend J. W. Stocks "one of the finest drivers of either racing or touring cars who ever lived." Why? "His experience on bicycles was of great assistance to him in motoring," said Edge.

Stocks had a stellar cycle racing career before he moved into motoring. He was "one of the greatest cyclists who ever rode; he was

Racing cyclist J. W. Stocks.

the first man to cover twenty-five miles in an hour," said Edge. Motoring pioneer Herbert Duncan called Stocks a "cycling lion."

In his self-penned entry in *Motoring Illustrated*'s 1903 listing of world motorists, Stocks said he took up motoring "after ten years of successful racing on the cycle path." His first cycle race was on the Hull Botanic Gardens cinder path in 1888, on a high-wheeler (he came second). In 1896 and 1897 he "held all records from one mile to one hour [including] the world record."

His motor-racing career started on motorised tricycles, but on familiar ground: the Crystal Palace cycling track. This was where he had finished his cycling career, with a world-record one-hour ride of 32 miles.

Stocks clearly had a speed fetish. Edge recounted the following anecdote about his friend:

> My old colleague of the road, J. W. Stocks, was once convicted of driving a motor tricycle at an excessive speed, although he produced conclusive proof that he was twenty miles distant from the spot where he was supposed to have committed the offence. The magistrate remarked that even if he were not driving at excessive speed at the place in question, he was doubtless doing so somewhere else!

Racing driver J. W. Stocks.
(The car is a Napier, designed by two racing cyclists).

&. MOTORING INFRASTRUCTURE

There's more to motoring infrastructure than roads alone. Cyclists had a hand in infrastructure such as the first British motor-racing track (it was built for bicycles) and the first multi-storey car park (it was built for horses, bicycles and new-fangled autocars). In the UK, the Cyclists' Touring Club still has the right to erect road signs, the same rights held by the Automobile Association and the Royal Automobile Club.

The first motor-vehicle museum was proposed by a bicycle magazine – Paris-based *Vélo Magazine* called for the establishment of a museum

> where all the old and experimental types of vehicles could be preserved and kept on exhibition. Many of these interesting first attempts are now lying neglected in storehouses or out-of-the-way places, where they are fast deteriorating. Steps cannot be taken too soon to rescue them and … and open a permanent motor vehicle museum.

The first British motor museum was set up by a cycling journalist. Edmund Dangerfield was the founder, in 1891, of *Cycling*, which is still published as *Cycling Weekly*. A lifelong cyclist, winner of cycling races and vice-president of the Bath Road cycling club, he was also the founder of *The Motor* magazine. His motor museum was situated on Oxford Street in London, and opened on May 31st, 1912 with over 40 vehicles on display. The exhibition was moved to Crystal Palace in Sydenham, South London, in 1914.

BEXHILL: BIRTHPLACE OF BRITISH MOTOR RACING

The first organised motor race in Britain was not staged on a circuit purpose-built for motoring, but on a circuit purpose-built for cycling – the Cycling Boulevard of Bexhill-on-Sea.

The Cycling Boulevard offered an excellent, off-carriageway circuit and the race was staged in the then fashionable seaside resort on a wet and windy day in May 1902. A local newspaper wrote that motor cars "teuf-teufed at a delightful rate here there and everywhere ..." Thousands of spectators marvelled at the novel sound of car horns sounding "Baw-don, Baw-don," and "Tworp, Tworp," said the delighted reporter, concluding "it was more like a Continental race meeting than the staid and decorous Bexhill on Sea."

Among the 200 racing-car drivers invited by the event organiser, the Automobile Club of Great Britain and Ireland, were Baron Henri de Rothschild, Charles Rolls, *Daily Mail* owner Alfred Harmsworth, Selwyn Edge and the fastest driver of the day, Léon Serpollet in his "Easter Egg" steam car.

A sleepy village was transformed into a happening resort by thrusting local aristocrat Reginald Sackville, the 7th Earl De La Warr. He built the Sackville Hotel in 1890, and a pier-end entertainment hall, the Kursaal. His younger brother, Viscount Cantelupe, wanted to cater to a new and affluent cadre of middle-class visitor so, in 1896, the peak year of the bicycle boom, he commissioned the Cycling Boulevard.

The future 8th Earl De La Warr – a "great enthusiast of our pastime," according to a high-society cycling journal – had good reason to encourage cycling: he was chairman of the Dunlop-owning Pneumatic Tyre Company. Cantelupe had been parachuted into the position by speculator Terah Hooley.

The Cycling Boulevard was laid out on De La Warr Parade, from the Sackville Hotel to the foot of Galley Hill, by Walter Pellant of the Humber Cycle Company. Bicycles could be hired, and cycling lessons booked, at the Cycling Chalet. A price list said that the Cycling Boulevard offered "pleasurable wheeling ... high-class instruction ... [and] freedom from road dangers."

Lady De La Warr rode on the boulevard on a Simpson patent Lever Chain cycle, with her initials and the De La Warr coat of arms on the frame, and a gold watch mounted on the handlebars. (Hooley, the promoter and conman, owned the Simpson company.)

The De La Warr's Manor House, away from the Cycling Boulevard, was used for cycling events. At bicycle gymkhanas in 1896 and 1897 the White Viennese Band entertained both locals and nobles. The De Le Warrs attracted royalty to the cycling events, including Grand Duke Michael of Russia and his wife, the Countess de Torby. Other aristocrats taking up the invitation from Lady De La Warr included the Duke and Duchess of Teck.

In 1902, desperate for funds, Earl De La Warr eagerly accepted the rental fee for turning the Cycling

The cycle chalet on the De La Warr Cycling Boulevard was later used as a timing hut for motor racing events.

Boulevard into a motor-racing circuit. The fees from the Automobile Club were welcome but short-lived. Bexhill's cycle track – in effect, a three-quarter-mile-long private road, next to but separated from the public highway on one side and a pedestrian promenade on the other – became increasingly unsuitable for the ever-faster racing cars of the day. In 1907, when the purpose-built Brooklands circuit was opened to great fanfare, Bexhill's time in the sun came to an abrupt end.

There's no sign of the Cycling Boulevard today. It is buried beneath the grass sward that separates the road from the promenade. Bexhill celebrates its role in British motor-racing history but the bicycling origins of the "motor racing track" are given no civic recognition whatsoever.

INDOOR CAR PARKS

James Cooper was ahead of his time. One hundred and seventeen years ago he commissioned a first-of-its-kind building, in my hometown of Newcastle upon Tyne. Until I started researching this book I had no idea James Cooper existed. He is not a celebrated Novocastrian. His far-sighted creation – now a building listed by English Heritage and with Hadrian's Wall beneath it – is not on the tourist trail. James Cooper's building was specifically designed to store and sell motor cars. It was an early motor

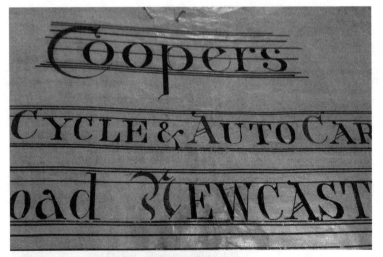

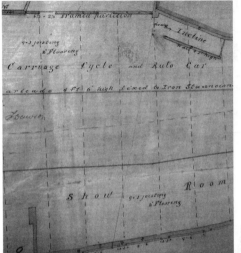

retail establishment but, because of the storage aspect, it was one of the first multi-storey car parks, probably the earliest in the world.

When, in 1897, Cooper commissioned the new three-storey building for his long-established auction business, motor cars had only been legally allowed on British roads for a matter of months. But James Cooper wasn't an "autocarist," one of the names for what would settle down as the noun "motorist." He hedged his bets. The building that still bears his name also sold horses and bicycles. In the late 1890s and well into the new century, bicycles, motor cars and horses co-existed on the roads of Britain. Aside from the fevered predictions of a small number of enthusiasts, there was no inkling that one of these forms of transport would soon supplant the others.

Cooper created a building that gave equal billing to all three forms of timetable-independent transport. A sign on the plans spelled it out: "Coopers Horse Carriage Cycle & Auto Car Repository."

A few hundred metres north of Cooper's building were the dominant transport modes of the time – trams

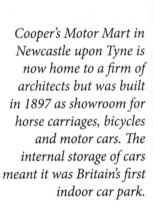

Cooper's Motor Mart in Newcastle upon Tyne is now home to a firm of architects but was built in 1897 as showroom for horse carriages, bicycles and motor cars. The internal storage of cars meant it was Britain's first indoor car park.

and trains, both reliant on rails. It made sense to be situated near the railway station, because train travel led to a huge demand for horses, helping to cart goods and people away from the stations.

The Cooper Horse Repository's manure pit can still be seen. A lift for motor cars, a radical innovation for the time, has been bricked up out-of-sight. The third-floor bicycle test track still has its original wooden floor, although today riding is trickier as you have to weave between desks, computer screens and bemused architects.

Ryder, an architectural firm, converted the building to its current use in 2010. Where James Cooper once stood, gavel in hand, auctioning horse flesh, is now a stylish reception desk. The first-floor gallery, where ladies could look down on toffs and toughs squabbling over prices, is still a seated gallery but the toffs and toughs are long gone (as is the manure).

The Coopers Horse Carriage Cycle & Auto Car Repository was built at a time when livery stables were facing an uncertain future. Livery stables were the car-rental garages of their day, hiring out horses and runabout carriages. Every large town or city had at least one horse repository.

There were livery stables similar to Cooper's in Hull and Norwich, but neither incorporated the storage and sale of motor cars and bicycles.

It's not clear how well James Cooper did with his prototype motor-car retail business. He may have been a little ahead of his time. Pre-1900 local newspaper adverts show that he advertised his bicycles for sale for some years, but not his motor cars.

MAPS

Motoring organisations eventually created their own, motoring-specific maps, but pioneer motorists relied on the maps produced for cyclists. The later motoring maps borrowed heavily from those produced for cyclists, and also benefitted from the on-the-ground intelligence that cyclists provided to mapping companies. In early 20th-century Britain, the Cyclists' Touring Club had a formal relationship with Messrs Bartholomew, an Edinburgh-based map publisher, for the provision of data. In 1898, John George Bartholomew, son of the founder of the map company, wrote to the secretary of the CTC proposing that club members should supply the firm with up-to-date information. This was an astute move – cyclists were prolific, well-travelled tourists and, out of necessity, mad keen on maps. In return for road intelligence from its 60,500 members, the CTC was provided with discounted maps. The crowd-sourcing enabled Bartholomew to update its maps every couple of years, unlike the slow-moving, state-owned Ordnance Survey, which relied on methodical surveys by its own staff.

With the help of cyclists, Bartholomew added detail to its maps, detail not on the stuffier Ordnance Survey maps. Bartholomew also classified roads, using quaint and rather eye-of-the-beholder terms such as "indifferent." It's fascinating to track Bartholomew road descriptions between Edwardian maps and those of the 1920s. Major through routes – routes which had very often been brought back to life by cyclists – morphed into what Bartholomew called "motoring roads", even though none had yet been built as such.

In America, turn-of-the-century motorists joined the main bicycle organisation in order to get hold of its maps, as evidenced by this extract from *The Automobile* magazine in 1899:

The example of the League of American Wheelmen in furnishing to its members systematic information … may well be followed. For instance, the Massachusetts Road Book, supplied to its members by the Massachusetts division of the League, is a model of its kind, containing not only excellent maps of the roads throughout the State, but lists of routes, and much compact information of the kind desired as to character of roads, gradients, etc. Since automobilists are interested in many of the same things that wheelmen are it has been suggested that mutual interests would be promoted if the former would join the L.A.W. It would, indeed, be a most advisable thing to do. The return for the small entrance-fee and annual charge is very large.

In the 19th century there were a great many maps and itineraries aimed at the Victorian leisured classes. There were many maps, guidebooks and itineraries for railway and steamship travellers but, due to a reduction in long-distance travel by carriages, far fewer for road travellers. Those that did exist were based heavily on 18th-century works, such as *Cary's New Itinerary* of 1798. Produced by map-maker John Cary, working on commission from Britain's Postmaster General, the *New Itinerary* contained maps, distances between towns, and stagecoach routes. When railways strangulated the stagecoach trade in the 1830s and 1840s, there was little use for maps of Britain's road network (indeed, little use for roads, either) – until cyclists came along.

Cyclists breathed new life into British roads, and there was an explosion in cycling-specific maps and guidebooks. *The Bicycle Roadbook* by Charles Spencer of 1878 was one of the first. *Wheaton's Map of the British Isles for Bicycle Tourists* cost "30 stamps, post free" and was produced by C. Wheaton, a Covent Garden-based maker of high-wheelers. James Wyld – "geographer to the Queen" – produced *Wyld's New Bicycle Map of the Roads of England, Wales and Scotland* which was "mounted on cloth, in limp cover" for the cyclist seeking to cover a lot of ground.

Of course, "a lot of ground" to cyclists was less so to motorists, many of whom craved non-stop speed above all else. Writing in 1907, the RAC Secretary Claude Johnson (later the lynchpin at Rolls-Royce) said:

> There are many excellent guide and road books already in existence, but few of these have been issued since touring in motor-cars has become general, and therefore they often lack the special points which are useful in a new form of travelling ... The pedestrian and cyclist often welcome a stop for a moment or two at a point where two roads meet, not only in order to leisurely consult their route book but to rest awhile ... The motorist nearly always resents delay. When faced by two roads he sometimes, indeed, prefers to take one at random rather than stop his career even for the brief moment necessary to carefully examine a direction-post or make an enquiry. I do not say that such haste and hurry is in any way admirable, but it must be reckoned with in the guide books of the future.

MOTOR DEALERS

Many early-1900s motor dealers had first been cycle dealers. It was a natural progression. Even those that didn't convert were able to repair the first motor cars, and many bike shops also stocked petroleum long before the concept of "filling stations."

In 1902, a writer for America's *The Automobile Magazine* described the cycle-industry origins of a number of well-known motor dealers. He talked about William Metzger of Detroit, America's biggest automobile retailer and "in Chicago I found Ralph Temple, of the Temple Austrian Company ... As a bicycle jobber Temple took the entire output of three factories. I know young Temple well, as we traveled together for over a year in Europe, and a more trustworthy and capable man than he is it would be hard to find." (It's highly likely Temple and the motoring-magazine writer – probably editor Angus Sinclair – spent time abroad together on a bicycle tour or two.)

In the early part of the 20th century, London's Holborn Viaduct was the go-to place if you were a motor car enthusiast in Britain. Before the First World War, almost every second building on "The Viaduct" contained a motor business, including offices of the major car brands and retail premises. Why did so many motoring concerns choose to locate on or near Holborn Viaduct? It was because of the road's earlier status as a "bicycle street." In a 1903 publication novelist and historian Sir Walter Besant said: "Holborn Viaduct is a favourite locality for bicycle shops."

At the end of the 19th century, Holborn Viaduct was home to many of the largest cycle shops in Britain, some of which remained as bike shops until the 1920s. Others became motor-car dealers, such as the London Cycle Mart which became Friswell's Automobile Palace, Britain's biggest car showroom before the First World War.

The first motor-car business to be located on Holborn Viaduct was Harry Lawson's Motor Car Club, at No. 40, where he and his associates planned the 1896 Emancipation Run. Lawson's pioneer motor-car business was on Holborn Viaduct because Lawson had long been involved with the bicycle industry and was connected with many of the individuals who managed the bicycle depots and stores on the street.

Holborn Viaduct – 1,400 feet long and 80 feet wide – was built between 1863 and 1869, and was the first "flyover" in central London. It was therefore seen as a progressive part of town, and bicycle retailers – selling the fastest and most progressive road vehicle of the day – clustered on or around the viaduct in the 1880s and 1890s.

The first cycle retailer on Holborn Viaduct was Thomas Smith & Sons, a long-established tool-maker in Birmingham. An 1880 advert for the company stated that it made the "celebrated Viaduct Bicycles", so it's probable that the Viaduct Bicycle Depot had been opened on Holborn Viaduct in 1879 or earlier. Nahum Salamon's Bicycle and Tricycle Supply Association opened in May 1881 at 27 Holborn Viaduct. It was both a supplier and a retailer. Other bicycle manufacturers and retailers soon followed.

Friswell's Automobile Palace had started life in 1893 as a bicycle shop. Charles Friswell & Co. made and sold bicycles from three premises: 97 Newgate Street in 1893, then 3 Holborn Viaduct and a repair outlet near the Old Bailey. The Holborn Viaduct store was within the London Cycle Mart. In 1899 the Holborn store was moved to No. 18 and, according to *The Autocar*, sold cars by Benz, Mors and de Dion. The motor-car shop was lined with French cycling posters. Charles Friswell had been "a racing cyclist of the early Paddington Track days" and was still attending events such as the Ripley Old-timers' Rally in 1917.

In 1902, Friswell's Automobile Palace was moved to a five-storey building in Albany Street, opposite Metropolitan Railway's Portland Road Station, and became Friswell's Great Motor Repository. Friswell later bought into Standard Motor Co. of Coventry and was knighted in 1909, becoming the first "motor knight."

ROAD CENTRE LINE

Edward N. Hines of Michigan devised the painted highway centre line, one of the world's most important road safety features. The first was installed on a rural highway in 1911, on the aptly-named "Dead Man's Curve" along the Marquette–Negaunee road in Michigan. Hines conceived the separation idea when he was a motorist but his interest in roads had started when he was a cyclist. Hines was Chief Consul of the League of American Wheelmen's Michigan division, a vice-president of the national organisation and also president of the Detroit Wheelmen cycling club.

Hines died in 1938 but was honoured in 2011 with the first Paul Mijksenaar Design for Function Award. The presentation was made at the University of Amsterdam in the Netherlands, with Michigan's State Transportation Director Kirk T. Steudle accepting the award on behalf of Hines's family. Steudle

Edward Hines, 2nd vice-president of the League of American Wheelmen.

said: "The highway centreline has been called the single most important traffic safety device in the history of automobile transportation, and Edward Hines originated it in Michigan."

In 1899, Hines listed 20 reasons why cyclists in Michigan ought to join the L.A.W., including securing funds to construct a "bicycle pavilion" on an island facing Detroit (it's still there, although it is now called the Athletic Pavilion) and work furthering the cause of Good Roads.

"We want more cycle paths, we want roads, we want danger signs erected, we want guides erected, we want to be fully protected at all times with our bicycles, we want our rights and privileges maintained," wrote Hines.

These privileges had been achieved earlier, with the passing of the County Road Law in 1893 and a change to Michigan's Constitution in 1894. In 1901, Hines served as the vice-president of the national L.A.W. His agitation for better roads secured his appointment (along with Henry Ford) to the Wayne County Board of Roads at its inception in 1903. In 1909, Hines – along with fellow L.A.W. official Horatio Earle – was responsible for the construction of the first full mile of concrete road in the world, a stretch of Woodward Avenue close to what would become the Ford factory in Detroit.

Hines, along with another member of the Detroit Wheelmen, former bike-shop owner William E. Metzger, co-founded the Detroit Automobile Club in 1916. Hines was a member of the Wayne County Road Commission until 1938.

ROAD SIGNS

In the UK, the placement of official, legally-sanctioned road signs is carried out by highway authorities. Road signs can also be erected by "prescribed bodies." Two of them are motoring organisations – the Automobile Association and the Royal Automobile Club. The third is a cycling organisation, the Cyclists' Touring Club. Why does a cycling organisation have the legal authority to erect road signs? It's because the CTC was the first to erect such signs, back in the 1880s, before the advent of motor cars.

Road markers, signposts and milestones have long been a feature of British roads but the first warning signs were erected for the safety of cyclists. High-wheeler cyclists required timely warnings because once they started on a descent they couldn't easily stop. The pedals were "fixed" to the hub on the large wheel – "freewheeling" had yet to be invented. Riders would dismount and walk the steepest hills.

Cast-iron warning signs were erected, from 1883 onwards, by both the CTC and the National Cyclists' Union. Prior to this, local cycling clubs had erected their own *ad hoc* signs. The CTC and the NCU produced standardised, cast-iron signs. The first signs read: "To cyclists this hill is dangerous."

By 1902, the roads of Britain were dotted with 2,331 "Danger" and 1,989 "Caution" boards. Pioneer motorists, in vehicles with not-yet-excellent brakes, relied on these boards. During the 1896 Emancipation Run, one of the drivers failed to spot a CTC warning sign on Handcross Hill in Sussex and shot down the hill:

> Whether M. Merckel saw the placard or not; he certainly approached the notorious descent of Handcross Hill with apparent indifference. To rush through the air at the speed of a torpedo-boat destroyer, down a narrow, curving road, enclosed with hedges, and without being able to see what was to the front of us, was a novel and thrilling experience.

Merckel was lucky; others were less fortunate. On July 12th, 1906, an omnibus driver descending Handcross Hill lost control and ten people were killed, including the local undertaker.

⚸ ROADS

REG: *"Well, yeah. Obviously the roads. I mean, the roads go without saying, don't they?"*
Monty Python's Life of Brian, 1979

&. MOTORING EVENTS & SHOWS

The majority of the world's early motoring events were either created or organised by cyclists. Motor cars were first exhibited in Britain and in France at cycle shows. Britain's Motor Show was founded by the editor of a tricycling magazine.

FIRST MOTOR CAR RACES

The world's first two motor-car races were organised by cycle journalists. The first, a race for road-going steam vehicles was organised and promoted by Paul Faussier, editor of the world's first cycling magazine, *Le Vélocipède Illustré*. This race was staged on April 28th, 1887, between Neuilly-sur-Seine and Versailles, but only one entrant turned up, the Compte de Dion in a De Dion-Bouton steam car.

The world's first combustion-engine motor car race was staged in 1894, between Paris and Rouen, a 127-kilometre test of endurance. The Competition for Horseless Carriages was created by Pierre Giffard, founder-editor of *Le Vélo* cycling magazine. Giffard was no stranger to organising races: in 1891 he created the 1,200-kilometre Paris–Brest–Paris cycle race. Giffard helped found the Automobile Club de France, many of whose co-founders were cyclists. Giffard's term for a bicycle – *la petite reine*, "the little queen" – has passed into common French usage. It refers to his bicycle book, *La Reine Bicyclette*, published in 1891.

HORSELESS CARRIAGE EXHIBITION, October 1895

The first large scale exhibition of motor cars in Great Britain was a parade of seven "road locomotives" held on the Agricultural Show Grounds in Tunbridge Wells on October 15th, 1895. This Horseless Carriage Exhibition was staged by Mayor Sir David Salomons, founder of the Self-Propelled Traffic Association. Salomons was a cyclist, and a trustee of the Cyclists' Touring Club. One of the all-French vehicles on show in Tunbridge Wells was a powered tricycle "exhibited by Monsieur Guedon for the Gladiator Cycle Co. of Paris."

STANLEY CYCLE SHOW, November 1895

Britain's main Victorian-era cycle exhibition was the Stanley Show, organised by the Stanley Cycle Club. In 1895 the exhibition was staged in the Agricultural Hall, Islington, and cycles were joined by motor cars. In effect, the 1895 Stanley Cycle Show was Britain's first indoor motor exhibition and gave Londoners their very first chance to view a motor car. There were only two on display, a Roger fitted with solid-tyred cycle wheels and the Panhard-Levassor that had been at the Tunbridge Wells motor show earlier in the month. At the following year's show *The Engineer* reported:

> The pressure on the space available was so great, that the two sections hitherto devoted to photographic apparatus and inventions have been abandoned. About 230 exhibitors, staging over 2,500 cycles are represented; whilst in the King Edward's Hall will be found the finest display of motor carriages which has yet been collected together in any building in this country.

The Stanley Cycle Show morphed into the Stanley Show, a motor exhibition, and was staged until 1906. It was put out of business by Charles Cordingley's Motor Show.

SALON DU CYCLE, December 1895

The first motor cars were made in Germany but the fledgling automobile industry was based in France. The first exhibition of motor cars took place at a cycle show, the third annual staging of the Paris-based Salon du Cycle.

According to *The Autocar*, "to the cycling enterprise in France must always remain the credit of assembling the first exhibition of autocars worth mentioning in the beginning of the renaissance of these vehicles of the future."

The show was staged at the Palais de l'Industrie on the Champs Élysées. When the Automobile Club de France organised its first motor-car show, in 1898, the show was called Le Salon de l'Automobile du Cycle et des Sports, a motor show combined with bicycles.

THE MOTOR SHOW, May 1896

Charles Cordingley was the organiser of the Motor Show at Islington's Agricultural Hall, first staged in August 1897. It grew out of Cordingley's laundry machine show and became known as the Cordingley Show. It was the main motoring show for some years. To promote his show, Cordingley also founded, in 1899, the *Motor-Car Journal*, Britain's first cheap motoring magazine. His entry into the world of automobiles had come via cycling, but with three wheels rather than two. In 1880, when he was just 18, Cordingley was editor of the *Tricycling Journal*, a "pioneer of cycling literature." Later, Cordingley was one of the founder members of the Automobile Club, and was one of those to bail out the fledgling club when it lost money on a motor exhibition of its own (the Club returned the favour by later becoming a patron of his annual Islington show).

INTERNATIONAL MOTOR EXHIBITION, Summer 1896

The International Motor Exhibition was housed at the Imperial Institute in Kensington, between May 9th and August 8th, 1896. It was staged by motoring and cycling pioneer Harry Lawson.

Former champion racing cyclist Selwyn Edge said Salomon's exhibition at Tunbridge Wells in 1895 "was not very accessible to the general public, but Lawson's exhibition was in the heart of London and he left no stone unturned to bring it to the notice of everyone." According to Edge, a pioneer racing driver, and erstwhile employee of Lawson, "London and the suburbs were literally plastered with posters, and glowing notices appeared in the press."

Harry Lawson was designing ground-breaking bicycles back in the 1870s and he invited many of his cycling chums to the now-famous London-to-Brighton Emancipation Run that would take place in November 1896. The varied motor vehicles on show at Lawson's summer exhibition had one thing in common: Lawson either controlled their sales in Britain or owned their patents.

The manager of Lawson's exhibition – which the Prince of Wales graced with his presence and his patronage, giving motoring the royal seal of approval – was Herbert Duncan, a former bicycle world champion racer and cycling promoter. In a self-published book – a fat tome – he described himself as "One of the best known and most successful cycle and motor pioneers." He was "Three times in succession Bicycle Champion of the World ... One of the few who really took part in the famous Brighton Ride of 1896 ... Founder of several Cycle and Motor Journals ... Builder of the Velodrome Buffalo at Paris."

EMANCIPATION RUN, 1896

"Old men who had seen the advent of trains held aloft children who would witness the coming of spaceships," wrote author Piers Brendon of the 1896 Emancipation Run. This is an evocative description of the cusp-like significance of British motoring's celebrated foundation event. The procession of pioneer motor cars from London to Brighton was a celebration of the just-passed "Emancipation Act," the over-turning of a law that had prevented, except under the most stringent of conditions, the use of motor cars on British roads. Contemporaries called it the "Magna Carta of Motoring."

Those who were part of the celebratory run to Brighton later took great pride in their attendance – to have been one of the participants in the kick-off event was something to boast about. And many of those who could do so were bicycle riders. Contemporary newspaper reports record that many of those who *watched* the event did so while leaning on their bicycles, but what wasn't reported was that a number of the drivers, some of the passengers and a great many of those at the slap-up evening reception in Brighton were leading members of the cycle industry or former champion cycle racers.

Thirty-three motor cars took part in the Run, on a damp, foggy November morning, seen off by a huge crowd including many cyclists.

Writing in *The Autocar*, a "cycling engineer" (undoubtedly editor Henry Sturmey) said the

THE MOTOR-CAR REVOLUTION: START FROM WESTMINSTER BRIDGE FOR BRIGHTON LAST SATURDAY.

Lawson in the lead car – on the right – at the Emacipation Run. From The Penny Illustrated Paper and Illustrated Times, *November 21st 1896.*

"huge and unwieldy crowd of decent and interested spectators ... [were] estimated to number upward of half a million ..." And they included: "High and low, rich and poor – the sweet athletic girl on her bicycle ... the squire, the publican and the prince – in fact, every shade and degree of the great British public were out awheel and afoot to see the autocars on the initial legal journey in this country." This "cycling engineer" – who followed the cars for part of the route, albeit on his bicycle – continued:

> Readers of *The Autocar* may take an old cyclist's word for this, he, in an endeavour to see as much of the trip as possible, having sampled the road throughout in his own proper person ... The writer, employing a motor which has run with but little failure for something like thirty-five years, joined the road where the Brighton Road proper may be said to commence, namely, at Croydon ... [The] cars were followed by a comet tail of cyclists.

The Emancipation Run, now re-enacted each year by the Royal Automobile Club, was organised by Harry Lawson. In 1879, he had been the creator of an early Safety bicycle, forerunner of today's rear-driven bicycles. The Rover Safety, designed by John Kemp Starley some six years later, is usually listed as the first modern bicycle but in some respects it was beaten to the punch by Lawson's machine, the Bicyclette. How did Lawson come to design a bicycle with smaller wheels than the high-wheelers of the day? Perhaps due to his height, which put him at disadvantage on high-wheelers? He was only 5 feet tall. Whatever his motivations, Lawson's Safety bicycle was ahead of its time.

His fashion sense wasn't, however, and during the Emancipation Run he wore a strange uniform. "Vanderdecken" of *The Graphic* magazine of London complained: "I sincerely hope that the costume *de rigueur* for 'moting' is not to be the Opera Comique yachting costume worn by Mr. H. J. Lawson; the crowning feature being a white yachting cap with a broad gold band and a badge ..."

(In the same article, "Vanderdecken" wrote: "One hears different opinions as to Mr. Lawson's claim to be the credit for inventing the 'Safety' bicycle, and I am able to say that his claim is perfectly justified. I personally inspected his invention in Brighton, where Mr. Lawson had his factory, in 1877, and it was then called the 'Safety'." Vanderdecken also said that motoring was a sporting concern, and very much from the world of bicycles: "on the Continent the motor-car has been in evidence in connection with long distance races; whilst in England the cycling interest has largely to do with it.")

It was as a financier – first of bicycle companies and later of motor car companies – that Lawson was to achieve fame. Or, rather, infamy. His motor-car syndicates and company flotations were often based on fraudulent claims. His prowess as a puffer of companies and as a publicist – skills honed in the bicycle industry – were apparent in his foundation of the British Motor Syndicate, a shell scheme which he aimed to promote by organising the Emancipation Run on November 14th, 1896. This procession to Brighton, Lawson told the Chief Constable of Sussex, was to provide a "practical demonstration of the capabilities and characteristics of the new vehicle."

Why Brighton? Because the London-to-Brighton road was a favourite of cyclists, and Brighton was where Lawson first lived when he started in the business of making bicycles, working with James Likeman, with whom he collaborated on his first bicycle patent in 1874.

The 60-mile Emancipation Run started outside London's Metropole Hotel at the corner of Northumberland Avenue and Whitehall Place. (Today, this is the Corinthia Hotel, and there are 55 "Boris bikes" outside.)

Cycle tourist and soon-to-be CTC council member William Rees Jeffreys, who would later become one of Britain's leading highway administrators, watched the motorists leave London. Racing driver and former champion bicycle racer Selwyn Edge joined the Run, but did so from his bicycle.

"It was foggy, dull and wet," he later wrote. "Just the kind of day which would make the modern motorist [of 1934] think twice before he would undertake such a journey in spite of all the advantages of a modern car [advantages such as a roof and a windscreen]."

Edge was made of stern stuff: "I had had more than one offer of a seat on a car, but as I was anxious to keep the whole procession in sight … find out what breakdowns occurred, and generally keep an eye on the whole event, I decided that I would be more favourably placed if I were to follow on a bicycle."

Edge wasn't the only one to follow the Emancipation Run on a bicycle. Claude Johnson, one of the key figures of early motoring, the hugely-influential first secretary of the Automobile Club, also rode to Brighton on a bicycle, as did former champion cyclist R. J. Mecredy.

"My old friend, R. J. Mecredy, who was at that time the editor of *The Irish Cyclist* and a director of the Dunlop Tyre company, shared my views, so we arranged to meet at the starting point and follow the procession through to Brighton," said Edge, continuing:

> I shall never forget the sight that met my gaze when I arrived on my bicycle, accompanied by R. J. Mecredy, at [London's] Hotel Metropole. The whole place was packed with people; they were occupying every window in the vicinity; boys had climbed up lamp-posts, hotel staffs were on the roofs, balconies were overcrowded, and only a small space [was] kept clear for the motor vehicles …

While Johnson, Edge and Mecredy rode their bicycles beside the pioneer motorists, other cyclists were part of the official procession, either as drivers or as passengers. All of the cars were numbered. Car number 1, a Panhard-Levassor, carried Lawson. Car number 7 was driven by former racing cyclist Herbert Duncan. Car number 11 was another Panhard-Levassor, driven by Charles McRobie Turrell, the secretary of Lawson's Motor Car Club and one of the organisers of the Run: he was formerly with the cycle company J. K. Starley and Co. of Coventry. Turrell's car carried Jack Dring of the Stanley Cycle Club. Car number 15 was a Daimler, driven by Charles T. Crowden, chief engineer of Humber, a bicycle manufacturer which later morphed into a motor car manufacturer. Crowden had been a designer of bicycles since the 1880s.

In a press car sat the Earl of Winchilsea, and writers for the *Daily Telegraph* and the *Pall Mall Gazette*, as well as Jerome K. Jerome, author of *Three Men in a Boat* in 1889 and the 1900 sequel *Three Men on the Bummel*, a tale of a cycle tour in Germany. Jerome had a nephew, the racing cyclist Frank Shorland, who would have been very familiar with the route taken by the cars earlier in the day – he was a London-to-Brighton record holder on his bicycle.

"The career of Frank William Shorland is exceptionally interesting in that, like many other pioneers of the motor industry, he made a wonderful name in the cycling sport and trade," said Duncan in his memoirs.

Shorland was a former professional racing cyclist – one of the best, in fact – and in 1896 was working for Raleigh Cycle Company, managing their London depot. Jerome joked that his nephew, thanks to cycling, was more famous than him. Shorland later moved into the motoring industry and in 1908 was appointed general manager of Clément-Talbot, making Talbot cars. "He was so successful that after two years of his able management, the works had to be considerably increased to cope with the enormous extension of trade," wrote Duncan. However, Shorland kept up his connections in the world of cycling and in 1925 was president of the Pickwick Bicycle Club, a cycling and lunching club.

Charles Rolls, a former racing cyclist and later to co-create Rolls-Royce, was in one of the Emancipation Run cars. American motor car manufacturer Frank Duryea, a former bicycle mechanic, drove another. Henry Hewetson, owner of the first car in Great Britain, drove his Benz on the day. Hewetson was proud of his cycling roots: in a 1904 motoring annual he said he had been the "first to ride a bicycle from London to Brighton."

Press baron and former cycling magazine editor Alfred Harmsworth was also one of the Emancipation Run participants. Another "emancipator" was Frederic W. Baily, who was one of the founding members

Frank Duryea knocked down and injured Miss Dyer of Crawley. She suffered a fractured skull. "A Child Seriously Injured by a Motor Car," Illustrated Police News, *November 21st, 1896.*

of the Automobile Club of Great Britain and Ireland, and a captain of the Anerley Bicycle Club between 1882 and 1890. He was the club president in the early 1900s, while running the Society of Motor Manufacturers and Traders' Automobile Exhibition at the Crystal Palace in London.

At an evening reception for the Emancipation Run participants in the Clarence Rooms at Brighton's Metropole Hotel, many more cyclists attended. Some of these were cycle manufacturers who had already or would soon become motor car manufacturers, but there were also cycle-industry executives who would only later become connected with motoring. Among the cyclists present were the Marquess of Queensberry; bicycle manufacturers Samuel Gorton, Dr. Illiffe and Rowland Hill of the New Beeston Cycle Company; Henry and James Jelley of the Beeston Tyre Company; Walter Phillips of cycle manufacturer Humber & Co.; Sir Somers Vine, director of the Imperial Institute and, according to *The Wheelwoman and Society Cycling News*, a very keen cyclist; and Herbert Duncan, the former cycle-racing champion.

Many of the cars that had taken part in the Emancipation Run were taken back to London and displayed at the 1896 Stanley Cycle Show at the Agricultural Hall. Immediately after that, many of the cars went on to another bicycle show, the rival National Cycle Show at the Crystal Palace.

DETROIT AUTO SHOW, 1899

Detroit – home to Chrysler, Ford, and General Motors – has had an automobile show since 1899, when it was staged at Beller's Beer Garden at Riverside Park. It was started by William E. Metzger, the co-founder and owner of Detroit's biggest bicycle shop, Huber & Metzger. Today the show is America's annual motor car jamboree, the North American International Auto Show.

Metzger opened the Huber & Metzger bicycle shop in 1891 and it grew to become one of the largest bike shops in the US (it was still selling bicycles in the 1920s), morphing in 1897 into one of America's first car dealerships. Metzger became a key motoring pioneer, involved in many aspects of the fledgling industry. His interest in self-propelled road transport had started when he became a cyclist in the 1880s. He was the first president of the Detroit Wheelmen cycling club and was active also in the L.A.W., being a champion of its Good Roads movement.

Metzger also helped create the Cadillac Motor Car Company, the Everitt-Metzger-Flanders motor car manufacturer – which was second in size only to Ford in 1911 – and the Metzger Motor Company.

Later, he started the first aviation show in Detroit. He was an associate of former Ohio bicycle-shop owners Wilbur and Orville Wright.

THE 1,000-MILE TRIAL, 1900

Since the 1930s, Britain's Veteran Car Club has fixated on the Emancipation Run as the starting event for motoring in Britain, re-enacting it every year as the London-to-Brighton Veteran Car Rally. The 1896 event might have been Britain's first (legal) motoring event but it certainly wasn't a terribly successful one from a reliability point of view. The run was ridiculed, both by those who turned out to watch and by the press. Selwyn Edge believed the event would have generated "very few converts to the cause of automobilism." The breakdowns and the limp-homes "served simply to increase the scepticism of those who had no faith in the future of the motor car."

The event that did a great deal more than the Emancipation Run to put motoring on the map followed four years later and was organised by the Automobile Club. The 1,000-Mile Trial proved that motor cars could be reliable over long distances. Starting on April 23rd, 1900, the well-publicised trial started in London and passed through Bristol, Birmingham, Manchester, Derby, Kendal, Carlisle, Edinburgh, Newcastle upon Tyne, Leeds, Sheffield and Nottingham before heading back to London, arriving on May 12th. At each stopover there was an exhibition promoting motoring. Sixty-five motor vehicles, of all shapes, sizes and nationalities, started the trial, which consisted of town-to-town processions, optional timed events and hill-climbing races. Thirty-five made it back to London.

Many of those who took part in the 1,000-Mile Trial, either in the vehicles themselves or as part of the promotional effort, had bicycling backgrounds. The former cyclists included champions of cycle-racing Charles Rolls, Alfred Harmsworth, Charles Friswell, J. W. Stocks, and Selywn Edge, driving and promoting a Napier. Tea entrepreneur, early motorist and even earlier cyclist Henry Hewetson also took part. Food magnate Sir Alfred Bird MP hosted a dinner at the Birmingham Conservative Club for all participants. Bird had been a very successful racing cyclist in his youth, and was one of the founding members of the Automobile Club. He was also a committee member, with a great interest in the improvement of roads. Bird developed this interest during his days as a cyclist. He had been an "energetic member" of the Cyclists' Touring Club and, before he became an MP, had been part of a CTC deputation to the Corporation of Birmingham to protest at the state of roads on behalf of cyclists, organised by the cyclists' Roads Improvement Association. Bird didn't give up cycling when he became a motorist. After his death (the motoring pioneer was knocked over by a motorist), his son endowed a prize fund in his father's memory. The Sir Alfred Bird Memorial Prize was offered by the CTC to "the inventor or producer of the greatest improvement in cycle design, construction, or equipment during any year." The prize medal – with a relief of Bird on one side – stated that Bird was "A cyclist of great renown who delighted in healthy exercise and fresh air. [He] loved the sport of cycling for its own sake and rode consistently from 1869 to his end in 1922."

Another cyclist who drove in the 1000-Mile Trial was Horace William Bartleet, friend to many cycling pioneers. Bartleet's collection of historic cycles was bequeathed to the City of Coventry and became the collection around which the car-centric Coventry Transport Museum was formed. In a 1904 motoring yearbook, Bartleet listed his hobbies as cycling and motoring and said he "took part in the 1,000 miles' trial of the Automobile Club in May, 1900, going through the three weeks' tour on a 3-h.p. air-cooled Decauville."

SMMT's AUTOMOBILE EXHIBITION, 1903

In order to stem competition from the long-established cycle shows that had displayed motor cars since 1896, the Society of Motor Manufacturers and Traders created its own show. The Automobile Exhibition at Crystal Palace in London, was staged from January 30th to February 7th, 1903. This was a sequel to the Crystal Palace Motor Show of the previous February. Both shows were organised by Frederic Wilfrid Baily.

Baily had taken in part in the Emancipation Run of 1896 and was one of the founding members of the Automobile Club of Great Britain and Ireland. He was also a bicyclist, and had been captain of the Anerley Bicycle Club between 1882 and 1890. "The Anerley" was one of the country's most famous cycling clubs, founded in 1881, and still exists. Baily – who was also the club's president in the early 1900s – had cut his organisational teeth on bicycle races for the Anerley. According to his entry in a 1903 guide to British motorists he "knew every rideable inch of his native country years before the arrival of teuf-teuf." ("Teuf-teuf" was an onomatopoeic French term for motor car.) Baily, the cyclist, had "a practical knowledge of motor men and machines second to none in this country."

Baily's SMMT show had competition from the Automobile Club's eighth annual Motor Show, in 1902 held at the Agricultural Hall in Islington, London, venue for many cycle shows and expositions over the years.

The growing number of competing motoring shows led *The Engineer* to reminisce:

"The vitality of the automobile industry is remarkable, and reminds one forcibly of the cycle boom of six or seven years ago."

❧ MOTORING ORGANISATIONS

Many automobile clubs started life as cycling clubs, or were founded by cyclists. A 1900 directory of automobile clubs in America's *The Automobile Magazine* had entries for clubs such as the Bicycle et Automobile Club de Lyon, Automobile Vélo of Nice, and the Veloce Club of Perigourdin. In Germany, there was the Radfahrer-und Automobilisten Vereinigung in Dresden and the Erster Stettiner Bicycle und Automobil Club in Stettin. Great Britain had the Motor and Cycle Trades Club in Birmingham and the Self-Propelled Traffic Association (with cyclists as lead players), as well as the London-based Automobile Club, which had many cyclists as founder members.

"Of provincial clubs the Automobile Club de Nice is undoubtedly the most active and important," wrote Charles Freeston in Sir Alfred Harmsworth's 1904 book on motoring, adding that the club had bicycling beginnings: "It was founded in 1897 as the Auto-Vélo Club."

Italy's motoring club was founded in 1897, as the Veloce Club e Club Automobilisti d'Italia – with the automobile section tagging on to an existing cycling club.

American motor clubs had many former bicyclists as prominent members. The Automobile Club of Syracuse, New York, "comprises some of the wealthiest and most influential residents of the Salt City," said *The Automobile Magazine* in 1902, adding that:

> It is interesting to note in the list of members the names of those who were formerly recognized … in the manufacture of bicycles for which Syracuse became known all over the world. The most prominent individual, no doubt, in this connection is E. C. Stearns, president of E. C. Stearns & Co., who were the makers of the once famous Yellow Fellow. The Barnes Cycle Company is likewise represented by Charles F. Saul, its former president, and William Van Wagoner, who made the Barnes White Flyer famous.

Automobile clubs were modelled on cycling clubs. "As it was with the wheel so will it be very largely in the case of the automobile," predicted *The Automobile Magazine.*

"In the early days of the bicycle there was perhaps one factor more than any other which contributed to the great demand for wheels," said the magazine. "That was the bicycle club."

In 1899, Britain's Automobile Club decided to take on the role of administering motor racing in Great Britain. It wasn't the first organisation to seek to do this and, in fact, it had to lobby hard to make sure it would be motor racing's governing body. The first organisation to suggest itself as the administrator of motor racing had been the National Cyclists' Union.

AMERICAN AUTOMOBILE ASSOCIATION

Formed at a meeting in Chicago on March 4th, 1902, the American Automobile Association was a federation of motor-car clubs, including the Automobile Club of America and automobile clubs from New Jersey, New York, Pennsylvania, Rhode Island and elsewhere. "Unite for better roads!" was the clarion call, a familiar message to many of those present at the Chicago Coliseum, where the AAA was

launched. Many of the officials who founded and steered the AAA, had earlier been officials in the League of American Wheelmen. They were therefore very familiar with L.A.W.'s Good Roads movement and would use broadly the same methods of agitation.

In 1904, the "Triple A" merged with the American Motor League, which had been the first American automobile organisation, founded in 1895. The American Motor League had been the creation of Charles Brady King, the first person to build and drive a car in Detroit. Brady King's inaugural run on March 7th, 1896 was followed by Henry Ford on his bicycle. Present at the first meeting of the A.M.L. was Sterling Elliott, former L.A.W. president (and inventor of the steering kingpin).

The A.M.L. was run by Isaac B. Potter, president of the L.A.W., publisher of the League's *Good Roads* magazine, an active wheelman since the 1880s, and also one of the early members of the Automobile Club. At a gala dinner, held in the Astor gallery in the Waldorf-Astoria hotel in New York in April 1900, and organised for the Automobile Club, Potter gave a talk where he "spoke of the interests of wheelmen in the [automobile] movement."

The A.M.L. continued the wheelmen's call for Good Roads and, when it was absorbed by the AAA, the A.M.L. formed the new organisation's highway lobbying arm. (Much of the rest of the organisation was concerned with motor-car racing, including organising and sanctioning races.)

Potter was the multi-term Chief Consul of the New York division of L.A.W., and had been elected National President in February 1897, after an acrimonious election battle with Sterling Elliott (both of these cycling officials would hold office in motoring organisations). The A.M.L. was modelled on the L.A.W. It was "an organization which would offer to its members the same protection in their rights upon the highways that the League of American Wheelmen gave its members in the pioneer days of cycling," said Potter.

In June 1903, *The New York Times* reported that

> The campaign of the American Motor League to extend its membership through the country is being conducted upon much the same plan employed by the League of American Wheelmen in its early days, and is under the direction of President Isaac B. Potter, an ex-President of the League of American Wheelmen … President Potter has secured the co-operation of many automobilists who formerly figured in the affairs of the League of American Wheelmen, and predicts that the same energetic campaign which brought that organization above the hundred-thousand mark will make the organized users of motor vehicles a body of great power and influence …

The A.M.L. didn't have to look far for promotional ideas: "The plan of the League of American Wheelmen of publishing handbooks, maps &c, and issuing them free to members will also be followed by the American Motor League. The first book of tours and routes for automobilists is ready for the press."

The League had some influential members: the Chairman of the League Committee on Technics was Charles E. Duryea, the bicycle-maker who, with his brother, produced America's first gasoline-powered motorcar.

The Automobile Club of America was originally a gentleman's club modelled on the even posher Automobile Club of Great Britain and Ireland (both clubs had restrictive membership rules and were not like today's motoring organisations, which are open to whomever pays for membership and are mainly road rescue providers). The Automobile Club of America was launched at New York's Waldorf-Astoria hotel in October 1899. Of the 20 or so individuals who met for the inaugural meeting, many had been cycling officials.

Automobile Club member Charles Ranlett Flint, the fabulously wealthy founder of the Computing-Tabulating-Recording Company, which became IBM, had been a L.A.W. consul. Jefferson Seligman had been a L.A.W. consul in 1897, and went on to become an official in the Automobile Club and then the AAA. Seligman became a vice-president of the organisation.

M. M. Belding, a silk manufacturer from New York, was a former L.A.W. consul who was an early member of the AAA.

These pioneer members of the Automobile Club were high-society figures, some of whom had been members of New York's exclusive Michaux Club. Founded in 1894, this was named after the French bicycle innovator of the 1860s. Some of New York's "best people," as *Munsey's Magazine* put it, were seen awheel. Rich socialites, such as the Rockefellers and the Roosevelts, were members of the Michaux Club. Within just a few years, high-society members of the club had transferred their affections to automobiles.

Another high-society cyclist-turned-motorist was Colonel John Jacob Astor. He was one of the wealthiest men of America's Gilded Age. Educated at Harvard, he thought highly enough of his own literary talents to write a science-fiction novel. This was published in 1894, a year before H. G. Wells's *The Time Machine*. Astor's book was not a bestseller, but some of his predictions – like those of H. G. Wells – are startling to modern eyes. He predicted that, by the year 2000, there would be high-speed magnetic railways, space travel, television, ground-penetrating radar, nuclear weapons, 500-miles-per-hour aeroplanes and an end to hunger thanks to solar power mills in the Sahara – and that the world would be ruled by the US and England. Like Wells, Astor also painted a world where there would be a great many bicycle paths.

Known as Jack, and noted for his love of motoring – he owned 20 cars at a time when owning just one was rare – Astor was one of the earliest members, and richest benefactors, of the Automobile Club of America. Before that he had been a benefactor of the L.A.W. "John Jacob Astor used to be one of us," said L.A.W. secretary Abbot Bassett in 1912. "He contributed liberally to our Good Roads fund."

Astor joined the L.A.W. in 1896 and renewed his membership every year until at least 1900. Clearly, he didn't give up on cycling when he joined the Automobile Club of America. It's also clear that Astor was a cyclist long before 1896 for, in 1889, he patented a bicycle brake – for a solid-tyred Safety bicycle.

Astor, an inventor, author and builder of deluxe hotels, and one of the wealthiest men in the world, was, by 1907, one of three members of the Automobile Club's Good Roads committee. As a former bicyclist and a member of the L.A.W., he would have been familiar with how cyclists were the first to agitate for better roads.

Another L.A.W. official to rise high in what was the successor to the Automobile Club of America was Amos G. Batchelder. He had been the official L.A.W. handicapper and chairman of the racing board of the National Cycling Association, and was one of the officials at the 1899 record attempt by Charles "Mile-a-Minute" Murphy, who rode a mile in 57 seconds on a bicycle paced behind a Long Island locomotive.

According to author Frank Parker Stockbridge, Batchelder was "one of the early members of the League of American Wheelmen." He became a member of the L.A.W. in March 1888. He was the sporting editor of the *Buffalo Courier*, becoming the secretary of the AAA in 1903. Leaving to become motoring editor of *The Evening Mail*, he was poached by William R. Hearst for his new magazine, *Motor*. In 1910, he returned to the Triple A as secretary, later becoming its executive chairman.

"To Batch belongs the chief credit for the national appropriation of $75,000,000 for highways and the financial part the government is now playing in good roads construction," said Abbot Bassett, editor of an L.A.W. publication, in 1921.

AMERICAN ROAD AND TRANSPORTATION BUILDERS ASSOCIATION

ARTBA is now thought of as an archetypal motoring-focused organisation, a leading part of the so-called "roads lobby". It was founded by Horatio "Good Roads" Earle who started his long career as roads champion with the Michigan division of the L.A.W. He was elected to the Michigan Senate in 1900, on an L.A.W. ticket. While still sponsored by a cycling organisation, Earle pushed through legislation to create a State Highway Department and pushed for the earliest freeways in America.

In 1901, Earle became the national president of the L.A.W. He lived in Detroit which, before it became Motown, a "motor town," was a "bike town." Detroit was a hotbed of cycle activism and a centre for bicycle manufacturing, too. Detroit was a hive of bicycle-based "Good Roads" activism, with Earle – and other Detroit wheelmen – key figures in pushing for better roads for all, not just cyclists.

In the 1920s the critical founding role of cyclists in the Good Roads movement was being forgotten or actively downplayed but Earle would have none of this, writing in his autobiography that "the bicycle is the father of the good roads movement in this country."

Earle remained a staunch L.A.W. supporter. "The League was the first organization that promoted the building of better roads," he insisted.

Earle's formation of American Road Makers (which would become the ARTBA) didn't get off to a very good start. Only three other people turned up: Earle had invited 200. This would not have deterred him. He was an organiser or, as the *Detroit Free Press* put it in 1899, "a hustler."

He was the sort who would engage anybody and everybody in conversation. One of his opening gambits, when meeting new people, was to talk to them about the League of Genial Lights, an organisation of his own creation. He had business cards printed to give to people, who would become "life members" of his organisation. (Presumably a hand-shake would reveal if the person he met was a Freemason, another organisation Earle "hustled" for.)

No doubt infused with the Christmas spirit, on December 26th, 1901, Earle wrote to 200 individuals he felt would be interested in creating a road-building association. Twenty-five replied and the three who turned up at the Cadillac Hotel in New York City on February 12th, 1902, formed, in Earle's opinion, "a large and honorable convention, because the purpose in view was both large and honorable."

Earle's letter to the 200 said that he was organising a plot to "overthrow a certain monarch ... and that monarch's name is Mud." He chose the name American Road Builders because the acronym ARM meant that the association "will never lower its arm until its purpose, 'The Capital Connecting Government Highway,' is attained..."

"The Capital Connecting Government Highway" was Earle's name for what would become the interstate highway system. He wanted ARM to be one part of the Capital Connecting Government Highway Commission, of which other members would include the Director of Public Road Inquiries and the president of the L.A.W.

While few turned up at the first meeting, the ARM was endorsed by Martin Dodge, Director of Public Road Inquiries. This body would become the Federal Highway Administration but in 1902 was still woefully funded and Dodge recognised that if Earle could organise professional road-builders and engineers into a professional body, funds for the cause of Good Roads would be easier to gain.

Earle became ARM's first president. In his autobiography, he wrote: "This organisation has wielded a mighty influence in the land, and without doubt, has been the principal factor in winning the national battle for better roads."

The organisation started by an L.A.W. president and which had just four people at its inaugural meeting saw 21,000 turn up at a session in 1928. "By gum, Michigan has shown the world how to build good roads," said Earle in 1929.

ANWB

The ANWB, or the Royal Dutch Touring Club, is the main motoring and road rescue organisation in the Netherlands. ANWB stands for *Algemene Nederlandse Wielrijders-bond*, or the General Dutch Cyclist Union. It was established in 1883 as a cycling club, before the advent of motoring. The founders were English, and modelled the Dutch cycling club on Britain's Cyclists' Touring Club – Charles Bingham became president of the new organisation and D. Webster became vice-president. The motoring side to ANWB was started in 1900. To begin with, motorists were provided with touring information. Within twenty years, motorists became the dominant force in the organisation.

The ANWB's club magazine was called De Kampioen (The Champion). *Today, the Dutch motoring organisation's house magazine is called just* Kampioen.

AUTOMOBILE ASSOCIATION

Today we tend to think of Britain's Automobile Association as a roadside rescue business. However, for much of its early history it was a radical campaigning organisation, a thorn in the side of the Government, and a rabble-rousing version of the more aristocratic Automobile Club. While the Automobile Club was founded by former cyclists, the Automobile Association was helped into life by cycling "scouts". See chapter 5.

(ROYAL) AUTOMOBILE CLUB

The Automobile Club of Great Britain and Ireland was founded in 1897. ACGB&I gained the Royal prefix, and shortened its acronym to RAC, when King Edward VII joined in 1907. To its first members, the posh and exclusive gentleman's club was known as the "Parliament of Motoring" and attracted affluent members, some of whom were aristocrats, while many were nouveau riche. Claude Johnson, the club's first secretary, said: "Anyone interested in automoblism is eligible for membership, though, naturally enough, we observe some social restrictions." The club claimed that it didn't admit "professional bicycle riders" but the restrictions were flexible, especially for founder members, such as Selwyn Edge, and Sir Alfred Bird MP.

Other Automobile Club founder members who had been bicycle racers included Herbert Duncan and the Hon. Charles Rolls.

Some of the committee members were cycling journalists, including Ernest Shipton and Henry Sturmey. Shipton was editor of the CTC magazine.

Many of the committee members of the Automobile Club had held similar positions with Britain's first motoring organisation, the Self-Propelled Traffic Association, and when this organisation merged with the Automobile Club in 1898 they came with it. One of these SPTA committee members was Sir Charles Vernon Boys, a professor of physics. In a 1904 motoring annual Boys described himself as "an enthusiastic motorist, and … fond of mechanics and cycling." Boys was a cyclist of long standing: he had started on high-wheelers and was intrigued by the science of cycling. "The extraordinary stability of the bicycle at high speed depends largely on the gyroscopic action of the wheels," he wrote in a scientific paper of 1884.

Boys remained a cyclist. Many other Automobile Club members didn't, including the club's prime mover Frederick Simms, importer of the Daimler engine and erstwhile associate of Henry Lawson. Simms had been a cyclist in his youth. He joined the CTC – along with his elder brother, Henry Bernard – in December 1880, before moving back to Germany to complete his education. Simms also founded, in 1902, the SMMT, and was elected its first president.

AUTOMOBILE CLUB DE FRANCE

"Believe me, gentlemen, the world is with us today," said the Comte de Dion in November 1895, "and the movement we are heading will be unstoppable." He was talking at his Paris home, during the foundation of the Automobile Club de France, the world's earliest motoring organisation. Twenty-four pioneer motorists were present, and a further 50 were later listed as founding members of the organisation. At least seven of these were active or former cyclists, and it's highly likely that many others were, too. Those with definite cycling credentials include racing drivers Fernand Charron and Chevalier René de Knyff. Charron was a former racing cyclist; Knyff was a cycle racing team manager. English motoring pioneer Sir David Lionel Salomons was also one of the first members. He was a life member and trustee of the Cyclists' Touring Club and president of the Tunbridge Wells cycling club. Cycle journalist Pierre Giffard was also a founding member, as were cycle-industry men Adolphe Clément, André Michelin and Armand Peugeot.

AUTOMOBILE CLUB DE MONACO

After Vatican City, Monaco is the smallest country in the world and is nestled on the French Riviera, close to Nice. Since its Monte Carlo casino opened in 1863 it has been a magnet for high-society and well-to-do ne'er do wells. Novelist W. Somerset Maugham said it was "a sunny place for shady people." It has been independent on-and-off for more than 800 years, a fortress home for the Grimaldi Royal family. Since 1911's staging of the first Monte Carlo rally the principality has been closely associated with motorsport, with the Automobile Club de Monaco organising some of the world's most important motor races, including the Monaco Grand Prix, first staged in 1929. But take a look at today's logo of the Automobile Club de Monaco – as well as a steering wheel and the fusily argent and gules, i.e., the Grimaldi family's trademark red and white diamond pattern, there's a bicycle. The Automobile Club de Monaco was founded in August 1890 as the Sport Velocipédique de la Principauté – the principality's bicycling club. It was a social and athletic club for Monaco's leading citizens, including friends of the royal family. At the request of the government the new club dropped the Principauté part of the name

and became Sport Vélocipédique Monégasque, or S.V.M. His Serene Highness H.S.H. Prince Albert 1st of Monaco became honorary president of the club on September 27th, 1905.

When its rich members took to the new sport of motoring the S.V.M. morphed into a motoring and cycling club (Prince Albert was a motorist, not a cyclist). In 1907 the S.V.M. added "automobile" to its name becoming the S.A.V.M., or Sport Automobile et Vélocipédique Monégasque. (The modern club logo features the initials S.V.M., not S.A.V.M.)

Club president Alexandre Noghès, a wealthy friend of the royal family and in charge of the principality's tobacco trade, created the glamorous Monte Carlo car rally in 1911. Fittingly, the first event was won by a former racing cyclist, Henri Rougier.

The Monaco Grand Prix was founded by Alexandre's son, Anthony. It was staged in 1929 by the Automobile Club de Monaco, which had dropped the cycling part of its name by 1925.

MOTOR TRADES BENEVOLENT FUND

"BEN is the UK's dedicated charity for those who work, or have worked, in the automotive and related industries, as well as their dependants," says the charity's website. BEN – the "Benevolent Fund" – is billed as "the automotive industry charity" and has five care centres dotted around England. It was created in 1905 as the Cycle and Motor Trades' Benevolent Fund, founded by long-time cycle journalist Arthur James "Faed" Wilson. (Faed was Wilson's pen name: it was deaf spelled backwards; Wilson was fully deaf from the age of 12.)

Wilson was a founder of the North Road Cycling Club in 1885 and one of the key founders of the cycling Road Records Association in 1888. In 1886, he and Dan Albone of Biggleswade – a stalwart of the North Road Cycling Club – designed the first practical tandem bicycle.

BEN's website doesn't mention its historic links to cycling but the charity's day-care centre in Coventry is called Arthur Wilson House. Wilson was honorary secretary and treasurer of the charity for many years. Wilson was still riding a tricycle in his seventies. In the 1890s and early 1900s Wilson worked for Dunlop, writing their advertising copy. In 1938, *The Cyclist* magazine said that Faed had made the world's first puncture repair kit, presumably in the early 1890s.

INSTITUTION OF AUTOMOBILE ENGINEERS

The Institution of Automobile Engineers of Great Britain was founded in 1906, merging with the larger Institution of Mechanical Engineers in 1946. The research side of the Institution of Automobile Engineers exists today as MIRA Ltd., at Nuneaton in Warwickshire. MIRA is the acronym for the Motor Industry Research Association, created in 1946. The testing and research company's origins go back beyond the Institution of Automobile Engineers. The IAE was originally the CEI, the Cycle Engineers' Institute, founded in Birmingham in January 1898.

According to *The Autocar* in 1899, "the Cycle Engineers' Institute looks upon the cycle and autocar manufacture as to a large extent sister branches of engineering, and it extends the privileges of membership to those concerned in the autocar trade."

The Autocar said that motor-car engineers were likely to join the Cycle Engineers' Institute because the "automobile branch of engineering has no representative body at present."

The Cycle Engineers' Institute was renamed the Automobile and Cycle Engineers Institute in 1904. The name was changed to the Institution of Automobile Engineers in 1906, (seemingly) severing the cycling connection.

The longest-serving council member of the IAE was George Douglas Leechman. At the time of his death in 1923 he was the organisation's vice-president. He had been a council member since 1899, when the organisation was still the Cycle Engineers' Institute.

Leechman was author of *The Autocar Handbook; A Guide to the Motor Car,* published in 1906, but a book written in 1895 shows one of his earlier interests: bicycling. For the cycling – and later motoring – publisher Iliffe and Son he wrote *Safety Cycling.* Leechman had been a bicycle designer since the 1880s, and was granted a number of British and US patents for "improvements to velocipedes." Leechman worked for the Success Cycle Co. of Limehouse, London, in the late 1880s and created Willesden Cycle Co. in 1891 after the former folded.

The Institution of Mechanical Engineers, incorporating the IAE, has another connection with cycling. Since 1914 it has awarded a student with the annual Starley Premium Award. This is to commemorate the work of John Kemp Starley, creator of the Rover Safety bicycle in 1885.

IRISH AUTOMOBILE CLUB

One of the founders of the Irish Automobile Club – and its chairman – was William Goff Davis-Goff of Glenville, Co. Waterford. (He was also a founder member of the Automobile Club of Great Britain and Ireland.) According to a 1901 guidebook, Goff had been "the second man in Ireland to ride a cycle." In the early 1890s, Goff built a cycle track in the People's Park in Waterford and donated it to the town.

(ROYAL) AUTOMOBILE CLUB OF VICTORIA

The Royal Automobile Club of Victoria is an Australian motoring club and mutual organisation. It was founded in 1903 and granted the Royal prefix in 1916. One of the RACV's founders was George Robert Broadbent. He became the organisation's tourist manager, a post he held until his retirement in 1937. His interest in road touring had blossomed when he was a bicyclist. Broadbent was a champion bicycle racer, "the finest road rider that Australia has ever produced." He was also a councillor of the League of Victorian Wheelmen in the 1890s and was active in the Australian Good Roads movement. In 1896, he issued a road map of Victoria, "prepared ... after some sixteen years riding and touring in all parts of the Colony." It became Victoria's standard road map, the basis of a continuous publishing programme by Broadbent's Official Road Guides Company.

In 1898, he became a motorist and contributed regularly to *The Argus* and *The Australasian* on both cycle touring and motoring. His second son, Robert Arthur, was also a cycling champion, representing Australia at the 1924 Olympic Games in Paris. Robert Broadbent succeeded his father as tourist manager of the RACV and established a map and guidebook business in his father's name.

Broadbent became vice-president of the Good Roads Association of Victoria in November 1912 and

MR. J. NAYLOR,
C.C. for Cheshire.

MR. W. COSENS,
R.C. for Herts.

MR. G. E. STANLEY,
R.C. for Worcester.

LT.-GEN. J. SPROT,
R.C. for E. Counties,
Scotland.

MR. C. E. DAWSON,
R.C. for Surrey.

REV. W. HAY FEA,
M.A.,
R.C. for Yorkshire.

SIR D. SALOMONS, BT.,
Life Membership
Trustee.

REV. C. E. RANKEN,
C.C. for Hereford and
Worcester.

MR. H. CROYDON
ROBERTS,
C.C. for Middlesex
and Herts.

MR. JOSEPH
PENNELL,
R.C. for U.S. of
America.

MAJ. C. H. L. BASKER-
VILLE,
R.C. for S.W. Grouped
Counties.

REV. T. H. ORPEN R.C. for
N. & E. Grouped Counties.

MR. J. JOHNSTON,
R.C. for Lanarkshire.

MR. J. WHITE,
C.C. for Dublin.

COL. F. E. B. LORAINE
C.C. for Hants and Isle of Wight

MR. W. F. BALL,
C.C. for Warwickshire.

SOME C.T.C. OFFICIALS.

*Motoring pioneer Sir David Salomons is in the centre of
this collection of officials with the Cyclists' Touring Club,
from* The Hub, *June 10th, 1899.*

was consulted regularly during the preparation of the Country Roads Bill.

While he became known for his role with the RACV he remained an avid cyclist. He "never allowed his familiarity with cars to make him forsake his first love," said *The Argus* in 1932. He told the newspaper: "Cycling is more than a sport and a pastime, it is healthful and it is a practical means of locomotion." It was certainly healthful for Broadbent, as he was still cycling in his eighties. "For touring he prefers the bicycle," said *The Argus* in 1946. "You can see more, and enjoy the scenery more, from a bike, he says."

SELF-PROPELLED TRAFFIC ASSOCIATION

The Self-Propelled Traffic Association was Britain's first motoring organisation. It was founded by Sir David Salomons, an electrical engineer, CTC trustee and pioneer motorist. At the SPTA's first meeting, held on December 10th, 1895 in a hotel in central London, Salomons was elected president.

There were other cyclists on the committee, including Ernest Shipton, secretary of the CTC and editor of the club's magazine; William Worby Beaumont, assistant editor of *The Engineer* and a member of the Cycle Engineers' Institute, later to become the IAE (in *Motoring*'s 1904 listing of the world's motorists, Beaumont said he didn't yet own a motor car and listed cycling as first among his hobbies); Sir Charles Vernon Boys, a professor of physics and a long-time cyclist; and Sir Benjamin Ward Richardson, a tricycle-riding public health specialist.

Henry Lawson was on the SPTA's committee for just one meeting: he and Salomons hated each other.

Most of the SPTA's committee members joined the committee of the Automobile Club when the two bodies merged in 1898.

Selwyn Edge said that Salomons was "numbered among that small band of men in England who foresaw the future of the horseless carriage." As well as creating the SPTA, Salomons was one of founding members of the Automobile Club de France.

While Lawson usually gets much of the credit for the agitation that led to the 1896 Emancipation Act it was actually Salomons who deserves most credit. He was very active behind the scenes, helping civil servants and politicians draft policy on the new form of locomotion. Motoring historian T. R. Nicholson said that Salomons had a "gift for influencing the wielders of power at the most critical point in the British motor movement's first days."

At his house at Broomhill in Tunbridge Wells Salomon built Britain's first private car storage area. He called this five-room garage his "motor stable." One of the five rooms was used as a "cycle house."

TOURING CLUB DE BELGIQUE

Belgium's motoring organisation was founded as the Touring Club de Belgique, quickly became Touring Club Royal de Belgique and, in 2004, morphed into the simpler Touring. The organisation was created in 1895 as a cycle touring club. It hasn't totally lost its cycling roots – as well as road rescue for motorists it has a road rescue service for cyclists.

❧ MOTOR MARQUES & THEIR BICYCLING BEGINNINGS

Cyclists and cycle manufacturers played a major part in the manufacturing, design and sale of the first motor cars in France, America and Germany – and, as an article published in 1902 shows, in Great Britain, too. "[A] large number of men who, having made their names in the sport and trade of cycling, are now engaged in the making, selling or driving of light cars," wrote a journalist for *Motor Cycling*.

In America, there was a members' organisation for "men who entered automobiling from the old field of cycling." At a gathering in 1911, 200 members showed up, including former bicycle shop owner William Metzger of the Everitt-Metzger-Flanders Company, one of the largest automobile manufacturers in the world in 1911, and Amos G. Batchelder, the long-time executive secretary of the American Automobile Association:

> The regular meeting of the "Old Guard" … was held in Madison Square Garden Tuesday, Jan. 17, and nearly 200 of the veterans gathered … In the party were William Metzger of the Metzger Motor Car Company; Harry Lozier, Lozier Bicycle Company in olden days and Lozier Motor Company today…A. G. Batchelder, ex-chairman of the N. C. A. racing board … Walter Wardrop, editor *Commercial Vehicle*; S. W. Merriliew, editor *Automobile Topics*; Fred Castle, the lamp manufacturer; Ezra Kirk of the Badger Brass Company; Fred Titus, known in the old days as handicap king and now a prominent motor car salesman, and many others.

"The cyclist and the cycle maker … paved the way for the autocar," said a front-cover editorial in an 1895 edition of the world's first weekly motoring magazine. Probably written by editor Henry Sturmey the piece in *The Autocar* added that the "wheelman has proved to a conservative nation the immense advantages of and economic gain obtained by the application of self-contained power as a means of propulsion."

The cycle manufacturer, said Sturmey, had "achieved a mechanical triumph in the combination of great strength to withstand internal strains with extreme lightness," skills and knowledge that were transferred directly to the manufacture of motor cars.

Not only had the cycle manufacturer "brought the science of road-carriage construction to [the] point of perfection," but the cyclist had also "accustomed the public mind to the sight of wheeled vehicles without horses."

Some of the world's most famous motor-car marques – such as Aston Martin, GMC, Chevrolet, and Rolls-Royce – were founded by racing cyclists. There are another sixty automobile companies with cycling backgrounds including Opel, Ford, and Land Rover. These are listed in the appendix.

CHAPTER FIFTEEN

FROM KING OF THE ROAD TO CYCLE CHIC

Farewell, farewell, my bicycle,
I've got a motor-car.

…

The times are changed, my bicycle,
Thou art not up-to-date.

…

I'll travel with the best,
For I shall turn a handle, and
The car will do the rest.

HARDWARE TRADE JOURNAL, JUNE 1897

Cyclists of the 1880s and 1890s were transport progressives. Many later morphed into motorists. When bicycles became affordable to the masses the social cachet of cyclists became but a memory. By the 1920s cycling was "poor man's transport" and in the 1960s it was thought that everybody would soon own a car, and that bicycles would become extinct. The resurgence of the bicycle took everybody by surprise and, today, cycling is on the march again.

The company that publishes the *Financial Times* began life as a small building contractor in Bradford, Yorkshire, in 1844. Weetman Dickinson Pearson expanded the firm founded by his grandfather and made a fortune in the Gilded Age by constructing mammoth projects such as the Admiralty Harbour at Dover, the Tehuantepec National Railway in Mexico and the Blackwall Tunnel under the Thames. In 1895, Pearson – by now knighted – was elected as Liberal MP for Colchester. At about the same time he bought Paddockhurst House in Sussex. For the master dining room of his country mansion Pearson commissioned an artwork, requesting "something bearing upon the source of his wealth." In 1897, the bohemian artist Walter Crane produced a "playful symbolic history of locomotion and transport" in a series of large and remarkable stucco frieze panels. The artwork, placed below the ceiling of the irregular shaped room, is chronological and features Bronze Age pedestrians, a canoe, the taming of the horse, a primitive cart drawn by oxen, a canal boat, a coach-and-four, a steam train and – the latest thing in 1897 – a number of motor cars. The frieze's concluding characters are Sir Weetman and Lady Annie Pearson themselves. The artwork is a sculpted snapshot of a time when plutocrats desired to be immortalised astride the most progressive vehicle of the day – the fabulously wealthy couple are shown riding bicycles.

In 1917, Pearson was elevated to the aristocracy as the 1st Viscount Cowdray. The dining room in what was Lord and Lady Cowdray's weekend residence is now part of Worth Abbey, home to an order of Benedictine monks since Michaelmas Eve, 1933. The frieze is still there; Sir Weetman and Lady Pearson – dressed to the nines – are still riding their bicycles, depicted from the front on one panel and from the back on another as they rush to reach one of their new-fangled motor cars. (See plates section).

Crane's sculpture was made from fibrous plaster pressed from a clay mould. It is detailed enough to show that the bejewelled front lamp of Lady Pearson's bicycle is etched with whirls and curls, as is the bicycle frame. This is a lifelike representation of the silver-plated bicycle that her husband bought from Tiffany & Co. of New York some time after 1895.

Crane, an illustrator of socialist publications, was given free rein on the artwork, but was asked to incorporate Lady Pearson's pride and joy. In his memoirs, Crane remembered that "Lady Pearson had a pet bicycle of silver ... which it was hoped I could introduce – that is to say, its portrait!"

The silver-plated bicycle, with its neo-rococo scrollwork and ivory handlebar grips, was an impulse purchase by Sir Weetman Pearson, who visited New York regularly. It was one of a number of similar high-society bicycles stocked by New York's top jeweller in the mid-1890s.

Such ostentation was indicative of an image problem – by 1896, for a bicycle to look like a high-status vehicle it had to be draped in ornamental silver. The Tiffany bicycle may have cost seven times as much as the usual top-of-the-range bicycle but its fine and costly decorations could only be seen at close quarters. Cycling's socially elevated status was waning. Bicycles were becoming affordable for the lower middle classes and, via credit or "tick", even blue collar workers were starting to cycle. The bicycle was now "the great leveller," editorialised a New York newspaper in 1896, "for not till all Americans got on bicycles was the great American principle, that every man is just as good as any other man ... fully realized. All are on equal terms, all are happier than ever before ..."

The first bicycles had been expensive and for elite use only. That well-paid workers could now afford bicycles, albeit not decorated, was the kiss of death for high-society cycling.

THERE'S NO denying motoring's revolutionary impact, but it's less well appreciated that the individualistic, go-anywhere bicycle helped punch a hole through the air for the motor car to follow. Many of the social benefits that motoring is said to have ushered in were, in fact, anticipated by cycling. For instance, motoring is often said to have reduced rural inbreeding because people could travel further for their trysts. Cycling got there first. There was a significant rise in the number of inter-parish marriages in south-west England after 1890 – even in those towns without railway stations. In a 1969 study it was concluded that the mobility provided by the bicycle was a major contributory factor.

In 1898, at a time when cars were becoming more popular, an article in an influential magazine discussed the leading scientific and industrial achievements of the age. The eminent scientist Professor W. J. McGee described American and European advances that were changing the world. McGee, who was also president of the American Association for the Advancement of Science, said there would soon be a new industrial and scientific revolution. He listed the many advances in geology, chemistry, medicine, astronomy, electricity, physics, telegraphy, bridge-building, photography, meteorology and anthropology. Land transport was also mentioned in McGee's 14-page article, with one form of transport being cited as a social revolutioniser. Twelve or so years after Carl Benz made his Patent-Motorwagen and two years after Ford made his quadricycle, America's leading scientist said that the social revolutioniser he had in mind "first aroused invention, next stimulated commerce, and then developed individuality, judgment, and prompt decision on the part of its users more rapidly and completely than any other device ..." McGee wasn't talking about the motor car. "The bicycle has broken the barrier of pernicious differentiation of the sexes and rent the bonds of fashion," he said, adding that, "weighed by its effect on body and mind as well as on material progress, this device must be classed as one of the world's great inventions."

The later success of the motor car overshadowed the regard in which bicycles were once held. In the 1890s and even into the early 1900s, when motor cars had yet to wow the world, bicycles had been seen as cutting-edge vehicles of social change.

In 1930 John Galsworthy, author of *The Forsyte Saga*, wrote of the bicycle's social significance in the explanatory *On Forsyte Change*, which described the influences on his famous book's characters, an upper-middle-class English family, similar to his own. Many of the upwardly mobile characters in the three Forsyte novels took to cycling: "Cicely and Rachel and Imogen and all the young people – they all rode those bicycles now and went off Goodness knew where."

Later, they took to motor cars, but it had been bicycles that had afforded them their first experience of freedom, said Galsworthy:

> Such historians as record the tides of social manners and morals, have neglected the bicycle. Yet would it be difficult to deny that [the bicycle] has been responsible for more movement in manners and morals than anything since Charles the Second ... Under its influence, wholly or in part, have wilted chaperons, long and narrow skirts, tight corsets, hair that would come down, black stockings, thick ankles, large hats, prudery and fear of the dark; under its influence, wholly or in part, have bloomed week-ends, strong nerves, strong legs, strong language, knickers, knowledge of make and shape, knowledge of woods and pastures, equality of sex, good digestion and professional occupation ...

Legs may have been stronger in the halcyon bicycle days, but not everybody wanted shapely pins. Writing about the joyful physicality of cycling in an 1889 book, American engineer Robert Pittis Scott showed that he was aware of the many experiments with powered propulsion, but he didn't expect them to supplant human power:

> That every rider will care for this extraneous assistance is doubtful, as the element of exercise would be eliminated to a great extent. For practical uses aside from exercise, as in the transaction of business, etc., other motors than that of human energy would be a boon in the present cycle, but they would never be used to the exclusion of the legs.

A writer in the L.A.W. magazine also ridiculed the idea that people would prefer to be propelled by a power source other than themselves:

> One of the prime pleasures of cycling, and one of its most beneficial attributes is the exercise afforded by the act of propelling a wheel driven by leg-power. No one would care to own an automatic gymnasium in which the Indian-clubs would swing themselves, and the dumb-bells go through their various evolutions without any muscular assistance. Exercise is something that cannot be obtained by proxy, and exercise is the very effervescence of the wine of motion.

Scott and the L.A.W. journalist were wrong – many people *did* want "extraneous assistance," and they cared little for the loss of exercise. In fact, the lack of exertion was one of the key appeals of motoring.

Victorian transport progressives may have adored their bicycles, but for many the love affair was fleeting – when it became practical to be propelled by a motor and not thighs, many of the cycling-besotted transport progressives switched camps. Writing in 1931, American political cartoonist Rollin Kirby remembered that the "novelty of effortless locomotion" was an almost instant attraction for those who had previously pedalled. He became misty eyed when thinking of the time when

> the whole world was awheel … Ramblers with their copper rims, Columbias, Victors with their spring forks, Iver Johnsons, Monarchs, Barnes White Fliers – how well we knew the different makes as they spun by with a great whirring of chains over the sprocket wheels.

The Pulitzer Prize-winning artist had been an "ardent, obsessed cyclist" in his youth but, like others, he eventually succumbed to the lure of the automobile. Part of the attraction was speed. When automobiles eventually became faster than bicycles those attracted to cycling because of its velocity transferred their affections to the swifter mode of transport.

The famous quote from motoring pioneer Hiram Percy Maxim about the bicycle creating motoring as it "directed men's minds to the possibilities of independent long-distance travel over the ordinary highway" referred partly to the fact that human propulsion was seen by some as slow and outmoded:

> … it came about that the bicycle could not satisfy the demand which it had created. A mechanically propelled vehicle was wanted instead of a foot propelled one, and we now know that the automobile was the answer.

In fact, the automobile was not the answer – at least not at first. Motor cars could not replace bicycles for the simple reason that not enough were manufactured. The Olds Motor Co. of Detroit was America's largest automobile manufacturer at the time but made just 2,500 vehicles in 1902.

Before the ascendancy of the motor car in the 1930s, it was the electrified tram, bus or underground railway which had enabled people to travel across towns and cities with only the minimum of effort. "In these days … few people walk much in towns," argued a British cycling magazine in 1899, "owing to the facilities existing for saving exertion and time." Similarly, an American article in 1901 complained about those seduced by trams:

> Why do we note a decline in wheeling? We think it has its root in the laziness of mankind. Time was when men wanted to get out and see the country and they employed the wheel. They had to work for it but they felt paid for all their labor in what they took in of scenery and fresh air. And now comes the trolley car and takes them out into the open country and they do no labor, get nearly all of it without work and for a nickel. We are such a lazy set that we use the nickel.

The "decline in wheeling", partly due to laziness, was precipitous. There were 103,293 members of the L.A.W. in its peak year of 1898. Seven years later there were just 2,874. With easy access to trams and buses – and only eventually motor cars – people no longer had to travel by engaging muscle-power. For most city dwellers this was bliss. It still is.

CYCLING WAS the in-thing in Britain for at least two social seasons. Writing in 1898, a year after the bicycle boom had ended, a cycling magazine recalled: "It would be hardly too much to say that in April of 1895, one was considered eccentric for riding a bicycle, whilst by the end of June, eccentricity rested with those who did not ride."

Three Men in a Boat author Jerome K. Jerome described high-society bicycling in Battersea Park in 1895:

> In shady bypaths, elderly countesses, perspiring peers, still at the wobbly stage, battled bravely with the laws of equilibrium; occasionally defeated, they would fling their arms round the necks of hefty young hooligans who were reaping a rich harvest as cycling instructors: "Proficiency guaranteed in twelve lessons". Cabinet Ministers, daughters of a hundred Earls might be recognised by the initiated, seated on the gravel, smiling feebly and rubbing their heads.

The upper middle classes had been bicycling for many more years than that. In 1891, *The Irish Times* reported that "the brotherhood of the wheel has increased a hundredfold within the last two or three years," and that cyclists now included "peers, judges, clergymen, barristers, medical men, solicitors, merchants and other respectable folk."

Workers were not yet on bicycles in great numbers. In 1888, R. J. Mecredy, the editor of the *Irish Cyclist* magazine and later to become an arch motoring journalist, recorded his faux irritation at learning that in a Dublin pub a tally was kept of which customers preferred the various cycling journals of the day. "How nice to have the merits of the paper discussed by Johnny the Shoeblack, on his hired crock, or the messenger boy from the grocer's up the road," he snarked.

Johnny the Shoeblack could not even afford to own a "crock", and the grocer's boy was riding a bicycle owned by his employer. However, in the Midlands – the centre of British cycle manufacturing in the 19th century – workers were more likely to own cycles, supplied to them at preferential rates, as happens with car factory workers today.

The first inklings that cycling might cut across all classes were contained in the 1887 book *Cycling*, Volume 7 of the aristocratic Badminton Library of Sports and Pastimes: "In Coventry, which may be looked upon as the peculiar home of cycling, it is fast becoming the custom for workmen to go home on their bicycles during the dinner-hour."

"WHERE IGNORANCE IS BLISS," &c.

He (alarmed by the erratic steering). "Er—and have you driven much?" *She (quite pleased with herself).* "Oh, no—this is only my second attempt. But then, you see, I have been used to a bicycle for years!"

Upwards of 300,000 cycles were sold in 1889. Cycles were expensive, and remained so until after the deflation of the bicycle bubble in 1897. That is, *new* models were expensive. "Last year's" model was far cheaper – Hoopdriver, the clerical-class cycling hero in H. G. Wells' 1896 cycling novel *Wheels of Chance*, bought "a machine with a past … it was perfectly sound, if a little old-fashioned." (By looking at his dated "crock", with "cushion" tyres and not pneumatics, the novel's bounder could tell at a glance Hoopdriver was from an inferior class.)

Bicycles could also be purchased on credit although, again, this was more for the aspiring lower middle classes rather than for, say, labourers. Nevertheless, the slow democratisation of cycling meant that by the end of the 1890s the bicycle was becoming an unreliable indication that the owner was wealthy. Those who wanted others to know they could afford the very latest in road chic gradually moved to motor cars, which were visibly and audibly expensive. The bicycle's fall from grace was not immediate. Cycling continued to be a popular form of leisure and transport for some of the moneyed classes for some years. For instance, the composer Edward Elgar began cycling in 1900. He explored the Malvern lanes close to his home until 1909, when his wife finally made him hang up his treasured Sunbeam in favour of a motor car.

At the end of the 1890s there appeared the first photographs of bicycle club members who appear to be from the skilled working class, but such photos are rare compared to photographs of middle-class cycling clubs and outings. (Cameras and cycling went very well together – the first photography magazines were published by cyclists.) In general, working people had neither the money nor the leisure time for weekend cycling.

The National Clarion Cycling Club, established in 1895, was ostensibly a socialist club aiming to get the working man out into the countryside, but the first club members were predominantly middle class and only later did it become a truly working-class club.

In 1909, thanks to blue-collar workers becoming daily cyclists, there were three million bicycles in regular use – but cycling was not yet a mass form of transport. (Motoring was even less so, with 48,000 motor vehicles in use.) One of the key spurs to getting more people on bicycles was the increase in leisure time, first for the clerical classes and later for the working classes. The 1911 Shops Act gave retail workers a weekly half-day holiday, the so-called "early closing day." In 1912, *Cycling* magazine reported that, "Roads [were] thronged with cyclists," because

> The Act is inducing people to spend their half holiday cycling … Many manufacturers [agree] that the Shop Hours Act has been the means of bringing large numbers of recruits into the ranks of cyclists.

An official from Dingley Brothers, a manufacturer of cycles in Coventry since 1890, told the weekly magazine: "We are decidedly of the opinion that the demand for bicycles among shop assistants has increased wonderfully since the introduction of the Shop Hours Act."

By the mid-1930s, exploring the countryside by bicycle had become a popular leisure pursuit for workers eager to escape the soot and grime of the cities. In 1926 the government estimated there were five million bicycles on the road. Ten years later there were twice as many. The cycle industry estimated that the 10 million mark had been reached much earlier, as pointed out in 1934 by H. N. Crowe, secretary of the National Cyclists' Union. He said that bicycles outnumbered motor cars by "five or six times … The output of the manufacturers has never been so big as it is now. The figure is round about 10,000,000 [bicycles in use]."

Crowe was speaking at an inquest into the death of a cyclist "tossed under a motorcoach." He told the coroner that now the "cycle is the poor man's vehicle." But, he remonstrated, that shouldn't make any difference to the cyclist's use of the public highway: "Why should a man who is not sufficiently well off to drive a car be deprived of the use of the streets?"

The coroner – almost certainly a car owner – was sympathetic to the dead cyclist's family: "It is a terrible thing for a wife to be suddenly bereft of her husband" – but Ingleby Oddie, coroner for the County of London, was less sympathetic to the continued use of the public highway by those daring to use what he considered "an out-of-date vehicle."

And these out-of-date vehicles now had to make way for the minority modern ones. "The time will come," predicted coroner Oddie, "when [bicycles] will not be allowed in the streets during the busiest hours."

Long before cycling became a minority mode of transport it was stigmatised by rich motorists as "poor man's transport". The marginalisation was quite literal – cyclists were forced to ride in the gutter by passing motorists even though many of the motorists had only very recently been cyclists themselves. Motorists certainly didn't want to share "their" roads with outmoded bicycles. Roads had very quickly become only for the powerful, with the agent of power being the accelerator pedal. Long before motoring became a mass form of transport it was viewed as normative, and motor cars were seen as the "natural" users of Britain's roads. Cycling was still the majority mode of transport but moneyed motorists portrayed it as abnormal.

LONDON-BASED American artist Joseph Pennell – who, along with his wife Elizabeth, was a long-time cycle tourer and successful travel writer – was upper middle class but even he had his nose put out of joint by the swaggering arrival of the new kings of the road. In 1902, he complained:

> It is only since the coming of the automobile that I have known what it is to be poor; only since the coming of the motor car that class distinctions have been set up all over the earth; only within the last two or three years that most of us have found that we belong to the submerged nine-tenths, the exposed tenth being composed mainly of motor makers and millionaires.

Pennell was wealthy enough to join the motoring crowd – he started with motor cycles – but most road users found themselves disenfranchised, their use of the road seen as deviant. The quietude of Victorian roads was now but a memory. Speeding cars and masses of cyclists were never going to mix very well. In America, cyclist numbers plummeted in the early 1900s and didn't recover until many years later but in Britain there were still millions of cyclists on the roads by the end of the 1920s. One of the people most responsible for getting the working man (and woman) on the bicycle was Sir Edmund Frank Crane of Smethwick, Birmingham. He inherited his family's failed bicycle business and in 1910, with his brother, turned the Petros Motor and Cycle Company into the Hercules Cycle and Motor Company, specialising in competitively priced bicycles for the lower middle classes. In 1922, just before the start of the working-class bicycle boom, the firm was making 700 machines a week. By the mid-1920s, a bicycle could be bought new for what the average labourer earned in two weeks – it was now an affordable luxury. (By contrast, a labourer in 1897 would have had to work for three months to afford a new bicycle.) By cutting prices even further and advertising the fact, Hercules sold 300,000 bicycles in 1928. Five years later this had risen to three million sales each year. In 1939, Hercules made six million bicycles, making it the largest cycle manufacturer in the world.

At the end of the 1920s, while manufacturers such as Raleigh and the other companies remaining from the mid-1890s bicycle boom continued to make and market bicycles for touring and leisure use, Hercules mostly made utilitarian bicycles, no-frills practical machines aimed squarely at the working-class market. A Hercules bicycle was a workhorse, cheaper than its rivals, but reliable.

With falling prices and rising wages, more and more people became able to afford bicycles. Yet the market growth came at the same time as the government and motorists were actively marginalising cycling. Cyclists, it was felt, had to get off the "motoring" roads. The marginalisation – framed by legislators as a safety concern – was highly successful and by the 1950s almost everybody had bought into the concept that bicycles had always been for poor people, even though the everyday use of bicycles by workers was little more than 20 years old.

History is rarely clean-cut. There are usually messy transitional stages between different eras. The worlds of cycling and motoring, once so intimate, pulled apart but the separation was slow, taking 20 or so years before the two-tribes mentality took over. If there's a single year that best represents the parting of the ways, it's 1906.

A faction within the Cyclists' Touring Club – including club secretary E. R. Shipton, a committee member of the Automobile Association and already a motorist with a speeding conviction – wanted to alter its 1887 constitution by broadening the membership to include motorists. Members present at the club's AGM in March 1906 voted by a margin of five to one to become the Touring Club, open to all road users. Such a change had taken placed in the Netherlands, with ANWB happily existing as a club for both motorists and cyclists (the motorists soon dominated, of course). However, the CTC was structured as a company and to change its memorandum of association required a petition before a judge. In December the case went before Mr. Justice Warrington.

In an affidavit put before the court, Shipton claimed that "touring on bicycles has gone out of favour chiefly on account of the introduction of motor cars, which, besides being more attractive in themselves, have to a great extent destroyed the pleasure of cycling, and have increased the risk of accident in the use of bicycles ..."

Judge Warrington may have concurred with Shipton's rather disloyal description of cycling being less attractive than motoring, but he did not agree that a company could promote the interests of what he felt were very different entities:

> If the business of catering to motorists is combined with this, the club could only protect bicyclists against the dangers arising from motors by taking measures against another class of its own members; and it seems to me that the result would be that it would be impossible to combine ... the business of catering for and protecting the rights and interests of motorists with the business of catering for and protecting the rights and interests on the roads of those who ride bicycles and tricycles.

The judge dismissed the application. Unlike in the Netherlands, the split between motorists and cyclists was now obvious for all to see. CTC officials and members may have remained middle class for some years to come (the CTC's post-WWI nickname was the "Collar and Tyre Club"), but cyclists as a whole were quickly becoming less so. A great many motorists clearly felt that the lower orders had to to make way for their betters. In the 1880s and 1890s Lucas of Birmingham made a cycling lamp called "King of the Road" which was used by wealthy and time-rich Victorian and Edwardian cyclists who had the roads largely to themselves. In the early 1900s Lucas used its road royalty brand name on headlamps for motor cars. Motorists, as Shipton made clear in 1906, were the new Kings of the Road.

MOTORISTS DIDN'T gain priority on roads just because of the greater speed and bulk of their vehicles, but also because they felt themselves to have superior *rights*. This entitlement syndrome was present from the first days of motoring, with motorists considering themselves the only rightful users of roads. In America and Britain, the highway superiority of motor cars was an unwritten rule. In Germany, it was quite explicit. While Adolf Hitler's Nazi party gets the credit for building autobahns and thereby creating a utopia for a tiny number of pre-war motorists, the concomitant desire to rid the ordinary streets of cyclists was not specifically fascist. Cyclists started to be treated as second-class citizens in Germany in the 1920s. Despite being in the majority, cyclists ought to be confined to cycle paths, suggested many motorists. The first cycle paths in Germany had been wide, well designed and constructed for the convenience of cyclists. The cycle paths called for in 1926 by the Research Association for the Construction of Automobile Roads (STUFA), and soon thereafter constructed by the *Zentralstelle für Radwege* (Central Office for Bike Paths), would be narrow, made from cheap materials and indirect. The inferior bike paths for Germany's 15 million cyclists were largely paid for by the cyclists themselves, via specific taxation. (In the Netherlands it was the other way round – a 1920s tax on cyclists paid for the construction of roads meant only for motorists.)

Ironically, STUFA had grown out of the work started by municipal engineer Dr. Henneking who had been the prime mover behind the superlative cycle paths in Magdeburg. 400 kilometres of these paths had been constructed in the early 1900s by the *Magdeburger Verein für Radfahrwege* (Magdeburg Association for Bicycle Paths), a cycling organisation made up of businesspeople, civil servants and city officials, founded in 1898. The new and inferior cycle paths were referred to as "the roads of the little man".

Use of cycle paths, when provided, became mandatory from October 1934, even if the path was poorly designed, surfaced or maintained. There was no outcry from cycling associations because they had been either outlawed or brought within the fascist fold as the Nazi-controlled *Deutscher Radfahrer Verband* (German Bicycle Association). In the run up to the Berlin Olympics of 1936, Nazi propaganda crowed: "Let us show the marvelling foreigners proof of an up-and-coming Germany … where the motorist has bicycle-free access not only to the autobahns but to all roads."

A road network freed of cyclists was also sought in Britain. Such an outcome was the ardent desire of motoring organisations, leading police officers, the Ministry of Transport, county council officials and the majority of other witnesses who gave evidence to the Alness parliamentary committee in 1938. Cyclists ought to be compelled to use cycle paths where provided, argued organisations other than cycling ones.

England's first cycle path was built in 1934, a 2¼ mile stretch of uneven concrete from Hangar Lane to Greenford Road in Ealing, London, kept separate from, but adjoining, Western Avenue. A cinema news snippet from British Pathé described the Western Avenue cycle track as "a new safety innovation" and claimed that "motorist users of the road will be equally appreciative of this new boon." (In 1934, British motorists owned 1.3 million motor cars – at the same time, there were 12 million cyclists.) A large crowd witnessed Leslie Hore-Belisha, the newly appointed Minister of Transport, cutting the ribbon at the official opening of the experimental "cycling track."

Hore-Belisha said that the cycle path, created at the behest of his predecessor, was for the "comfort and safety" of cyclists. Hore-Belisha was no fan of cycling – he believed cyclists were "the most dangerous people on the roads today" and, in parliament in July 1934, when Viscountess Astor asked whether a "system could be devised to prohibit pedal cycling in very crowded areas" he answered "I quite appreciate her humanity of view." Opposition to the Western Avenue path came from both the CTC and the NCU. Later in 1934, Hore-Belisha described cyclists as "hysterical prima donnas." *The Perils of the Cycle Path*, a CTC leaflet produced in 1935, made it plain that cyclists did not want to be fobbed off with substandard bike paths, and feared being compelled to use them, as had happened in Germany and America (when most of the famous Coney Island Cycle Path was converted to a motor road after 1911 cyclists had nowhere they could legally ride – in 1896 they had acquiesced when the Park Commissioner banned cycling on all parts of the Ocean Parkway except the Cycle Path because they felt the "reasonable regulation … in no way interfered with their needs in that section.")

The few urban "cycling tracks" provided to English cyclists in the 1930s were a poor substitute for the rural roads cyclists were used to riding on. Even one of the designers wasn't impressed. Eric Claxton, then a junior engineer in the Ministry of Transport, was an everyday practical cyclist, not a racing or touring cyclist. The cycle tracks he worked on in London were, he felt, sub-standard. "As a cyclist they gave me no satisfaction," he admitted.

> They were too narrow. They were made of concrete and suffered from either cracking or construction joints. They provided protection where the carriageway was safe but discharged the cyclists into the maelstrom of main traffic where the system was most dangerous. For me worst of all the tracks were uni-directional either side of the dual carriageways; thus if for any reason one needed to retrace one's way, one was compelled to run the gauntlet of crossing the streams of traffic on both carriageways to return on the far side – woe betide the person who left money, keys, books, tools or even lunch behind.

But it wasn't just cyclists who thought the 8ft-6in-wide path on Western Avenue disjointed and bumpy. The AA, the RAC, the police and many others also said the experimental cycle path was poorly executed.

Better ones should be provided, were "segregation" to be compelled by law, the parliamentary committee chaired by Lord Alness was told in 1938. When the committee's report was published, one of the chief recommendations was that cyclists should be provided with wide, well-surfaced cycle tracks, separated from fast-moving motor vehicles.

Despite CTC and NCU opposition to the uneven Western Avenue cycle track, often crowded with pedestrians, the Ministry of Transport ordered more cycle tracks to be built. By 1938, 45 miles of new arterial roads had cycle paths running beside them, with a further 68 miles "under construction."

Cycle paths built in the early 1930s – like many of those in Britain today – didn't form a usable network. Quite apart from the poor surface cyclists had to give way frequently, interruptions that increased as more and more housing and industrial developments sprouted up beside the new arterial roads. Cloverleaf intersections for motorists could be designed but similar intersections for cyclists would be "impossible" or "too costly", town planners told the six peers on the Alness committee. (The Automobile Association submitted plans to the committee with underpasses and other features the like of which only started to become commonplace in the Netherlands from the 1970s.) In evidence given to the committee, witness after witness attested to the dire nature of England's cycle paths but, apart from cyclist witnesses, most wanted cyclists to be forced to use the paths.

Cycle champion to motor executive Frank Shorland got back on his bike but most of the middle classes rejected cycling.

When questioning witnesses, the peers on the committee – the Lords Iddesleigh, Birkenhead, Brocket, Rushcliffe, Addison and Alness – made frequent mention of their love of motoring, a bias not lost on interested parties. In a parliamentary debate welcoming the Alness report, Lord Sandhurst said:

> … the editor of *Cycling* finds it necessary to invent a new body of your Lordships' House, which he calls the Peers Road Council. Having invented it, he then elects four members of the Select Committee to it – the noble Lords, Lord Reading, Lord Iddesleigh, Lord Birkenhead, and Lord Brocket – and then, having described them as keen motorists, he says, "Let us see what this Committee recommends for cyclists." What is the idea? Obviously they are trying to get at their not too well educated public and suggest that this is such a biased Committee that no attention need be paid to their recommendations.

The motoring bias of the report is as obvious today as it was then. Motoring organisations and magazines were very much in favour of almost all the report's 281 recommendations. *Commercial Motor* described the report as "the finest of its sort that has ever appeared" and applauded its victim-blaming approach:

> The case for the fair-minded motor driver has been put forward admirably. There is little need to read between the lines to appreciate that the Committee is fully aware how the good driver is constantly "nursing" the careless pedestrian and, often, the cyclist … Exception is taken to "a popular fallacy … that the motor driver, being in control of what is sometimes termed a lethal weapon, is usually to blame when an accident occurs." This is a destructive attitude, whilst the Report throughout is constructive. Its compilers obviously realize that progress, represented by fast road transport, is desirable, that the change of conditions following in its train must be accepted, that the mode of life of the people must be modified in accordance and adapted to the new conditions, and not that progress should be checked in order that that mode of life may remain unaltered.

There was palpable excitement from the peers at the prospect of German-style autobahns being built in Britain – free of cyclists, pedestrians and animals – and frustration when cyclist and pedestrian groups said they recommended that motorists who went fast on motor specific roads should be restrained on ordinary roads.

Soon after being built, many of the 1930s cycle paths were narrowed to make more room for motor vehicles. Yet cycling was booming. Six million more people had taken to riding bicycles since 1928, the peers were told – a fact that "staggered" Lord Alness. Cyclists were largely "proletarian", said one Lord in the debate launching the Alness report in 1939, and so were not deemed to be as valuable to the economy – or the war effort – as motorists. (In the 1930s the motor industry was cosseted because it was expected that car production would be shifted to military vehicle production; bicycle factories, such as the Raleigh plant, were also converted for armaments production but Sturmey–Archer gears couldn't power tanks. And roads, unlike the railways in the 1926 General Strike, couldn't be brought to a standstill by powerful unions.)

In evidence given to the Alness committee, CTC officials had stressed that the main objection was to the *quality* of cycle paths and not just the principle of being able to continue riding on the carriageway, the hard-won right of cyclists since 1888. The CTC feared that legislation would be brought in that would make it compulsory to use cycle paths even before a useable network had been built, and that, going by the poor provision of paths in the previous five years, there was little likelihood that the paths of the future would be of decent quality.

The following exchange between the peers and CTC secretary George Herbert Stancer shows the antagonism between the parties, although the CTC man remained polite throughout.

Lord Alness: Your Association is, if I may say so, broad-minded enough to regard motor traffic as necessary and proper development?

Stancer: Yes, my Lord. Of course we have grown up with the motor movement and I think that during the whole of that period we have treated it with perhaps more tolerance than we have always received at the hands of the people who have been concerned with motoring.

Lord Alness: Is your Club in favour of the construction of motorways?

Stancer: Yes, my Lord, we have been advocating that for many years.

Lord Alness: Is your Club in favour of the provision of separate cycle tracks for cyclists?

Stancer: No, my Lord, we are not. Our feeling is that cycle paths at the side of the road do not, in the present circumstances, and never can, provide the same facilities for enjoyable cycling as are provided by our present road system.

Lord Alness: I should have thought personally that it would be more enjoyable to cycle on the cycle track on the Great West Road than to cycle on the highway there?

Stancer: Those people who are not accustomed to cycling always tell me that and I think that it must be a general view ... The fact of it is that the existing experiments in the construction of cycle paths are, I think, most unsatisfactory and they have created a bad impression amongst cyclists.

Lord Alness: Assume the track was adequate in dimensions, in breadth, as in Germany, 9ft let us say, and its surface was good, do you not approve of the experiment at least being made?

Stancer: The difficulty is not so much a matter of width or surface. It would be essential to provide a sufficiently wide track and most of the tracks we have knowledge at present are too narrow and the surface is very unsatisfactory. On most of them even if we had a sufficient width and an excellent surface there is still the disadvantage that the track by the side of the road is constantly being interrupted and broken by the passage of other tracks coming from houses or whatever it may be. Every time there is a private house with a garage or there is a filling station or there is a way into a field or way into a shop ... everything has to come across the cycle path; so that while on the carriageway you get a perfectly straight, smooth, unbroken, uninterrupted course for whatever vehicle is using it, the cyclist has always got something coming across.

Lord Alness: But he is not submitted to the same dangers as when he is cycling on the highway on the Great West Road?

Stancer: No, my Lord. My suggestion is that those dangers ought to be removed.

Lord Alness: Is that not a counsel of perfection? The removal of the dangers seems rather idealistic?

Stancer: The other alternative seems to be a counsel of despair: "The law is powerless to preserve you on the road now; you must get off the road." That is roughly what it comes to.

The six Lords were disappointed with the answers from Stancer, so recalled him five days after his first appearance. Showing how far the erosion of non-motorists' rights had gone, Lord Brocket asked, in all seriousness: "Then you consider that cyclists and motorists have an equal right to the road?"

Stancer: Yes.

Lord Brocket: But you realise that motorists pay for the upkeep of the roads to a certain extent?

Stancer: I realise that they frequently say so but in point of fact the main costs of the roads is borne by the ratepayers, and the ratepayers include cyclists. I know to my cost that I pay an enormously large sum in rates for the use of roads which have been rendered much more costly by the requirements of motorists. Pedestrians and cyclists … are paying excessively for the provision of roads which are mainly intended for the use of motorists … It is unfair to say motorists pay for roads.

Earl of Iddesleigh: If we could enable you to avoid the great motor roads and provide for you really satisfactory roads on which you would not have to compete with a great deal of fast moving traffic, there would be a gain in enjoyment?

Stancer: If it were possible to provide facilities that are equal to those that we enjoy now, with the additional advantage that they would not be shared by motorists, I think that cyclists would have no objection …

Earl of Iddesleigh: Are the two grounds upon which you are against cycle tracks these? First, because the cyclist insists on his abstract right to the use of the highway, and secondly, because it is less pleasant to use a cycle track than a highway?

Stancer: The second one you have mentioned is far more important. Cyclists would never insist upon their abstract rights if it were not that they are losing the chief pleasure of cycling by being forced on to the paths. If the paths are by any miracle to be made of such width and quality as to be equal to our present road system, it would not be necessary to pass any laws to compel cyclists to use them; the cyclists would use them.

The Alness Report recommended that children of ten and under should be banned from the public highway on bicycles, and that segregation on the roads should be carried out with utmost urgency. Cyclists, said the report, should get high-quality cycle tracks and should be forced to use them. Pedestrians were also to be fined for daring to cross the road at points other than designated crossing points. Motorists, decided the motoring Lords, should be treated with a light touch by the law, and should be provided with motorways and many more trunk roads. (Naturally, there were no recommendations that motorists should be restricted to motorways alone – today this would mean motorists would have access to only two percent of the roads in Britain.)

Britain's cycle-path network was growing and, being 60 percent funded by the Ministry of Transport, likely to grow further. The Alness report recommended that the building of a fully segregated transport network should be accelerated, with cyclists and pedestrians given protected slices of the newly minted highways. The House of Lords committee published its findings in March 1939; in September war was declared and the construction of a national network of cycle tracks ground to a halt. The Alness report – derided by one Labour MP as a "tale of deaths and manglings … and extraordinary conclusions," – was mothballed. After the war a House of Commons select committee dusted it down. Many of the recommendations in the Alness report were taken forward, especially the pro-motoring bits, but, for a while at least, there would be no new roads and certainly no provision of cycle paths. Post-war austerity

The Western Avenue cycle path of the 1930s was a curate's egg: good in parts. But not for long.

killed off putative plans for a national network of cycle tracks. But while there would be no building of cycle paths, post-war politicians were still urged by motoring organisations and newspapers to force cyclists off the roads "for their own safety," even though cyclists were still by far the most numerous actors on the roads, probably *because* cyclists were still the most numerous actors on the roads.

Faced with calls to take action, politicians did what they often do best: nothing. Cyclists were still a force to be reckoned with. It was easy for politicians to pick a fight with the CTC or NCU, as these organisations were tiny compared to the rich motoring organisations; but to impose restrictions on all of the country's 12 million cyclists would have been folly. One of the witnesses to the original select committee said as much, showing how a powerful minority had no qualms over extinguishing the rights of a majority: "[Cyclists] ought to be forced to use [tracks]. The only reason they escape is because there are so many of them. There is a vague idea on the part of Governments that they would lose the cyclists' vote." This was the claim of Lord Newton, who repeated the claim when the report was published: "[cyclists] form a very formidable body, of which all Party politicians are very much afraid. That is the sole reason why they have not been regulated up to now, and I hope sincerely that that state of things will come to an end."

By not banning cyclists from the road, as many organisations demanded, politicians avoided antagonising cyclists. By building roads with no cycle facilities it was motorists that did the antagonising. 1949 was to be the peak year for cycling in Britain. In the 1950s the increasing number of motor cars slowly forced cyclists off many roads, and not just the arterial ones.

Motorways – roads long championed by the CTC as a means of removing fast-moving traffic from the ordinary roads of Britain – started to be built at the end of the 1950s but it was well into the 1960s before motorway mania took hold, with many trunk roads also being built or old roads widened, straightened and made less friendly for cyclists. None of the new arterial roads had cycle paths built beside them.

In 1958, Professor Sir Colin Buchanan, Britain's top town planner, wrote:

> The meagre efforts made to separate cyclists from motor traffic have failed, tracks are inadequate, the problem of treating them at junctions and intersections is completely unsolved, and the

attitude of the cyclists themselves to these admittedly unsatisfactory tracks has not been as helpful as it might have been.

Some modern bicycle advocates suggest that it was the opposition of conservative cycling organisations to the cycle path experiments of the 1930s that prevented national take-up of these paths. A typical claim is that if only CTC and the NCU had supported the Western Avenue experiment, a Dutch-style cycle network – suitable for all ages, from 8 to 80 – might have later evolved. This is impossible to prove. Cycling organisations may have been opposed to the paths but they had little to do with their failure. Utilitarian cyclists didn't use the paths because the paths weren't very good, and post-war austerity meant no new paths were built, nor were existing ones improved to the standard that CTC and NCU said would be required. The "right to use the road" concept was common among middle-class cycling officials (most of whom owned cars and thought of cycling as recreation rather then transport) but this was academic to the bulk of "cloth cap" cyclists, riding to and from factories and who, because of their numbers, dominated on the roads at certain times anyway.

Many of the CTC and NCU officials were elderly in the 1930s and could remember the halcyon days of cycling on car-free roads in the 1890s. There was a strong belief from the cycling old guard that the right to the use of the *rural* highway had been so hard-fought that it should not be given up. Evidence given to the Alness committee had suggested that this right to the highway need not be lost at all. D. H. Brown, the County Surveyor of Warwickshire, had told the six peers:

> Engineers look upon the highway as the whole width between the forecourt fences, i.e. the outside boundary wall or the front wall of the houses. We do not draw a distinction like the cyclists do, that they are driven off the highway if they are driven off the carriageway ... Railings should be put beside footways ... and the pedestrian should not stray on the carriageway but should be confined to his own section of the highway, in the same way that cyclists should be ... The underlying idea is of segregation of the highway ... We believe that the expense of putting [cycle] tracks down in a proper way – and they are of no use if they are not serviceable – is so great that the use of them when they are made should be compulsory ... As engineers we cannot understand the attitude of the cyclist who will not ride on the special track provided ... the cycle track is part of the highway.

However, organised cycling feared that only a very few highways would be segregated and that the width given over to cyclists would be insufficient; motorists would then consider the rest of the (unsegregated) road network to be off-limits to cyclists. Campaigners worried that provision of "off the carriageway" cycle paths would reinforce the impression that cycling on the road was somehow wrong and would lead to cyclists being "punished" deliberately or otherwise. H. R. Watling, director of the British Cycle and Motor-cycle Manufacturers and Traders Union, had voiced this fear at one of the Alness hearings:

> I think cyclists in general fear that if cycle tracks are provided in certain places the psychology of the motorist will be affected adversely ... they will regard the cyclist as more and more an undesirable person on the road, and it may lead in some cases to an increase in the degree of carelessness exhibited by drivers of all types.

Cyclists need not have worried – there was little appetite to provide anything at all for them despite the fact they far outnumbered motorists. Post-war politicians and planners were deeply dismissive of "proletarian" mass cycling because they themselves were motorists and wished to provide for their own kind. They were also attracted by the economic potential of motoring and it was felt that cycling was outmoded and not suited for the motor era. And the great British public seemed to agree – people wanted to own and drive motor cars and when they could give up their bicycles, they did. Cycle use in the 1950s fell off a cliff.

Colin Buchanan's highly-influential report of 1963, *Traffic in Towns* – which was also a best-selling Penguin paperback – mentioned cyclists only in passing, and, like many other traffic engineers, Buchanan clearly believed that urban cycling would wither to nothing:

> … it is a moot point how many cyclists there will be in 2010 … [This] does affect the kind of roads to be provided. On this point we have no doubt at all that cyclists should not be admitted to primary networks, for obvious reasons of safety and the free flow of vehicular traffic … It would be very expensive, and probably impracticable, to build a completely separate system of tracks for cyclists.

Yet, in 1960 Buchanan had warned about allowing car use to go unrestrained:

> … much of our future happiness and well being depends on the extent to which we can control the motor vehicle … [Urban areas would become] horrible uncivilised places under the influence of motor traffic …

He made similar warnings in *Traffic in Towns* but these were largely ignored in the rush to build more facilities for motorists. *Traffic in Towns* was also influential in the Netherlands, a country with a strong history of cycling, where national identity is tied up with cycling. The Buchanan report was one of the guiding influences behind Dutch town planners reining back the car in residential streets. While in the

UK Professor Buchanan's ideas were used to build more urban motorways, in the Netherlands they helped inspire "woonerven", the "liveable" streets where motorists were required to drive slowly, often at walking pace. Traffic engineers in the Netherlands tamed the car (and improved the existing and extensive cycle path network); traffic engineers in the UK designed only for the car.

The bicycle's status as "poor man's transport" was vividly demonstrated in 1975 on the front cover of the Pelican edition of *Class in a Capitalist Society: A Study of Contemporary Britain* by eminent sociologists John Westergaard and Henrietta Resler. This featured a Rolls-Royce and a utilitarian bicycle. The inference that bicycles are low status vehicles would have been as obvious with any motor-car marque.

CAR OWNERSHIP is high in the Netherlands but there's a societal recognition that, for many short journeys, bicycles are best. High levels of car use and low levels of cycle use, typical in Britain, are not inevitable – they are the wholly predictable outcome of urban planning policies that promote motor vehicle use and relegate cycling. Walking often suffers the same fate.

Today in Britain bicycle and pedestrian advocates push for more consideration from planners and politicians but fear with dread certainty that the creeping, incremental provision for motorists isn't likely to end any time soon. Given that roads were quickly considered as "motoring roads" even when motoring was a minority pursuit this is no wonder. In many places in Britain, the rural A roads from town to town are often the only highways available and have to be shared by all users, but there has been little provision put in place for anything other than motorists. These roads often have speed limits of 50 miles per hour, making them hazardous for road users not able to reach such speeds. In effect, these useful roads – usually with no footpaths or cycle paths beside them – have become motor-only roads.

In America, it's often far worse, with many cities having been retrofitted – or designed from scratch – almost exclusively for the use of motor cars. Residential areas in some US localities don't even have sidewalks – the expectation is that everyone will drive. The result is usually equal to the design expectation – life as a non-motoring road user in some parts of America can be exceedingly difficult. However, there's a growing awareness that auto-centrism has gone too far and, if left unchecked, can only lead to gridlock. The modern equivalent of the Good Roads movement is the Complete Streets Coalition, a movement for more "liveable communities":

> The streets of our cities and towns … ought to be for everyone, whether young or old, motorist or bicyclist, walker or wheelchair user, bus rider or shopkeeper. But too many of our streets are designed only for speeding cars … or creeping traffic jams … Instituting a Complete Streets policy ensures that transportation planners and engineers consistently design and operate the entire roadway with all users in mind …

The movement was suggested in 2003 by Barbara McCann, then working for America Bikes, a coalition of bicycle advocacy groups, including the League of American Bicyclists, today's version of the L.A.W. Complete Streets quickly became about much more than bicycles, just as the L.A.W. in the 1890s recognised that the Good Roads movement would be more powerful if allied with other interests. The National Complete Streets Coalition, founded in 2005, was led by America Bikes and roped in a number of influential and mainstream non-cycling organisations. McCann became Executive Director, before moving in January 2014 to become a Director at the US Department of Transportation. This segue into central government bears an uncanny resemblance to the moves L.A.W. officials made in the 1890s, when they started working for the Federal Office of Road Inquiry. While these 19th century cycling officials morphed into 20th century motorists, perhaps McCann will be able to push the 21st century liveability agenda and help transform at least some of America's roads into highways for all?

She will have a tough job. Car culture was started by elites but now motoring is endemic and, arguably, it's even more deeply embedded in poorer communities where automobiles are potent status symbols. The car-free, or car-lite, lifestyle can be characterised, perhaps unfairly, as middle class, elitist and white – politically active cyclists are very often part of the so-called "creative class". In many ways today's cycle advocates look and act a lot like their Victorian counterparts. London Cycle Campaign's "space4cycling" municipal elections campaign in 2014 targeted councillors, pressing them on their cycling policies – almost identical campaigns were carried out by the L.A.W in American cities in the 1890s.

While many modern cycle advocates stress that building bicycle infrastructure will attract the "masses" to start cycling the placement of such infrastructure is often in gentrified areas of town rather than on "sink estates". As sociologist Dave Horton has shown in a number of studies, cycling is not considered as an attractive option by many lower-income groups in British society. For instance, bike paths built to and from a working-class estate don't tend to persuade residents to ride bicycles: bikes, for them, are toys, cycling is for children, and bikes are perceived to be a very low status transport option for adults.

Paradoxically, while the wealthy can afford to reduce their car dependency, those motorists on low incomes often cannot. Motor cars are not just status symbols and signifiers of supposed responsible adulthood for those on low incomes they often provide transport to and from (multiple) jobs where

Cycling's 1890s cachet was lost in the 1920s, it's now back. But does cycling need to become "classless" to achieve Dutch-style ubiquity?

public transport may not reach. They also provide protection against street aggression, and in extremis, a car can be used as living space should somebody lose the roof over their head. Bicycles may be swift and efficient users of urban streets but they offer poor shelter in the rain.

CYCLING CAN be emblematic of political dissent, a signifier of environmental responsibility and a rejection of consumerism yet it can also be the opposite of all three. The current flowering of bicycle movements around the globe – from Critical Mass to World Naked Bicycle Rides, and from cycle chic to bike blogs – points to cycling going mainstream. Some motorists may continue to think that cyclists are socio-economically challenged ("get a car!" is a common shout), and some are, but the numbers of "middle-aged men in Lycra" on expensive, carbon-framed commuter bicycles doesn't appear yet to have peaked. Oddly, there's no settled name for the female equivalent of the MAMIL but more women are getting on bikes, too.

The arrival of hipster cyclists, the appearance of ever more boutique bicycle brands, the demand for "Dutch bikes", the renaissance of the cargo bike and the staging of Tweed Runs and "die-ins", as well as the growing clamour for urban cycling infrastructure, are, at least partially, manifestations of middle-class lifestyle choices. Those who choose to use bicycles as transportation for lifestyle reasons are likely to enjoy the experience rather more than those who cycle out of necessity.

Naturally, in the Netherlands, it's different – all classes cycle, partly because of the superlative cycling infrastructure but also because of the 100-year old national identification with the bicycle. In the 1960s cycle use dropped in the Netherlands when motor-centric infrastructure was installed (much has since been ripped out and replaced by bike networks which offer safety, directness, coherence, comfort and attractiveness) but there were so many "everyday cyclists" that the reduction in cycling was less dramatic than the cliff-drop in Britain. Cycle advocates stress that the Netherlands isn't a nation of cyclists, it's a nation of people who use bicycles, a subtle but critical difference.

Dutch cycle advocates are amazed to discover there's so much hatred directed against cyclists in

Britain and America. There are many examples of such blind hate on social media – for some commenters it's culturally acceptable to vilify people for choosing non-motorised transport.

Such outpourings of dehumanising bile – for example, "joking" about killing cyclists – could be due to cycling's increasing visibility and an irrational fear that everybody will be forced to cycle whether they want to or not. (They won't be.)

Cycling was eccentric in the 1970s but has become far less so today. The "other" is now often the "me". Cycling is rising in popularity in places hitherto thought toxic to two-wheel travel. London, Paris and other world cities are planning to spend billions on catering to an "out-group" that's rapidly becoming an "in-group". Cities such as Seville in Spain are "going Dutch" with a vengeance. Naturally, the transformation of our streets, the so-called "reallocation of road space" will not happen overnight, and is happening too slowly for many "liveability" advocates, but it *is* happening. Motor-centric infrastructure was introduced by stealth over a great many years, and the reimagining and eventual remodelling of our towns, cities, villages – and the linear spaces between them – will also take a great many years.

CURRENTLY, MOTORISTS get the lion's share of highways cash even in places where they are not majority users of roads. This is blindingly obvious in the Developing World but even in cities such as London pedestrians far outnumber motorists (a jaw-dropping 38 percent to 13 percent, in fact) yet still the needs of motorists are usually considered first. A number of cities are making some of their roads less intimidating to those not in motor vehicles. In 2012, Michael Bloomberg, the then mayor of New York City, recognised that cyclists and pedestrians (and, to a lesser extent, buses and trams) are efficient users of public highways and need to be given more consideration. "Our roads are not here for automobiles," he said when cutting the ribbon on a 20 miles per hour slow-zone. "Our roads are here for people to get around."

To most politicians – and, of course, the majority of planners, and much of the general population, too – roads are deemed to be for transport only, for *movement*. The "place" elements of roads and streets, the supremely important non-transport uses, the "liveability" factors, were only rarely considered in the past, leading to the dystopian sterility of the "concrete jungle" that has blighted cities for many years. Similarly, roads in rural areas have long suffered from being treated, by some motorists, as race tracks. (Driverless cars cannot come quickly enough.)

Roads are social constructs and throughout history they have had multiple functions, and were not just for passage and carriage. The mono-functionality of most of today's roads is neither fair nor sustainable, something recognised by the United Nations Environment Programme. "Despite the high societal costs, increasing the road space for cars continues to be a priority for investors and governments," stated the UNEP's "Share the Road" report in 2010, warning that this is folly, hastening climate change, and leading to danger, death, inequality, and economy-damaging congestion. "Roads must be designed with all users in mind," concluded the organisation's report.

Sky-cars for the elite, as imagined by by French writer and illustrator Albert Robida. "A Visit to the Opera in the year 2000," is from La vie électrique, *1890.*

In 1925, US architect Harvey W. Corbett imagined a future with cars underground and where pedestrians had regained control of the streets – there are no cyclists "in the way".
From Popular Science, *August, 1925.*

EPILOGUE

Never has there been a more exciting time to be alive, a time of rousing wonder and heroic achievement. As they said in the film Back to the Future, *"Where we're going, we don't need roads".*
Pʀᴇsɪᴅᴇɴᴛ Rᴏɴᴀʟᴅ Rᴇᴀɢᴀɴ, Sᴛᴀᴛᴇ ᴏғ ᴛʜᴇ Uɴɪᴏɴ ᴀᴅᴅʀᴇss, 1986

"Get off the road!" – an angry epithet some motorists shout at cyclists – ought to become the longer, but historically more accurate, "hey, cyclists, thanks for the roads and the cars!" (Don't hold your breath.)

Had H. G. Wells' Time Machine been real and had he been able to transport himself to the modern day, what would he think about today's blacktops, autoscapes, and fast cars, and the survival of cycling?

I should imagine he would be incredibly surprised that cycling had survived; yet, at the same time, he would consider it perfectly normal that dentists, doctors and brain surgeons spent so much money on fancy-schmancy carbon-framed bicycles. He would be utterly amazed that people on the lowest incomes felt they had to spend so much of their disposable income on motor cars they can ill afford. Part of this mainstream desire to be motorised is for reasons of status, convenience, comfort, security, pleasure, warmth, and orthodoxy, but much of it is also by design: long, linear parts of the "public realm" were remodelled for motors, and yes, despite my book's title, plenty of roads *were* specifically built for cars.

It's unlikely many Edwardians – even motorholics such as Lord Montagu – ever imagined society would become quite so utterly dependent on automobiles. Most would have been horrified by the concept. Motoring, for them, was elitist. Their extrapolations predicted faster cars on open roads built for the upper classes, but motoring for the masses would have been a detestable concept to most of the automobile pioneers.

One of the few to see what was coming was Susan Jeune, Baroness St. Helier. Like others of her class, she was an enthusiastic motorist; and, also like others of her class, she had first been an enthusiastic cyclist. She wrote glowing articles about motoring in books and magazines, just as she had earlier written very similar articles about cycling. In 1895, Lady Jeune wrote that cycling as an exercise was "a very delicious one." For a how-to book on motoring, published in 1905, she contributed a chapter on the joys of motoring, but she realised that when everybody owned a car, there would be less joy to share around:

> When cars can be made [cheaply] then we may talk of the social effect of motoring on modern life, and the effect will not, I think, be a pleasing one. The country will be invaded by vast numbers of small cheap cars through which the larger and more powerful ones will thunder with more or less disastrous results, for no time limit will then exist, because the roads will not be in possession of the South African millionaire, the rich stockbroker, or the rich autocrat, but Demos will have taken the road, at his own pace, and for his own pleasure, and no County Council will dare stay his headlong progress.

With this power-to-the-people prediction Lady Jeune beat the professionals. H. G. Wells predicted a future of fast-moving automobiles, but in his utopias – and the various others imagined by authors and planners alike – there were no brutal concrete flyovers creaking and decaying into dust, no traffic jams, no poisonous exhaust particulates, no above-ground heat-absorbing flood-causing car parks, no auto asphyxiation, no motor myopia, no morgues full of "vulnerable road users." By stealth, we've built a

---

❧ EVILS BROUGHT BY THE PNEUMATIC TYRE

CERTAIN IS that few inventions of major importance exist which have not resulted in some evil, if not by reason of their own nature, then because they have been put to evil ends; indeed, the vast majority of them have much to answer for, since they become the blind tools of human nature, which is at once both good and evil …

The pneumatic tyre then, in common with most other inventions, has its measure of evil to account for … It has done more than most things to change the aspect and the tempo of human existence.

Let it be remembered that in 1888 the railway was supreme, whilst the highways were falling into grass-grown disuse … The pneumatic tyre, first by making popular the cycle, and then the motor car

and coach … revealed [countries] to their peoples. Surely an unalloyed benefit? And yet before this invention there were no laws or societies for preventing the desecration of rural England by this mass invasion, no wastes of … litter, nor was the sweep of the Downs scarred with by-pass roads, its beauties desecrated with advertisements.

[Another evil] is the vast mortality [on the] roads. More than a hundred lives a week, a figure so terrible that one wonders whether, if … Dunlop in his Belfast stable-yard or Welch in his father's workshop, had had the power to see into the future, they would have fathered and foster-fathered this strange child of theirs.

ARTHUR ROY DU CROS, 1938

car-dependent world, with roads retrofitted for those with motors only. This is the new normal, and to suggest that motorists – such as myself; just because I cycle doesn't mean I don't own a car – ought not to enjoy unbridled use of comfortable space-inefficient armoured transportation bubbles is to be accused of "taking civilisation back to the Stone Age."

I'M NOT the first to wonder what the motoring pioneers – many of them brought into motoring by the bicycle – would have thought about such a car-dependent society. And nor am I the first to fret about a world where automobile dependence is leading inexorably to gridlock, obesity and climate change. Read the two warnings below, issued 70 years apart.

Arthur Roy Du Cros was the grandson of William Harvey Du Cros, populariser of the pneumatic tyre. In 1938, he wrote a thought-provoking essay warning that the benefits of motoring may be cancelled out by the "evils" of motoring.

William Clay Ford Jr. is the great grandson of Detroit's most famous cyclist. He has been the executive chair of the Ford Motor Company since 1999. When reading his words, delivered at a TED conference in 2011, remember this wasn't the CEO of Greenpeace talking, this was a man with the blood of Henry Ford – and tyre magnate Harvey Firestone – coursing through his veins.

🔖 A FUTURE BEYOND TRAFFIC GRIDLOCK

WHAT HAPPENS when the number of vehicles on the road doubles, triples, or even quadruples? [The] good news is we are tackling the big issues, of cars and the environment … We're pushing fuel efficiency to new heights … But unfortunately, as we're on our way to solving one monstrous problem … another huge problem is looming … And that is, the freedom of mobility that my great grandfather brought to people is now being threatened … The problem … is one of mathematics. Today there are approximately 6.8 billion people in the world, and within our lifetime, that number's going to grow to about nine billion … Our transportation system simply won't be able to deal with [this]. We're going to create the kind of global gridlock that the world has never seen before … It's clear that the mobility model that we have today simply will not work tomorrow. Frankly, four billion clean cars on the road are still four billion cars, and a traffic jam with no emissions is still a traffic jam … So what's going to solve this? The answer isn't going to be more of the same. [The] answer to more cars is … not to have more roads. When America began moving west, we didn't add more wagon trains, we built railroads … Today we need that same leap in thinking … The solution is not going to be more cars, [or] more roads … We must have an infrastructure that's designed to support [a] flexible future.

WILLIAM CLAY FORD Jnr., 2011

ACKNOWLEDGEMENTS

This book took four years to research, write and publish – far longer than I had planned. For their patience, thanks are due to my wife Jude, and my children Hanna, Ellie, and Josh Reid. My parents, Albert and Jean Reid, helped by being there when it mattered – and my mum spotted some glaring typos before the text went across to Martin Rickerd, my copy-editor, who saved even more of my blushes. Indexer Nicola King helped squash some textual inconsistencies. Beta readers Dave Cox, Joy Roberts and Ted Timmons suggested some improvements which I was happy to incorporate.

Cycle history errors were expertly spotted by historians Professor Hans-Erhard Lessing and Nicolas Clayton. Naturally, any mistakes that remain in the book are mine.

As much of this book is original research it has involved wading through personal papers and dusty archives. Librarians in America and the UK proved to be exceptionally helpful. It was wonderful – albeit distracting – to work in gob-stoppingly beautiful libraries such as the Library of Congress, Washington, D.C., and the library at the Royal Automobile Club in London. I paid numerous (fruitful) visits to the National Cycling Archive at the Modern Records Centre at Warwick University, and while this doesn't have the architectural splendour of the former libraries it more than made up for it in the wonderful array of records deposited by the Cyclists' Touring Club and other bodies. The Salomons Library of Canterbury Christ Church University provided some key information on the early links between cycling and early motoring. The Historical Associations of Detroit and Martin County in the US and Oystermouth in the UK helped with picture research.

I've also got to thank Google. With judicious key-word searches it's now possible to drill down into obscure journals and long-forgotten books in a way not available to scholars in previous decades. This works picture research, too – how else would I have spotted God riding a penny farthing globe? Source: *Le vingtième siècle: la vie électrique*, Albert Robida, 1893.

A great number of individuals helped with idea-bouncing, research, translations and more:
Rachel Aldred, Steve Bagley, Michael Barnstijn, Les Bowerman, Patrick Brady, Joe Breeze, Marco Brommelstroet, Klaas Brumann, Kathy Chaney, Nick Clayton, Ralph Dadswell, Phillip Darnton, Chris Davey, Nick Dey, Stuart Dinsey, Lisa Djahed, Trevor Dunmore, Alice Gould, Steve Graham, Alan Kind, Edmund King, Katja Leyendecker, Adam Lovell, Stephen McNally, John Powell, Brenda Puech, Andrew Ritchie, Paul Robson, Oliver Schick, Todd Scott, Brian Smith, Teresa Stokes, Jack Thurston, Mark Treasure, Peter Walker, Roberta Wedge and Sophie Wuerger.

HISTORY OF ROADS TIMELINE

700 B.C.	Bitumen and brick used for a processional road in Assur. Parking restrictions put in place in Nineveh, the capital of Assyria – King Sennacherib ordered the placing of signs saying "Royal Road – Let no man decrease it." The penalty was death.
400 B.C.	Romans start paving their roads.
312 B.C.	Romans start the construction of Via Appia, the Appian Way, the "Queen of Roads."
45 B.C.	Julius Caesar bans certain wheeled vehicles from the centre of Rome at certain times of the day and introduces one-way streets and off-street parking measures.
A.D. 50	Claudius I extends wheeled vehicle restrictions to all Roman towns.
125	In an attempt to limit congestion, Hadrian limits the number of wheeled vehicles allowed to enter Rome.
c. 200	Roman road system at its peak, with 50,000 miles of paved roads.
850	Caliph Abdorraman II paves the streets of the Moorish city of Cordoba in Saracen-controlled Spain.
950	Road widths defined by Norse law.
1135	Henry I rules that English roads should be two carriages in width.
1184	Paris paves some of its streets
1285	Edward I's Statute of Winchester codifies the "right of way", specifies road maintenance duties for manors, and rules that some roads have to be maintained to a width of 200 feet.
1300	The Strand in London is paved.
1356	England introduces a vehicle tax to raise money for road construction.
1415	Stone setts used in Paris for the first time.
1555	"Acte for the mendyng of Highe Wayes … being bothe verie noysome & tedious to travell in & dangerous to all Passengers and Cariages …"
1614	Great North Road in Islington, London, is provided with a sidewalk.
1635	Establishment of a mail coach between London and Edinburgh.
1663	Wadesmill, 25 miles north of London, erects first English turnpike toll gate.
1680	Christian Huygens designs an internal combustion engine (bang! – it's powered by gunpowder).
1703	English parliament introduces toll act, although "turnpike mania" didn't start until 1751.
1710	First use of bollards to separate pedestrians from wheeled vehicles.
1722	London Bridge introduces a "keep left" rule.
1747	*École Nationale des Ponts et Chaussées*, the National School of Bridges and Highways, founded in Paris.
1761	Introduction into Britain of granite setts.
1766	London introduces policy to create more sidewalks.
1769	Nicolas-Joseph Cugnot produces three-wheeled *fardier à vapeur*, "steam dray."
1801	Richard Trevithick runs his steam "road locomotive" in Camborne, England.

1804	Trevithick's steam-powered railway locomotive runs, briefly, on Pen-y-Darren Line near Merthyr Tydfil, Wales.
1814	George Stephenson builds "Blutcher," the world's first practical steam-powered railway locomotive, at Killingworth Colliery.
1817	Baron Karl von Drais introduces his "running machine", a steerable velocipede without pedals.
1825	Stephenson's "Locomotion" runs on Stockton–Darlington railway.
1829	Stephenson's "Rocket" wins Rainhill Trials to find best self-propelled engine for Liverpool–Manchester line, which opens in 1830, kickstarting "railway mania".
1835	English Highway Act specifies width of cartways, formalises left-hand driving, introduces local government taxation for roads, prevents carriages from "driving" or parking on footways. The law is still in force, although largely ignored.
1841	Mail carried on British railways.
1845	Robert Thomson patents "aerial wheel … elastic bearings … for tires of carriage wheels," the first air-filled tyres. They flop.
1861	English Locomotives Act, "An Act for regulating the Use of Locomotives on Turnpike and other Roads."
1865	English Locomotives Act 1865 introduces requirement for "road engines and traction engines" to be in control of at least three people, including one to precede the vehicle waving a red flag.
c. 1865	Pierre Lallement (or Pierre Michaux – the history is disputed) attaches cranks and pedals to a velocipede to create the world's first bicycle. Both Lallement and Michaux were based in Paris. Lallement moved to America, where he patented his machine in 1866.
1872	Friedrich Fischer mass produces steel ball bearings.
1877	James Starley patents the differential gear for tricycles. This technology later transferred to automobiles.
1878	National Cyclists' Union established in London on February 16th. It is now the British Cycling (Federation). Bicycle Touring Club founded in Harrogate on August 5th. It is now CTC, the Cyclists' Touring Club, a registered charity. English Highways and Locomotives Amendment Act – requirement that road locomotives had to be preceded by a person waving a red flag abolished in most counties, but attendant still had to walk in front of vehicle. Taylor v Goodwin results in cycles becoming classified as "carriages" thereby "legalising" cycling in Britain.
1862	Alphonse Beau de Rochas patents four-stroke internal combustion engine.
1880	League of American Wheelmen founded in Newport, Rhode Island.
1884	National Cyclists' Union creates the Midland Road Fund to pay for road maintenance and to lodge a court case against local highway surveyors.
1885	Carl Benz buys cycle parts from the House of Bicycles, Germany's biggest bike shop, to create his *Patent-Motorwagen*, the world's first motor car, and patents it the following year.
1886	Cyclists' Touring Club and National Cyclists' Union create Roads Improvement Association. John Kemp Starley introduces his Rover Safety Bicycle.
1888	John Boyd Dunlop patents (reinvents) the pneumatic tyre. League of American Wheelmen form National Committee for Highway Improvement, which became the Good Roads movement.

1895	Sir David Lionel Salomons, a life member and trustee of the Cyclists' Touring Club, becomes one of the original members of the new Automobile Club de France, the world's first motoring organisation. A number of cycle racers, bicycle manufacturers and cycle journalists helped found the club. In the same year Salomons also created the Self-Propelled Traffic Association, Britain's first motoring organisation. Also on the SPTA committee was Ernest Shipton, secretary of the CTC.
1896	Locomotive Act of 1878 was further amended now allowing motor cars to legally drive on the roads of Britain. Pioneer motorists called this the "Emancipation Act" and the "Magna Carta of Motoring." In November, Henry Lawson organised the London–Brighton "Emancipation Run".
1902	Foundation of the American Automobile Association. L.A.W. president Horatio Earle creates American Road Makers, which is now the American Road and Transportation Builders Association
1903	English Motor Car Act. Speed limit raised from 12 to 20 miles per hours. Owners of motor cars now had to pay a registration fee. Bicycle builders Orville Wright and Wilbur Wright fly the first heavier-than-air powered aircraft.
1908	Introduction of the Model T Ford.
1909	Creation of the Road Board in the UK.
1916	US Federal Road Act signed by cycle tourist, motor enthusiast and US President Woodrow Wilson.

MOTOR MARQUES & THEIR BICYCLING BEGINNINGS

*On the shoulders
of giants?
From* The Automobile
magazine, 1902

The following brands – there are more than sixty of them – were involved in cycle manufacturing before becoming automobile manufacturers. Such a long list would have been even longer had I included motorbike firms that evolved from bicycle companies, or motorbike companies – such as Harley-Davidson – which also produced bicycles. (Many did but that's almost a given.)

I haven't included every company that made bicycles and then automobiles. For instance, I've omitted Herbert Austin's Wolseley. Austin – founder of the Austin Motor Company – was a cyclist and his Birmingham factory made bicycle parts, but I felt the bicycle element was lacklustre. Austin is said to be have designed a bicycle but as it didn't go into production I didn't feel I could include Wolseley in my list of brands.

All of the brands listed were created in the Victorian or Edwardian eras. I haven't included any of the more modern automobile companies that started as bicycle manufacturers. For instance, Kia Motors of South Korea started life as Kyungsung Precision Industry, founded in 1944 as a manufacturer of steel cycle tubing and bicycle parts. By 1951 the company was making complete bicycles, moving into motorbikes later in the 1950s and soon thereafter into automobiles.

The majority of the brands listed went out of business – or were absorbed and retired – relatively early, thanks to cut-throat competition and corporate consolidation. However, some of them are still major players today, although their bicycling backgrounds are almost totally hidden from view.

ADLER
Heinrich Kleyer of Frankfurt-am-Main created the Adler brand of motor car. By 1928, only Opel and BMW sold more cars in Germany than Adler. Before diversifying into automobiles – and motorbikes and aircraft – Kleyer's firm was Germany's first large-scale producer of bicycles.

Kleyer's life in the locomotion business began when he started importing high-wheeler bicycles from England in 1880. He had been inspired to do so while working in America as an engineer for a textile machinery maker. At Boston's celebrations for the Fourth of July in 1879 Kleyer saw a speed demonstration of high-wheelers, a parade staged by Colonel Albert Pope, who had started producing Columbia bicycles the year before. Amazed by the speed of the machines, Kleyer surmised that there would be a demand for bicycles in Germany. He arranged a meeting with Pope at his Boston bicycle factory, retail outlet and riding school.

Unable to meet domestic demand, Pope told Kleyer that he could not sell him even one bicycle at that moment but that English makers had larger supplies. Kleyer departed for England and, from Coventry Machinists, secured a batch of high-wheelers, and bagged the exclusive agency for the English brand in Germany. He also secured the agencies for Singer and Starley Bros. cycles.

He opened Maschinen & Velocipede Handlung in Frankfurt on March 1st, 1880. Like Pope, Kleyer knew that if he was to make headway, he had to promote the concept of bicycling. In April 1881 he created the Frankfurter Bicycle Club, which organised races. This club became one of the largest and most important in Europe (Kleyer was still a member of the club in the 1920s). Kleyer also built a riding school and a racing track.

Also in 1881 he commissioned engineering company Spohr & Krämer to produce his German-built bicycles, branded Herold, Frankfurt and Jugend.

After four years of steady growth, Kleyer had prospered enough to buy land on Gutleutstrasse and he built Haus des Fahrrades, the House of Bicycles, a Pope-style all-in-one factory-style showroom, the "best of its kind in the world." The nine-storey building could house 5,000 high-wheelers and, just as in Pope's original facility, the top floor was a riding school and bike test-ride area. (See illustration on page 13.) Next door to the Haus des Fahrrades was Germany's first indoor cycling track.

In 1885, via his Mannheim agents, Maschinenhandlung Max Rose & Cie., Kleyer supplied cycle wheels, and probably other cycle parts, to Carl Benz, helping to create the Benz Patent-Motorwagen, the world's first motor car.

Heinrich Kleyer.

By 1887, Adler had outgrown the House of Bicycles, and Kleyer built a larger store on the outskirts of town. With the move, and production of a new Safety bicycle, came a new brand name, Adler – "eagle" in German, an imperial symbol of strength.

Kleyer was also active in cycle sport. He was president of the German Cycling Union and was an official of the International Cycling Association, the first cross-border body for cycle racing. The ICA was created by Henry Sturmey and its first meeting was held in the Royal Agricultural Hall, Islington, London in November 1892.

Adler diversified into typewriters and motorbikes in 1898 and, the following year, motor cars, a throwback to the day when Kleyer had played a part in creating the world's first true automobile. The cars were produced under the long-established Adler name. In 1908 Adler started producing engines for Zeppelin airships and other aircraft. Before the outbreak of the First World War, the expanded Adler factory employed around 7,000 people.

Adler cars were built until the Second World War. As part of war reparation agreements with the Allies, Adler was forced to hand its motorbike manufacturing plant over to Britain's BSA. (The Birmingham Small Arms company had made bicycles since the 1890s.) Adler's drawings and machines were later used by Britain's Ariel to produce their Arrow and Leader motorbikes. (Ariel was a bicycle brand name from the 1870s.) Without its motorbike division, Adler focused on the manufacture of office equipment and was taken over by Grundig in 1957, and later by Olivetti.

ALLARD & CO.

Allard & Co. was a small Coventry-based motor-car manufacturer, making cars at the end of the 1890s. It merged with another company and lived on until just before the First World War. It was founded and staffed by cyclists. Frederick William Allard was a professional bicycle and tricycle racer of the late 1880s and early 1890s. He created Allard & Co. as a cycle manufacturer in 1889 after having worked at Coventry Machinists, the venerable old cycle-maker. His partner in the business was George Pilkington. By 1899 the company was making the Allard Rapid motor car. In 1901 the company merged with Birmingham Motor Manufacturing to create Rex Motor Manufacturing of Coventry, which made motorbikes. The managing director of the new company was Billy Williamson, another bicycle racer, winner of hill climb competitions, and a former bicycle shop manager.

ARGYLL MOTORS

Scotland's biggest car marque was Argyll Motors, which manufactured cars from 1899 to 1930. At its peak in 1906 the company employed 1,500 in a palatial purpose-built factory in Alexandria, by the banks of Loch Lomond, near Glasgow. Argyll Motors was run by Alex Govan, who moved into motor-car manufacturing from the bicycle industry. He and his brother-in-law, John Worton, had designed the Worvan, a bicycle produced for them by the Scottish Manufacturing Company of Glasgow.

By the early 1890s Govan had moved to Redditch to become the foreman for Eadie Manufacturing Co., a manufacturer of bicycles, sewing needles and rifle parts. In 1897, Govan was given the task of stripping down a number of motor cars. From this he realised that he could make his own and he returned to his native Glasgow, opening a small engineering company. In 1900, he started producing the Argyll Voiturette in the same factory that had made the Worvan bicycle. The chassis was made of tubular steel shaped on the factory's bicycle-tube formers. The business prospered but the move to its plush new factory eventually crippled the company.

ARIEL MOTORS

The Ariel was an English motor car manufactured in Selly Oak, Birmingham from 1902 to 1917 and took the place of the Ariel bicycle marque made by the Ariel Cycle Company (the firm also made motorbikes). Both companies were run by designer Charles Thomas Brock Sangster, who became a stalwart of the British motor industry and president of the Motor and Cycle Trades Benevolent Fund in 1921. Sangster's career started when he was apprenticed to the maker of Whippet cycles of London. In 1893, he left to join the long-established New Howe Machine Co. in Glasgow. His next move was south to the Rudge cycle factory in Coventry but he didn't stay long – he was poached for the top design post at the positively historic Coventry Machinists Co. He designed the company's Swift cycles for 1895, revamping the firm's image in the process.

His fame in the cycle industry was now such that he made the leap from designer to works manager of a large new factory at Selly Oak set up by the new Cycle Components Manufacturing Co., a cycle-parts maker created by, among others, Harvey Du Cros of Dunlop. This factory made tubing and it was natural to spin-off a house brand: this was the Ariel, under the direction of Sangster. Ridden to victory in the world championships of 1897 by J. W. Stocks, who later became a top racing driver, Ariel rapidly achieved commercial success.

Soon after the passing of the Emancipation Act in 1896, Sangster acquired a De Dion motor tricycle. He made numerous improvements to the design, creating the Ariel motor tricycle. This work led to the creation of the Ariel motor car. Sangster was managing director of the Ariel factory for 30 years. The company made motor cars and motorcycles until its collapse in 1932, never having stopped making bicycles and parts for them.

ASTER

The first Aster cars were made in London in 1922. It was a luxury marque, a favourite of the Duke of York, who later became King George VI. The marque sprang out of Begbie Manufacturing Co. of Wembley, importers of the French Aster stationary engine. The company was run by Sydney Dawson Begbie, a former champion racing cyclist. Among Begbie's world records was the 100-mile tandem tricycle record of 1894, ridden with T. G. King.

ASTON MARTIN

The Aston Martin company was founded in 1913 by Lionel Martin and Robert Bamford. Both were racing cyclists and members of the Bath Road Club. Martin, a rider since 1891 when he started at Eton College, was the swifter of the two, and the holder of a number of long-distance records, including on tandem and tricycle.

Martin and Bamford became specialists in taking ordinary cars and "souping" them up to go faster. The Aston Martin name came from a hill-climb race at Aston Clinton in Buckinghamshire. Martin drove a modified Singer car very fast up this climb in 1914 and when Bamford & Martin Ltd. needed a name for the new car brand the decision was made to link the words Aston and Martin. The company's first advert was in a cycling magazine, *Bath Road News*, the journal of the Bath Road Club: "If you must sell your birthright for a mess of petrol, why not purchase your car ... from Bamford & Martin Ltd, the most humorous firm in the motor trade."

Martin was a tricyclist to his dying day – literally. He was killed in October 1945 after being knocked from his tricycle by a motor car on a suburban road in Kingston upon Thames.

AUTOBIANCHI

Autobianchi, an Italian motor car manufacturer, was created in 1955 by Fiat, Pirelli and Bianchi. F.I.V. Edoardo Bianchi S.p.A was founded in Milan in 1885 as a bicycle manufacturer. Company founder Edoardo Bianchi died in a car smash in 1946. From the early 1900s to 1939, Bianchi built motor cars and trucks. A 1917 advert for "The Italian Bianchi" placed by the company's London agent described the Bianchi as "The Car of the Connoisseur." In 1927, Bianchi was Italy's second-biggest car manufacturer (Fiat was first). Pope Pius XI was driven in a Bianchi.

Bianchi cars (and motorbikes) were raced by Grand Prix legend Tazio Nuvolari. Ferdinand Porsche called Nuvolari the "greatest driver of the past, the present, and the future." Il Mantovano Volante, "the Flying Mantuan", won his first automobile race in a Bianchi, later driving for Ferrari and for Alfa Romeo, which also has a bicycling back-story. Nuvolari was inspired to become a racing driver thanks to his uncle, Giuseppe Nuvolari, a bicycle racer and several times winner of the Italian national track championships. Nuvolari's father was also a top cycle racer but it was his uncle who taught him to ride a motorcycle. Bianchi's involvement with motorsport had followed the company's earlier successes in cycle racing. Bianchi's first sponsored cycle racer was Giovanni Tomaselli, the 1899 winner of the prestigious Paris Grand Prix, considered the European road cycling championships.

THE ITALIAN
BIANCHI
"*The Car of the Connoisseur.*"

12 H.P.   14/20 H.P.   18/30 H.P.   25/40 H.P.

Guaranteed for 50,000 miles.

18/30 H.P. BIANCHI CABRIOLET.

Telegrams:
"BIANCHAUTO,
LONDON."

BIANCHI
MOTORS Ltd.,
26, ST. JAMES'S ST.

Telephone:
5660
REGENT.

Famously, Bianchi sponsored Fausto Coppi, the *Campionissimo* – "Champion of Champions" – the first rider to win the Tour de France and Giro d'Italia double, achieving this in 1949, and repeating the feat in 1952.

Bianchi is still one of the world's top cycling brands, celebrated for its "celeste" turquoise. Picasso had a Bianchi bicycle in his studio in Vallauris, France. He described it as "one of the most beautiful and purest sculptures in the history of art."

CHARRON Ltd

VOITURE LÉGÈRE 14 H.P. (4 cylindres)
Toute équipée : 8.800 francs

USINES ET BUREAUX Rue Ampère Puteaux
Magasins d'Exposition et de Vente
2, Rue de la Paix ··· 100, Av^{ue} des Champs-Elysées

AUTOMOBILES CHARRON

In October 1897, Fernand Charron and his business partners Léonce Girardot and Carl Voigt launched the Agence Générale des Automobiles with shops close to the Arc de Triomphe and Avenue de la Grande Armée. This was one of the first French car dealerships. The business partners also created an automobile manufacturing company: Charron-Girardot-Voigt, or CGV.

Senior partner Charron had been a racing cyclist, winning the *Championnat de demi-fond*, a French middle-distance race, in 1891, beating Henry Fournier into second place. Fournier became Charron's mechanic when the cycle-racing champion turned to motor cars in the mid-1890s.

Charron's success on a bicycle was bettered by his success at the new sport of motor racing. He won the Marseille–Nice and Paris–Amsterdam–Paris races, both in 1898. Most importantly, this former racing cyclist won the inaugural Gordon Bennett Cup, a motor car race on public roads between Paris and Lyon. This 1900 event was the precursor to modern motorsport. Charron's first racing victories came in Panhard et Levassor motorcars. Charron, Girardot and Voigt's CGV motorcar marque was established in 1901.

CGV became Automobiles Charron in 1906 when Girardot and Voigt left the firm. Automobiles Charron remained in business until 1930.

Charron was married to Jeanne Clément, daughter of cycle – and later motor – manufacturer Adolphe Clément.

BANKER BROTHERS

Banker Brothers Co., of Pittsburg, Pennsylvannia, was a multi-store automobile dealership that made an own-brand motor car as early as 1895 and made a short-lived electric car for children in 1905. Banker Brothers Co. was originally a bicycle dealership. The shop had been founded in the 1880s, with the three sons of W. H. Banker taking over in the 1890s.

George Banker financed the push into motor cars with the money he won from a successful cycle-racing career in Europe. Banker was the travelling companion of Arthur Augustus Zimmerman, the world's most famous and richest racing cyclist in the mid-1890s. A member of Pittsburgh's high-society Keystone Bicycle Club, George was the youngest of the three brothers. Albert and George Banker were also racers, winning many local races, but it was George who did the most to spread the popularity of the Victor bicycle, the brand of bicycle sold in the family shop.

Banker won his first race in 1892, on a high-wheeler, in Brownsville, 35 miles from Pittsburgh. He set out for Europe in 1894 to race as a professional, on a Safety bicycle. He won the Grand Prix de Paris as well as races in other European cities. In 1895, he was stricken with typhoid and withdrew from racing, returning to the pro circuit in 1898 when he won the world sprint track championships in Vienna. He retired in 1899, ploughing his winnings into Banker Brothers Co., turning it into one of Pennsylvania's dominant automobile businesses.

BINKS

In 1905, Charles Binks designed a motor car for Roydale Engineering Company. It bombed, but his work on the car's carburettor paid off – he launched it as a stand-alone product and it became one of the leading carburettors of the 1920s and 1930s. Binks was formerly a bicycle and tricycle engineer, and a partner in a mid-1880s partnership with Alfred Lilwall (Lilwall and Binks).

BOSCH

From 1890 onward, Robert Bosch (see left) – founder of the world's largest car-accessories company – used a bicycle to visit his customers. "It not only got him there faster, but also saved him money," said a Bosch corporate history.

BRITISH GERMAIN MOTOR COMPANY

Belgium-based Germain was a builder of railway equipment that diversified into motor cars and trucks in the early 1900s. The British distributor for Germain motor cars was John Harris Adams, who in the 1880s was a record-breaking cyclist. Representing the Lewisham Bicycle Club, Adams broke the Land's End to John O'Groats record by two days in May 1884, riding on a Facile, a "dwarf" high-wheeler. *Wheeling* thought the ride was "by far the biggest thing ever done in the history of cycling, and proves Mr Adams the best road rider in the world." In October the same year Adams broke the 24-hour record, riding for 266 miles. By 1902 he was the owner of British Germain Motor Company.

BRITISH MOTOR SYNDICATE

The British Motor Syndicate made cars in the late 1890s – sort of. It had two factories in Coventry. One of them was a cycle factory and is now an Ibis hotel, with "Cycle Works" still visible in the brickwork. The other was known as the "Motor Mills" and was home to Daimler, the Great Horseless Carriage Company, the Beeston Pneumatic Tyre Company and the Humber Cycle Company. The plan was for the British Motor Syndicate to have a monopoly on the manufacture and sale of motor cars in Britain. But it was all smoke and mirrors and very few cars were made. While the reality turned out to be very different to the promises, the British Motor Syndicate, founded in 1895, stimulated others to do things the right way. The syndicate's founder was fond of doing things the wrong way – Harry Lawson was a superb promoter, but not such a good entrepreneur.

The British Motor Syndicate's factory in Coventry is now an Ibis hotel.

As well as being a pioneer of the motor industry, albeit eventually a shamed one, Lawson had been an interesting player in the bicycle business, although he overcooked his importance by claiming to be more pivotal than he ever was in reality. Nevertheless, Lawson made a great deal of money out of the bicycle business and planned to do the same in motor cars. He bought up a great number of automobile patents and hoped that, by controlling them, he could dominate the fledgling motor-car market. Many of the patents turned out to be worthless or indefensible, but many inventors weren't too worried about that and pocketed tidy sums anyway. While he was unscrupulous – despite being the son of a Calvinistic Methodist minister – Lawson claimed that money didn't motivate him. Rather, he was a control freak – he wanted to dominate the markets he was involved with, forming a complex web of companies to grow and protect his empire.

Herbert Duncan, a high-society old-time cycle racer who worked as Lawson's bicycle and motor agent in France, said that Lawson's British Motor Syndicate was formed to "corner the British side of the motor industry by buying up all past, present, and future patents in the expectation of running across some master patents ... the fees secured from royalties and manufacturing and selling licences would cause a continual flow of dividends and eventually raise the price of shares beyond the imagination of the most sanguine holder."

Lawson's real claim to fame isn't the Safety bicycle he claimed to have invented before John Kemp Starley, or the motor car he claimed to have patented in the 1880s, but his organisation of the London-to-Brighton Emancipation Run of 1896. Thanks to lobbying he undertook via a public exhibition of motor cars, he claimed much of the credit for the passage of the so-called Emancipation Act – which allowed motor cars on to the roads of Britain – but, in reality, the real work was done behind the scenes by CTC trustee Sir David Salomons. However, few today have heard of Salomons, but many know about the annual "old crocks" run of pre-1905 motor cars from London to Brighton.

Lawson's interest in road transport started with bicycles. In his home base of Brighton, in 1876, he patented a pre-Safety Safety bicycle – the Sussex Giant – and in 1879 produced the Bicyclette. This Safety-style bicycle wasn't quite as radical as J. K. Starley's later Rover Safety but it employed a chain-drive to the rear wheel, so it was certainly an interesting development.

His entry into the world of high finance came in 1887 when he refinanced the long-established Coventry-based Haynes and Jeffries by turning it into the publicly-traded Rudge Cycle Company. If many of his early financial deals bordered on the fraudulent, his later deals were wholly fraudulent. Boom markets always attract speculators willing to gamble with other people's money. In the mid-1890s Lawson converted other bicycle firms into publicly listed companies, making fortunes for himself and for investors. Some of the deals would be described as Ponzi schemes today. One of his promotional tactics was to appoint aristocrats as directors of his companies. These figures, many of them in dire need of funds, added a veneer of respectability to Lawson's companies. Few of them had any business sense, none made any real cash and all of them were to rue getting involved with the bicycle-maker from Brighton.

Lawson was an inveterate promoter of novel products. As well as companies, he founded organisations, including the Motor Car Club, headquartered at 40 Holborn Viaduct, which was then London's premier bicycle retailing street.

Lawson bought the rights to market the Daimler Motor Company in Britain. Herr Daimler was present on Lawson's Emancipation Run in November 1896. Securing the rights for Daimler meant employing Frederick Simms, the Daimler rights holder. A more savvy entrepreneur – Dunlop's Harvey Du Cros, for instance – could have used the Daimler rights to build a useful empire, but Lawson believed his own hype and thought he could do better than control just one brand. Simms went on to found the Automobile Club.

While Lawson's Motor Car Club was a club in name (the full name was the Motor Car Club Syndicate Ltd.), it was also part of Lawson's complex financial empire as part owner of the publicly listed Great Horseless Carriage Company. While some pioneer automobile entrepreneurs were full of bluff and never made a single motor car, Lawson did actually produce cars. One of them was the only British-made car in the 1896 Emancipation Run, constructed in a Coventry bicycle factory that still stands (the Ibis hotel mentioned above).

Lawson pulled the wool over the eyes of greedy investors (some of whom made money, at first) but his reputation as a shyster was well known in the City. The *Stock Exchange Gazette* warned: "The fact that Harry J. Lawson is the controlling spirit [of Daimler] is a very bad omen for the company and augurs a speedy acquaintance with the bankruptcy court."

This was sound advice. The Daimler marque lives on, but Lawson's company doesn't: it was wound up in 1903 and in 1904 Lawson was sentenced to a year's hard labour after being found guilty of conspiracy to defraud. He died in 1925, penniless and forgotten.

BROWN BROTHERS

Brown Brothers Distribution is today based in Stowmarket in Suffolk, and is owned by a multinational. It supplies paints to the automotive trade market and has had a colourful history. In the early 1900s it was based in London and made motor cars; for much of its history it made bicycles, too. The company was founded in 1889 by Ernest and Albert Brown, selling accessories to the booming bicycle trade. Brown Brothers went public in 1897 – shares were three times oversubscribed – and, spotting the potential in the fledgling automobile market, it opened a motor department in 1898. The company produced its first motor car, a quadricycle, in 1899. Other models followed, including the Brown Voiturette. Four Brown-branded motor cars were listed in the Brown Brothers catalogue for 1901.

The company diversified into aeroplanes, prams and other sidelines but the mainstay of the business remained wholesaling accessories to the cycle and motor trades. Car manufacture continued until the 1930s.

Via leading women's rights campaigner Myra Sadd, the firm had a connection to the suffragette movement, a movement intimately connected to bicycling. (The non-militant National Union of Women Suffrage Societies even marketed an NUWSS bicycle.) Myra Sadd married Ernest Brown, meeting him through their shared interest in cycling.

CADILLAC

Henry Martyn Leland created the Cadillac and Lincoln auto brands and the self-starter motor, and established the first major school for automobile mechanics. He was a machinist who developed interchangeable car parts with exceptionally close tolerances at a time when most car parts were hand-made by craftsmen and couldn't be easily transferred between cars, even of the same make. Before he made car parts, Leland made bicycle parts. His machine shop's mass produced close-tolerance interchangeable parts for shaft-drive transmissions were used on bicycles made by Colonel Albert Pope's Columbia bicycles. Pope was banking on shaft-drive technology to boost flagging bicycle sales. The close-tolerance technology didn't rescue bicycle sales but shaft-drives transferred to automobiles, including those later made by Pope.

"[In 1896] Harry M. Leland, then busy with his machine shop, was still more interested in bicycles than in motor cars," said a biography of Leland, "and till the close of the century he had no idea that he would be concerned with making them."

Leland started his own machine shop after a varied career as an apprentice machinist, fireman, policeman, gun-maker, sewing-machine factory supervisor and travelling salesman, as well as working for Brown & Sharpe, one of America's leading machine-tool makers. He was also an inventor, creating, among other things, electric barber's clippers. Originally from Vermont, Leland settled in Detroit in 1890 following financial backing from lumber entrepreneur Robert C. Faulconer and Detroit hardware seller Charles A. Strelinger. Strelinger's hardware business had done an "immense trade in bicycles."

Detroit in the 1890s was an expanding industrial town, famous for making railway carriages, ships and marine engines. It was also known for its high-precision machining, which attracted bicycle-makers to town. Detroit also had a thriving cycling scene, with the Detroit Bicycle Club being just one of many active clubs. Leland's company – Leland & Faulconer Manufacturing – grew quickly from 12 employees to 60. One of the company's later employees was Horace Dodge, who would set up his own machine shop, initially making bicycles and later engines for Henry Ford, and who would go on to create the Dodge car brand.

At the turn of the century, L&F was making engines for Ransom E. Olds' Olds Motor Vehicle Company and, on its own account, created the Cadillac automobile.

Cadillac – named after Frenchman Antoine Laumet de La Mothe, sieur de Cadillac, the founding father of Detroit (he established a fort there in 1701) – has another connection with cycling. Its most successful early salesman was William E. Metzger, co-founder of Detroit's Huber & Metzger bicycle shop. Metzger was a vice-president of Detroit's Wheelman's Club and also founded the Detroit Auto Show, as well as opening one of America's first car showrooms. When working for Leland, Metzger took orders for 2,700 Cadillac cars at the New York Auto Show of 1903 (a show he had founded).

CALCOTT BROTHERS

James and William Calcott of Coventry started making motorcycles in 1910 and diversified into motor cars in 1913, continuing to make cars until the death of James in 1924, when the firm was taken over by Singer, the motorcycle and motor-car manufacturer founded in 1875 to make Challenge high-wheeler bicycles. Calcott Brothers also had a bicycling background. It had been founded in 1888, making the X.L. range of Safety cycles. James Calcott had started in partnership with Enoch John West (who had been working at Singer Cycle Co.), forming Calcott Bros & West in 1888. West left in 1891 to set up his own company, E. J. West & Co Ltd, and in 1897 began designing cars, quadricycles, tricycles and motorcycles.

Calcott Brothers remained at is premises in Far Gosford Street, one of Coventry's medieval thoroughfares. The factory's offices are now listed and form part of a student hall of residence. A large graphic in a downstairs window features a black-and-white photograph of the interior of the car factory.

CAMERON BROTHERS

The first cars used by the US Mail service operated in Boston. There were two of them and they were steamers made by Cameron Brothers of Brockton, 20 miles south of Boston. Everett and Forrest Cameron, originally from Nova Scotia, produced their first gasoline car in 1903, with a unique air-cooled internal combustion engine (that would later prove useful on aeroplanes).

Cameron cars were light and fast, winning events around the world, including on the new, purpose-built Brooklands race circuit in England.

While still in their teens, the Cameron brothers had started their first business in 1894 as Cameron Brothers, Bicycles and Repairing. They made bicycles as well as repairing them. Cameron racing bikes – made under the Eclipse brand – were renowned for being lightweight, yet strong.

In 1899, the Cameron brothers built their first car, the Eclipse Steam Buggy, used by the US Mail. 500 of their innovative air-cooled gasoline cars were sold in 1904 and by 1906 the brothers had their own factory in Beverley, Massachusetts, and another in Attica, Ohio.

CHAMPION SPARK PLUG

Paris–Roubaix winner Albert Champion created the world's best-known spark plug brands.

The world's two best-known brands of spark plug were both created by Albert Champion, a French bicycle racer. Champion, a track racer, switched disciplines in 1899 to win the famously bumpy Paris–Roubaix one-day race. In the early 1900s he moved to America, where the prize purses were greater. (He may have also moved to avoid conscription.) When in America he did what lots of bicycle racers did – he became a racing driver. A crash ended that particular line of work, so he moved into the allied world of motoring, and took existing technologies to make a better spark plug. He returned to cycling in 1904, becoming French motor-paced champion at Henri Desgrange's Parc des Princes velodrome. In the same year he founded the Champion Ignition Company to make spark plugs. After a spat he left that company and started another, the AC Spark Plug Company, named after Champion's initials. Today the brand is known as ACDelco.

In the 1960s, the managing director for Champion Spark Plugs in the UK was Hubert Granville Starley, great grandson of James Starley, "father of the cycle industry." Starley Jnr. clearly had some cycling blood coursing through his veins – in 1967, Champion Spark Plugs was a headline sponsor of six-day cycle track racing in the UK.

CHATER LEA

London-based Chater Lea Manufacturing Company made motor cars from 1907 to 1922 and motorbikes from 1900 to 1936. The firm was founded in 1890 by cycle racer William Chater-Lea, who had been an engineer with Linley and Biggs, makers of the Whippet cycle. Chater-Lea's firm started out making bicycle parts, progressing to bicycle frames and then parts for motorbikes and finally full machines. The firm's first car was the two-seater Carette of 1907.

CHEVROLET

On November 3rd, 1911 in Detroit, Swiss racing car driver Louis Chevrolet partnered with William C. Durant (founder of General Motors) and two others to create the Chevrolet Motor Car Company. The Chevrolet name had cachet – Chevrolet was a famous driver with a French-sounding name at a time when French motor-car companies were still renowned for being early on the scene. American companies would soon usurp them, and Chevrolet would be shortened, unofficially, to Chevy. Born on Christmas Day 1878, the son of a clock-maker from the Jura Mountains – the heartland of Swiss watch-making – Louis Chevrolet emigrated to America and, after a stint as a chauffeur, became one of America's best-known racing drivers. Less well known is that Chevrolet had a successful career as a champion bicycle racer in France and owned a bicycle brand before he fronted a car brand.

Chevrolet's large family moved from Switzerland to Beaune in eastern France when he was six. As a young teenager he became a mechanic at the Roblin bicycle shop in the centre of Beaune and started winning cycle races, sponsored by the Gladiator bicycle brand. The Roblin shop was close to the luxury Hôtel de la Poste. A Chevrolet family legend relates that in 1898 a rich American guest at this hotel had his motor tricycle fixed by the 20-year-old Louis Chevrolet and that the gentleman, who was also 20, remarked that someone so gifted with their hands would do well in America. The family legend says this gentleman was William Kissam Vanderbilt II – grandson of the railway magnate and later to become the first key patron of motor-car racing in America – and that Chevrolet was inspired to emigrate by the chance meeting.

Perhaps. What's certain is that, before he moved to America, Chevrolet and his brothers Gaston and Arthur created their own brand of bicycle, making them in the winter and selling them in the summer under the name Frontenac, after the 17th-century governor of France's North American colonies.

In 1899, Chevrolet moved with his family to Paris to become a Gladiator-sponsored track rider, the prize money from which helped to support his siblings. Gladiator had been founded in 1891 by Alexandre Darracq, who became an automobile manufacturer after 1896 and sold Gladiator to cycle racer and entrepreneur Adolphe Clément. Through his links with Gladiator, Chevrolet landed a job with Darracq and he retired from cycle racing.

In 1900, at the age of 22, Chevrolet emigrated to Canada. He found work as a chauffeur and car mechanic (at the time this was one and the same job). The following year he moved to Brooklyn in New York to work as a mechanic and designer for French car manufacturer, De Dion-Bouton, then one of the world's leading makes of automobile.

His motor-racing career started in 1905. At Sheepshead Bay, New York, he went up against – and beat – Barney Oldfield, one of the top drivers of the day (Oldfield was another former cycle racer). Chevrolet's racing frame brought him the deal with Durant, creating the Chevrolet car brand.

After a falling out, Chevrolet and his brothers created the Frontenac Motor Corporation in 1916, using the name first used for their bicycle brand. The Frontenac Motor Corporation made racing parts for Henry Ford's Model T.

CLÉMENT-PANHARD

Frenchman Adolphe Clément was a passenger in the winning automobile in the world's first competitive motor event, the Concours des Voitures sans Chevaux ("Competition for Horseless Carriages"), an 1894 race on public roads from Paris to Rouen, organised by cycle journalist Pierre Giffard. Clément went on to become a millionaire automobile manufacturer with the majority stake in one of the leading global car brands of the day.

A 1904 profile of Clément said he was a self-made man who...

> ... started and built up a bicycle manufacturing establishment which, in 1894, was considered one of the finest in France. In time this developed into the finest cycle manufactory in that country ... In 1899, Clement contracted with Panhard & Levassor to manufacture under their patents, and in 1900 he made a most successful light vehicle of four horse-power. Since then he has developed his automobile factory ...

He also had a hand in making pneumatic tyres, motorcycles, aeroplanes and airships. Arthur Du Cros, of Dunlop fame, called Clément, "the Dick Whittington of Paris."

His start in motoring came through bicycle racing, via a cycle-repair business he founded in Bordeaux at the age of 21. Moving to Marseille, he made steel tubes for bicycles. In 1877, he moved to Lyon and began manufacturing bicycles under the name Clément SA cycles. The following year he moved to Paris to open a bike factory, A. Clément & Cie., near the Place de l'Étoile. Clément was also still racing at the time, including partnering cycling champion Charles Terront at six-day events at the Agricultural Hall in Islington, London. Also in 1878 he opened a larger shop in Paris and advertised his by-now successful bicycle marque with an innovative poster campaign.

Clément's fortune was made thanks to his share in the Dunlop business, in which he invested during 1889, which was later sold at great profit.

By 1890, Clément was the leading cycle brand in France. In 1893 the company owned the Vélodrome de la Seine, which was frequented by personalities such as the artist Toulouse-Lautrec, originally famous for his bicycle posters. One of cycling's most famous cycling posters – not a Lautrec – was produced for a brand that Clément invested in. This was the Gladiator Cycle Company, founded by Alexandre Darracq and Paul Aucoq in 1891. (Darracq would later go on to produce motor cars.) The poster featured a flame-haired siren flying with a bicycle. Clément pumped money into the business in 1893, thanks to advice from his future son-in-law, Fernand Charron, a champion cyclist, who became France's leading motor-racing driver. The Belle Époque poster of a flame-haired, buck-naked nymph propelled through the starry night on a Gladiator bicycle with wings in place of pedals is probably the thing for which the company is best known today. (See plates.)

Clément's first powered vehicle was produced in 1895, a naphtha-powered tricycle made by Gladiator. Clément became one of the dominant players in the French and European motoring industry up until the 1920s. He and other former cyclists became co-directors of multiple interconnected motoring companies. In a company prospectus published in 1901 for a London motor-car firm, he was still listed as "cycle maker." His fellow directors in this company were ex-racing cyclist and pneumatic tyre promoter Harvey Du Cros of Dunlop, motor-racing driver Selwyn Edge, and the Hon. Derek Keppel, the second of the three sons of the 7th Earl of Albemarle, who was the president of the National Cyclists' Union in the 1880s and 1890s and author of the aristocrats' book about cycling. Derek Keppel, Equerry to the Prince of Wales, was a keen cyclist, as was his wife.

In 1903, Clément was indirectly responsible for the creation of the Tour de France cycle race. Clément was one of the advertisers in Pierre Giffard's cycling-and-general-interest magazine *Le Vélo*. Giffard was a Dreyfusard. The Dreyfus Affair gripped France at the turn of 20th century. Alfred Dreyfus, a Jewish captain in the French army, had been jailed over a trumped-up espionage charge and, after Émile Zola wrote his famous *J'accuse* letter in a liberal newspaper in 1898, French society was split between those, usually left-wing, who supported Dreyfus and those who didn't (usually right-wing). Among the anti-Dreyfusards were motoring pioneers and business associates Comte Jules-Albert de Dion and Adolphe Clément. Both advertised in *Le Vélo* – which was printed on green paper – and both pulled their adverts. A tussle at a horse-racing track in 1899 between Giffard and de Dion led to the President of France being rapped on the head with a walking stick by de Dion. Comte de Dion was jailed for 15 days. Infuriated, de Dion and Clément – and tyre manufacturer Michelin – conspired to put Giffard out of business by funding and publishing a rival newspaper. *L'Auto-Vélo* was an all-sports newspaper majoring on motoring. It was printed on yellow paper. A court forced the new newspaper to drop the *Vélo* part of the name but the newspaper still promoted itself as a newspaper for "Automobile et Cyclisme." The industrialist owners appointed as editor Henri Desgrange, who had worked for Clément on public relations projects, and was a former cycle racer. Despite generous funding, the fledgling newspaper wasn't a commercial success. With sales flagging, and the industrialist backers getting impatient at the clearly thriving *Le Vélo*, Desgrange, speaking about Giffard, said: "What we need is something to nail his beak shut."

Le Vélo was famous for staging cycles races such as the Paris–Roubaix. During a restaurant lunch, Géo Lefèvre, a writer poached from *Le Vélo*, suggested that *L'Auto* ought to organise a rival, a more ambitious race – around France. This was launched in 1903 and became an instant success, with the cycling event radically changing the fortunes of the supposedly motoring-focused newspaper. The Tour de France, with its yellow leader's jersey – so coloured because of *L'Auto's* yellow pages – finally led to the nailing shut of Giffard's beak: *Le Vélo* closed in 1904. Very possibly that would have pleased Clément.

CLULEY CARS

Cluley & Company made 2,000 or so motor cars in the 1920s. The business later made textile machinery and lasted until 1987. It was established in Coventry in 1884 as Clarke, Cluley & Co. as a manufacturer of cycles, a partnership between Ernest Clarke and Charles J. Cluley and two other associates. The company was also making motorcycles by 1901 but, according to trade directories, was only producing bicycles in 1912. The firm made cycles under the Globe brand name and Cluley-branded motor cars between 1921 and 1928.

CLYDE MOTORS

George H. Wait of Leicester-based Clyde Motors made motorbikes and motor cars from 1900 to 1926. Wait was "a clever mechanic, and an old cyclist," according to *Motor Cycling* magazine. He had worked as a design engineer for the cycle-maker Humber.

COLUMBIA

Despite being into bicycles early and, for a time, being the leading player in the fledgling motor-car industry with ultra-efficient factories that Henry Ford visited and copied, Colonel Pope's Pope Manufacturing Company failed to capitalise on its advantages and had abandoned the automobile industry by 1915. Not all popes are infallible. (See chapter 2.)

The first-ever presidential motorcade, Hartford, Connecticut, August 22nd 1902. President Roosevelt (left) is sitting in a Columbia Electric Victoria Phaeton by bicycle firm Pope Manufacturing. The policemen are riding on Columbia chainless bicycles.

CRYPTO CAR

The two-seat Crypto three-wheeler car was produced for three years or so by Crypto Works Co. of London. The company also produced motorbikes, although by 1917 it was making only engines. The company had been founded in 1872 by William Gilbert James, "at one time a successful cycle-racer, contemporary with Mr. S. F. Edge," according to a 1904 motoring annual. This also revealed that James was a member of the Bath Road Cycling Club – as were many other motor pioneers, such as Napier, Edge, Martin and Bamford – and he believed in "the courteous consideration of other users of the road."

James's Crypto Works was making cycles, including tricycles, by 1884. His most famous cycle was the Crypto Bantam, a favourite of Henry Sturmey. This was an eccentric bicycle with pedals connected to the front wheel like a high-wheeler but, thanks to the Crypto Dynamic two-speed gear, it was much smaller than a high-wheeler. It was produced while the high-wheeler was going out of fashion – it was almost dead by 1891 – and the Safety was all the rage. The Bantam offered the best of both worlds. It was also fast, ridden by cycle and later motor executive Frank Shorland in many record rides.

GOTTLIEB DAIMLER & WILHELM MAYBACH

In 1885, Gottlieb Daimler and his co-worker Wilhelm Maybach attached a breakthrough gasoline engine to a wooden-framed two-wheel single-track cycle with small outrigger wheels either side for stability, creating the world's first motorbike, albeit one with "training wheels." The *Reitwagen*, or "riding wagon", looked like an 1817 Draisine *Laufmaschine* "running machine", not an 1885 bicycle. It had wooden wheels and straight forks: it couldn't turn very well. This slow machine wasn't designed to be a vehicle in its own right, but was a test platform for the German twosome's "grandfather clock" engine. (Daimler is the name that has come down more prominently through history but it's likely that Maybach was the greater innovator of the two. Daimler was the organisational brains, Maybach the more inspired engineer.)

In 1886, Daimler and Maybach placed an improved version of their engine on a modified horse carriage, creating a motor car. But, as it was an adapted vehicle and not one built from scratch, most motoring historians do not consider this to be the world's first automobile. Most conclude that it was Carl Benz – working in Mannheim, 56 miles from Daimler and Maybach – who made the first true automobile because his 1886 tricycle-with-an-engine was purpose-built and, give or take an iteration or two, ready for sale.

Daimler and Maybach's third vehicle, much later called the *Stahlradwagen* ("wire-wheel car"), was a quadricycle, and, unlike the pair's modified horse carriage vehicle, was – thanks to Maybach's insistence – built from cycle parts and consequently lightweight. "Similar to the first Benz Patent Motorcar of 1886, this vehicle would be unthinkable without bicycle technology," wrote automotive historian Erik Eckermann in a book published in 2001 by the Society of Automotive Engineers.

In the Meyers encyclopedia of the 1880s, Germany's leading reference work, Daimler's automobile was listed in the "bicycle" section. The automobile's steel frame was made by cycle manufacturer Neckarsulmer Stahlfabriken of Riedlingen (this would later become NSU Motorenwerke, a motorbike manufacturer from 1901 that built motor cars from 1905).

The Daimler/Maybach quadricycle – unlike the Roger/Benz Motorwagen – wasn't displayed at the 1889 Paris Exposition but it was taken there later in the year, securing interest from Panhard & Levassor. Panhard & Levassor, then a woodworking machinery company, acquired the rights to make the quadricycle and these were assigned first to bicycle-maker Peugeot which, in 1890, made its own version of the Daimler/Maybach quadricycle. This was the start of the French automobile industry and, in effect, the start of the world automobile industry.

The Daimler agency for Britain was picked up by Frederick Simms, a CTC member who, after a stint working for Harry Lawson, founded the Automobile Club of Great Britain and Ireland.

DARRACQ

Automobiles Darracq was founded in 1896 by Alexandre Darracq and was soon one of France's top motor car marques. Branching out into Italy, a new company was formed in 1906, Società Anonima Italiana Darracq. By 1909, the Italian Darracq cars were selling slowly so S.A.I.D. was dissolved and a new company was formed, with the same staff, still with Darracq in partnership. This was Anonima Lombarda Fabbrica Automobili, the "Lombard Automobile Factory". S.A.I.D. had become A.L.F.A. and, in turn, this became Alfa Romeo.

"Darracq ... made the first moderate priced automobile in France," said a 1904 profile. "He is now the engineer and manager of one of the biggest factories in the world." The car that starred in *Genevieve*, the 1953 movie about a re-enactment of the London-to-Brighton Emancipation Run, was a 1904 Darracq.

Alexandre Darracq was formerly a bicycle manufacturer, founding the Gladiator Cycle Company in 1891. This had a cycle-racing team managed by Thomas Charles Willis Pullinger, who was a cycle racer and cycle maker. Pullinger, who had made lightweight bicycles under the Parade brand, became a designer at Darracq and, after working on Gladiator bicycles, moved on to Gladiator motor cars. Herbert Duncan said that Pullinger "constructed one of the first (if not the first) small cars with ... tubular frame and two seats side by side."

In 1896, Darracq sold Gladiator to cycles-to-automobiles entrepreneur Adolphe Clément.

DE DION-BOUTON

De Dion-Bouton was a French automobile manufacturer founded in 1885 by Comte Jules-Albert de Dion and steam engineers Georges Bouton and Charles Trépardoux. Originally it made steam cars but was quick to latch on to the potential of the combustion engine developed in Germany. By 1900, De Dion-Bouton was the largest motor-car manufacturer in the world. One of its most flamboyant employees was Herbert Osbaldeston Duncan. Author of the self-published *The World on Wheels* published in 1926, a three-kilogramme tome that must have cost a small fortune to produce, H. O. Duncan was one of early motoring's most vigorous promoters. His 1,200-page book is packed with anecdotes showing his personal connections with the key figures in motoring and cycling from the 1890s to the 1920s. It also featured a great deal about H. O. Duncan himself.

Duncan, with some aristocratic blood coursing through his veins, and always a smart dresser, certainly had fingers in lots of pies. Known to his friends as H.O.D., in 1894 he was living in Paris and held the rights to sell the German Hildebrand & Wolfmüller motorbike in France and Belgium. The H&W was one of the first mass-produced motorbikes in the world. With colleague Louis Suberbie, Duncan opened a factory in Croissy to manufacture the H&W Pétrolette. Duncan Suberbie & Co. failed after faults were found with the early motorbikes and Duncan returned to England, seeking out his old cycling friend Harry Lawson, and in 1896 becoming the manager of London's first motor-car exhibition; later the same year he was one of the pioneer motorists on the London-to-Brighton Emancipation Run. At the dinner held to celebrate the motor cars arriving in Brighton, Duncan sat at the top table. To those interested in motoring, "H.O.D. is a household word," claimed French pianist and motoring enthusiast Ernest Vavin in a foreword to Duncan's book.

Duncan worked for Lawson and his British Motor Syndicate, managing the Motor Exhibition at the Imperial Institute in South Kensington. Later he represented the diminutive businessman's automobile interests in France but, no doubt anticipating the collapse of Lawson's business, he left in 1898 to become the Paris-based manager of De Dion-Bouton. The company also made gas-explosion engines for upwards of 150 other motor-car manufacturers. Duncan was at the centre of all this.

Duncan created the short-lived *Motor Review Journal* but three of his earlier publications – French-language books published in 1890 and 1898 on the sport of cycling and a magazine, *The Véloceman*, first published in 1885 – show how, before he became a prominent promoter of motoring, he was doing the same for bicycling.

Grandson of a Master of the Quorn Hunt in Leicestershire – a fact he provided in his memoirs in order to explain his middle name, his good breeding and his love of sport; his grandfather, who died penniless, was a colourful minor aristocrat with a penchant for fast living – Duncan started riding high-wheel bicycles in 1877, at age 15, "at his country home at West Drayton," just north of what would much later become Heathrow airport. Duncan was a gentleman racer and in his memoirs describes how at his "London home," a grand townhouse in Notting Hill, he met and befriended a fellow gentleman rider, Baron Frédéric de Civry, a minor French aristocrat with a "beautifully nickel-plated bicycle" who "blew a plated bugle … much to the discomfort of other neighbours."

Duncan and de Civry joined the Belgrave Bicycle Club: "We invested in the club's uniform – tight fitting breeches, a black-braided tunic and a cap with leather chin strap."

The two joined up with Paul Médinger, another high-wheel rider. "The three of us raced together throughout France, Germany and Austria," said Duncan. "On the Continent we were styled 'the celebrated trio of champions.'"

Duncan won the 50-mile time trial championships in the following three years. Duncan's memoirs said he

Herbert Duncan in his cycle racing clothing, and below, in his motor executive days.

was "three times in succession Bicycle Champion of the World, [and] Bicycle Champion of France, London and Middlesex."

Thanks to his friendship with de Civry and Médinger, Duncan settled in France, first in Montpellier and later in Paris. He lived in France for most of his life but always kept well abreast of developments in the country of his birth. As an Englishman living in France he became a conduit for the spread of technological innovations between the two countries. When he was still one of the top high-wheel racers Duncan was quick to spot the potential of J. K. Starley's Safety bicycle, introduced in 1885. Duncan sang its praises in France, and was partly responsible for the speedy acceptance of the innovation in his adopted homeland, promoting first the Rudge bicycle and later the Humber.

He joined Rudge in 1887, soon after retiring from racing. As well as taking a position as a globe-trotting cycle salesman, he became a cycle journalist and publisher. Later he became a cycle-racing manager, and in 1892, the brains behind the first velodrome in Paris, the Velodrome Buffalo, located in Neuilly-sur-Seine near the Porte Maillot. Duncan persuaded Clovis Clerc, director of the Folies Bergère to finance the track. Henri Desgrange, later to help found the Tour de France, set the first "hour" record on this track in 1893 and it was also a favourite haunt of Belle Époque artist Henri de Toulouse-Lautrec (many of his posters were of races in the Velodrome Buffalo).

De Civry and Médinger became friendly "rivals in the cycling business," said Duncan:

> When our racing days were over … Frédéric de Civry became manager for France of the Rudge Cycle Co.'s Paris shop … Médinger was manager for France for the Coventry Machinists Co. Ltd. at their Paris shop. [I] was manager for France at the Paris shop of Humber & Co. Ltd.

The rivalry continued into cycle sport. De Civry was manager of racer Pierre Jiel-Laval, who rode a Clément bicycle with Dunlop pneumatics; Duncan was manager for Charles Terront, France's first great cycling star. In September 1891, with Duncan as his promoter, manager and equipment provider, Terront won the first Paris–Brest–Paris cycle race on a Michelin-equipped Humber.

"To successfully manage a cycle business at this period, one had to be a journalist and a sportsman as well as a business man," wrote Duncan. And, as the motoring pioneers later discovered, borrowing from cycling, "the best method of advertising was the winning of important races."

Duncan sponsored some of the best French cyclists of the day and "nearly all the principal events were won on Beeston Humber cycles," boasted Duncan.

He was the Paris-based manager of De Dion-Bouton from 1898 to 1916, when he moved to London to become chairman of De Dion-Bouton in Britain, responsible for sales to Britain and overseas.

DODGE

Dodge is an American car, SUV and truck brand owned by Chrysler. It was founded as an accessories maker in 1900 by brothers Horace Elgin Dodge and John Francis Dodge from Detroit, with the first complete car made in 1914. As well as having their own auto business they were major investors in the Ford Motor Company. By the time of their death in 1920, Dodge was America's second-biggest car brand, after Ford.

In the 1890s the brothers had been keen cyclists and in 1897, with Canadian Fred Evans, had founded their own bicycle business in Windsor, Ontario, making the Evans and Dodge bicycle, based on a dirt-resistant ball-bearing assembly the brothers had patented the year before. (Horace also worked part-time for Henry M. Leland at the Leland and Faulconer Manufacturing Company in Detroit, which made high-precision parts for the bicycle industry.) Leland went on to establish the Cadillac Motor Car Company in 1903. In 1899, the Evans and Dodge brand was purchased by Toronto-based National Cycle. Horace stayed in Windsor to look after the machine shop while John moved to Hamilton, Ontario to manage another bicycle factory that National Cycle had acquired.

The Dodge brothers dissolved the partnership with Fred Evans in 1900 and used their share of the proceeds to establish their own machine shop in Detroit, making parts for the rail industry and the fledgling automobile industry. When National Cycle was itself bought out, and soon thereafter failed, the Dodge brothers acquired its machining equipment and tools, and moved them to Detroit. A contract to supply to Ransom Olds, maker of the then leading car in America, the Oldsmobile, made the brothers' firm into one America's biggest auto-parts suppliers.

When Henry Ford came calling, Horace and John kept him on a tight credit leash (two of his earlier auto businesses had failed), and they became shareholders when he needed capital for expansion. From the founding of the Ford Motor Company in 1903 until 1914, the Dodge brothers supplied about 60 percent of the total value of the cars that Ford built. Only later did the Ford factories make almost everything on site.

Ford might have been Detroit's most famous cyclist but the Dodge brothers were even keener. A "Mr. Dodge" was a stoker in a two-mile tandem race on the Detroit banked track in 1897 and the brothers were active members of the Detroit Wheelmen, volunteering to be race judges and timers. Well into the period when they were making fortunes from the automobile business the Dodge brothers were still active in cycling. In 1905, John Dodge ran for a position on the Detroit Wheelmen board and Horace was elected the club's second vice-president the following year. The brothers were still visiting the Detroit Wheelmen's clubhouse in 1908.

Charles Duryea.

DURYEA

Two bicycle mechanics built the first motor car to splutter along Washington D.C's Pennsylvania Avenue. It was made by the Duryea brothers of Illinois and was a circus freak, leading out a promotional parade by Barnum and Bailey's Greatest Show on Earth on May 11th, 1896. The motor car was upstaged by eight baby elephants and a gorilla called Joanna.

Charles Edgar Duryea was the designer of the first-ever American-made, commercially-available "mass-produced" gasoline-powered car: 13 identical machines were built in 1896.

(Charles had designed a gasoline-powered engine in 1891, but didn't progress with it.)

Charles, the elder of the two, trained as a mechanic and after completing his studies he worked in H. S. Owen, a bicycle shop in Washington, D.C., in the mid-1880s. By the end of the decade he had designed and patented a number of bicycle innovations, including a hammock saddle and, to take the sting out of the rough roads of the day, a variety of frame-mounted spring-suspension devices.

He was talent-spotted by bicycle-maker Harry G. Rouse of Peoria, Illinois and the two went into business together as the Rouse-Duryea Cycle Company. This company – via gun- and sword-maker Ames Manufacturing of Chicopee, Massachusetts – made the Sylph spring-suspension "comfort" bicycle for men and women.

An 1892 trade catalogue for the company said: "Our Mr. C. E. Duryea is well known as one of the most prolific practical cycle inventors in America, and as the originator of [a] number [of] cycling features of great value."

Charles's brother Frank – who had joined the Rouse-Duryea Cycle Company – carried on working on the gasoline-powered engine, and perfected it.

In the meantime, Charles visited the Chicago World's Fair in 1893, and in the Transportation Building was transfixed by a quadricycle motor car designed by Daimler. The visit inspired Duryea to push on with his vehicle. A local journalist was briefed on his work and a prescient newspaper report duly appeared:

> A new motor carriage, which, if the preliminary tests prove successful as is expected, will revolutionize the mode of travel on highways, and do away with the horse as a means of transportation, is being made in this city. The carriage is being built by J. F. Duryea … The vehicle was designed by C. E. Duryea, a

bicycle manufacturer of Peoria, Ill., and he communicated his scheme to his brother, who is a practical mechanic in this city.

A week later, on September 21st, 1893, in Springfield, Massachusetts, Charles Duryea made the first trip in an American-made, gasoline-powered automobile. It featured parts from a Columbia tricycle – including a differential gear – bought from the Pope Manufacturing Company.

Duryea may have constructed a motor car, but he remained a cyclist. He was a member of the League of American Wheelmen. Writing in the club magazine, he showed his pre-automobile interest in roads:

> From the dawn of history to the present, civilization and roadways have been linked together. Whether landways or waterways, whether traversed by ships or slaves, canal-boats or camels, canoes or cyclers, the progress of any country has been reflected by its system of roads.

By 1896 – while still working in the bicycle trade – Charles and Frank Duryea offered for sale the first commercially-available automobile in the US. One of these was bought by Henry Wells of New York. On May 30th, 1896 Wells drove his Duryea Motor Wagon into New York City to take part in a horseless-carriage race organised by *Cosmopolitan* magazine. While racing, on public roads, he crashed into Evelyn Thomas, riding a Columbia bicycle on Broadway near West 74th Street. Wells became the first motorist arrested for what would later become known as "dangerous driving."

Ms. Thomas had been planning to attend a Civil War Memorial Day service but was instead hospitalised with a fractured leg. While in hospital, she was visited by Horatio Earle, the leading light of the League of American Wheelmen. Thomas related her story to Earle and they agreed that cyclists' rights on the highway would need protecting from a new menace on the road.

Frank Duryea took two Duryea motor cars to England for the 1896 Emancipation Run. There were some controversial press reports at the time claiming that one of the Duryea cars was first to arrive in Brighton. This was not a claim made by Duryea.

In 1897, Charles Duryea met America's leading bicycle-maker, Colonel Albert Pope. Pope was interested in selling the Duryea car but the businessmen couldn't agree terms. "Thus ended the possibility of a Pope-Duryea combination," wrote motoring pioneer Herbert Duncan in 1926. "It is interesting to speculate what such an amalgamation of inventive and manufacturing genius might have accomplished under happier auspices."

DÜRKOPP

Dürkopp of Bielefeld in Germany made motor cars – and trucks – from 1894 to 1929. The firm had previously been a manufacturer of bicycles, starting in 1885. Just like many other cycle firms, Dürkopp had begun as a maker of sewing machines. In 1945, the company made bicycles again, and motorbikes. Production stopped in 1961. The company still exists today, although with multinational corporate owners and makes industrial sewing machines.

E.M.F.

The Everitt-Metzger-Flanders Company made 26,000 motor cars in 1911, making it one of the largest automobile manufacturers in the world at the time. It had been started by motor-car big hitters Byron Everitt, Walter Flanders and William Metzger. Everitt was a bodywork specialist; Flanders was an engineer, who had masterminded the initial production of Ford's Model T; and Metzger had opened, in Detroit, America's first automobile retailer. In the 1890s, Metzger had co-founded Detroit's Huber & Metzger, one of America's biggest and best bicycle shops. In 1902, *The Automobile* wrote:

> While in Detroit the other day, I paid a visit to W. E. Metzger, one of the brightest and most energetic

young men in the automobile business. Like many of the other good ones in the automobile trade, Mr. Metzger graduated from the bicycle business and is a pioneer automobile dealer. His present palatial establishment on Jefferson Avenue is the result of things accomplished already, and an abiding faith in the future of the automobile. As a bicycle agent, W. E. Metzger was a bright light among lesser luminaries in his city. I remember when he was selling bicycles at Christmas when his competitors persuaded themselves that it was an off season and were not trying to do any business; he is doing the same thing in the automobile business to-day.

The Henry Ford

Detroit's most famous cyclist: Henry Ford.

FORD

At just after 11 pm on March 6th, 1896 the first motor car on the streets of Detroit was piloted to a stop on Woodward Avenue. This car was driven by its builder, 28-year-old mechanical engineer Charles Brady King. King's horseless carriage was followed by a tall, slim man on a three-year-old bicycle. This bicycle – brand unknown – was Henry Ford's pride and joy. Three months after riding behind King, Ford knocked out the wall of his home workshop at 58 Bagley Avenue in downtown Detroit and went for a drive in his first automobile. This was Ford's Quadricycle, featuring a great many bicycle parts, including tubular steel for the chassis, 28-inch wire-spoked bicycle wheels and pneumatic tyres.

Ford sold this car to his friend Charles G. Annesley for $200. (The first used car sale in America had a cycling connection: Annesley sold the Quadricycle to A. W. Hall, a bicycle shop owner.)

Annesley, like Ford, was a cyclist. Annesley was nephew of one of the wealthiest men in Detroit and was friends with Barton L. Peck, son of a wealthy industrialist and another of Detroit's wheelmen. Annesley and Peck were rich and educated. Ford was neither but the three had a joint interest: their bicycles. Annesley and Peck could afford the latest models, while in 1896 Ford was still riding on the bicycle he had bought in February 1893.

Ford rode to work at one of Detroit's Edison electric plants on his bicycle. William Simonds' 1946 biography of Ford said: "As became an engineer making a good salary, Mr. Ford wore a handsome moustache, and could be seen frequently on his bicycle pedalling on some errand."

Simonds also recounts how, as a practical joke, Ford "borrowed" a Rambler bicycle a co-worker had on a test ride: "Mr. Ford was seen rounding the corner of State Street. He laughed so hard he fell off the bicycle …"

Ford also cycled to work when he was developing the Model N, precursor to the Model T of 1908. He may be known now as the kick-starter of the US automobile industry but he was careful with his money and knew that his trusty bicycle could get through Detroit quicker than the town's trams.

In his dotage Ford was still a cyclist. *Time*, in August 1940, reported that, on his birthday, the 77-year-old automotive billionaire "took a ride … on the light (12-lb.) English bicycle on which he likes to take a three-mile spin every evening after supper."

GARRARD

Garrard Manufacturing Company of Birmingham, England, was a motor-car firm that had produced an electric car as early as 1893. After seeing a run of the Garrard Electric Phaeton in 1894, *The Cyclist* made the bold claim that this would be "The Carriage of the Future." The Phaeton's frame was made of steel bicycle tubes and it was the first British car to be shod with pneumatic tyres. Company co-founder Charles Riley Garrard was a former cycle-factory foreman and a racing cyclist. He was tenth in the 100-mile national championships in 1882. He patented his electric car with his business partner Thomas William Blumfield. The electric car was ahead of its time and didn't gain traction. Instead, in 1894 Garrard moved to Paris to build Gladiator motor tricycles for Adolphe Clément of Clément Cycles. Clément – another cycle racing man – had taken over the Gladiator bicycle and motors brand in partnership with Harry Lawson and Lord Charles Chetwynd-Talbot, 20th Earl of Shrewsbury. In 1896, Garrard & Blumfield was absorbed into Lawson's Great Horseless Carriage Company. From 1902 to 1905, Garrard was back in Birmingham making Clément-Garrard motorbikes and cars. He was president of the Cycle Engineers' Institute, which later became the Institution of Automobile Engineers. In the 1891 census Garrard was listed as "Cycle Examiner, Turner and Fitter." In the 1911 census he described himself as an automobile engineer.

GEORGE & JOBLING

Starting in 1902, George & Jobling was a manufacturer of motor cars, based in Newcastle upon Tyne. In 1904, the company occupied part of the factory that had previously been used by locomotive engineers Robert Stephenson and Company. Originally making an own-brand car, the company soon became a motor agent – for brands such as Darracq, Hillman and Ford – and was a bodywork modifier. The firm was founded by Arthur Edward George and Robert Lee Jobling and initially made bicycles.

George was a champion cyclist, having raced from the age of 17. In 1897, he won the national mile championships at North Durham. George also raced in France, America and Canada, before moving to live in South Africa with his uncle John George. He became national cycling champion of South Africa and represented that country at the 1899 track cycling world championships in Montreal, Canada.

In the Second Boer War, George served with the Cape Colony Cyclist Corps from 1901 to 1902. On his joining-up papers he was described as a "Cycle Mechanic" who "Supplies own bicycle."

George became a racing driver, driving a Darracq and achieving third place in the 1908 RAC Tourist Trophy. As with many cyclists who became motorists, he also became a keen aviator. He didn't stop cycling, though. In 1926, he went on a cycle tour across Morocco, during the Rif war, a series of mountain skirmishes between Berber tribesman and Spanish soldiers. For his 72nd birthday he piloted a plane and went on a cycle ride.

GMC

Now one of America's top SUV and truck brands and owned by General Motors since 1909, GMC was originally the Rapid Motor Vehicle Company. Before Rapid was founded, in 1902, by brothers Max and Morris Grabowsky, it was the Grabowsky Motor Vehicle Company. This is when the corporate history of the brand starts but that's not when the Grabowsky brothers got into the transport industry. Their first business was Grabowsky Manufacturing, a "bicycle sundries" maker. In 1899 it was based at 380 Woodward Avenue, Detroit. It's likely the business was at least two years old at this point. The brothers were keen cyclists and in 1896 Morris was on the entertainment committee of the Detroit Wheelmen cycling club. This club had 450 members and was rich enough to afford a $40,000 clubhouse, complete with exterior bike rack and the club's logo on the exterior in stone. The clubhouse had an auditorium, a bowling alley, billiard and card game tables, baths, a library, a kitchen and a dining room.

HILLMAN

The first car I can remember from my childhood is the Hillman Imp. I used to sleep on its back shelf. Hillman started as a cycle company: Hillman & Herbert, co-founded in 1875 by William Hillman. Earlier a business associate of James Starley, Hillman was one of the pre-1870 pioneers of the high-wheeler bicycle. Hillman and Starley had both worked for marine-engineering company John Penn of Greenwich – Hillman as an engineer, Starley as Penn's gardener. Starley, a self-taught engineer, moved to Coventry to exploit an improvement he had made to sewing machines. Both men joined the Coventry Sewing Machine Co., which became Coventry Machinists, the earliest British maker of velocipedes, a French innovation. Starley and Hillman left to form their own partnership and in 1870 introduced the industry-shaping Ariel high-wheel bicycle. Its steel backbone and large, wire-spoked wheels kickstarted the first cycle revolution.

Hillman left the partnership in 1872 and, in 1875, with capital from William Henry Herbert, created Hillman and Herbert, a maker of high-wheelers. The pair took on a third partner in 1880 and became Hillman, Herbert and Cooper. This business was best known for the Kangaroo, a geared-up, front-driven chain-drive "dwarf" high-wheeler introduced in 1884. Later, it produced Safety bicycles which the chain-drive Kangaroo had helped to spawn.

In 1887, Hillman created the Auto Machinery Company to make cycle components and, later, ball and roller bearings, the manufacture of which made Hillman a millionaire, enabling him to buy a Coventry mansion, the grounds of which would later be used to build a car factory.

Meanwhile, in 1891, Hillman and his partners incorporated as the Premier Cycle Company. By the time of the mid-1890s bicycle boom, it was one of the largest cycle manufacturers in the world, employing 600. Hillman stepped down from the day-to-day running of the business in 1896, with the firm steered by his sons-in-law, but behind the scenes he still pulled many of the strings.

With sales riding high, even after the bicycle bubble burst, Hillman saw no pressing need to do what other cycle manufacturers were doing – attaching motors to bicycles and tricycles. He waited until 1902 before experimenting with his first motorbike but by 1907 Premier was producing large motor cars, designed by Frenchman Louis Coatalen, who would become one of British motoring's leading automobile designers. Coatalen married one of Hillman's six daughters. Coatalen had been working at the long-established Humber factory, a field away from Hillman's mansion. The Hillman–Coatalen Motor Company was incorporated in 1907. Coatalen left in 1910 to join Sunbeam, another car brand with bicycle beginnings and the company became the Hillman Motor Company.

By the time of his death in 1921, Hillman had become – like many of the Coventry cycle entrepreneurs – a fabulously wealthy man. His career had spanned half a century of dizzying technological change. In 1925, the Hillman Company was absorbed by Humber and by 1928 Hillman was the leading brand in the portfolio of the Rootes Group of motor-car marques, alongside other former bicycle brands Humber, Sunbeam and Singer. The Hillman Minx was the group's leading car in the 1930s. The Hillman Imp, like me, was a child of the 1960s. The last Hillman car was the Avenger, introduced in 1970 and made until 1981.

HOUPT-ROCKWELL

New York's famous yellow cabs are connected to cycling twice over – first in the few years before the First World War, and then in the 1970s. The original yellow taxi cab appeared in 1909. It was made by Rockwell, a car company with bicycle roots. The Houpt-Rockwell company developed from the New Departure Manufacturing Company of Bristol, Connecticut. New Departure became one of the largest accessory makers within General Motors but had started, in 1888, as a maker of bicycle bells. The company was founded by Edward Rockwell and his brother, Albert. The New Departure Bell Company also made ball bearings and an innovative freewheeling hub brake, the "coaster" brake that, in the early 1970s, was resurrected to be used on the first "klunkers" in Marin County, California – the downhill race machines that morphed into cross-country mountain bikes.

The first company to use Rockwell-made cabs was Wyckoff, Church and Partridge, a company which was absorbed in 1910 by the Connecticut Cab Company, operated by Rockwell and other directors from the New Departure Manufacturing Company. In 1912, Rockwell incorporated the Yellow Taxicab Company, and the colour of New York's cabs was set.

HUMBER

Humber was the first British mass producer of motor cars. Prior to the First World War, the Humber car was the third most popular in Britain. Humber's first production car rumbled into life in 1896 thanks to commissions from Harry Lawson of the British Motor Syndicate. Humber-badged cars were made until 1976.

The company was founded by Thomas Humber of Nottingham. The young Humber originally worked for sewing-machine manufacturer William Campion in Nottingham. In 1867, while exhibiting his sewing machines at a show in Paris, Campion saw and purchased a velocipede and brought it back to Nottingham in order for Humber to copy. In 1868, Humber saw an article about an improved velocipede in *English Mechanic* magazine and believed he could improve it still further. He set up in business for himself, making the "Spider" high-wheeler.

Bearded Thomas Humber and business partner T. Harrison Lambert on a Humber tandem tricycle.

At first, Humber made these in a shed at the back of his house in Nottingham. The business was expanded in 1875 when Humber was joined by Thomas Rushforth Marriott. When Fred Cooper joined in 1877, the firm was renamed Humber, Marriott and Cooper.

By 1880, the Humber works in Beeston, near Nottingham, employed 1,200 people. In 1885, Cooper and Marriott left the partnership, and later sold bicycles made for them by Rudge of Coventry. Unusually, and unwisely, Humber allowed them equal rights to the Humber name, as well as use of the old partnership's patents, which later led to a legal dispute, won by Cooper and Marriott.

In the same year, Humber entered into partnership with T. Harrison Lambert, his riding partner in a famous illustration of the pair on a Humber tandem tricycle. In 1896, C. H. Shacklock, the manager of Humber's Wolverhampton factory, designed a motor car. The same year, Harry Lawson bundled the Humber business with three other firms, floating the new Humber company for a tidy sum, mainly for Lawson. Lawson would attempt to pull similar tricks in the fledgling motor-car industry.

The Lawson-controlled company moved into motorbikes and motor cars in 1896, thanks to Walter Phillips, a former manager with Rudge cycles and a long-time cyclist. A Humber cycle was fitted with a Pennington engine, the first true British motorbike. When it started to make Beeston-Humber motor cars at the turn of the century, the Humber works at Beeston employed 2,000 people.

Humber continued to make bicycles. In 1905, a company advert showed 62 members of royalty, nobility and high society on Humber cycles. In 1932, Humber was taken over by Reginald and William Rootes – and they sold the cycle division to Raleigh.

In 1935, King George VI ordered his first Humber car. In the Second World War, Humber's car factories were converted to military production although the company also made army staff cars, including General "Monty" Montgomery's "Old Faithful." After the war, the former bicycle company won the contract to produce luxury cars for Britain's embassies overseas. In the 1950s and early 1960s, Humber was also the car of choice of British prime ministers. Chrysler acquired the Humber brand from the Rootes Group in 1967, and buried it in 1976.

"Father of the British tractor industry" Dan Albone raced on bicycles made at his Ivel Cycle Works of Biggleswade.

IVEL MOTOR WORKS

On February 15th, 1902, Dan Albone of Biggleswade, Bedfordshire, in the agricultural east of England patented his Ivel Agricultural Motor. London's Science Museum says this was "the first successful light internal-combustion engined agricultural tractor." It was far lighter than the steam traction engines used on farms at the time. Albone also produced an armoured version of his tractor, a forerunner to the military tank. Three years earlier Albone's firm had made bespoke motor cars. A town plaque says "Biggleswade's most famous son" was "Father of the British tractor industry." There are plans to erect a monument to Albone in the town – a plinth and a reconstruction of the world's first tractor – but, for now, there's the Dan Albone Memorial Car Park.

Car park? It ought to be a cycle parking stand, because Albone's background was in making and racing bicycles.

He had been a pioneer cyclist, receiving a boneshaker two-wheeler on his ninth birthday, a hand-me-down from his cousin. In 1873, at the early age of 13, Albone built his first bicycle, a high-wheeler. By the age of 20, "Smiling Dan" Albone had started his own business from home, advertising high-wheeler bicycles for sale, which he manufactured in the outbuildings of the Ongley Arms. He named his firm the Ivel Cycle Works after River Ivel, which flows through Biggleswade. In 1880, to encourage the take-up of cycling in the area – and to create a demand for bicycles in his first year of business – he started the Biggleswade and District Cycling Club. This was both a racing and a touring club, using the (largely deserted) Great North Road as its stamping ground.

His firm later also made tricycles and, in 1886, a Safety bicycle. In the following year he produced a women's Safety bicycle, one of the first made, and in 1891 he patented a forward-facing wicker child-seat for a bicycle, ahead of its time.

After his mother's death in 1883 Albone took over the tenancy of the Ongley Arms. Ten years later he also became landlord of the adjoining Ivel Hotel, rebuilt by a local brewing company, Wells and Co. The town's brewer built back-of-the-hotel premises for Albone's cycle works. The Ivel Cycle Company was employing almost 100 men by 1887, a sizeable and important business for a small market town.

Both the Ongley Arms and the Ivel Hotel were watering holes for the growing number of cyclists on the Great North Road, many of them attracted by the manufacturing and racing fame of their host, "whose cheery nature is proverbial, and who understands the Bohemian and unconventional habits of the record-breaker …"

Albone rode cycles of his own manufacture when racing – first high-wheelers, then tricycles and eventually Safeties. His greatest victory was achieved in September 1888, when he won an international five-kilometre tricycle scratch race in the coastal resort of Scheveningen in the Netherlands.

His business went under, briefly, in 1893 when a recession led to reduced demand for his bicycles but after the peak of the bicycling boom in 1897 his firm was financially solid, and able to use the profits from the sale of bicycles (and, presumably, beer and victuals to cyclists) to explore the potential of the internal combustion engine.

Albone started making motor cars in 1898, selling an early one to the Duke of Bedford. He also made motorbikes, including one for women, hoping to recapture the commercial and critical success of his women's Safety bicycle. (It flopped.)

In April 1899, Albone led a "motor carists … meet at Bedford" where "a party of local pressmen was afterwards taken for short rides … before the motor carists proceeded to Biggleswade, dinner being served at the Ivel Hotel." The party found "the roads in good condition …" as this was "the haunt of record-breaking cyclists."

One of the "motor carists" at Albone's meet was his cycle-racing friend and motor pioneer, Selwyn Edge. He became a director of Albone's Ivel Agricultural Motors and along with fellow pioneer motorist Charles Jarrott they made efforts to interest the British government in both the Ivel tractor and the prototype tank.

JEEP

American satirist P. J. O'Rourke is from Toledo, Ohio. He says his hometown is now a shadow of its former self, partly because many of the automotive jobs the city had long relied on seeped away. Toledo, like Detroit, was once a major centre for making cars. Why? Bicycles. As O'Rourke explained in 2013, this is because "Toledo was America's bicycle capital, with 22 bicycle manufacturers in 1898. Then came the automobile."

"Twenty-two" bicycle manufacturers is pushing it. There were 14 or 15 in the peak year of 1898 (depending how a couple are counted) but there's no disputing that Toledo was one of America's foremost bicycle manufacturing centres, and this was the reason for the later auto factories being in town. In most cases these weren't new concerns building new factories – Toledo's auto factories were set up by bicycle businesses and used bicycle parts to craft the early automobiles, most of which were steam powered. (Steam and electricity were briefly more popular than petrol in the late 1890s and early 1900s.)

Toledo's first automobiles were built in 1899 by the Albert Pope-owned American Bicycle Company. In ABC's Lozier factory, 1,600 workers made bicycles alongside automobiles. ABC – a collection of down-on-their-luck companies united by Pope – became the largest cycle-manufacturing concern in the US. At the Madison Square Garden Auto Show in New York in 1901, ABC – with its Pope-Toledo gasoline-powered car brand – was the largest exhibitor.

Other bicycle makers in Toledo also made automobiles. The Snell Fittings Company partnered with the Kirk Manufacturing Company – two of the largest US manufacturers of bicycle accessories – to produce, in 1903, the Yale automobile.

Following the collapse of ABC a former bicycle man, John North Willys, bought Pope's bicycle plant to make cars for the Overland Motor Company. It was the Overland Motor Company that, in 1941, won the contract to manufacture "Jeeps" for the US military in the Second World War. The Willys MB Jeep, made in a former bicycle factory, is the oldest off-road vehicle and SUV brand. The Jeep inspired a number of other 4x4 vehicles, including the Land Rover, made by the Rover car company of the UK – another car firm that started life as a bicycle company.

LEA-FRANCIS

Between 1922 and 1963, Coventry's Lea & Francis – and variants thereof – made 10,000 or so motor cars, having earlier made motorbikes. The company was founded as a cycle manufacturer in 1895. Graham Inglesby Francis had earlier worked for William Hillman's Auto Machinery Company. Richard Henry Lea had been works manager for cycle manufacturer Singer since 1878. In 1903, Lea-Francis built cars, under licence, for the Singer company.

LEAMINGTON MOTOR CAR WORKS

In 1903, Charles Thomas Crowden supplied Leamington Corporation with its first motorised fire engines. Crowden later built fire tenders for other cities. Earlier, he had made cars, too, and had been involved with Harry Lawson's Great Horseless Carriage Company at the Motor Mills in Coventry. Like Lawson, Crowden had previously been a bicycle designer. In 1884, he had been granted letters patent for a Safety bicycle he produced with Herbert J. Pausey. In 1896 he was chief engineer at Humber, one of Britain's top cycle manufacturers. In 1898, he patented a technique for jointing bicycle tubes using water pressure. This patent was bought by company promoter – and fraudster – Ernest Terah Hooley. The Humber and Hooley connections brought Crowden into contact with Lawson. Crowden became lead engineer at the Motor Mills at the very start of British motor manufacturing, working to produce vehicles by Daimler, Humber and Pennington. The Autocar reported in 1897 that "... great progress is made in the factory of the [Great Horseless Carriage Company]. It is only two months since Mr. Charles Crowden got to work at Coventry, and we have seen the first half-dozen of the carriages that are being put through."

Falling out with Hooley and Lawson – an astute move – Crowden left the Motor Mills in 1898 and by the following year was described as a motor car manufacturer, owner of the Leamington Motor Car Works.

LEWIS

"I beg to apply for permission to use a motor vehicle in the city of Adelaide," wrote Vivian Lewis to the mayor of the South Australian city in 1900. The request for permission was sought in retrospect for Lewis had already started driving his own make of motorised tricycle. Lewis started his business in 1893 as Ormonde Bicycle Depot, changing this to Lewis Cycles Works and, in 1907, to Lewis Cycle and Motor Works.

In 1899, an Australian magazine noted:

> One of the novelties of cycle building has recently been turned out by Mr. Vivian Lewis, of Adelaide. It is a motor triplet cycle, which has been tried in Adelaide streets, found to work admirably, and caused quite a little stir, whilst going through a series of movements in Freeman Street. Mr Lewis is certainly up-to-date at all times, but this – his latest triumph in cycle building – speaks volumes for his work in this colony.

Lewis made motorbikes and motor cars until the 1930s.

MARLBOROUGH ENGINEERING

Marlborough Engineering of New Zealand made Marlborough motor cars from 1912 until the 1920s. Between 1922 and 1928 the firm made the Carlton brand of motor car. Company founder John North Birch was a bicycle-maker in the 1880s and 1890s, latterly working from the Foleshill Cycle Works near Coventry, England. He emigrated to New Zealand in 1905.

MORRIS

What was it about 1930s motor barons and strong national government-by-dictator? Ford admired Hitler (the feeling was mutual) and Oxford's William Richard Morris admired English fascist leader Oswald Mosley – so much so that he bankrolled him.

Morris and Ford were cut from the same cloth – small-town founders of micro businesses that grew massively and who wouldn't hand corporate control to others. Like Ford, Morris had been a keen cyclist in his youth. Morris was a successful racing cyclist in Oxfordshire and surrounding counties. In 1900, he took part in a ten-mile time trial in Oxford that Lionel Martin also entered. Morris beat the later co-founder of Aston Martin by a tiny margin. In later life, the many cycling trophies Morris had won took pride of place in his spartan office.

In 1955, Morris's biographers Andrews and Brunner noted:

> Everyone knows something of the story of the apprentice in a bicycle repairing shop, who soon came to have a bicycle shop of his own, then a flourishing garage, and then became one of the largest motor vehicle manufacturers in the country. Lord Nuffield has become a legend in his own lifetime … Anyone who expects to meet a big industrial magnate sitting in a luxurious office will have a shock … [Lord Nuffield's office is a] narrow, plainly furnished room … The really prominent feature of the room … is a glass case hanging over the fireplace, which contains numerous medals and badges, which recall vividly one activity of their owner – his considerable prowess as a cyclist.

By the 1930s, Morris was Europe's biggest automobile manufacturer and had made a fortune. He gave away much of this money, especially to medical charities. For his benevolence – despite his fondness for the blackshirts – he was later ennobled as Viscount Nuffield.

His first enterprise was a bicycle repair shop, started in 1893 and operated from a brick shed behind his parents' house in Oxford. He also made his own brand of bicycle, and raced it too, becoming county champion over distances from one to 50 miles. Morris met his wife through a cycling club. He and Elizabeth Maud Anstey went on many cycle tours together.

Through graft and guile Morris built up a successful bicycle business, with rented premises in Oxford. The entry "William Richard Morris, cycle maker," appeared for the first time in the Oxford commercial directories for

1896–7. He outgrew his home business. In the 1901 *Oxford Directory* he advertised himself as "W. R. Morris, Practical Cycle Maker and Repairer, 48 High Street and … James Street, Oxford. Sole maker of the celebrated Morris cycles." Morris built an oversize 27-inch frame bicycle for the rector of a local church, which was a rolling advertisement for his business. Andrews and Brunner describe this bicycle as the "first Morris vehicle."

Morris won his last cycle race in 1904 and had interests in bicycle retail businesses in Oxford until 1908. The profits from his bicycle shops enabled Morris to invest in making motorbikes with Joseph Cooper, an old cycle-racing friend. In 1912, Morris started making small cars from a factory in Cowley, Oxford. By 1924, Morris held a 51-percent share of the domestic market for motor cars.

Despite his fame as Britain's biggest car magnate, Morris remained connected with the bicycle industry. He was a member of the exclusive and still extant Pickwick Bicycle Club, the world's oldest cycling club. Members are known by pseudonyms taken from *The Pickwick Papers* by Charles Dickens. Morris was "Joseph Smiggers."

Cycle racer William Morris ploughed the profits from his bicycle shop into a motor business, rising to become one of Britain's richest men. He was ennobled as Lord Nuffield.

NAPIER

Before Rolls-Royce became Britain's leading brand of luxury car – thanks to the Silver Ghost – that position was occupied by the Napier motor car. Napier was a company that, since 1895, had produced parts for the growing bicycle industry. Montague Napier bought his grandfather's engineering business from the executors of his father's estate. Napier & Son relaunched by producing machine tools for bicycle manufacturers. In 1899 his friend – and fellow cyclist – Selwyn Edge suggested that Napier ought to produce parts for the new motor-car industry. This developed into a company making upmarket automobiles. Napier started by copying Edge's Panhard-Levassor motor car. Edge and Napier became business partners. Edge drove a Napier car to victory in the 1902 Gordon Bennett Cup, the first British victory in an international motor race. Later Napier built aircraft engines. By the mid-1920s, half of all British aircraft were powered by Napier engines. Napier – like Edge – was a member of the Bath Road Cycling Club.

The Winning Napier with S. F. Edge, the Driver, and Mr. Napier, the Constructor of the Vehicle

Montague Napier and Selwyn Edge were both former racing cyclists.

The Opel brothers Carl, Wilhelm, Heinrich, Fritz and Ludwig.

OPEL

The Opel company started making cars in 1899. Prior to that the company made bicycles, and it continued to do so alongside automobiles until February 1937. Opel was one of the top manufacturers of bicycles in Europe, having sold nearly three million since making its first in 1886. The firm went on to become one of the top automobile makers in Europe. The company was founded by Adam Opel, originally as a sewing machine maker. He did not live to see the company's first automobile.

His sons – Carl, Wilhelm, Heinrich, Friedrich and Ludwig – were all champion bicycle racers on Adam Opel bicycles. Wilhelm took over the company after his father's death and started the production of automobiles.

In 1926, Herbert Duncan said: "As in other countries, the cycle played an amazing part in launching many men into the automobile industry; and this is particularly the position in Germany. The Opel family must be especially mentioned ..."

Friedrich (or Fritz) was the most successful cyclist among the Opel brothers, winning more than 180 races, including the 620-km Basel–Kleve race in 1894. Wilhelm founded the Academic Cycling Club at the Technische Hochschule (Technical University) at Darmstadt, which later became the Corps Franconia Darmstadt, a right-wing student fraternity.

ORIENT

It is one of history's givens that Henry Ford's Model T sold in its millions because it was the first automobile marketed to the masses, at a time when all other motor car manufacturers only made luxury cars for the elite. In fact, like much of the received wisdom concerning Ford, it's plain wrong. Five years before the introduction of the Model T, the Waltham Manufacturing Co. of Waltham, Massachusetts, was advertising "The Lowest Priced Automobile in the World!" The

Waltham Manufacturing Company's Victoriette, 1900.

1903 $450 Orient Buckboard was light and cheap, and quickly became one of the top-selling automobiles of the day, with strong domestic and overseas sales. "They sell like bicycles," claimed a 1903 advert.

And Waltham Manufacturing Co. would know all about bicycles because the Orient had been one of America's best-known brands of bicycle throughout the 1890s. The Orient brand was the brainchild of cycle racer, engineer and inventor Charles Herman Metz. Metz was a Utica, New York, bicycle champion and bicycle-parts manufacturer who upped sticks to Massachusetts in 1893, buying into Waltham Manufacturing Co. in order to exploit the technical expertise of Waltham's precision engineers (it had been a watch-making town) and to expand his production capacity. Back in New York, Metz had worked for the Orient Fire Insurance Company, giving him the inspiration for the name of his upmarket bicycle brand, which at first specialised in lightweight racing bikes, with parts designed by Metz. He was granted more than 20 patents for his bicycle innovations, including improvements to pedals, frames, handlebars and, in 1900, gears.

Metz was a prime mover behind the creation of the Waltham Bicycle Park, a dirt racing track where a great many speed records were broken, including on Orient bicycles. In 1898, Metz placed a motor on the back of an adapted tandem to be used as pacer cycle in front of track cyclists. Metz later claimed that the Orient-Aster was, in effect, the first American "motor cycle." Metz certainly had the salesman's touch – as a publicity stunt, the Waltham Manufacturing Co. produced a ten-seater cycle in 1898, the Oriten.

Metz moved into automobiles in 1898 (while still manufacturing the Orient range of bicycles), testing out his ideas for motorised quadricycles and tricycles, and also creating an electric car. Metz used the Aster gasoline motor from France. Waltham Manufacturing Co. was the engine company's American agent.

In 1900, *Automobile* said that the Orient "autogo" was:

> … the first vehicle of this sort to be made in this country, and is the product of French ingenuity linked with the best American mechanism. Easily handled, it represents a style of motor vehicle destined to become popular … of interest more particularly, perhaps, to the cycling enthusiast who has graduated from the push and whose enthusiasm has commenced to drift towards the self-propelled vehicle.

The Orient Runabout, the company's first commercially available motor car, was introduced in 1901, priced at $875. Metz left the Waltham Manufacturing Co. in 1902, becoming technical editor of the trade magazine *Cycle and Automobile Trade Journal*. He returned in 1908 (having meanwhile been making the C.H. Metz brand of track-pacing motor cycles, as used by the National Cycling Association). Despite producing the cheapest automobile in America, the Waltham Manufacturing Co. wasn't very profitable and Metz was charged with turning round its fortunes. By 1915, Metz Company had produced over 7,200 cars, but competition from the Ford Model T – and the fact the American government claimed his aeroplane factory during the First World War – eventually put Metz out of business. He produced his last automobile in 1923.

OVERMAN AUTOMOBILE

In the 1890s, the most important American bicycle barons were former Civil War colonels – Albert Pope and Albert Overman. Both would diversify into motor cars. Overman's bicycle brand was the Victor. Overman's short-lived car was also called the Victor and was produced by the Overman Automobile Company between 1900 and 1904. Overman plumped for steam as the motive force, while Pope favoured electricity. Pope and Overman hated each other but they could agree on one thing – the cyclist-led campaign for improved roads. In the 1890s, both were funding the Good Roads campaign spearheaded by the League of American Wheelmen.

PEUGEOT

France's Peugeot, in the milling business since 1810, produced a steam-powered carriage in 1889. Only four were made. By 1890 the company was making a gasoline-powered motor car. But this wasn't Peugeot's first road vehicle

– that had been a high-wheeler bicycle, Armand Peugeot's "Le Grand Bi," built in 1882. The Peugeot company would produce both bicycles and motor cars until 1926, when Cycles Peugeot split from the motor-car company. In 1895, *The Autocar* said: "The peculiar adaptability of the cycle trade for the construction of [autocars] has already been recognised in France, Messrs. Peugeot being already well-known as cycle builders …"

PIERCE-ARROW

Pierce-Arrow motor cars of Buffalo, New York, were deluxe vehicles favoured by pashas, princes and presidents. The firm made its large cars from the early 1900s to 1938. Prior to 1901, Pierce-Arrow was a bicycle manufacturer. The founder company was established in 1865 as Heinz, Pierce and Munschauer, a maker of gilded bird cages and bath-tubs. In 1872, George N. Pierce bought out Heinz and Munschauer, and changed the firm's name to George N. Pierce Company. By 1888 the firm was making cycles, famous for the arrow frame badge. It didn't give up making two-wheelers when it started to make automobiles, and carried on making bicycles until 1915.

PUCH

Puch of Austria started making motor cars in 1904. Its luxury models were supplied to the Austrian royal family. Much later the company became known for its motorbikes and mopeds but Puch was originally a bicycle brand.

Company founder Johann Puch, from Slovenia, made his first cycles in 1889 in a small workshop in Graz. Erste Steiermärkische Fahrradfabrik – or the First Styrian Bicycle Company – was absorbed into Austro-Daimler in 1928 to become Austro-Daimler-Puchwerke. Another merger in 1934 saw the company become Steyr-Daimler-Puch.

RAMBLER

The Thomas B. Jeffery Company of Kenosha, Wisconsin made Rambler-brand motor cars between 1902 and 1916. In the first year of production, the Rambler became the second best-selling automobile in America, after Ransom Old's Oldsmobile. Thomas Buckland Jeffery named his motor car the Rambler because that's what he had called his Safety bicycle. Jeffery – along with school friend R. Phillip Gormully – started producing cycles in 1881.

In 1902, *The Automobile* praised Jeffery for his Rambler automobile and stressed that it followed Jeffery's 20 years'

A full-page advertisement in The Automobile *magazine in 1900 had two former bicycle manufacturers next to each other.*

experience making bicycles or, as the magazine called them, "manumotive vehicles":

> Wherever in the world a bicycle is ridden there is the name of Thomas B. Jeffery known. What the Rambler bicycle was to the manumotive vehicle the Rambler automobile will be to the motor one. The Thomas B. Jeffery who designed and built the Rambler bicycle did the same thing for the Rambler automobile, and the more than twenty years he spent in the study of the manumotive vehicle has not been lost sight of in the three years he has devoted to perfecting the automobile …

The first Jeffery-and-Gormully cycle – "The American" – was a high-wheeler, a copy of Starley and Hillman's "Ariel." Jeffery was born in Devon, England, emigrating to America at the age of 18 and settling in Chicago. In 1879, while visiting the land of his birth, he saw his first high-wheeler cycle. As a maker of scientific instruments he figured he could make his own cycles and went into partnership with Gormully, initially importing parts from England and assembling cycles in America.

The Gormully & Jeffery Manufacturing Company became America's second biggest cycle company, after Pope. The Rambler name was applied to Gormully & Jeffery's first Safety bicycle. Jeffery designed his first motor car in 1897. The Gormully & Jeffery Manufacturing Company was the forerunner to the Thomas B. Jeffery Company, which became Nash Motors, and so was one of the ancestor companies of American Motors and Chrysler.

RILEY

The Riley car was produced in Britain from 1905 to 1969. The brand is now owned by BMW. The firm began as the Bonnick Cycle Company in Coventry, which was bought out by William Riley Jr. in the 1880s. Riley had been in the weaving business and when this went into decline he sought a way into the cycle industry thanks to his enthusiasm for cycling. In 1898, his sons took the business into the manufacture of automobiles.

ROLLS-ROYCE

The daredevil aristocrat Charles Stewart Rolls, third son of the Welsh 1st Baron Llangattock, was an early racing driver, motor-car promoter and aviator. His partnership with Henry Royce of Manchester led to the creation in 1904 of Rolls-Royce. Rolls had become a motorist ten years earlier, having been shown his first motor car by motoring pioneer and cyclist Sir David Salomons of Tunbridge Wells.

"Rolls grew up in the age of the bicycle and readily embraced the spirit of individualism, science, and speed which it symbolized," says his profile in the Oxford Dictionary of National Biography. Herbert Duncan wrote in 1926 that "Like all prominent motorists, [Rolls] was a speedy cyclist." In 1895 Rolls began a mechanical and applied science course at Trinity College, Cambridge, and became a competitive cyclist, on solo bikes as well as tandems and a four-man cycle. By 1897 he was captain of the university cycle racing team and earned a "half blue" university sports award for his cycling.

Rolls attended the International Road Congress in 1908 as a delegate of the Royal Automobile Club and the Roads Improvement Association. Also in 1908 Rolls travelled to Le Mans in France to meet the aviation pioneer – and former bicycle shop owner – Wilbur Wright. Rolls was one of the first to fly with Wright. On July 12th, 1910, while taking part in a flying tournament at Bournemouth, the 32-year-old Rolls crashed, becoming the first Briton to be killed in a fixed-wing smash.

ROOTES

The Rootes Group was a dominant British automobile manufacturer, and parent company of many well-known British marques, including Hillman, Humber, Singer and Sunbeam. These all began life as bicycle brands. The

Rootes Group – a name that ultimately disappeared when it became part of Chrysler Europe – was founded from a Kent bicycle shop. William Rootes Snr started a bicycle business in the early 1890s, making and selling the Trusty brand of bicycle. His son, also called William, became Baron Rootes thanks to the creation of a motor business that, by 1960, had an annual output of 200,000 motor vehicles. The roots of the Rootes Group can be traced to Goudhurst, a village in Kent, where Rootes Snr. traded from Church House.

His son William was born in 1894 in Goudhurst, ten miles from Tunbridge Wells, the venue for Britain's first motor show, held in October 1895 and staged by CTC trustee Sir David Salomons. Rootes Snr. visited this Horseless Carriage Exhibition and became interested in motor cars. In 1898, he moved his bicycle business to the nearby village of Hawkhurst and, from a building that now houses a picture framing business, started stocking motor accessories, too.

His sons William and Reginald turned the business into a motor agency, selling Singer cars. By the mid-1920s Rootes Ltd was one of the largest motor car distributors in Britain. By the end of that decade, the Rootes brothers had started acquiring marques – first Hillman and Humber, then Sunbeam and eventually Singer.

ROVER

John Kemp Starley, one of Britain's most unsung engineers, designed an early motor car, a battery-powered tricycle developed in 1888. However, his greater claim to motoring fame is for using the name Rover. Today's Land Rover – a brand known all over the world – can be traced back to J. K. Starley's Rover Safety bicycle, the machine that, according to later company adverts, "set the fashion to the world." The 1885 Rover Safety went through a number of important changes before becoming, in 1888, a recognisably modern bicycle.

Starley's Rover bikes were so called because their riders were free to rove.

Starley & Sutton Co. was based in Coventry thanks to John Kemp's uncle, James Starley, one of the key pioneers of cycling. In 1889, the company became J. K. Starley & Co. and, in the late 1890s, it became the Rover Cycle Company. This started manufacturing Rover cars in 1904, three years after J. K. Starley's death. Rover was later managed by J. K. Starley Jnr., who kept up a connection with the bicycle trade via membership of the Pickwick Bicycle Club.

An early Rover Safety bicycle. It has solid tyres. The equestrian is included in the illustration to show that a Safety bicycle could outpace a galloping horse.

SIDDELEY

John Davenport Siddeley founded the Siddeley Autocar Company in 1902. Later moving into equipping the armed forces, Siddeley received a knighthood in 1932 for the engine supplied to Vickers for their tanks. Siddeley engines powered the majority of the RAF's bombers in the First World War. Fabulously rich, in 1937 Siddeley purchased Kenilworth Castle and in the same year was raised to the peerage. Baron Kenilworth started his career as a shirt cutter (his father was a hosier) but, via his interest in cycle racing with the Anfield Bicycle Club, he studied at night school to become a design draughtsman and by 1891 was working as a cycle designer for the Humber Cycle Company of Beeston, Nottingham. He also organised Land's-End-to-John-O'Groats record rides, by Humber riders, in 1891 and 1892. He joined the riders at some locations, pacing them by riding his own lightweight racing bicycle. For a time, Siddeley was also manager of the Rover Cycles' race team. In 1897, he became managing director of the Clipper Pneumatic Tyre Company, which licensed the bicycle clincher tyre patent owned by the company that produced Dunlop cycle tyres. Via Clipper tyres, he entered the motor trade, forming the Siddeley Autocar Company to produce cars licensed from the French bicycle-and-motor car brand Peugeot. During the First World War he won government orders for Siddeley-Deasy military motor cars and trucks, and moved into the production of aero engines.

In 1919, Siddeley-Deasy merged with Armstrong-Whitworth to become Armstrong Siddeley and, in the 1920s, Siddeley started making the Armstrong Siddeley luxury motor car, a brand that lived on until 1960.

SINGER

Lionel Martin, the racing cyclist who co-founded Aston Martin, first succeeded in the motor business by souping up a Singer motor car and winning the Aston hill-climb in 1914. Singer was founded in Coventry in 1874 by George Singer, who started by making high-wheeler bicycles.

Singer was born in Dorset and moved to Coventry to join William Hillman and James Starley at the Coventry Sewing Machine Company. All three had worked for marine engineering company John Penn in Greenwich. At the company that became Coventry Machinists they made early high-wheeler bicycles. Hillman and Starley left to form their own company in 1870, while Singer stayed until 1874 before doing the same. In 1878, Singer patented a type of raked fork, a design still used on many bicycles today. Singer was mayor of Coventry between 1891 and 1893.

In 1896, the high-society magazine *Cycling World Illustrated* said:

> The makers of cycles and their component parts … are at the present time enjoying a period of entirely unexampled prosperity. In Coventry, the home of the trade … this wonderful activity has been more especially noticeable … Of Messrs. Singer's cycles and methods of manufacture … it is difficult to speak without seeming to over praise …

In 1901, Singer motorised a tricycle, his company's first foray into motor car manufacturing. Four years later, Singer built a car under licence from Lea-Francis. Lea had earlier worked for Singer. George Singer died in 1909. The company was by then producing cars designed in-house. Singer cars were made, latterly as part of Rootes Group, until 1970.

STAR MOTOR COMPANY

The Star Motor Company of Wolverhampton made motor cars from 1898 to 1932. At its peak, Star produced around 1,000 cars a year. In later years more than a quarter of Star's production was exported, mainly to Australia and New Zealand. Writing in a bicycle magazine, racing driver Selwyn Edge said in 1900 that the Star was "the best car of its class yet produced."

The Star Motor Company started life in 1883 as the Star Cycle Company, founded by racing cyclist Edward Lisle, who had built his first bicycle in the mid-1870s. In 1876, he went into partnership with Edwin John Sharratt, with whom he made high-wheeler bicycles in the former Humber factory on Pountney Street in Wolverhampton. When the partnership foundered, Lisle created the Star Cycle Company. At the peak of the bicycle boom in 1896, the company was producing 10,000 bicycles per year.

In 1898, engineers at the Star Cycle Company disassembled and copied a Benz Velocipede motor car, marketing it as a Star-Benz. While Lisle ran the Star Motor Company, Lisle's son – also called Edward – took over the running of the Star Cycle Company. Confusingly, this company also made motor cars, badged as Starlings.

SUNBEAM

Before the First World War Sunbeam of Wolverhampton made its name by producing the fastest cars in the world. Designed by Frenchman Louis Coatalen – who had earlier worked for Hillman, another car brand with bicycle roots – Sunbeam racing cars had powerful engines and, importantly, pencil-shaped aerodynamically efficient "wind-cutting" exteriors, a new idea. Sunbeam cars won the French Grand Prix in 1923 and the Spanish Grand Prix in 1924. The Sunbeam 350hp established land-speed records in 1922 and was bought by Malcolm Campbell, who renamed it the Blue Bird. In 1924, Campbell set a new record speed of 146.16 miles per hour, raising the mark the following year to over 150 miles per hour. A 1,000-hp Sunbeam captured the record in 1927 at Daytona Beach, USA, the first car to exceed 200 miles per hour. Despite setting all these speed records – a sales ploy to sell its standard touring cars – Sunbeam also made cycles, and had done so since 1887. Sunbeam continued to make bicycles alongside motor cars until the brand's demise in 1937.

Sunbeam was founded in 1887 by John Marston, from an old land-owning family. He was also the owner of a japanning factory, which made black lacquered pots and plates with gold trim, and decided to make cycles because he was a keen tricyclist. The japanware factory was renamed Sunbeamland. Sunbeam added motor cars to its range in 1903.

Sunbeam's most famous customer was the composer Sir Edward Elgar, who bought a Royal Sunbeam bicycle in 1900 and called it "Mr. Phobeus." (He bought another in 1903 and called that Mr. Phobeus, too.) Sunbeam bicycles were nearly twice the price of other bicycles – and were painted black, with gold trim.

Marston founded the Villiers Cycle Components Company in 1898 to make pedals and cycle components for Sunbeam. It was Villiers – based in a former coach-house in Upper Villiers Street, Wolverhampton – that made the first Sunbeam motor cars.

Marston became the first president of the Wolverhampton Automobile Club, but he preferred cycling to driving. Each morning an employee in uniform would set off to Marston's house, riding a cycle and holding the chairman's cycle as it wheeled alongside. Marston would then mount the proffered cycle and pedal to Sunbeamland, the employee riding discreetly behind.

TRIUMPH MOTOR COMPANY

Triumph is a famous English motor-car and motorbike marque. The company was founded in 1886 by a German, Siegfried Bettmann, who moved to England at the age of 20. Bettmann made bicycles and operated the Triumph Cycle Company and the Gloria Cycle Company. During Queen Victoria's Diamond Jubilee in 1897, Bettmann presented the diminutive monarch with two silver-plated Triumph bicycles. Bettmann moved into motorbikes in 1902, becoming Britain's leading maker by 1918. In 1913, Bettmann became mayor of Coventry, his adopted home city. Triumph, while still making bicycles, started making motor cars in the 1920s. The cycle division was sold to Raleigh in 1932, much to Bettmann's chagrin (he tried to buy it back in 1936). Triumph motorbikes sold well in America, and are still sold today. Triumph made its last car in 1981. The trademark has been owned by BMW since 1994.

UNIC

UNIC was a French truck manufacturer. It sprang from Société des Cycles Georges Richard, an 1890s bicycle manufacturer. (See plates.) Georges Richard started building cars in 1900, originally under licence from Vivinus of Belgium. He raced his own cars but was ousted from the company (partly for racing his own cars). In 1905, he formed Société Anonyme des Automobiles UNIC, which later specialised in commercial vehicles. It's now part of the IVECO group.

WINTON MOTOR CARRIAGE COMPANY

The Winton Motor Carriage Company of Cleveland, Ohio placed one of the first automobile adverts ever seen in a mainstream American magazine. It appeared in *Scientific American* in 1898, backing up favourable editorial copy, and told readers that they could now "dispense with a horse" thanks to a "handsomely strong" vehicle that had "Suspension Wire Wheels. Pneumatic Tires. Ball Bearings." These three sales points for the Winton Motor Carriage were technology transfers from the bicycle. The company was founded and run by Alexander Winton, a Scottish-born bicycle manufacturer who had created the Winton Bicycle Company in Cleveland in 1890.

The 1898 coverage in *Scientific American* worked: Winton sold 22 hand-built cars that year, at $1,000 a pop. Horses, it seemed to some, were history. In 1897, long before worries about sexual discrimination, a Cleveland newspaper wrote:

> Alas! Poor equine. If the anticipations of Alexander Winton, of the Winton Bicycle Co., will be ultimately realised, the horse will slowly but inevitably drop into oblivion. Mr Winton has succeeded in perfecting a carriage which can be operated [even] by a woman … The carriage, which is at present at the works of the Winton Bicycle Co., Cleveland, is a peculiar but not ungainly looking object …

In an 1896 issue of *The Horseless Age*, Winton was described as the mechanical superintendent at the Winton Bicycle Company; in fact, he was company founder and part-owner. He had been born in 1860 in Grangemouth, Scotland and served an apprenticeship in the shipyards of the Clyde. He arrived in America, along with other

Alexander Winton.

family members, at the age of 20. He worked first at an iron works in New York City before moving in 1884 to be with his sister in Cleveland. He found work at the town's Phoenix Iron Works. Six years later, and by now an enthusiastic cyclist, he started making his own bicycle parts, some of which used his improved and patented means of installing ball bearings. With cash support from his brother-in-law Thomas W. Henderson, he founded the Winton Bicycle Company in 1890, making complete bicycles. He patented a number of bicycle innovations, one of which – a split bottom bracket of 1892 – was cited in a patent by Cannondale Bicycle Corporation as late as 2010. His advertising motto was "The Winton is a Winner" and Winton bicycles were described as "flush-joint beauties" which were "light, strong, easy-running, durable."

Later a specialist in bevel-gear shaft-drive bicycles, Winton would use shaft-drives in his early motor cars. He made his first motor car in 1896, the same year that Henry Ford produced his Quadricycle. Like the Quadricycle, Winton's first car used a great many bicycle parts.

In a book about Winton, Bernie Golias wrote that "people tend to equate Henry Ford with all the major automotive accomplishments, but if you take a look at the early patents, Winton held the groundbreakers in automotive development."

There are other connections with Detroit's most famous cyclist. In 1899, Leo Melanowski, Winton's chief engineer, invited Ford to Cleveland for an interview at the Winton auto works, but he wasn't hired; and in 1901 Winton and Ford raced their cars on the Detroit Driving Club's race track at Grosse Pointe, Michigan, competing against each other to see who had the fastest and most reliable car. Thanks to an assumed mechanical failure, Ford won, even though Winton was one of the most successful – and fastest – racing drivers of the day. In a second race the following year bicycle racer Barney Oldfield raced a Ford against Winton, besting him again.

The Winton Motor Carriage Company was incorporated in March 1897, with Henderson as vice-president. To prove his car's durability, Winton drove one on an 800-mile endurance run from Cleveland to New York City, later repeating the trip with newspaper sponsorship and a journalist on board to write up the trip in daily dispatches – a publicity coup for Winton and, because the newspaper articles were syndicated across America, a coup for the reliability of automobiles in general. In 1903, a Winton became the first car to cross America coast to coast, with Dr. Horatio Nelson Jackson, Winton's mechanic, and a dog they acquired in Idaho. Bud the dog didn't like the dust thrown up from the roads, so was provided with his own motoring goggles.

Long-time cycle journalist Henry Sturmey wrote in Britain's *The Autocar* that the 1899 Winton Motor Carriage was "substantially built, exceedingly easy to ride in, and well calculated to stand the rough work of American roads." Winton, the bicycle builder, was now the biggest gasoline-powered car-maker in the US, beaten in size only by electric car specialist Colonel Albert Pope. Winton's first cars used tillers to steer; in 1900 he started to use steering wheels, an innovation he gifted to Henry Ford.

In the early 1900s Winton was one of a number of famous motorists who took part in races in Europe, such as the annual Gordon Bennett Cup. His name was mentioned in breathless newspaper and automobile prose alongside former racing cyclists such as Belgium's Chevalier René de Knyff, France's Fernand Charron and England's Selwyn Edge.

Winton carried on making cars until 1924 but, as a craftsman builder, he was unable to keep pace with mass-market specialists such as Henry Ford. Perhaps if Winton had hired Ford back in 1899, history might have turned out very differently.

APPENDIX C

KICKSTARTER SUPPORTERS

Thanks to the following individuals for their support of the pre-publication book. These names are in pledge-type order, not alphabetical. I've left the names as they were typed rather than correct for capitalisation and so on. Not everybody supplied a second name on their pledger details; some gave avatar names.

Philip Benstead
Nik Windle
Ines Carvalho de Azevedo
Rob Archer
William Kennedy
Kass Schmitt
Robert Addison
Albert Reid
Rachel HolmesLudovic Roguet
Eric Joanis
Dorr St.Clair
Michael Josephy
Elijah Rayfield
jinjer Stanton
Sally Robertson
gary ryan
Troy Donovan
Strangeway
Nicholas Bignell
Bryan Lorber
Sergey Kozyr
Ralph Dadswell
Niels
Kevin Hasley
James Robb
Matija Nalis
Eric Damon Walters
Chris Dent
Stuart Trigg
Luca Reina
Mike Hartley
Angus Hewlett
Ben Bowskill
Eifion Francis
Jon H Ballentine
victor fagence
Clare Causier
Kris Wills
hillary weisman
Gregory 'Profeta' Chauvet
drew
David Frederick Swindells
B.J. Green
Sam Pearce
Alex Norelli
Clive Matthews
Christopher Orme
Jeffrey Miles-Shenton
Bridget Kahn

Aaron E. Bradshaw
Sarah Eveline King
David Alan Greening
Kathryn Reid Moore
Richie Brian
Jonathan Frascella
Matt Thyer
Roy
Melvin Bailey
The Warmans
Karey Harrison
Tom Sulston
Christopher Fox
Steve Nielson
Tim Stredwick
Hester Wells
Scott Dedenbach
Kelly McNamara
naath
Marsha Jackson
Jesper Berggreen
Jacqueline Campbell
Jerry McKinley
Richard Evans
steve
tedder
Peter Carpenter
Martin Packer
Juan Miguel ExpÃ³sito
Hans-Peter Hemmer
Sindre
Edmond Rosen
Marc Vendetti
Simon Proven
Stephen Metcalfe
Stephen Taylor
Kerry White
Robert Hedges
Paul Keiffer
John-Patrick Stacey
T
Chris Dorling
Anthony McDougle
Jules Graybill
Allen Dickie
Karen Dalby
Bradley Dean
Stuart Duckworth
Bob Imrie

Nigel Clark
antony arnold
simonmilligan
Peter March
Maggi
Michael Charland
Craig Drown
Fiona Cooper
Luke Smith
Stewart Duncan
David Churchill
Mark Philpotts
Joseph Farthing
Trent Fisher
Sandy Brelsford
David Houghton
Paul Myers
Phill Price
Naomi Rush
Kevin Hopps
Martin
Mark Stallard
Bob MacQueen
Seamus Kelly
Jon Sparks
Paul j Walsh
Ashley Burrows
Stepan Chizhov
Robert Dunlop
Rod Whitworth
David Gallagher
Vivian Sayward
Andreas Kambanis
Tara Goddard
Dipesh Navsaria
Rick Rubio
Ben Wooliscroft
Paul Shealy
Michael Berg
Chip Smith
Margaret Batson
Edd Cochran
Victoria Shockey
Richard Boggs
gisella_a
David Hunter
Monika Gause
Nevin Liber
Jonathan Streete

g. gnielka
Don Springhetti
Victor A Eichhorn
Pento Stefano
Oscar Velarde
Erin McWalter
Bryce Bederka
Bill Turner
Sylvia Lindman
Bryan Beretta
Heath Dayrit
Pim Zwaard
Mark von Wodtke
Ho-Sheng Hsiao
Paul Megson
Deborah Cole
Michael Drew
Jim Baltaxe
Lea Tui
J.E. Sawyer
Mark Carlson
John Wills Lloyd
Patrick Brady
Gavin Bell
dave robinson
Stephen M. Greenberg
Eric Norris
Frances Chaloner
Simon Daw
Sam Joslin
Vincent Docherty
Martin Ashby
natb
Chelle Destefano
John Grocoick
Mike Gordon
Michael Prescott
David Robertson
Greg thomas
Brad W. Bartlett
Tina Bach
Karen Canady
Peter Moisan
Anthony Morley
Martin Lucas-Smith
Andrew Knights
Terry Duckmanton
Jeremy Strutt
Pierre Riteau

Jack Thurston
Ian Walker
Steven Hope
Gaz
Stephen Psallidas
Paul Timlett
Graham Clark
Matthew Hardy
Dave Barter
Jez Higgins
Dave Warnock
Peter Watson
Andrew Curry
Keith Robertson
Peter Whitelegg
Christopher Peck
Mad Biker
Graham Fereday
Alex Ingram
Jonny Haynes
John Krug
Steve Worland RIP
Terry Coaker
Sarah G Palmer
Mike Hall
Susan E Spinks
Richard Williams
Philip Johnston
Rich Cassidy
David Ryan
Paul Holdsworth
Norman Oxtoby
Pascal Desmond
JCorvesor
Paul Jakma
Paul Kohn
james holloway
Greg Collins
Peter Wilson
David Smith
Tim Mullett
Chris Davey
Justin
Nadya Labib
Christopher Juden
Nigel Shoosmith
Robert Weeks
Peter Owen
Peter Bull
Roger John Davis
Dennis Fitton
Toby Churchill
Ivor Hewitt
Colin Jago
howard sprange
road.cc
Tom Finnie
Parimal Kumar
Greg Hodgson
John Broderick
Adam Pride
Martin Lucy
Dario Demarco

Darryl Rayner
Dave Holladay
Abby Hone
Dave Minter
David Wellbeloved
TJ Alexander
christian wolmar
Gerald Wyatt
Mike Trinder
Jim Stuart
Russell Merry
Richard Palmer
Yoav Tzabar
Stephen Ball
Paul Robison
Timothy Harris
John Olson
David Fong
Philip Passmore
Brian Brunswick
Christopher Sauvarin
Yannick Read
Gary Dawes
Konrad Kielczykowski
Peter Hawkins
Keith Day
Harriet Bazley
Jonathan Simpson
Paul Sims
Thomas Bennett
Gregory Cowan
Gregory Williams
Alan Jones
Michael Davis
Steve Woodward
GODtower
Michael Pospieszalski
Rob Hague
Steve Bradley
Marc Eberhard
Scott Wall
Colin Howden
Sigurd Gudd
Roy McNeill
Ian Bray
Owen Smith
Simon Bannister
James Clarke
Sue Abbott
Jonathan
David MacArthur Scott Kinnen
Guy B Roebuck
COLIN ROLLAND
Michael Kidd
David Mundow
David StephenCrampton
Ron Fellows
Martin T Randall
Colin Campbell
Richard Warren
Magnus Lagher
Peter G. Taylor-Anderson
Ed Loach

Shannon Robalino
Ian Jones
Mike Croker
Michael Gaze
Chris Jones
Martyn Legg
David Gibbon
David Winch
Robert Pugsley
Tony Raven
Nick Hubble
John Woodruff
Andy Hunter
Robert O'Brien
John Bacon
Robert Harber
Daniel Hones
Ian Pretswell
Jenni Gwiazdowski
John Drydon Edwards
David Oxley
BRUCE MACRAE JEFFREY
Jonathan McGarry
Alexander Allan
Michi Mathias
David Moerel
ian t
Peter Kidd
Tony Hewson
Pete Ruse
Viv Marsh
Richard Gordge
nunuboogie
Tim Blackwell
Tibs
Kieran Taylor
Neil Mansfield
David Warner
Robert Dingwall
Peter Lyons-Lewis
Nick Lewis
Andrew Harker
James Speakman
John Daniels
Lorenzo Hermoso
Ian Denton
Mark Dempsey
Jessica Hawkins
Shane de Jersey
Patrick Carr
Shana Worthen
Francis King
Robert Nolan
Alan Robinson
James Orloff
Simon MacMichael
Gary Bandy
Christopher Kenmore
MARK ANDREW HARRISON
Mr Chris Robson
Samanfur
Carl Pettman
Phil Wain

Keith Byrne
James Cobb
Julian Fox
Rob Brewer
Tom mcclelland
Thom Sanders
Jonathan Sanderson
Scott Dawson
Samuel Quemby
Steve Pineger
Barry Bogin
Mark Drury
Rachel Aldred
Adam Burgess
Steve Scanlan
Beth Nobles
Andy Arthur
Oscar Montiel
Michael Roth
Derryl Cocks
Kasey van Puijenbroek
Lyneke Onderwater
Kerry Palmer
Heikki Rautanen
BeeDee
David Palan
Santiago Gorostiza Langa
David Tuttle
Peter Snoeren
Iain Cummings
Mark Homewood
David kuehn
Dale Calkins
Todd Scott
Peter Goodman
Alan Nordin
Mark Hartsuyker
Clement T. Cole
Mark Dwight
Jim Vance
Frode P. Bergsager
Steve & Donna Hess
tstarback
Carlos Saul Duque
Joseph RJ Studlick
Paul Deaton
David Hartley
Davide Zulli
K.A. Moylan
KEN AUSTIN
Jon M. Riddle
Miguel Aguado
Stephen Karamatos
Thomas Hoffmann
Charles Webb
Hugh Wilson
Tore Simonsen
PurpleCyclist
Tristan Broomhall
Jamie Thornton
James P Baross Jr
Spurcycle
Fiona Campbell

Jeffrey Dallas Moore
Alvaro Remesal
Greg Hostetler
Lisa Kane
Craig Lewis & Carrie Newbold
Alasdair Sinclair
Michael Levesque
Jim Stahl
WoolSports, Inc.
Nick Andrew
Erik Daems
Kostakis Nikolaos
Jason McDowell
Christopher Thompson
Patrik Lundquist
Kreg Hasegawa
Cedric Kaltenrieder
Minh-Tam Nguyen
Doug McClellan
Roland Tanglao
Elaine Bradtke
Sarah Hill
Carol Wise
Nathalie Beauregard
JB Humphreys
Kenneth Pinto
Herbert Tiemens
Konrad manning
Philip Lee
Christian Amoser
Denis Wood
Heather Darrah
Stephen Hawkins
Paul Wilkinson
yo yehudi
Anthony Cartmell
Rich Lee
Lindsay Chapman
Kevin M Ablitt
Peter Greenwood
Nick Rearden
Shaun McDonald
James Spinks
Tom Ryan
Eviltoystealer
Will Crocombe
Michael Kidd
David Cox
Klaas Brümann
Mark Hirst
Malcolm Bracken
Sylvia Aitken
Bruce Devlin
Mike Thomson
shirley ripullone
Tim O'Malley
Gwallter Arkimedes Rixon
Chris Begg
Jonathan Bennett
M Hanson
Alan T Anderson
John Conway
Adrian Briggs

John Waterworth
Mathieu Davy
Chris Routledge
Chris Walton
Jerry Ash
Toby Adam
Mike Hewison
Chris Hinchliffe
Edward Thomas Burke
Paul Champion
Chris Harrison
Peter Rohde
David Cardus
Graham Burton
Graham Robinson
Ben Fields
Andrew Martin
Brenda Puech
Simon Bird
Alec McCalden
Richard Gibson
Anthony Lister
Robflyte
Taylor Rivera
radar s matt
Lorenz Zahn
Matt Moritz
Thorin Messer
Matt Clifford
Leah Cosgrove
Lexi
Constantine Kousoulis
filias
Ben Martin
Nicky Dey
Maree Carroll
joe ruf
Jonathan Ward
Thomas L. Bowden Sr.
Johanna D. Henderson
David Bernstein
Angela van der Kloof
Luke Iseman
Tim Johnson
James J Ferrari
Nicole Snyder
Craig Shanklin
Janne Pirttilahti
David Williams
Ken Eng
Colin Campbell
Mark Redmond
Aaron Spencer
Liz Sachs
Dean Wisleder
Sean Morrissey
Doug Ingram
Andrew Reeves-Hall
Charles Halliday
Mark Pinto
Lin Tuff
Steve knattress
Adam Tandy

Tim Kirk
John Cromwell
Greg McDougall
Graham Smith
Luke Turnbull
Sarah
Roland Backhouse
Phillip Darnton
Joe Farler
Simon Duane
Jeremy Bradsell
john galbraith
Jose Manuel Nunes Calaça
Rupert Shute
Howard Peel
Jonathan Dow
Robert Prior
Mark Appleton
Philip Fletcher
James Moss
Michael Schooling
Mark Martin
fred_dot_u
Jessica
SumMin Yi
Michael Dunn
Gary
Peter Michaelson
Larry Pizzi
Graham Bradshaw
Charles S. Lawrence
David Lewis
Christopher Reader
Greyson
Todd Herrick
John Marshall
HanoverFiste
JMatt Peterson
Jim Vincent Jr.
Martha Van Inwegen
Ian Cull
John Reese
jimmy egan
Michael Barnstijn
Ian Brett Cooper
Denis CARAIRE
Dave Walker
Peter Berkeley
Joe Breeze
john Simpson
Patrick Russell Knox Sr.
Trevor Parsons & Hackney Cycling Campaign

BIBLIOGRAPHY

Cycling's contribution to motoring history is woefully neglected by academic and general authors alike. At best there may be a line or two about cyclists having founded the Good Roads movement or that some automobile manufacturers started life as bicycle manufacturers. The best study of the Good Roads movement is a PhD thesis from 1956. Even classics such as Robert Smith's social history of cycling in America give the Good Roads movement little more than a passing mention. As far as I am aware there has never been a book or study comparing the British and American roads improvement organisations created before motoring existed. I have been guided and inspired (and sometimes infuriated) by the following books, with many more cited in the notes.

Ways of the World, Maxwell G. Lay, Rutgers University Press, 1992.

English Local Government; The Story of the King's Highway, Sidney & Beatrice Webb, Longmans, Green and Co., 1913.

The Kings Highway, William Rees Jeffreys, Batchworth Press, 1949.

Wheels of Fortune, Sir Arthur Du Cros, Chapman and Hall, London, 1938.

Peddling Bicycles to America: The Rise of an Industry, Bruce D. Epperson, McFarland, 2010.

A Social History of the Bicycle, Robert A. Smith, McGraw-Hill Book Company, 1972.

On Your Bicycle, Jim McGurn, Facts on Files, 1987.

America and the Automobile: Technology, Reform and Social Change, 1893-1923, Peter J. Ling, Manchester University Press, 1992.

The League of American Wheelmen and the Good Roads Movement 1890-1905 [PhD thesis], Phillip Mason, The American University, 1957.

Cycling and Society, Edited by Dave Horton, Paul Rosen, and Peter Cox, Ashgate, 2007.

The Romance of The Cyclists' Touring Club, James T. Lightwood, CTC, 1928.

Motors and Motor-driving, Viscount Alfred Harmsworth Northcliffe, Longmans, Green, 1902.

The Motor Car and Politics: 1896-1970, William Plowden, The Bodley Head, 1971.

Dirt Roads to Dixie: Accessibility and Modernization in the South, 1885-1935, Howard Lawrence Preston, University of Tennessee Press, 1991.

Bicycle design: an illustrated history, Tony Hadland, Hans-Erhard Lessing, The MIT Press, Massachusetts, 2014.

Bicycle: The History, David V. Herlihy, Yale University Press, 2004.

The Motoring Century: The Story of the Royal Automobile Club, Piers Brendon, Bloomsbury Publishing, 1997.

The motorway achievement, Thomas Telford, Ron Bridle, Peter Baldwin, John Porter, Robert Baldwin, 2004.

Down the Asphalt Path: the Automobile and the American City, Clay McShane, Columbia University Press, 1994.

My Motoring Reminiscences, Selwyn Francis Edge, GT Foulis & Company, 1934.

City of Cities: The Birth of Modern London, Stephen Inwood, Pan, 2005.

Death on the Streets, Cars and the Mythology of Road Safety, Robert Davis, Leading Edge Press, 1992.

The King's Best Highway, Eric Jaffe, Simon & Schuster, 2010.

The condition of England, Charles Frederick Gurney Masterman, Faber & Faber, 1909.

R. J. Mecredy: The Father Of Irish Motoring, Bob Montgomery, Dreoilin Publications, 2003.

For love of the automobile: looking back into the history of our desires, Wolfgang Sachs, University of California Press, 1992.

Drive on!: a social history of the motor car, Leonard John Kensell Setright, Granta Books, 2002.

The Birth of the British Motor Car, 1769-1897, T. R. Nicholson, Palgrave Macmillan, 1982.

NOTES

Full and copious notes for this book can be found at www.roadswerenotbuiltforcars.com/notes

INDEX

Italic text is used for titles publications and other media. If not printed matter the type is given afterwards in brackets. **Bold** text is used to identify the pages where illustrations appear. Plates are identified as pl. i, pl. ii etc. Pre-modern counties are used to locate towns and cities in the UK.

310

ABOUT THE AUTHOR

Carlton Reid is the executive editor of trade magazine BikeBiz.com. His travel pieces have appeared in *National Geographic Traveller* and *The Guardian*. His previous books include *Adventure Mountain Biking* (Crowood Press, 1990); *Complete Book of Cycling* (contributor, Hamlyn, 1997); *I-Spy Bicycles* (Michelin, 1998); *Discover Israel* (Berlitz, 1993); *Lebanon: A Travel Guide* (Kindlife, 1995); *Classic Mountain Bike Routes of the World* (contributor, Quarto Publishing, 2000); *Bike to Work Book* (Front Page Creations, November 2008) and *Family Cycling* (Snow Books, 2009).

Island Press | Board of Directors